Anonymous

Democratic Campaign Book

Congressional election 1894

Anonymous

Democratic Campaign Book
Congressional election 1894

ISBN/EAN: 9783337425807

Printed in Europe, USA, Canada, Australia, Japan

Cover: Foto ©Suzi / pixelio.de

More available books at **www.hansebooks.com**

Anonymous

Democratic Campaign Book
Congressional election 1894

ISBN/EAN: 9783337425807

Printed in Europe, USA, Canada, Australia, Japan

Cover: Foto ©Suzi / pixelio.de

More available books at **www.hansebooks.com**

DEMOCRATIC

CAMPAIGN BOOK.

CONGRESSIONAL ELECTION 1894.

BY AUTHORITY OF DEMOCRATIC CONGRESSIONAL COMMITTEE.

WASHINGTON, D. C.:
HARTMAN & CADICK, PRINTERS.
1894.

What the Democratic Congress Did.

It repealed the Sherman Silver Law which required the Government to purchase annually 54,000,000 ounces of silver and pay for the same in gold obligations, thereby menacing the credit of the Government, and imperiling the stability of our commercial, manufacturing and financial interests.

It removed from the statutes the Federal Election Law, the most odious and undemocratic measure ever enacted, and thereby restored to the people of the sovereign States full and complete control over their elections, free from the intervention of supervisors and deputy marshals, whose sole duties, under Republican supremacy, had een to intimidate, arrest and imprison electors before they had cast their ballots.

It reduced the expenditures of the Government below those of the last Republican administration more than $28,-000,000, thereby relieving the people from the payment of that immense sum into the Federal Treasury to stimulate extravagant jobs.

It reformed the abuses in the various Departments, and by the aid of the heads of the same dispensed with useless positions, thereby reducing the salary list more t $1,000,000 annually.

It repealed that most obnoxious, ill-formed and c pi sive measure called the McKinley Law, and substitute its stead a measure of revenue reform that will re trade and restore prosperity.

3

It destroyed the policy of paying out of the public funds in the Treasury, derived from taxes collected from the people, millions of dollars annually in the way of bounties to aid private individuals in the prosecution of their private industries.

It provided for the taxation, by States, counties, and municipalities of more than three hundred millions of taxable values which had heretofore not only been exempt from taxation, but had enabled unscrupulous persons, by fraudulent practices, to escape from their just share of the burdens of domestic government.

It placed upon the statute books the most drastic measure against combinations, trusts, and monopolies engaged in foreign commerce ever enacted.

It provided for an Income Tax upon the wealth of the country, thereby placing upon the shoulders of the rich a due share of the burdens of government.

It recognized the dignity of labor by providing by law a National Holiday in the District of Columbia upon which the working people may cease from toil and unite in a peaceful celebration of their achievements and triumphs.

It enacted more than two hundred laws for the benefit of the people in different sections of the country.

Cause of Panic of 1893.

The Inevitable Result of Four Years of Republican Maladministration.

REVENUES FALL—EXPENDITURES RISE.

The False Cry of Fear of Tariff Legislation and Democratic Rule.

The strenuous effort made by protectionists to impress upon the minds of the people that the depression of last year was caused by the fear that the tariff would be reformed and that all that was necessary to insure a speedy return of good times was to cease the agitation of this question, in the light of the history of the last few years under high protection, was supremely ridiculous.

Could it be possible that the mere accession of the Democratic party to power in all the departments of the Government, upon the profession of principles under which the civilized people of every country of the world, which has practised them, including ourselves, had accumulated wealth and attained a higher degree of prosperity, had the effect, in so short a space of time, to convert a prosperous people into a helpless and dependent state? Is it not more credible that the great disaster which came upon us was the outgrowth of a false system of economy which, with all our matchless resources, we were unable to longer stand? Will not future genera when they look back to our times to draw lessons of wisdom to guide hem direction in which they should go, rather ascribe our reverses to our follies i of our fears? Are the advocates of a restrictive policy ready to confess tha withstanding our unparallel d resources, thirty years of protection had fai establish our industrie- upon a foundation sufficiently firm to withstand e proposition looking to a conservative modification of its structure?

5

If ever the influence and operation of a protective tariff could have brought wealth and happiness to a people, or measurably, have preserved the same from destruction by the ingress of injurious competition, most assuredly the last twenty should have been years of uninterrupted prosperity. Have they been? We challenge the advocates of protection to point to a period of like duration in the history of this or any other country during which there has been so many depressions, such serious conflicts between employers and employees, more factories closed, or a greater number of commercial failures recorded. From 1873 to 1882, inclusive, the number of failures was 74,978, with liabilities aggregating $1,648,310,-517. From 1883 to 1890 we were constantly on the verge of a financial crash. The Secretary of the Treasury was continually forced to purchase bonds and prepay interest to check the alarm. With all however that could be done, we had the stringency of 1883, the panics of 1884 and of 1890.

The number of failures during this period, including the years 1883 and 1890, exceeded 82,000, with liabilities more than $1,250,000,000. The failures, which numbered 6,738 in 1882, arose to 9,184 in 1883, and 10,907 in 1890, with liabilities aggregating $189,856,964. Not since the tariff revision of 1883 went into effect has the number of failures fallen below 9,000 in a single year.

During this period the conflicts between employers and employees increased until riots and bloodshed became so numerous as to excite but little interest except in the most extreme cases. During the years 1883, 1884, 1885, and 1886, we had 2,977 strikes in 17,271 establishments, embracing 1,039,011 employees. The number of strikes increased from 471, affecting 129,591 employees in 1881, to 1,411, affecting 499,489 employees in 1886. During the years 1882 to 1886, inclusive, lockouts occurred in 2,214 establishments, affecting 175,270 employees. The estimated wage loss to employees by reason of strikes and lockouts during these six years aggregated $59,972,440.

In 1890 the McKinley law went into operation and note the result:

Under the operation of this act the number of failures arose from 10,907, with liabilities aggregating $189,856,964, in 1890, to 12,273, with liabilities aggregating $189,868,693 in 1891, and the conflicts between employers and employees, which had theretofore culminated only in combats and riots, became battles between great forces armed with rifle and cannon. The number of failures in 1892 was 10,270, while in 1893 it reached the maximum height, 15,560, with liabilities aggregating $462,000,000, as against assets amounting to $262,000,000. In no country has there been such a disturbed and unsettled condition as we had. We reached a point when idleness became so common that the feats of the tramp were considered laudable avocations.

Since the passage of the new tariff act trade has become active, idle factories are starting up and the hopes of the people are once more animated by the belief that a long period of solid prosperity is in store for them. The trouble was not that tariff legislation was threatened, but rather that it was not an accomplished fact. The long delay was the result of Republican opposition in the Senate, and to that party should be charged the increased misery and suffering which resulted from the same.

The Cause of the Panic of 1893.

The commercial depression and monetary crisis which swept over the country in 1893, and from the effects of which we have but partially recovered, has been persistently charged, by the leaders and the press of the Republican party, as the result of Democratic success at the last election, and the fear that the policies espoused by that party would be carried into effect by Congressional enactments. It is not the purpose of this chapter to enter into any labored argument to prove the absurdity of this accusation, but simply to recall the facts which preceded our reverses and leave the student to draw his own conclusions. Before tracing the commercial and financial history of the last ten years, which cast a flood of light on this question, it is in order to remove a few fallacies which have found lodgment in the minds of a great many sincere persons.

Silver Money.

Not a few believe that the disaster which came upon us last year was the result of the limited silver policy which had been pursued since the demonetization of the white metal in 1873. On the 1st day of July, 1893, we had in silver coin, $496,687,573, and in Treasury notes, issued in payments for purchases of silver bullion, under the Sherman act of 1890, $140,855,611, making a total circulation of $637,543,187. This is by far the largest volume of silver ever in use as a part of our circulation. We have, in times past, enjoyed the greatest prosperity with a much less supply, and it cannot, therefore, be said that the crash of last year was the result, solely, of a deficiency in the volume of silver money. Whatever influence the silver question had upon our prosperity, and, it is not intended to here claim or argue that it did not have an important one, it is certainly evident that it was not solely because of a scant supply of silver money.

Ample Currency.

Again, many were firmly of the opinion that the result was caused by an insufficient supply of money, and this belief was strengthened by the fact that a large amount of clearing-house certificates and other substitutes had to be issued to tide over the stringency. The scarcity of currency, however, was the result and not the cause, as these certificates were soon retired by the return to circulation of the money, which, at the first approach of the storm, had sought safety in retirement. That this opinion was erroneous is fully established by the fact that on the 30th day of June, 1892, we had a total circulation, including gold, silver and paper money, of $1,753,953,744; the largest per capita in the history of the country.

In what has been said as to the quantity of silver and the total circulation per capita, it has not been the purpose to argue to any one that we have all the silver we can use, or that the volume of our circulation is fully adequate to the requirements of the people. These are questions entirely outside of the purview of this chapter. All that it is intended to here impress upon the mind of the student is, that the recent panic resulted from causes other than simply the scarcity of silver money, or an insufficiency in the volume of our circulation.

Real Cause.

What, then, was the primary cause? Was it the result of a fear upon the part of the people that the Democratic party would carry into effect the policies it had advocated? Did the great business interests of the country become alarmed at the election of Mr. Cleveland, in 1892?

The people in the great commercial and financial centers of the country endorsed him in such a decisive manner as to demonstrate, beyond controversy, the supreme confidence they had in the wisdom of the policies he represented. Even if this had not been the case, if the Democratic party had succeeded to power under the leadership of an untried captain, and the great business interests of the country had harbored forebodings as to the future, does any one believe that a collapse from a sound, stable and healthy prosperity could, for that reason, have come upon the country so suddenly and with such terrible force.

That the disaster which so soon followed upon the advent to power of the Democratic Administration was the direct result of the preceding four years of Republican rule can be demonstrated as clearly as any fact in governmental affairs can be established.

A comparison of the receipts and expenditures of Mr. Harrison's with Mr. Cleveland's first term presents many striking contrasts.

Comparison of receipts and expenditures, exclusive of postal, for four years beginning June 30, 1885, and ending June 30, 1893.

CLEVELAND'S.

Years.	Receipts.	Expenditures.	Surplus.
1886	$336,439,727	$242,483,138	$93,956,589
1887	371,403,277	315,835,428	55,567,849
1888	379,266,074	259,653,958	119,612,116
1889	387,050,058	281,996,615	105,053,443
Total	$1,474,159,132	$1,099,969,139	$374,189,907

HARRISON'S.

Years.	Receipts.	Expenditures.	Surplus.
1890	$403,080,982	$297,736,484	$105,344,498
1891	392,612,448	355,372,685	37,239,763
1892	354,937,785	345,023,331	9,914,454
1893	385,819,628	383,477,894	2,341,734
Total	$1,536,450,843	$1,381,610,397	$154,840,449

It will be seen from the foregoing table that for the four years of Mr. Cleveland's administration, the total receipts were $62,291,711 less; the total expenditures, $281,641,253 less, while the surplus was $219,349,548 more than during Mr. Harrison's. Still more important facts may be noted by a further examination. The revenues increased every year during Mr. Cleveland's term, beginning with $336,439,723 in 1886, and ending with $387,050,058 in 1889, while the reverse, with the exception of a single year, is true of Mr. Harrison's. During the latter's term the revenue fell from $403,080,982 in 1890, to $354,937,785 in 1892, and $385,819,626 in 1893, and the surplus revenues from $105,344,496 in 1890, to $2,344,674 the last year of his term.

It is an unquestioned fact that an increase in the revenues of the Government is the highest evidence of the prosperity of its people while a diminution of the same is a sure indication of depression.

A table of the imports and exports of gold coin and bullion during the respective terms is equally significant.

Statement of the imports and exports of gold coin and bullion by fiscal years from March 1, 1885, to March 1, 1889, and from March 1, 1889, to March 1, 1893, and from March 1, 1893. to June 30, 1894.

Fiscal Years	Imports.	Exports.
1885, March to June...	$3,333,625	$3,486,161
1885–6	20,743,349	42,952,191
1886–7...	42,910,601	9,701,187
1887–8...	43,934,317	18,376,234
July, 1888, to March, 1889, ...	7,386,187	20,808,768
Total	$118,308,079	$95,324,541
1889, March to June...	$2,898,671	$39,143,507
1889–90..	12,943,342	17,274,491
1890–91..	18,232,567	86,362,654
1891–92..	49,700,454	50,195,327
July, 1892, to March, 1893, ...	11,043,720	59,832,578
Total	$94,818,754	$252,803,557
1893, March to June...	$10,120,661	$42,235,575
1893–94...	72,453,066	77,038,729

MINT BUREAU, *July* 10, 1894.

It will be seen from the foregoing table that the net imports of gold during Mr. Cleveland's administration was $22,788,538. Only during two of the years of his term did the exports exceed the imports, and then not to the extent of the domestic production. During Mr. Harrison's administration there was not a single year that the exports did not exceed the imports; the total reaching the startling sum of $157,980,803. During the last three months, December, January, and February, of the latter's term, the net exports were over $36,000,000, being at the rate of more than $12,000,000 a month, or $140,000,000 a year; while during the first four months of Mr. Cleveland's present term it was but a little over $32,000,000, and during the fiscal year ending June 30, 1894, only $4,584,663. The whole administration of Mr. Harrison, with the exception of the first year, which was in some respects prosperous, as a result of the great impetus given to it by the four preceding years of sound economical administration, was that of falling revenues, increasing expenditures, and a heavy flow of gold from the country. Any of these was calculated to excite apprehension but the three combined were sufficient to and did destroy private confidence as well as the public credit.

The sound financial condition of the Treasury at the time Mr. Cleveland delivered his great trust to Mr. Harrison, enabled the latter to glide smoothly through the first year of his administration, but when he returned it to the hands from whence he received it there was nothing but an impaired credit and an empty purse.

Is it not, therefore, apparent that the great depression of last year was born, gathered its strength and started upon its course of devastation and ruin during th· Republican administration and gained such a velocity that Mr. Carlisle was unable to at onc · stay its progress?

False Statement of Account.

At the very beginning of Mr. Harrison's administration a feeling of unrest an I insecurity began to show itself in financial centers and continued, with slight intervals, to the end of his term. During the year 1890 the financial stringency became so great that Secretary Windom was compelled to purchase Government bonds to the amount of $73,694,850, for which he paid premiums amounting to $21.222,894. During the last months of Mr. Harrison's administration all sor s of rumors were in circulation. The report was current that an issue of bonds had been contracted by Secretary Foster in order to protect the gol l reserve in the Treasury, and, but for the assistance of the New York bankers, such a transaction certainly would have been necessary. He had, in fact, given orders for the preparations of the plates upon which the bonds were to be printed.

It was only by a change in the form of the statements and a juggling with the funds that Secretary Foster was able to show an apparant balance at the end of his term. Under the provisions of an act passed by the 51st Congress, the fund in the Treasury for the redemption of the national bank notes was made an asset instead of a liability. The surplus in the Treasury was in this way inflated by the transfe of $54,207,975 from one side of the ledger to the other. Not a single cent was by this change added to the assets nor a single penny taken from the liablities, yet there was an apparent increase of the surplus of more than fifty millions of dollars.

The subsidiary silver coin, being a legal tender for sums not exceeding five dollars, had been considered, prior to Mr. Harrison's administration, as unavailable for the payment of the obligations of the Government, and, therefore, had not been counted as an available asset. This was likewise transferred from the column of unavailable to that of the available assets, and the surplus was again augmented without the addition of a farthing. Had this system of stating the accounts been in us· at the end of Mr. Cleveland's term, the surplus in the Treasury, including the reserve, would have been $183,827,190, instead of $148,903,158. Whatever, therefore, of these two funds was on hand at the end of Mr. Harrison's administration should have been deducted from the surplus as stated in order to have arrived at the true balance. The amount of the National Bank Redemption Fund on hand March 1st, 1893, was $22,272,061, and of fractional silver, $10,971,875, the aggregate of the two being $33,243,936. Deducting these sums from the balance stated March 1-t, 1893, to wit: $24,128,087, an I there was a real deficiency of $9.115,849.

This was the condition when Secretary Carlisle took charge. The surplus had been squandered; our gold was being transported to Europe at the rate of $12,000,000 a month; the expenditures had been increased more than $60,000,000 a year, while the revenues had fallen off $18,000,000, and yet h· was expected, and Republicans affect to be surprised that he was not able, to at once fully restore public confidence and give prosperity and financial stability to every industry and enterprise throughout the country.

Injurious Influences.

What, the question may be asked, brought about this collapse during Mr. Harrison's administration? No one will dispute the fact that the financial disturbances in South America, which resulted in the failure of the great banking firm of Baring

Brothers, had a depressing influence upon our credit and our commerce. The capitalists of Great Britain have for many years been large holders of American stocks and securities. They have furnished the money to build and equip our railroads, to develop our mines, to carry forward our great improvements, and hence we are and have been largely in their debt. Having large investments in South America when the stress in the Argentine government began to be felt, it was but natural that they should throw upon the markets our stocks and securities, which were the best in the world, and that our people who were interested in upholding their values should be forced to become heavy purchasers. No doubt the effort to fill this sink first started the large exports of gold to Europe in 1890. The effects of this, however, would have been but temporary had it not been for the harmful and extravagant legislation of the Fifty-first Congress, which so closely followed it. That Republican Congress assembled with a determination to so modify our revenue laws as that no surplus should remain at the end of the year as a protest against a high tariff.

The House immediately entered upon its unbridled course, and within less than four months Members began to ask of each other, when some measure requiring an expenditure was under consideration, "Where is the money to come from?" The McKinley act, which increased the taxes of the people but reduced the revenues of the Government, was rushed through under cloture. The Sherman law, which stopped the coinage of silver and required the Government to purchase 4,500,000 ounces of silver bullion each month and to pay for the same in Treasury notes redeemable in gold, was likewise forced through. By the McKinley act the burdens of the people were increased while the receipts of the Government were diminished, and by the Sherman law, silver was reduced to the level of a commodity and the Government forced to purchase large quantities of it every month and pay for it with gold obligations.

The effect of these two measures was to so impair the credit and cripple the commerce of the country as to augment instead of allay the fears of the people. Under the Sherman law $156,000,000 in Treasury notes were issued and immediately became a charge against the gold reserve in the Treasury. This constantly and rapidly increasing menace, with a promised deficiency, was more than the credit of the nation could stand, and hence during the last year of Mr. Harrison's administration there was an actual deficiency of $9,115,849, while the balance of trade, which, under reasonable conditions, should always be in our favor, at the end of the fiscal year, was $18,735,728 against us. The Sherman act, in compliance with the Chicago platform, was repealed, but not until serious damage had been done to both public and private credit. The repeal of this measure, while it may not have had the immediate beneficial effects that were predicted, was certainly an important factor in allaying the fears of the people and staying the course of the panic. The net exports of gold during the last fiscal year was only $4,585,603, as against $86,807,275 the year previous.

The repeal of this measure, although an imperative necessity, left the country without any means of increasing its volume of money except by additions to its stock of gold or an increase of national bank currency. The disturbed condition of affairs has made it impossible for the Democratic party to mature a satisfactory plan for the reformation of our financial system, but after the settlement of other questions, now pressing for solution, this great desideratum will unquestionably be successfully accomplished.

IMPORTATION OF LABOR BY CONTRACT---A REPUB-LICAN MEASURE.

The subject of legislation affecting the interests of the laboring classes has become an important matter.

Our wage-workers are in a great measure an organized class, and as such have become a most potent factor in educating and influencing the masses upon political questions. All parties, therefore, are making great efforts to win their approbation and support. The most ardent professions for their interest and welfare have been and will be expressed in platforms and proclaimed upon the stump.

This class of our citizens, however, have long since realized that but little faith could be put in the pledges of platforms or the profession of politicians, and that the only sure guide to the principles which control a party is to be found in the record which it has made.

The members of the Republican party are boastful in their professions of devotion to the interests of American labor. They profess to be its special protectors, and without their guardianship one would conclude, from their pretensions, that our laboring classes would long since have been reduced to a condition of dependency and servitude more deplorable than that of the poorest-paid labor of Europe.

It is not intended at this time to do little more than call attention to some of the legislation which seriously affected the welfare of our laboring classes, so that they may readily fix the responsibility for their enactment or non-enactment where it rightfully should be.

In 1864, Congress passed an act substantially entitled an act to encourage immigration. This was its ostensible purpose, but its real object was to clothe contractors, mine owners, and manufacturers with power to contract with and import laborers from Europe to supplant American workmen, and to reduce the price of American wages.

Mr. E. B. Washburn, in reporting the same to the House, said:

The vast number of laboring men, estimated at nearly on · million and a quarter, who have left their peaceful pursuits and patriotically gone forth in defence of our government and its institutions, has created a vacuum which is becoming seriously felt in every portion of the country. Never before in our history has there existed so unprecedented a demand for labor as at the present time. This demand exists everywhere. It exists in the agricultural districts of the northwest ; in the central States; in New England, and among the shipping interests of the lakes and the seaboard, and is felt in every field of mechanical and manufacturing industry. The dearth of laborers is severely felt in the coal and iron mines of Pennsylvania ; in the coal mines of Ohio, Indiana, and Illinois ; in the lead mines of Galena; and in the gold and silver mines of California, Nevada, Idaho, and Colorado. * * * It is believed that the demand for laborers on our railroads alone will give employment for the entire immigration of laborers in 1863.

The second section provides that contracts may be made whereby immigrants shall pledge the wages of their labor to repay the expenses of their immigration, and further provides for the enforcement of the contracts, and that it shall operate as a lien upon any land acquired by the immigrant when recorded in the county where the land is situated.

So drastic were the provisions of this measure that it gave to the importer of

The fact that this statute remained in force nearly twenty years, eighteen after the war had closed, and that every effort to repeal it in the interest of American labor was thwarted is sufficient to satisfy the most skeptic person that it was fashioned and framed in the interest of the contractor and manufacturer. From the time of the enactment of this law till its repeal over 6,500,000 immigrants came to our shores. How many of these left their native land and came to us voluntarily upon their own resources because of their admiration for our institutions, and how many debased and vicious characters were brought here under this contract system cannot be told. Laborers were imported under the provisions of this law up to the time of its repeal, and the statutes now in force prohibiting the same are still being evaded in many ways by the men who cry loudest "protection to American labor!" The Republican party, supreme in all the departments of the Government, was cognizant of the fact, that while honest laborers were unable to secure employment, importations under contract were constantly being made, but no step was taken to protect them from this competition

Dump all the paupers and criminals of Europe and all the Mongolians of Asia in here. What cared the operator and manufacturer? Labor was made more dependent and wages cheaper. This was the policy of the Republican party. Open wide the doors for the importation of cheap labor, but close them tight against the importation of cheap clothing and cheap food. Let us see if the attention of the Republican members of Congress was ever called to this matter.

On the 13th of December, 1869, Senator Wilson, of Massachusetts, introduced a bill (S. 378) to regulate the importation of immigrants under contract. This bill was called up by him on the 22d of April, 1870, and its consideration urged; but Senator Ferry, of Michigan, objected and the bill was referred to the Committee on Commerce, a majority of whom were Republicans, who reported against its passage. They were unwilling to consider a bill to even regulate the subject four years after the war was over.

On the 5th of February, 1870, Senator Wilson introduced another bill (S. 539) to make the importation of immigrants under contract unlawful. He made several efforts to secure consideration of the same without reference to a committee, but objections were made, and on December 12, 1870, it was referred to the Committee on Education and Labor and was never heard of again. No power was strong enough to carry a bill through the committee; the ears of Republicans were deaf to all appeals. They saw American workmen out of employment, wages going down, strikes and lock-outs daily occurring, but none of these aroused their attention. I remained for a Democratic House of Representatives to repeal this odious and injurious measure, and to force the Republican Senate to take action before anything could be accomplished. On the 8th of January, 1884, Mr. Foran of Ohio introduced a bill (H. R. 2550) to prohibit the importation of foreign labor under contract. This bill passed the House on the 19th of June, 1884.

The bill was sent to the Senate where it was referred to the Committee on Education and Labor. It was reported back at an early day, and repeated but fruitless efforts made to secure consideration of it until in February, 1885, when it finally passed that body. Let every intelligent workingmen in the country examine without prejudice this record and if he does not come to the conclusion that those who upheld this law for the importation of contract labor for so many years were not his friends, we shall doubt his ability to select them.

laborers not only a lien upon any land that they might enter, but upon the wages they might earn.

Senator Sherman, in reporting this measure to the Senate, very adroitly tried to conceal its real purpose, but inadvertently disclosed the secret before concluding his statement. He said:

"The special wants for labor in this country at the present time are very great. The war has depleted our workshops and materially lessened our supply of labor in every department of industry and mechanism. In their noble response to the call of their country our workmen in every branch of the useful arts have left vacancies, which must be filled or the material interests of the country must suffer. The immense amount of native labor occupied by the war calls for a large increase of foreign immigration to make up the deficiency at home. The demand for labor never was greater than at present, and the fields of usefulness were never so varied and promising."

It was true, as stated by Senator Sherman, that there was "a noble response to the call of their country" by the workingmen, but while absent fighting its battle their vacant places should not have been filled with cheap laborers imported from Europe under contract. Paupers unable to get to this country under the terms and provisions of this law could virtually enslave themselves in foreign countries to American contractors and American manufacturers, and the contract would be enforced here to the fullest extent.

The second section of this law reads as follows:

SEC. 2. *And be it further enacted,* That all contracts that shall be made by emigrants to the United States in foreign countries, in conformity to regulations that may be established by the said Commissioner, whereby emigrants shall pledge the wages of their labor for a term not exceeding twelve months, to repay the expenses of their emigration, shall be held to be valid in law, and may be enforced in the courts of the United States or of the several States and Territories; and such advances, if so stipulated in the contract, and the contract be recorded in the recorder's office in the county where the emigrant shall settle, shall operate as a lien upon any land thereafter acquired by the emigrant, whether under the homestead law when the title is consummated, or on property otherwise acquired until liquidated by the emigrant; but nothing herein contained shall be deemed to authorize any contract contravening the Constitution of the United States, or creating in any way the relation of slavery or servitude." (U. S. Stats. at Large, vol. 13, 1863-65.)

The extent to which the authors of this measure knew they were going is apparent from the last lines of this section—"but nothing herein contained shall be deemed to authorize any contract, contravention of the Constitution of the United States, or creating in any way the relation of slavery or servitude."

A further provision of this law exempted the immigrants imported under contract from military service. The American workman might be taken from his place in the shop at any time, but the imported laborer was in no danger.

When we ask Republicans why they took advantage of the absence of the wage-workers who were in the Army, they say it was necessary. Labor was scarce and wages were high! Will they answer why, when the war was over, when the armies disbanded and the men returned home to take their places, this law was not repealed? Will they inform us why, when a half million or more of men were discharged from the mills or factories in 1873, this law was kept upon the statute books? Will they answer why during that long period of depression, when hundreds of thousands of men were out of employment and seeking work, it was necessary to import as was done under this law, large numbers of European laborers?

LABOR DAY A HOLIDAY.

Made One by a Democratic Congress for the Benefit of the Workers.

Be it enacted by the Senate and House of Representatives of the United States of America in Congress assembled, That the first Monday of September in each year, being the day celebrated and known as Labor's Holiday, is hereby made a legal public holiday, to all intents and purposes, and in the same manner as Christmas, the first day of January, the twenty-second day of February, the thirtieth day of May, and the fourth day of July are now made by law public holidays.

Approved, June 28, 1894.

RESTRICTING CHINESE IMMIGRATION.

All Legislation to that end has been Secured by the Democratic Party.

Not only the Pacific coast, but our entire country is vitally interested in the sub-ject of Chinese immigration, and the most casual examination of the *Congressional Record* will show that our toilers owe all the beneficial legislation that has been had upon this subject to the Democratic party, and while many Republican converts have been made of late years, their change of heart is due to the persistent work accomplished under Democratic leadership.

The efforts to restrict Chinese immigration as far as Congress is concerned began December 6, 1869. Upon that date Senator Williams of Oregon introduced a bill to regulate immigration and to prevent importation of coolie labor. This bill was in-definitely postponed upon motion of Senator Zach. Chandler, a Republican.

In January, 1870, Representative Johnson California introduced a joint resolu-tion to restrict this immigration, but the Republican committee refused to re-port it.

On June 6, 1870, Senator Stewart of Nevada introduced a bill to prohibit contracts for servile labor. Also defeated.

On June 7, Representative Sargent (California) introduced a similar bill in the House. No report was made.

On July 7, 1870, Representative Mungen (Ohio introduced a resolution for the protection of American labor against Chinese. This was killed in committee.

On July 9, 1870, Representative Cake Pennsylvania introduced a resolution against the importation of Chinese coolies and directing an investigation. This bill also failed in committee.

On December 18, 1871, Representative Coughlan (California introduced a bill to prohibit contracts for servile labor, which was referred to the Judiciary Committee. This committee was discharged from further consideration and the bill referred to another committee, which reported a substitute never considered.

On April 30, 1872, Senator Casserly (California) introduced a bill to prohibit con-tracts for servile labor, which also died in committee.

In 1879, Mr. Willis, our present Minister to the Hawaiian Islands, reported to the House a restriction bill. He took strong grounds against Chinese immigration. He concluded his statement in these words: "No self-governing country can afford to diminish or destroy the dignity, welfare and independence of its citizens. Justice to the people of the Pacific coast, the dictates of common humanity and benevo-lence, as well as the plainest suggestions of practical statesmanship, all demand that the problem of Chinese immigration shall be solved while it is yet within the legis-lative control. Governed by these views, your committee present and recommend the passage of the bill accompanying this report."

When this measure was adopted, Mr. Garfield (afterwards President) proposed an amendment to prevent the bill from going into effect until the Chinese Empire was apprised of the termination of the then treaty. The amendment being declared out of order, the bill was ordered to engrossment and a third reading. On its passage under a call from the yeas and nays, Mr. Garfield failed to vote, and the measure was passed by 155 yeas to 72 nays. (*Record*, Forty-fifth Congress, third session, p. 801.) Of the affirmative votes 104 were Democratic and 51 Republican. Those voting in the negative were 56 Republicans and 16 Democrats.

The Senate considered and passed the bill on the 15th of February. In that body 22 Democrats and 19 Republicans and 1 Independent voted in the affirmative, and 20 Republicans and 8 Democrats in the negative.

The Senate made certain amendments, and when the bill was reported back to the House, Mr. Willis moved that the bill be taken up and that the House concur in the Senate amendments.

Mr. Garfield called for separate votes on each amendment. The motion was made to lay the bill and amendments on the table. This vote was lost by 95 yeas to 140 nays, Mr. Garfield voting yea.

The measure was vetoed by President Hayes, and failed to pass over the veto—the House vote being, yeas, 110, nays, 96. As prominent a Republican as General Garfield lead the negatives. (*Record*, Forty-fifth Congress, third session, p. 2277.)

Of the 110 members who voted to pass the measure over the veto were 88 Democrats and 22 Republicans. The negative vote was composed thus: Republicans 81, Democrats 15.

In September, 1880, a new treaty was negotiated by which the United States were given the right to restrict immigration, and in 1882 a bill suspending immigration of Chinese laborers for the period of twenty years passed the House by a vote of 167 to 66. This vote was divided as follows: Yeas, Democrats 98; Greenbackers 8; Republicans 61. Nays, Republicans 62; Democrats 4; total, 66. In the Senate: Yeas, Democrats 31; Republicans 6; total, 37. Nays, Democrats none; Republicans 28; Independent 1; total, 29. This bill was vetoed by a Republican President, and upon the question of passing it over his veto the Senators voted just as they did upon the original question. This, of course, defeated it.

Thereupon a new bill in which the term of exclusion was limited to ten years and which was really the first positive exclusion act, was passed. Upon this measure the vote in the House was, yeas: Democrats, 103; Republicans, 91; Greenbackers, 7; total, 201. Nays: Republicans, 34; Democrats, 3; total, 37.

In the Senate, yeas: Democrats, 31; Republicans, 9; total, 40. Nays: Republicans, 24; Democrats, none; Independent, 1; total, 25.

This measure is known as the act of May 6, 1882.

Afterwards the Federal judges in California held that Chinamen who were subjects of countries other than China were not within the restrictions of this law, and thereupon another act of July 5, 1884, was passed, for the purpose of remedying the defect. The vote upon the act of 1884 in the House was as follows: Yeas, 184; nays, 13. The nays were all Republican.

The bill was reported favorably by the Committee of Foreign Affairs of the House by a strict party vote, and the record show that every voice raised against it, as well as every vote, was Republican. Its fate in the Senate was exceedingly dubious until the pressure of campaign necessities forced it through.

When the act of 1884 was under consideration, ex-President Harrison, who was then a member of the Senate, failed to record himself, but he voted against the act of 1882 and also voted to strike out the section which prohibited naturalization of the Chinese. (See record of t e Senate of April 25th, 1882.)

It will thus be seen that three Republ can Presidents, viz : Hayes, Garfield, and Harrison, did not sympathize with the efforts made by the Democratic party to exclude Chinese coolie competition, and the same was true of President Arthur.

The following declaration of two very eminent Republicans tend clearly in the same direction.

Senator Oliver P. Morton, who investigated the Chinese question by persona inspection in California, presented a report to the body of which he was a member, entitled : Senate Mi . Doc. No. 20, 2d session, 44th Congress. Among other things he said : " But before entering upon the discussion of any other principle, I may be permitted to observe that in my judgment the Chinese cannot be protected in the Pacific States while remaining in their alien condition. Without representation in the legislature or Congress, without a voice in the selection of officers, and surrounded by fierce, and in many respects, unscrupulous enemies, the law will be found insufficient to screen them from persecution. Complete protection can be given them only by allowing them to become citizens and acquire the right of suffrage, when their votes would become important in elections and their persecutions in great part converted into kindly solicitation."

Senator Hoar of Massachusetts, in a speech delivered in the Senate March 1, 1882, declared that the Chinamen who obey the law was entitled " to go every where on the surface of the earth that his welfare may require." He further asserted that " this privilege is beyond the rightful control of government." His Democratic colleagues ably and completely refuted this argument.

The following views of the leading San Francisco Republican papers further illustrate this position :

(San Francisco Call, April 10, 1882.)

Notwithstanding that most of the Republican Senators, except those who represent the States of the Pacific, opposed the passage of the anti-Chinese bill, which President Arthur vetoed, there is a studied effort to deceive our people by saying that Democratic Congressmen are trying to defeat the passage of another anti-Chinese bill. We have reason to believe there is not a word of truth in it, for did not nearly all the Democratic Senators and Representatives in Congress do their utmost to pass the bill which the President, instigated by his stalwart friends, vetoed?

(San Francisco Call, April 5, 1882.)

The recent exercise of the veto power by President Arthur in reference to the Chinese bill, is, perhaps, the most arbitrary act an American President has ever performed. The message is worse for the President and his party than if he had based it on an excessive term of prohibition. It is a flat contradiction of the platform on which he was elected, and raises the question whether the anti-Chinese plank in the Republican platform was not a deliberate deceit practiced on the people of this Coast.

(San Francisco Bulletin, April 3, 1882.)

The opposition exhibited to the Chinese by these facts has been extending instead of decreasing. It is, in short, the development of a great labor question,

which no public man can face and continue in or enter public life. It has already been formulated as protection to American labor, which is just as necessary as protection to American manufactures.

(San Francisco Bulletin, March 30, 1882.)

This state is to be saved by wise limits to Chinese immigration or it is to be hopelessly cursed by immigration which is irredeemable and outside of all future improvement. The journals and the politicians who prefer the latter alternative are not the friends of this country, and no argument of their assumed philanthropy can make them such. The forces and the influences which are at work to-day in favor of unrestricted Chinese immigration are hostile to the Pacific Coast and to the best interests of the whole country. He who is not with us is against us. Hostility to the proposed measure is hostility to the prosperity of the Pacific States

(San Francisco Call, February 9, 1882.)

We fear that it is not quite so certain that a bill restricting Chinese immigration will be passed during the present session of Congress, as some of our contemporaries seem to anticipate. Certain it is that Republicans alone cannot pass it, for they have not a majority in both houses of Congress, and it is also known that some Republicans will oppose any and all bills. No bill can possibly pass Congress unless it be approved by a majority of the Democratic members of the Senate and the House of Representatives. Of this our citizens may be assured; but as the Democratic party is proverbially the friend of labor, there cannot be any doubt that they will favor the passage of such a bill as will relieve this coast of its present troubles.

(San Francisco Bulletin, April 29, 1882.)

The bill for the exclusion of the Chinese passed the Senate yesterday by a vote of 32 to 15—22 Democrats, 9 Republicans, and David Davis, president *pro tem.*, voting for it. All the Democratic Senators from the West and those from the South voted for the bill. Ingalls, of Kansas, was inclined to assist us, but the missionary sniveling was probably too much for him, and he voted against the bill. Of the 15 votes in the negative 11 were furnished by New England—all its Senators but one. This indicates that the area of Chinamania is confined principally to that section, with a queer extension in the direction of Georgia. This area is also that which is devoted to the manufacture of cottons for the Chinese trade. The other four negatives were:

Harrison, of Indiana;
Ingalls, of Kansas;
Lapham, of New York;
Sherman, of Ohio.

The bill which went through the Senate, was passed by the House by the enormous vote of 201 to 37, 6 more than two-thirds of the whole body. Of the 201, 107 were Democrats and 94 Republicans. We will have the law on our side to stop the yellow tide, and the people of California will see that the law is executed. No technicalities, evasions, or loop-holes will be tolerated on this coast.

(San Francisco Bulletin, March 10, 1882.)

The bill suspending Chinese immigration passed the Senate yesterday. *   *
The great body of the negatives were Republicans. It is proper to state that two of them—Edmunds and Ingalls—would have voted for the bill if the term of suspen-

gion had been reduced to ten years. The only real Democratic vote in the negative—for Davis, of Illinois, is an unknown political quantity—was Brown, of Georgia. * * * It is quite apparent from the above vote that if the Republicans in the House cannot be rallied to the support of the measure more generally than in the higher chamber, there is some danger of the failure of the bill. Only a fifth of the Republican Senators voted against it. If these proportions are maintained in the House, the shave by which the bill is likely to pass will be very slight, unless, indeed, broader views are more generally accepted there.

(San Francisco Call, March 10, 1882.)

The anti-Chinese bill has passed the Senate by a majority of nearly two to one of the Senators voting—29 to 15. It is a matter for congratulation that but fifteen Senators were willing to place themselves on record in opposition to the right of government to regulate immigration. The position taken by the opponents of the bill would have required us to sit quietly down and let foreign hordes crowd into our country without regard to their fitness to share with us the responsibilities of government.

On March 16th, 1888, President Cleveland sent to the Senate for consideration a treaty by the terms of which Chinese laborers were to be excluded for a term of twenty years. The Senate made two amendments of an immaterial character, but the Chinese Government refused to ratify the treaty as amended. Thereupon the act of October 1, 1888, was passed. This statute was known as the Scott exclusion act, and excluded all Chinese laborers not then in the United States. Mr. Cleveland, in approving this statute, sent a very clear and succinct statement to Congress demonstrating that the cause of the conduct of the Chinese government in refusing to act upon the treaty submitted it was necessary to affirmatively legislate to the end that this country might be protected from Mongolian competition. Mr. Cleveland thus demonstrated that he cordially sympathized with the efforts of the people of the Pacific coast to protect themselves from the threatened danger. The act of 1888 was essentially a Democratic measure.

On May 5, 1892, the Geary law was approved. This also proceeded from a Democratic source and was pushed by Democratic effort. Under its provisions all Chinese laborers within the United States and entitled to remain, are required to register and procure a certificate of registration from the proper officer of the United States. This act was designed to make it practically impossible for Chinese laborers who unlawfully entered the United States after the expiration of the time for registration to remain therein. Not having a certificate their identification is easy. The Chinese in California contested the validity of this statute, but the Supreme Court of the United States, by a divided bench, declared it valid. The time for registration having expired the act of November 3, 1893, was passed, extending the registration privilege six months. This statute contains a valuable though stringent addition to earlier legislation. It requires that the certificates of residence to be issued thereunder must contain the photograph of the applicant, together with his name, local residence and occupation, and that a copy of such certificate with a duplicate of the photograph must be filed in the office of the local collector of internal revenue, and that such photographs and duplicate shall be furnished by each applicant in such form as may be prescribed by the Secretary of the Treasury. This statute was passed by a Democratic Congress and signed by a Democratic President.

THE RECENT TREATY WITH CHINA.

On March 17, '94, a convention was concluded at Washington between the United States and China concern'ng the subject of immigration. Upon being presented to the Senate it was carefully considered and was ratified upon August 13, following.

Criticisms have been made for partisan purposes upon this treaty, but an investigation of its terms will readily silence opposition and demonstrate the wisdom of its negotiations.

Prior to this treaty our diplomatic relations with China were disagreeably strained, and while we cannot afford to take any steps which will place our people in competition with coolie labor, we must neverthless do our best to deserve the respect and confidence of every nation, wheth·r civilized or otherwise.

This treaty is almost identical with that which was ratified in 1888, and which China finally refused to accept, the impo.tant difference between the two documents being that the present engagement permits only *registered* Chinese laborers to return to the United States and expressly recognizes the duty of all Mongolians within our borders to comply with the acts of May 5, 1892, and November 3, 1893, while the rejected treaty contained no reference to the important subject of registration. Hence the present compact is more favorable to the United States than former, as we are willing and anxious to ratify the treaty of 1888. No reason can be assigned to justify questioning the wisdom of accepting that of 1894.

Protests were filed by various parties againts the ratification of the treaty, but all of them were based upon misappprehension of its terms. It may be well to briefly state some of these objections :

1. It is urged that article 2 gives the right to return to every registered Chinese laborer who has a lawful wife, child or parent in the United States or property therein of the value of $1,000, or debts of like amount due him and p·nding settlement.

In the absence of the treaty these laborers have a right to live and die in the United States, there is no law demanding their exit and it is not perceive l why a Chinaman whom we concede may stay with us permanently shall not be allowed to temporarily absent himself.

We must, or ought to be, rational concerning this as well as other matters. In the next place no harm can be done by the enforcement of such a provision. Suppose every Chinaman now in the United States were to forwith avail himself of the privilege granted and visit China for one year, and then return, would our laborers be injured because of his trip ? Would they be better off if the Mongolian had not made the visit and had remained in this country to compete with them ? If we desire to rid ourselves of these people for good can we afford to object to even temporary relief ?

2. It is further argued that Chinese laborers who have no property and no debts owing to them will, by perjury, impose upon our officers and obtain the privilege of going from and returning to the United States. The answer to this is twofold. Proper Treasury regulations administered by our own officials will make successful fraud rare. And secondly, for the reasons already given, if all resident Chinamen were allowed the benefit of a visit, regardless of their pecuniary or family condition, no harm would follow.

The fact is that Chinese laborers have been coming into the United States in vio-

lation of the Scott Exclusion Act, because of the difficulties of identification.   But
the registration provided for by the act of 1894, and especially the photographic
and descriptive certificate will make it perilous and unprofitable to further press the
importation of Chinese not entitled to land.

There are no other objections worthy of the name to the second article.

The third article of the treaty has been criticised because it permits persons who
are not officials, teachers, students, merchants or travelers for curiosity or pleasure, enter the United States.

In the first place such is the law without the treaty.

Article 3 confers no advantage upon Chinamen which they do not at present enjoy.   If the treaty were obliterated these people could enter under the sixth section
of July 5, 1884.   This act forms the basis of this treaty provision, and was properly
considered at the time it was adopted as the most rigid exclusion measure theretofore proposed.   All the votes cast against it in the lower House of Congress were
cast by Republicans, and the only argument advanced by them was that the act
was unduly severe.

Moreover none of the persons described in the third article can enter the United
States without the approval of our consular officers.

It has been said by those who are probably entirely ignorant of the provisions of
the treaty, that it overrules the Geary and McCreary laws.   The absurdity of this
pretense becomes manifest when the fifth article is examined, which explicitly recognizes the validity of those acts and binds both governments to their enforcement.

It has also been urged that it is undignified for the United States to permit a foreign government to acquiesce in the enforcement of our laws.

This would be absurd in any case, but it is particularly so in this instance, since
the Supreme Court of the United States sustained the registration law by a bare
majority, and since that time one of the judges whose vote was necessary to the decision and who concurred therein has died, and his able successor has never been
called upon to express an opinion upon this topic.

The advantages of the treaty are manifest.   Outside of the relief which it affords
us in the removal of the imputation that we have disregarded diplomatic usages in
the violation of antecedent treaties, it binds both governments to absolute exclusion.

The very first article says : "The high contracting parties agree that for a period
of ten years, beginning with the date of the exchange of the ratifications of this convention, the coming, except under the conditions hereinafter specified, of the Chinese laborers to the United States shall be absolutely prohibited."

The only exceptions are as to registered laborers who have relations in this country, or assets of the value of one thousand dollars, who are permitted to go to China
and return.   No Chinese laborer not now in the United States can ever come here.
Hence when demagogues assert that this treaty let down the bars and that thousands
of Mongolians will enter the United States under it, they make a declaration as silly
as it is untruthful.

It has been said that the certificate to be given the laborer upon his departure
may be used by another.

These certificates will be properly prepared.   The laborer's photograph will be
retained, and an adequate description of his person, so that such fraud will not be
practicable.

But if the certificate is transferred, it is evident that it cannot be divided, and if the Chinaman who leaves the United States manages to find his double, he will lose his own right to return.

The treaty will, when ratified by China, be supplemented by legislation making an imposition or attempted imposition of this kind a crime, and it will not pay to take the risk of severe penalties, especially as the opportunity for the discovery is so favorable.

Mr. Cleveland has done more than any other President to deliver the country from the perils of Mongolian immigration.

The following is the treaty to which reference has been made :

Whereas, on the 17th day of November, A. D. 1880, and of Kwanghsü, the sixth year, tenth moon, fifteenth day, a Treaty was concluded between the United States and China for the purpose of regulating, limiting or suspending the coming of Chinese laborers to, and their residence in, the United States; and

Whereas, the Government of China, in view of the antagonism and much deprecated and serious disorders to which the presence of Chinese laborers has given rise in certain parts of the United States, desires to prohibit the emigration of such laborers from China to the United States; and

Whereas, the two governments desire to co-operate in prohibiting such emigration, and to strengthen in other ways the bonds of friendship between the two countries ; and

Whereas, the two Governments are desirous of adopting reciprocal measures for the better protection of the citizens or subjects of each within the jurisdiction of the other;

Now, therefore, the President of the United States has appointed Walter Q. Gresham, Secretary of State of the United States, as his Plenipotentiary, and His Imperial Majesty, the Emperor of China, has appointed Yang Yu, Officer of the second rank, Sub-Director of the Court of Sacrificial Worship, and Envoy Extraordinary and Minister Plenipotentiary to the United States of America, as his Plenipotentiary; and the said Plenipotentiaries, having exhibited their respective Full Powers found to be in due and good form, have agreed upon the following articles :

ARTICLE I.

The High Contracting Parties agree that for a period of ten years, beginning with the date of the exchange of the ratifications of this Convention, the coming, except under the conditions hereinafter specified, of Chinese laborers to the United States shall be absolutely prohibited.

ARTICLE II.

The preceding Article shall not apply to the return to the United States of any registered Chinese laborer who has a lawful wife, child or parent in the United States, or property therein of the value of one thousand dollars, or debts of like amount due him and pending settlement. Nevertheless every such Chinese laborer shall, before leaving the United States, deposit as a condition of his return, with the collector of customs of the district from which he departs, a full description in writing of his family, or property, or debts, as aforesaid, and shall be furnished by said collector with such certificate of his right to return under this Treaty as the laws of the United States may now or hereafter prescribe and not inconsistent with the provisions of this Treaty, and should the written description aforesaid be proved to be false, the right of return thereunder, or of continued residence after return, shall in

each case be forfeited.   And such right of return to the United States shall be ex
ercised within one year from the date of leaving the United States, but such right
of return to the United States may be extended for an additional period, not to
exceed one year, in cases where, by reason of sickness or other cause of disability beyond his control, such Chinese laborer shall be rendered unable
sooner to return, which facts shall be fully reported to the Chinese consul at the
port of departure, and by him certified, to the satisfaction of the collector of the
port at which such Chinese subject shall land in the United States. And no such
Chinese laborer shall be permitted to enter the United States by land or sea without producing to the proper officer of the customs the return certificate herein
required.

ARTICLE III.

The provisions of this Convention shall not affect the right at present enjoyed of
Chinese subjects, being officials, teachers, students, merchants or travelers for
curiosity or pleasure, but not laborers, of coming to the United States and residing
therein.   To entitle such Chinese subjects as are above described to admission into
the United States, they may produce a certificate from their Government or the
Government where they last resided vised by the diplomatic or consular
representative of the United States in the country or port whence they depart.

It is also agreed that Chinese laborers shall continue to enjoy the privilege of
transit across the territory of the United States in the course of their journey to or
from other countries, subject to such regulations by the Government of the United
States as may be necessary to prevent said privilege of transit from being abused.

ARTICLE IV.

In pursuance of Article III of the Immigration Treaty between the United States
and China, signed at Peking on the 17th day of November, 1880, (the 15th day of
the tenth moon of Kwanghsü, sixth year) it is hereby understood and agreed that
Chinese laborers or Chinese of any other class, either permanently or temporarily
residing in the United States, shall have for the protection of their persons and
property all rights that are given by the laws of the United States to citizens of
the most favored nation, excepting the right to become naturalized citizens.   And
the Government of the United States reaffirms its obligations, as stated in said
Article III, to exert all its power to secure protection to the person and property of
all Chinese subjects in the United States.

ARTICLE V.

The Government of the United States, having by an act of the Congress, approved May 5, 1892, as amended by an act approved November 3, 1893, required
all Chinese laborers lawfully within the limits of the United States before the passage of the first named act to be registered as in said act provided, with a view
of affording them better protection, the Chinese Government will not object to the
enforcement of such act and reciprocially the Government of the United States recognizes the right of the Government of China to enact and enforce similar laws
or regulations for the registration free of charge, of all laborers, skilled or un-
skilled (not merchants as defined by said act of Congress), citizens of the United
States in China whether residing within or without the treaty courts.

And the Government of the United States agrees that within twelve months of
the date of the exchange of the ratifications of this convention and annually there-

after it will furnish to the Government of China registers or reports showing the full name, age, occupation, and number or place of residence of all other citizens of the United States, including missionaries, residing both within and without the treaty courts of China, not including, however, diplomatic and other officers of the United States residing or traveling in China upon official business, together with their body and household servants.

ARTICLE VI.

This convention shall remain in force for a period of ten years, beginning with the date of the exchange of ratification, and, if six months before the expiration of the said period of ten years, neither government shall have formally given notice of its final termination to the other, it shall remain in full force for another period of ten years.

In faith whereof, we, the respective plenipotentiaries, have signed this convention and have hereunto affixed our seal.

Done, in duplicate, at Washington, 17th day of March A. D., 1894.

WALTER Q. GRESHAM, [SEAL.]
YANG YU. [SEAL.]

IMMIGRATION LAWS.

Their Strict Enforcement Has Benefitted the Working Classes.

The enforcement of the laws enacted by Congress for excluding from our shores undesirable immigrants and alien laborers imported under contract has a very important bearing upon the interest of American workingmen. While the manufacturers of the country have been "protected" by a tariff, enacted at their behest, the laboring part of our population were for a long time unprotected from the danger of being superseded by underpaid and underfed laborers, imported from overstocked hives of industry in the Old World. In other words, our industrial population were subject to free trade in labor while they had to pay protection prices for the means of subsistence.

The law now prohibits the immigration of laborers under contract, with a few exceptions, such as skilled workmen for new industries, labor for which cannot be otherwise obtained, actors, artists, lecturers, singers, and personal or domestic servants. It also excludes idiots, insane persons, paupers, persons suffering from a loathsome or dangerous contagious disease, persons who have been convicted of a felony or other infamous crime or misdemeanor involving moral turpitude, and polygamists. It having been found difficult in many cases to prove a specific contract under which an alien laborer could be barred, a special statutory provision has been made that any *assisted* immigrant, or any alien whose ticket or passage has been paid for with the money of another, shall be barred *ipso facto*, unless it is affirmatively and satisfactorily shown on special inquiry that he does not belong to one of the excluded classes, including alien contract laborers.

Federal legislation on this subject began in 1882. It has grown into quite a code of laws, which however, lack clearness and precision and need amendment in many respects. The difficulty in their enforcement is largely inherent in the subject but has been enhanced by the greed of steamship companies, to secure steerage passengers, and their connivance, in the past, at least, with agents, bankers, and padroni in this country, who make a business of supplying foreign laborers to employers—corporations, mines, railroads and factories.

About eighty per cent of all the immigrants arrive at the port of New York. Prior to 1890 the New York State Government had charge of immigration at that port; but in that year the Secretary of the Treasury assumed control and appointed a Federal Superintendent of Immigration for the port. In 1891 an act of Congress was passed which enlarged the Government's control of the subject of immigration. Under it a general Superintendent of the Bureau of Immigration, with an office at Washington, was appointed, and commissioners were appointed at New York and several other ports by the Secretary of the Treasury. A large immigration station was erected at

Ellis Island, so that all steerage passengers could be brought there with their baggage, for the purpose of full inspection and quasi-judicial determination of their right to land. In 1893 the immigration laws were further amended by providing that it should be the duty of every inspector of arriving immigrants to detain for special inquiry every person who might not appear to him to be clearly and beyond doubt entitled to admission, and that the issue should be tried and determined by a board of four inspectors, whose decision should be final, subject, however, to appeal to Washington. The Commissioner of Immigration at each port is charged with supervising his force of inspectors and other employees, and the work is of great magnitude.

The number of immigrants applying for admission during the fiscal year 1891–2 was 445,967. The number of arrivals for the year 1892–1893 was 343,422, of whom 814 were barred, 458 being alien contract laborers. The number of arrivals for 1893–1894 (July 1st to July 1st) was 219,046, of whom 2,013 were barred, 1,444 being alien contract laborers.

A Democratic Bureau of Immigration took charge of the execution of the immigration laws in the spring of 1893, soon after President Cleveland's inauguration, when a new superintendent of the general bureau at Washington was appointed, as well as a new commissioner at the principal port of New York. The efficiency of the Democratic over the Republican admini tration has been marked. The effect of the rigid enforcement of the laws is shown in various ways : First, by the decrease of immigration secondly, by the improved quality of the immigrant now arriving; thirdly, by the unprecedent dly numerous exclusions, both in actual numbers and proportionately, of intending immigrants, who have been forced to return to Europe by the watchful gatekeepers of our country; and fourthly, by the refusal on the part of the steamship companies to sell tickets to intending immigrants whose eligibility to land was not obvious, such refusal being due to the fact that under the new law the steamship companies must assume full responsibility for embarking undesirable immigrants. The systematic importation of laborers under contract has been practically stopped by the unceasing vigilance of the present Democratic officials.

The Hon. John G. Carlisle, Secretary of the Treasury, has issued his warrant under the act of 1888, and has caused to be deported alien contract laborers who have not been in the United States over a year, thereby establishing a precedent and affording to American labor a protection not heretofore accorded.

All aliens who have become a public charge within a year of their landing, who are insane or suffering from a loathsome disease, or who are permanently disabled from earning a living, are deported at the expense of the steamship companies who brought them here, or at the expense of the immigrant fund, thereby relieving our insane asylums and alms-houses of this burden. It is confidently asserted that during this administration our insane asylums and almshouses are getting no alien pauper patients who were landed within a year, and it is the intention of the immigration officials in future to save our eleemosenary institutions from this crying evil.

The immigration service has been more than self sustaining, and is supported entirely from the head tax paid by the immigrants; so that it is no charge upon the people.

The decrease in immigration is unquestionably due to a very great extent to the strict inspection of immigrants insisted upon by the Democratic administration, in lieu of the tax and often collusive methods of their predecessors. The increased effici ncy has been rendered possib e by a revision of the regulations, a reorganization of the service, and the substitution of highly competent, conscientious and sagacious employees for superannuated drones and "inspectors" who encumbered the offices without ever really inspecting. The greatest efforts are now made to detect and send back those alien passengers who leave their homes in Europe under contracts which make slaves of them, to take the places of American workmen at reduced wages, without debarring *bona fide* immigrants who come of their own free will because they are dissatisfied with European conditions, and are willing to take their fair and natural chance here. Those who are returned become, of course, anti-immigration agents in their own countries of the most effective type; and not even the enactment of the sternest imaginable statute could be more restrictive of undesirable immigration than these natural regulators of the ebb and flow in the tide of aliens.

Many bodies of organized American workmen have made specific acknowledgement of the fact that their trades had been materially benefitted by the manner in which the law has been enforced for the last eighteen months, such as cigar makers, tailors, hatters, shoemakers, etc.

The executive boards of many organiz tions, including the general executive boards of the American Federation of Labor, and the Knights of Labor, have visited Ellis Island during the Democratic administration and carefu ly observed the manner of inspecting immigrants and searching for violators of the law. Their satisfaction at the methods adopted and the results achieved was apparent, and resulted, in a number of instances, in formal resolutions to that effect, which were transmitted to the Department.

The work of the Supervisory Bureau of Immigration at Washington, under its distinguished Democratic chief, has been performed in such a manner as to give the greatest satisfaction.

The Secretary of the Treasury recently appointed the Hon. Herman Stump the Superintendent of Immigration, Dr. Joseph H. Senner the Commissioner of Immigration at the port of New York, and Edward F. McSweeney, Esq., the Assistant Commissioner, a commission to investigate and report to him information under the following five heads :

1. What changes, if any, in the rules and regulations now in force are necessary in order to secure a more efficient execution of existing laws relating to immigration and the laws prohibiting the importation of alien laborers under contract.

2. Whether said laws are defective in any particular, and what practical difficulties, if any, have been encountered in their execution.

3. What effect, if any, immigration has had upon the wages of labor or opportunities for employment in the United States, and whether or not the existing industrial condition of the country is attributed in any degree to the influx of laborers from abroad.

4. Whether any measures, and, if so, what, can be adopted under existing legislation to discourage the concentration of immigrant laborers in particular localities and to secure a better distribution of immigrants whose admission to the country is not prohibited by law.

5. Whether the "Padrone" system exists in this country, and, if so, to what extent and among what class of immigrants, and what measures can be taken under existing laws to break it up and protect American laborers against its evil effects

upon wages and at the same time improve the social and economic condition of the immigrants.

The Commissioners have also been directed to secure and report such information, from all available sources, as will enable the Department to employ its official force in the most effective manner for the enforcement of the immigration and contract-labor laws according to their true intent and purpose, and to suggest such amendments as experience may have shown to be necessary in order to adapt them to existing conditions.

This investigation is now in progress and has already resulted in the accumulation of a vast amount of documentary information and recommendations, which a e being sifted. The Commissioners are also visiting various sections of the country for the purpose of personally receiving the benefit of the practical knowledge of local heads of trades organizations. It is anticipated that these efforts will lead to important amendments to the laws and regulations, so that the sifting process, by which only desirable immigrants shall be admitted and all the undesirable classes shall be utterly excluded, will be perfected in all its workings. Certainly no criticism can be made that the present officers of the Immigration Service are in any-wise lacking in zeal, energy, or capacity, in dealing with this complex subject. On the other hand, their efforts are being daily supplemented by the assistance of intelligent and appreciative workmen throughout the whole United States, whose co-operation has been sought. The Democratic party has every reason to congratulate itself upon the successful efforts of its appointees to regulate immigration in accordance with the best interests of the whole people and without unworthy discrimina-

COMPARISON OF RATES

Of Duties between the McKinley Act and the New Tariff Law.

	Rates of duty under—		Average ad valorem under—	
	McKinley law.	New law.	McKinley law.	New law.
SCHEDULE A.—CHEMICALS, OILS AND PAINTS.				
Acids:			*Per ct.*	*Per ct.*
Acetic or pyroligneous—				
Specific gravity not exceeding 1.047..............lbs...	1½ c. per lb	20 per cent......	} 13.19	} 20
Specific gravity exceeding 1.047..............lbs...	4 c. per lb		(22.36	
Boracic..............lbs...	5 c. per lb	3 c. per lb......	95.12	57.06
Chromic..............lbs...	6 c. per lb......	4 c. per lb......	32.69	21.80
Citric..............lbs...	10 c. per lb......	25 per cent......	28.73	25
Tannic or tannin..............lbs...	75 c. per lb......	60 c. per lb......	181.28	145.03
Tartaric..............lbs...	10 c. per lb......	20 per cent......	32.91	20
Alcoholic perfumery, including cologne water and other toilet waters, galls	$2 per gall...... and 50 p. c.	$2 per gall...... and 50 per c.	61.77	61.77
Compounds, alcoholic, not specially provided for..............galls...	$2 per gall...... and 25 p. c.	..............do..........	163.43	188.43
Alumina, alum, alum cake, patent alum, sulphate of alumina, and aluminous cake, and alum in crystals or ground..............lbs...	6-10 c. per lb...	4-10 c. per lb...	37.18	24.79
Ammonia:				
Carbonate of..............lbs...	1⅜ c. per lb...	20 per cent......	26.56	20
Muriate of, or sal ammoniac..lbs...	¾ c. per lb......	10 per cent......	15.20	10
Sulphate of..............lbs...	½ c. per lb......	20 per cent......	22.21	20
Blacking of all kinds..............	25 per cent......	..............do..........	25	20
Bone char, suitable for use in decolorizing sugar....................	..............do..........	..............do..........	25	20
Borax, crude, or borate of soda, or borate of lime (a)..............lbs...	3 c. per lb......	2 c. per lb......	119.47	79.64
Borax, refined..............lbs...	5 c. per lb......	..............do..........	42.31	16.92
Camphor, refined..............lbs...	4 c. per lb......	10 per cent......	12.20	10
Chalk:				
Prepared, precipitated, French and red..............lbs...	1 c. per lb......	20 per cent......	32.02	20
Chalk preparations, all other, not specially provided for..............	20 per cent......	..............do..........	20	20
Chloral hydrate (no data)....................	50 c. per lb......	25 per cent......	....	25
Chloroform..............lbs...	25 c. per lb......	25 c. per lb......	19.64	19.64
Coal-tar colors or dyes, not specially provided for..............	35 per cent......	25 per cent......	35	25
Cobalt, oxide of..............lbs...	30 c. per lb......	25 c. per lb......	19.23	16.02
Collodion, and all compounds of pyroxyline..............lbs...	50 c. per lb......	40 c. per lb......	63.91	49.13

Comparison of rates of duties between McKinley act and new law.—Continued.

	Rates of duty under—		Average ad valorem under—	
	McKinley law.	New law.	McKinley law.	New law.

SCHEDULE A—CHEMICALS, OILS, AND PAINTS—Continued.

	McKinley law.	New law.	McKin ley law.	New law.
			Per ct.	*Per ct.*
In finished or partly finished articles......lbs...	60 c. per lb..... and 25 p. c.	45 per cent......	43.44	45
Rolled or in sheets, but not made up into articles......lbs...	60 c. per lb.....	50 c. per lb.....	87.08	72.57
Coloring for brandy, wine, beer, or other liquors......	50 per cent......	50 per cent......	50	50
Barks, beans, berries, balsams, buds, bulbs, and bulbous roots, and excrescences, such as nutgalls, fruits, flowers, dried fibers, grains, gums, and gum resins, herbs, leaves, lichens, mosses, nuts, roots, and stems, spices, vegetables, seeds (aromatic, not garden seeds), and seeds of morbid growth, woods used expressly for dyeing, and dried insects, any of the foregoing which are not edible, but which have been advanced in value or condition by refining or grinding or by other process of manufacture......	10 per cent......	10 per cent......	10	10
Ethers:				
Sulphuric......lbs...	40 c. per lb.....	40 c. per lb.....	400	400
Nitrous, spirits of (no data).........	25 c. per lb.....	25 c. per lb.....		
Of all kinds, not specially provided for......lbs...	$1 per lb........	$1 per lb........	35.88	35.89
Fruit ethers, oils, or essences.lbs...	$2.50 per lb....	$2 per lb........	238.28	190.62
Logwood and other dyewoods, extracts and decoctions of......lbs...	⅜ c. per lb.....	10 per cent......	11.43	10
Sumac:				
Extract of......lbs...	......do...........	......do...........	23.24	10
Bark for dyeing or tanning, extracts of Other than hemlock, not specially provided for......lbs...	⅜ c. per lb.....	10 per cent......	8.28	10
Fish glue or isinglass:				
Valued at not above 7 cents per pound......lbs...	1¼ c. per lb...	25 per cent......	25.12	25
Valued at above 7 cents and not above 30 cents per pound..lbs...	25 per cent......	......do.........	25	25
Valued at above 30 cents per pound......lbs...	30 per cent......	......do.........	30	25
Gelatin:				
Valued at not above 7 cents per pound......lbs...	1¼ c. per lb...	......do.........		25
Valued at above 7 cents and not above 30 cents per pound..lbs...	25 per cent......	......do.........	25	25
Valued at above 30 cents per pound......lbs...	30 per cent......	......do.........	30	25
Glue:				
Valued at not above 7 cents per pound......lbs...	1¼ c. per lb...	......do.........	26.16	25
Valued at above 7 cents and not above 30 cents per pound..lbs...	25 per cent......	......do.........	25	25
Valued at above 30 cents per pound......lbs...	30 per cent......	......do.........	30	25
Glycerin:				
Crude, not purified......lbs...	1¾ c. per lb...	1 c. per lb......	32.62	19.64
Refined......lbs...	4½ c. per lb...	3 c. per lb......	52.54	35.03

Comparison of rates of duties between McKinley act and new law.—Continued.

	Rates of duty under—		Average ad valorem under—	
	McKinley law.	New law.	McKinley law.	New law.
			Per ct.	*Per ct.*
SCHEDULE A.—CHEMICALS, OILS AND PAINTS.				
Ink of all kinds and ink powders.......	30 c. per lb.....	25 per cent......	30	25
Iodoform...............................lbs...	$1.50 per lb...	$1 per lb.........	40.45	26.97
Licorice, extracts of, in paste, rolls, or other form.............................lbs...	5½ c. per lb...	5 c. per lb......	46.32	42.10
Magnesia:				
Calcined.............................lbs...	8 c. per lb......	7 c. per lb.......	40.71	35.62
Carbonate of, medicinal.......lbs...	4 c. per lb......	3 c. per lb......	53.12	39.84
Sulphate, of, or Epsom salts.lbs...	3-10 c. per lb...	1-5 c. per lb....	38.34	25.51
Morphia, or morphine, and all salts thereof...............................oz...	50 c. per oz.....	50 c. per oz.....	47.09	47.09
Oils:				
Alizarine assistant, or soluble oil, or oleate of soda, or Turkey red oil—				
Containing 50 per cent or more of castor oil...............galls...	80 c. per gal	30 per cent......	30	30
All other................galls...	30 c. per gal			
Castor.................................galls...	80 c. per gal...	35 c. per gal ...	100.35	43.87
Cod-liver ....galls...	15 c. per gal...	20 per cent......	28.65	20
Flaxseed or linseed, raw, boiled, or oxidized....................galls...	32 c. per gal.	20 c. per gal...	95.14	59.46
Poppy-seed oil, raw, boiled, or oxidized...........................galls...	...........do......		54.37	33.93
Fusel oil or amylic alcohol....lbs...	10 per cent......	10 per cent......	10	10
Hemp seed and rape seed...galls...	10 c. per gal...	10 c. per gal...	24.12	24.12
Olive, fit for salad purposes.galls...	35 c. per gal...	35 c. per gal...	26.92	26.92
Peppermint..............................lbs...	80 c. per lb...	25 per cent......	47.07	25
Seal.....................................galls...	8 c. per gal.....	..........do..........	23.45	25
Fish, not specially provided for, galls.......................................	...........do......	...........do.........	32.12	25
Whale, not specially provided for....................................galls...	...........do......	...........do.........	33.90	25
Opium:				
Aqueous, extract of, for medicinal uses, and tincture of, as laudanum, and all other liquid preparations of, not specially provided for....................lbs...	40 per cent......	20 per cent.......	40	20
Crude or unmanufactured, and not adulterated, containing 9 per cent and over of morphia...	Free...............	Free...............	Free.	Free.
Prepared for smoking, and opium containing less than 9 per cent of morphia.........................lbs...	$12 per lb........	$6 per lb..,......	169.65	84.82
Paints and colors:				
Baryta, sulphate of, or barytes, including barytes earth—				
Manufactured.................tons...	$6.72 per ton..	$3 per ton......:	50.25	26.45
Blues, such as Berlin, Prussian, Chinese, and all others containing ferrocyanide of iron—				
Dry or ground in or mixed with oil.........................lbs...	6 c. per lb.......	6 c. per lb.......	20.03	20.03
Blanc fixe, or satin white or artificial sulphate of barytes...lbs...	¾ c. per lb.....'	25 per cent.....	47.54	25

Comparison of rates of duties between McKinley act and new law.—Continued.

	Rates of duty under.—		Average ad valorem under—	
	McKinley law.	New law.	McKinley law.	New law

			Per ct.	Per ct.
SCHEDULE A—CHEMICALS, OILS, AND PAINTS—Continued.				
Paints and colors—Continued.				
Black, made from bone, ivory, or vegetable, including boneblack and lampblack, dry or ground in oil or water..............lbs...	25 per cent......	20 per cent.......	25	20
Chrome yellow, chrome green, and all other chromium colors in which lead and bichromate of potash or soda are component parts—				
Dry or ground in or mixed with oil..............................lbs...	4½ cts. per lb..	3 cts. per lb....	30.84	20.56
Ocher and ochery earths—				
Ground in oil....................lbs...	1½ cts. per lb..	1¼ cts. per lb..	19.04	16.37
Sienna and sienna earths—				
Ground in oil....................lbs...	1½ cts per lb..	1¼ cts. per lb.	21.14	17.62
Umber and umber earths—				
Ground in oil....................lbs...	..... do	........do	25.80	21.50
Ultramarine ....lbs...	4½ cts. per lb..	3 cts. per lb.....	46.15	30.77
Spirit varnishes..................galls...	$1.32 per gall. and 35 p. c.	$1.32 per gall. and .5 p. c.	69.56	59.56
All other, including gold size or Japan,..... ....galls...	35 per cent......	25 per cent......	35	25
Vermilion red, and colors containing quicksilver, dry or ground in oil or water........lbs...	12 cts. per lb...	20 per cent	26.77	20
Vermilion red, not containing quicksilver, but made of lead, etc........	25 per cent......	6 cents per lb..	25	....
Wash blue containing ultramarine............................lbs...	3 cents per lb...	3 cents per lb..	20.33	20.33
Whiting and Paris white—				
Dry ....lbs...	½ cent per lb...	¼ cent per lb..	142.48	71.24
Ground in oil (putty).........lbs...	1 cent per lb...	½ cent per lb..	189.50	94.75
Zinc, oxide of, and white paint containing zinc, but not containing lead—				
Dry ....lbs...	1¼ cts. per lb..	1 cent per lb...	31.44	25.15
Ground in oil....................lbs...	1¾ cts. per lb..	........do............	40.47	23.15
All other paints and colors—				
Dry or mixed, or ground in water or oil, including lakes, not specially provided for, and artists' colors of all kinds, in tubes or otherwise..............	25 per cent......	25 per cent . .	25	25
Mixed or ground with water or solutions other than oil, and commercially known as artists' water-color paints............	30 per cent......	......do............	30	25
Crayons	25 per cent......	......do	25	25
Smalts and frostings......................	......do	......do	25	25
Brown—				
Spanish, Indian red, and colcothar or oxide of iron	......do	....do	25	25
Vandyke, Cassel earth, or Cassel brown..........................	......do	.......do	25	25
Paris green and London purple (no data).................	25 per cent......	12½ per cent...	12.50	25

Comparison of rates of duties between McKinley act and new law.— Continued.

	Rates of duty under—		Average ad valorem under—	
	McKinley law.	New law.	McKinley law.	New law.
SCHEDULE A.—CHEMICALS, OILS, AND PAINTS—Continued.			*Per ct.*	*Per ct.*
Lead, acetate of—				
Brown (b)..................................lbs...	3¼ cts. per lb..	1¾ cts. per lb...	....	....
White...lbs...	5¼ cts. per lb...	2¾ cts. per lb...	78.04	39.02
Litharge..lbs...	3 cents per lb...	1½ cts. per lb...	94.91	47.45
Lead, nitrate of...........................lbs...	do	do	18.23	9.11
Orange, mineral.........................lbs...	3¼ cts. per lb...	1¾ cts. per lb...	78.80	39.40
Red..lbs...	3 cents per lb...	1½ cts. per lb...	91.17	45.59
White, dry or in pulp, and ground or mixed in oil, and white paint containing lead....................lbs...	do	do	59.21	29.60
Phosphorus....................................lbs...	20 cts. per lb...	15 cts. per lb...	40.79	30.59
Potash—				
Chromate and bichromate of..lbs...	3 cents per lb...	25 cent per...	36.72	25
Hydriodate, iodide and iodate of lbs...	50 cts. per lb...	25 cts. per lb...	19.68	9.84
Nitrate of, or saltpeter, refined, lbs...	1 cent per lb...	½ cent per lb...	21.32	10.66
Pussiate of—				
Red ....lbs...	10 cts. per lb...	25 per cent......	29.04	25
Yellow.......................................lbs...	5 cents per lb...	do	25.40	25
Preparations, medicinal, including medicinal proprietary preparations—				
Of which alcohol is a component part, or in the preparation of which alcohol is used (a)...lbs...	50 cts per lb...	50 cts. per lb...	15.51	15.51
Of which alcohol is not a component part	25 per cent......	25 per cent	25	25
Calomel and other mercurial preparations.........................lbs...	35 per cent......	do	35	25
Preparations or products known as alkalies, and alkaloids, and all combinations of the same, and all chemical compounds and salts, by whatever name known	25 per cent......	25 per cent	25	25
All other essential oils, and combinations of ....lbs...	do	do	25	25
All other fixed or expressed oils, and combinations of.......galls...	do	do	25	25
All other rendered oils and combinations of ....galls...	do	do	25	25
Bicarbonate of potash............lbs...	do	do	25	25
Preparations used as applications to the hair, mouth, teeth, or skin, such as cosmetics, dentifrices, pastes, pomades, powders, and tonics, including all known as toilet preparations not specially provided for.........	50 per cent	40 per cent	50	40
Santonine, and all salts thereof containing 80 per cent or over of santonine....................lbs...	$2.50 per lb......	$1 per pound...	163.35	65.34
Soap:				
Castile...lbs...	1¼ cts. per lb...	20 per cent......	19.48	20
Fancy, perfumed, and all descriptions of toilet ....lbs...	15 cts. per lb...	35 per cent	36.66	35

Comparison of rates of duties between McKinley act and new law—Continued.

	Rates of duty under—		Average ad valorem under—	
	McKinley law.	New law.	McKinley law.	New law.
Schedule A.—Chemicals, Oils, and Paints—Continued.				
Soap—Continued.			*Per ct.*	*Per ct.*
All other, not specially provided for	20 per cent	10 per cent	20	10
Soda:				
Bicarbonate of, or supercarbonate of, or saleratus......lbs	1 cent per lb	½ cent per lb	60.47	30.24
Hydrate of, or caustic.........lbs	......do	......do	42.75	21.37
Bichromate and chromate of..lbs	3 cts. per lb	25 per cent	45.59	25
Soda ash.................lbs	¼ cent per lb	¼ cent per lb	20	20
Sal, or soda crystals ....lbs	......do	⅛ cent per lb	29.06	14.53
Silicate of, or other alkaline silicate.................lbs	¼ cent per lb	⅜ cent per lb	43.50	32.62
Sponges	20 per cent	10 per cent	20	10
Seamoss or Iceland moss (no data)	Free	10 per cent	Free.	10
Strychnia, or strichnine, and all salts thereof ....ounces	40 cts. per oz	30 cts. per oz	93.79	70.34
Sulphur, sublimed, or flowers of tons	$10 per ton	20 per cent	28.66	20
Sulphur, refined ....tons	$8 per ton	20 per cent	34.23	20
Sumac, ground ....lbs	4-10 ct. per lb	10 per cent	19.81	10
Tartar—				
Cream of, and patent ....lbs	6 cts. per lb	20 per cent	21.45	20
Tartars and lees crystals, partly refined...............lbs	4 cts. per lb	......do	31.07	20
Tartrate of soda and potassa, or Rochelle salts.................lbs	3 cts. per lb	2 cts. per lb	16.49	11
Total Schedule A, chemicals, oils, and paints............			31.61	24.44
Schedule B.—Earths, Earthenware, and Glassware.				
Earthen, stone and China ware:				
Brick and tiles—				
Brick fire—				
Not glazed, enameled ornamented or decorated in any manner......tons	$1.25 per ton	25 per cent	25.15	25
Glazed, enameled, ornamented or decorated tons	45 per cent	30 per cent	45	30
Brick, other than fire—				
Not glazed, ornamented, painted, enameled, vitrified, or decorated...M	25 per cent	25 per cent	25	25
Ornamented, glazed, painted, enameled, vitrified, or decorated..M	45 per cent	30 per cent	45	30
Magnesic fire brick (not enumerated ; no data)	25 per cent	$1 per ton	25	....
Not glazed, ornamented, painted, enameled, vitrified, or decorated	25 per cent	25 per cent	25	25
Ornamented, glazed, painted, enameled, vitrified, or decorated, and all encaustic	45 per cent	40 per cent	45	40

Comparison of rates of duties between McKinley act and new law—Continued.

	Rates of duty under—		Average ad valorem under—	
	McKinley law.	New law.	McKinley law.	New. law.

SCHEDULE B.—EARTHS, EARTHENWARE, AND GLASSWARE—Continued.

	McKinley law.	New law.	McKinley law.	New law.
			Per ct.	*Per ct.*
Cement:				
Roman, Portland, and other hydraulic, in barrels, sacks, or other packages..........lbs...	8 c. per 100 lbs	8 c. per 100 lbs	24.09	24.09
Other ....lbs...	20 per cent	10 per cent......	20	10
Lime ....lbs...	6 c. per 100 lbs	5 c. per 100 lbs	30.41	25.34
Plaster of Paris:				
Calcined.........................tons...	$1.75 per ton..	$1.25 per ton...	25.11	17.97
Ground..........................tons...	$1 per ton......	$1 per ton	6.07	6.07
Clays or earths:				
Unwrought or unmanufactured, tons..	$1.50 per ton .	......do	19.72	13.15
China clay, or kaolin...........tons...	$3 per ton......	$2 per ton	39.56	26.38
Wrought or manufactured, not specially provided for......tons...	....do	......do	22.35	14.90
Brown earthenware, common stoneware, and crucibles not ornamented or decorated in any manner..	25 per cent......	20 per cent......	25	20
China, porcelain, parian, bisque, earthen, stone, and crockery ware, including plaques, ornaments, toys, charms, vases, and statuettes—				
Painted, tinted, stained, enameled, printed, gilded, or otherwise decorated or ornamented in any manner............................	60 per cent......	35 per cent......	60	35
Clocks, china, chief value.............	......do	25 per cent......	60	25
Plain white, and not ornamented or decorated in any manner	55 per cent......	30 per cent......	55	30
Gas retorts...........................No...	$3 each............	20 per cent......	20.22	20
Bottles and vials, flint and lime:				
Empty—				
Holding more than 1 pint.lbs...	1 c. per lb	¾ c. per lb.....	61.27	45.95
Holding not more than 1 pint and not less than ¼ pint, lbs	1½ c. per lb...	1⅛ c. per lb...	81.30	60.97
Holding less than ¼ pint, gross	50 c. per gross	40 c. per gross	50.34	40.27
Other on which specific duty would be less than 40 per cent................	40 per cent......	40 per cent......	40	40
Filled—				
Holding more than 1 pint.lbs...	1 c. per lb.......	¾ c. per lb.....	87.79	65.84
Holding not more than 1 pint and not less than ¼ pint, lbs	1½ c. per lb...	1⅛ c. per lb...	116.05	87.04
Holding less than ¼ pint, gross	50 c. per gross	40 c. per gross	119.80	95.84
Other on which specific duty would be less than 40 per cent................	40 per cent......	40 per cent......	40	40
Bottles and vials, green and colored, molded or pressed:				
Empty—				
Holding more than 1 pint.lbs...	1 c. per lb......	¾ c. per lb.....	70.17	52.63
Holding not more than 1 pint and not less than ¼ pint. lbs	1½ c. per lb...	1⅛ c. per lb...	85.67	64.25

Comparison of rates of duties between McKinley act and new law—Continued.

	Rates of duty under—		Average ad valorem under—	
	McKinley law.	New law.	McKinley law.	New law.

SCHEDULE B.—EARTHS, EARTHENWARE, AND GLASSWARE—Continued.

	Rates of duty under—		Average ad valorem under—	
	McKinley law.	New law.	McKinley law.	New law.
Bottles and vials, &c.—Continued. Empty—Continued.			*Per ct.*	*Per ct.*
Holding less than ¼ pint, gross	50 c. per gross	40 c. per gross	64.47	51.58
Other on which specific duty would be less than 40 per cent	40 per cent	40 per cent	40	40
Filled—				
Holding more than 1 pint.lbs.	1 c. per lb	¾ c. per lb	71.48	53.61
Holding not more than 1 pint and not less than ¼ pint, lbs	1½ c. per lb	1⅛ c. per lb	114.42	85.81
Holding less than ¼ pint, gross	50 c. per gross	40 c. per gross	148.08	118.46
Other on which specific duty would be less than 40 per cent	40 per cent	40 per cent	40	40
Demijohns and carboys (covered or uncovered):				
Empty—				
Holding more than 1 pint.lbs.	1 c. per lb	¾ c. per lb	37.91	28.43
Other on which specific duty would be less than 40 per cent	40 per cent	40 per cent	40	40
Filled—				
Other on which specific duty would be less than 40 per cent	do	do	40	40
Flint and lime, pressed glassware, not cut, engraved, painted, etched, decorated, colored, printed, stained, silvered, or gilded	60 per cent	do	60	40
Articles of glass, cut, engraved, painted, colored, printed, stained, decorated, silvered, or gilded, not including plate glass silvered, or looking-glass plates	do	do	60	40
Chemical glassware for use in laboratory, and not otherwise specially provided for	45 per cent	do	45	40
Thin-blown glass, blown with or without a mold, including glass chimneys	60 per cent	do	60	40
All other manufactures of glass, or of which glass shall be the component material of chief value, not specially provided for	do	35 per cent	60	35
Heavy-blown glass, blown with or without a mold, not cut or decorated, finished or unfinished	do	40 per cent	60	40
Porcelain or opal glassware	do	do	60	40
Cylinder, crown and common window glass, unpolished:				
Not exceeding 10 by 15 inches square lbs.	1⅜ c. per lb	1 c. per lb	47.47	34.48
Above 10 by 15 inches, and not exceeding 16 by 24 inches...lbs.	1⅞ c. per lb	1¼ c. per lb	106.19	70.79

Comparison of rates of duties between McKinley act and new law—Continued.

	Rates of duty under—		Average ad valorem under—	
	McKinley law.	New law.	McKinley law.	New law.
SCHEDULE B.—EARTHS, EARTHENWARE, AND GLASSWARE—Continued.				
Cylinder, crown, &c.—Continued.				
Above 16 by 24 inches, and not exceeding 24 by 30 inches...lbs...	2⅜ c. per lb...	1¾ c. per lb...	*Per ct.* 120.66	*Per ct.* 88.90
Above 24 by 30 inches, and not exceeding 24 by 36 inches...lbs...	2⅞ c. per lb...	2 c. per lb......	124.97	86.93
All above 24 by 36 inches......lbs...	3⅛ c. per lb...	2⅛ c. per lb...	116.79	79.41
Cylinder and crown glass, polished, unsilvered:				
Not exceeding 16 by 24 inches square....sq. ft...	4 c. per sq. ft..	2½ c. p. sq. ft..	20.07	12.50
Above 16 by 24 inches, and not exceeding 24 by 30 inches...sq. ft...	6 c. per sq. ft..	4 c. per sq. ft..	27.58	18.39
Above 24 by 30 inches, and not exceeding 24 by 60 inches...sq. ft...	20 c. per sq. ft..	15 c. p. sq. ft..	63.84	47.88
Plate glass, fluted, rolled, or rough (excess of 1 pound per square foot, dutiable at same rates):				
Not exceeding 10 by 15 inches square....sq. ft...	¾ c. per sq. ft..	¾ c. p. sq. ft..	23.08	23.08
Above 10 by 15 inches and not exceeding 16 by 24 inches...sq. ft...	1 c. per sq. ft..	......do	56.58	42.43
Above 16 by 24 inches and not exceeding 24 by 30 inches...sq. ft...	1½ c. p. sq. ft..	1 c. per sq. ft..	64.19	42.90
All above 24 by 30 inches...sq. ft...	2 c. per sq. ft..	1½ c. p. sq. ft..	48.74	36.51
Plate glass, fluted, rolled, or rough, ground, smoothed, or otherwise obscured (excess of 1 pound per square foot, dutiable at same rates):				
Not exceeding 16 by 24 inches square....sq. ft...	5 c. per sq. ft..	5 c. per sq. ft..	20.76	20.76
Above 16 by 24 inches and not exceeding 24 by 30 inches...sq. ft...	8 c. per sq. ft..	8 c. per sq. ft..	34.97	34.97
Above 24 by 30 inches and not exceeding 24 by 60 inches...sq. ft...	25 c. per sq. ft..	20 c. p. sq. ft..	48.03	38.43
All above 24 by 60 inches...sq. ft...	50 c. per sq. ft..	35 c. p. sq. ft..	91.32	63.91
Plate glass, cast, polished, finished, or unfinished, and unsilvered:				
Not exceeding 16 by 24 inches square....sq. ft...	5 c. per sq. ft..	5 c. per sq. ft..	22.22	22.22
Above 16 by 24 inches and not exceeding 24 by 30 inches...sq. ft...	8 c. per sq. ft..	8 c. per sq. ft..	33.22	33.22
Above 24 by 30 inches and not exceeding 24 by 60 inches...sq. ft...	25 c. per sq. ft..	22½ c. p. sq. ft	97.49	87.74
All above 24 by 60 inches...sq. ft...	50 c. per sq. ft..	35 c. per sq. ft..	174.45	122.11
Plate glass, cast, polished, silvered:				
Not exceeding 16 by 24 inches square....sq. ft...	6 c. per sq. ft..	6 c. per sq. ft..	20.39	20.39
Above 16 by 24 inches, and not exceeding 24 by 30 inches sq. ft....	10 c. per sq. ft.	10 c. per sq. ft.	26.06	26.06
Above 24 by 30 inches, and not exceeding 24 by 60 inches sq. ft....	35 c. per sq. ft.	23 c. per sq. ft.	51.97	34.14
All above 24 by 60 inches......sq. ft...	60 c. per sq. ft.	38 c. per sq. ft.	49.39	31.28
Cylinder and crown glass, polished, silvered, and looking-glass plates:				
Not exceeding 16 by 24 inches sq. ft....	6 c. per sq. ft..	6 c. per sq. ft.	19.34	19.34

Comparison of rates of duties between McKinly act and new law.—Continued.

	Rates of duty under—		Average ad valorem under—	
	McKinley.	New law.	McKinley law.	New law.
SCHEDULE B.—EARTHS, EARTHENWARE, AND GLASSWARE—Continued.				
Cylinder and crown glass, polished, silvered, etc.—Continued.				
Above 16 by 24 inches, and not exceeding 24 by 30 inches..sq ft...	10 c. per sq. ft.	10 c. per sq. ft	*Per ct.* 28.68	*Per ct.* 28.68
Above 24 by 30 inches, and not exceeding 24 by 60 inches..sq. ft...	35 c. per sq. ft.	23 c. per sq. ft.	49.77	32.70
All above 24 by 60 inches.....sq.ft...	60 c. per sq. ft.	38 c. per sq. ft.	43.88	27.79
Cylinder, crown, and common window glass, unpolished, when ground, obscured, frosted, sanded, enameled, beveled, etched, embossed, engraved, stained, colored, or otherwise ornamented or decorated:				
Not exceeding 10 by 15 inches square ....lbs...	1⅜ c. per lb. and 10 p. c.	1 c. per lb. and 10 p. c.	19.84	17.15
Above 10 by 15 inches, and not exceeding 16 by 24 inches.....lbs...	1 ⅞ c. per lb. and 10 p. c.	1¼ c. per lb. and 10 p. c.	53.60	39.07
Above 16 by 24 inches, and not exceeding 24 by 30 inches.....lbs...	2 ⅝ c. per lb. and 10 p. c.	1¾ c. per lb. and 10 p. c.	100.42	76.62
Above 24 by 30 inches, and not exceeding 24 by 36 inches.....lbs...	2 ⅞ c. per lb. and 10 p. c.	2 c. per lb. and 10 p. c.	73.33	54.06
All above 24 by 36 inches......lbs...	3 ⅛ c. per lb. and 10 p. c.	2⅛ c. per lb. and 10 p. c.	87.27	62.54
Cylinder and crown glass, polished, unsilvered, when ground, obscured, frosted, sanded, enameled, beveled, etched, embossed, engraved, stained, colored, or otherwise ornamented or decorated:				
Not exceeding 16 by 24 inches square ....sq. ft...	4 c. per sq. ft. and 10 p. c.	2½ c. per sq. ft. and 10 p. c.	24.99	19.36
Above 16 by 24 inches, and not exceeding 24 by 30 inches sq. ft..	6 c. per sq. ft. and 10 p. c.	4 c. per sq. ft. and 10 p. c.	31.79	24.60
Above 24 by 30 inches, but not exceeding 24 by 60 inches sq. ft..	20 c. per sq. ft. and 10 p. c.	15 c. per sq. ft. and 10 p. c.	61.45	48.58
Cylinder and crown glass, polished, silvered, when ground, obscured, frosted, sanded, enameled, beveled, etched, embossed, engraved, stained, colored, or otherwise ornamented or decorated:				
Not exceeding 16 by by 24 inches square ....sq. ft...	6 c. p. sq. ft. and 10 p. c.	6 c. p. sq. ft. and 10 p. c.	23.67	23.67
Above 16 by 24 inches, and not exceeding 24 by 30 inches sq. f	10 c. p. sq. ft. and 10 p. c.	10 c. p. sq. ft. and 10 p. c.	16	16
Above 24 by 30 inches, and not exceeding 24 by 60 inches sq. ft..	35 c. p. sq. ft. and 10 p. c.	23 c. p. sq. ft. and 10 p. c.	36.49	27.14
All above 24 by 60 inches..sq. ft...	60 c. p. sq. ft. and 10 p. c.	38 c. p. sq. ft. and 10 p. c.	40	29

Comparison of rates of duties between McKinley aet and new law—Continued.

	Rates of duty under—		Average ad valorem under—	
	McKinley law.	New law.	McKinley law.	New law.
SCHEDULE B.—EARTHS, EARTHENWARE, AND GLASSWARE—Continued.				
Plate glass, cast, polished, silvered, when ground, obscured, frosted, sanded, enameled, beveled, etched, embossed, engraved, stained, colored, or otherwise ornamented or decorated:			*Per ct.*	*Per ct,*
Not exceeding 16 by 24 inches square...................sq. ft...	6 c. p. sq. ft. and 10 p. c.	6 c. p. sq. ft, and 10 p. c.	14.80	14.80
Above 16 by 24 inches, and not exceeding 24 by 30 inches..sq. ft...	10 c. p. sq. ft. and 10 p. c.	10 c. p. sq. ft. and 10 p. c.	29.54	29.54
Above 24 by 30 inches, and not exceeding 24 by 60 inches sq. ft..............	35 c. p. sq. ft. and 10 p. c.	23 c. p. sq. ft. and 10 p. c.	20.55	16.93
All above 24 by 60 inches.....sq. ft...	60 c. p. sq. ft. and 10 p. c.	38 c. p. sq. ft. and 10 p. c.	39.48	28.67
Plate glass, cast, polished, unsilvered, when ground, obscured, frosted, sanded, enameled, beveled, etched, embossed, engraved, stained, colored, or otherwise ornamented or decorated:				
Not exceeding 16 by 24 inches square....................sq. ft...	5 c. p. sq. ft. and 10 c. p.	5 c. p. sq. ft. and 10 c. p.	24.52	24.52
Above 16 by 24 inches, and not exceeding 24 by 30 inches..sq. ft...	8 c. p. sq. ft. and 10 p. c.	8 c. p. sq. ft. and 10 p.c.	30.98	30.98
Above 24 by 30 inches, and not exceeding 24 by 60 inches .sq. ft...	25 c. p. sq. ft. and 10 p. c.	23 c. p. sq. ft. and 10 p. c.	65.32	60.89
All above 24 by 60 inches...sq. ft...	50 c. p. sq. ft. and 10 p. c.	38 c. p. sq. ft. and 10 p. c.	51.95	41.88
Spectacles and eyeglasses, or spectacles and eyeglass frames.....gross...	60 per cent......	40 per cent......	60	40
Lenses costing $1.50 per gross pairs, or less ....gross pairs...	......do..........	35 per cent......	60	35
Spectacle and eyeglass lenses with their edges ground or beveled to fit frames.....................gross...	......do..............	......do..............	60	35
Stained or painted window glass and stained or painted glass windows, and hand, pocket, or table mirrors not exceeding in size 144 square inches, with or without frames or cases, of whatever material composed.................	45 per cent......	......do..............	45	35
(a) Lenses of glass or pebble, wholly, or partly manufactured, and not specially provided for, and fusible enamel.....................	......do..............	......do..............	45	35
Marble and stone, and manufactures of marble:				
In blocks, rough or squared, of all kinds ....cu. ft...	65 cents per cubic foot.	50 cents per cubic foot.	39.20	30.15
Veined marble, sawed, dressed, or otherwise, including marble slabs and marble paving tiles...cu. ft...	$1.10 per cubic foot.	85 cents per cubic foot.	60.90	47.06
All manufactures of, not especially provided for.....................	50 per cent	45 per cent......	50	45
Clocks, marble, chief value.............	......do..............	25 per cent......	50	25

Comparison of rates of duties between McKinley Act and new law.—Continued.

	Rates of duty under—		Average ad valorem under—	
	McKinley law.	New law.	McKinley law.	New law.
SCHEDULE B—EARTH, EARTHENWARE, AND GLASSWARE— Continued.				
Freestone, granite, sandstone, limestone, and other building or monumental stone, except marble, not specially provided for—			*Per ct.*	*Per ct.*
Undressed or manufactured cu. ft.	11 c. p. cu. ft.	7 c. per cu. ft.	34.41	21.89
Hewn, dressed, or polished	40 per cent	30 per cent	40	30
Grindstones, finished or unfinished tons	$1.75 per ton	10 per cent	13.74	10
Slates, slate chimney pieces, mantels, slabs for tables, and all other manufactures of slate	30 per cent	20 per cent	30	20
Slate roofing	25 per cent	do	25	20
Total Schedule B, earths, earthenware, and glassware			51.50	35.21
SCHEDULE C.—METALS AND MANUFACTURES OF.				
Iron ores.				
All other ore tons	75 cents per ton.	40 cents per ton.	42.70	22.77
Iron in pigs, kentledge, spiegeleisen, ferromanganese, and ferrosilicon:				
Ferrosilicon tons	$6.72 per ton	$4 per ton	26.66	15.87
Spiegeleisen and ferromanganese tons	do	do	25.54	15.44
All other tons	do	do	40.94	24.97
Scrap iron and steel, waste or refuse, fit only to be remanufactured:				
Iron, wrought and cast tons	$6.72 per ton	$4 per ton	47.83	38.47
Steel tons	do	do	43	25.59
Bar iron, rolled or hammered, comprising—				
Flats not less than 1 inch wide nor less than ⅜ of one inch thick lbs	8-10 c. per lb	6-10 c. per lb	36.30	27.22
Round iron not less than ¼ of 1 inch in diameter, and square iron not less than ¾ of 1 inch square lbs	9-10 c. per lb	do	24.57	16.38
Flats less than 1 inch wide or less than ⅜ of 1 inch thick; round iron less than ¾ of 1 inch and not less than 7-16 of 1 inch in diameter; and square iron less than ¾ of 1 inch square lbs	1 cent per lb	do	52.63	31.58
Bars or shapes of rolled iron not specially provided for, and round iron in coils or rods, less than 7-16 of 1 inch in diameter lbs	1 1-10 c. per lb.	8-10 c. per lb.	61.77	44.93
Bars, blooms, billets, or sizes or shapes of any kind, in the manufacture of which charcoal is used as fuel tons	$22 per ton	$12 per ton	56.82	30.99

Comparison of rates of duties between McKinley act and new law—Continued.

	Rates of duty under—		Average ad valorem under—	
	McKinley law.	New law.	McKinley law.	New law.

SCHEDULE C.—METALS AND MANUFACTURES OF.—Continued.

	McKinley law.	New law.	McKinley law.	New law.
			Per ct.	*Per ct.*
All other, and slabs, blooms, or loops..............................lbs...	35 per cent......	5-10 c. per lb..	35	8.29
Beams, girders, joists, angles, channels, car-truck channels, TT columns and posts, or parts or sections of columns and posts, deck and bulb beams, and building forms, together with all other structural shapes, of iron or steel... lbs...	9-10 c. per lb...	6-10 c. per lb...	74.64	49.76
Boiler or other plate, iron or steel (except saw plates) not thinner than No. 10 wire gauge, sheared or unsheared, and skelp iron or steel, sheared or rolled in grooves :				
Valued above 1 cent and not above 1 4-10 cents per pound, lbs....................................	65-100 c. per lb..	......do..............	49.47	45.66
Valued above 1 4-10 cents and not above 2 cents per pound, lbs....................................	8.10 c. per lb...	30 per cent.....	54.35	30
Valued above 2 cents and not above 3 cents per pound.....lbs...	1 1-10 c. per lb.	......do..............	44.45	30
Valued above 3 cents and not above 4 cents per pound.....lbs...	1 5-10 c. per lb.	......do......... ...	40.58	30
Valued above 4 cents and not above 7 cents per pound.....lbs...	2 c. per lb......	25 per cent......	37.77	25
Valued above 7 cents and not above 10 cents per pound.....lbs...	2 8-10 c. per lb.	......do..............	31.02	25
Valued above 10 cents and not above 13 cents per pound.....lbs...	3½ c. per lb...	......do..	32.03	25
Valued above 13 cents per pound, lbs......................................	45 per cent......	......do......... ..:	45	25
Forgings of iron or steel, or forged iron and steel combined, not specially provided for..................lbs...	2 3-10 c. per lb.	1½ c. per lb.(*a*)	44.95	29.30
Hoop, band or scroll, or other iron or steel, valued at 3 cents per pound or less, 8 inches or less in width, and less than 3-8 of an inch thick :				
Not thinner than No. 10 wire gauge...................................lbs...	1 c. per lb	30 per cent.....	45 70	30
Thinner than No. 10 and not thinner than No. 20 wire gauge...................................lbs...	1 1-10 c. per lb.	......do..............	41.41	30
Thinner than No. 20 wire gauge, lbs...	1 3-10 c. per lb.	......do..............	49.52	30
Bars or rails for railways :				
Flat rails punched—				
Iron or steel.................tons...	$13.44 per ton..	7-20 c. per lb...	44.38	25.88
T rails and other railway bars—				
Iron................. ....tons...	......do..............	......do.........	50.09	29.22
Steel or in part of steel ...tons...	......do..	......do.........	58.24	33.99

Comparison of rates of duties between McKinley act and new law—Continued.

	Rates of duty under—		Average ad valorem under—	
	McKinley law.	New law.	New law.	McKinley law.
SCHEDULE C.—METALS AND MANUFACTURES OF—Continued.				
Sheets of iron or steel, common or black, including iron or steel known as common or black taggers' iron or steel. and skelp iron or steel, valued at 3 cents per pound or less:			*Per ct.*	*Per ct.*
Thinner than No. 10 and not thinner than No. 20 wire gauge..lbs...	1 c. per lb......	7-10 c. per lb...	48.90	34.23
Thinner than No. 20 and not thinner than No. 25 wire gauge, lbs..............................	1 1-10 c. per lb.	8-10 c. per lb..	39.46	28.69
Thinner than No. 25 wire gauge, lbs..............................	1 4-10 c. per lb.	1 1-10 c. per lb.	70.24	55.19
Corrugated or crimped.........lbs...	....do.............	......do............	25.24	19.83
Sheets or plates of iron or steel (excepting what are commercially known as tin plates, terne plates, and taggers' tin), galvanized or coated with zinc or spelter, or other metals, or any alloy of these metals:				
Thinner than No. 10 and not thinner than No. 20 wire gauge, lbs..............................	1¾ c. per lb...	95-100 c. per lb.	40.48	21.97
Thinner than No. 20, and not thinner than No. 25 wire gauge, lbs..............................	1 85-100 c. per lb.	1 5-100 c. per lb.	72.70	41-26
Thinner than No. 25 wire gauge, lbs..............................	2 15-100 c. per lb.	1 35-100 c. per lb.	49	30.76
Sheets and plates pickled or cleaned by acid or by any other material or process, and cold rolled, smoothed not polished:				
Thinner than No. 10 and not thinner than No. 20 wire gauge, lbs..............................	1¼ c. per lb...	825-1000 c. per lb.	34.73	22.92
Thinner than No. 20 and not thinner than No. 25 wire gauge, lbs..............................	1 35-100 c. per lb.	925-1000 c. per lb.	44.46	30.45
Thinner than No. 25 wire gauge, lbs..............................	1 65-100 c. per lb.	1 225-1000 c. per lb.	72.79	54.04
Sheet iron or sheet steel polished, planished or glanced.............lbs...	2½ c. per lb...	1¾ c. per lb...	45.93	32.15
Tin plates: (a) Sheets or plates of iron or steel, or taggers iron, or steel coated with tin or lead, or with a mixture of which these metals are a component part, by the dipping or any other process, and commercially known as tin plates, terne plates and taggers' tin—				
Lighter than 63 pounds per 100 square feet ....lbs...	2 2-10 c. per lb.	1 1-5 c. per lb.	78.44	42.32
All other ....lbs...	......do.............	......do............	73.20	39.86
Tin, manufactures of :				
All manufactures of, not specially provided for......................	55 per cent......	35 per cent......	55	35
Foil....................................	......do.............	......do............	55	35

Comparison of rates of duties between McKinley act and new law—Continued.

	Rates of duty under—		Average ad valorem under—	
	McKinley law.	New law.	McKinley law.	New law.

SCHDULE C.—METALS AND MANUFACTURES OF—Continued.

Steel ingots, cogged ingots, blooms, and slabs, by whatever process made; die blocks or blanks; billets and bars and tapered or beveled bars; steamer, crank and other shafts; shafting; wrist or crank pins; connecting rods and piston rods; pressed, sheared or stamped shapes; hammer molds or swaged steel; gun-barrel molds not in bars; alloys used as substitutes for steel tools; all descriptions and shapes of dry sand, loam, or iron-molded steel castings; and steel in all forms and shapes not specially provided for:

	McKinley law.	New law.	McKinley law.	New law.
			Per ct.	*Per ct.*
Valued at 1 cent per pound or less ....lbs...	4-10 c. per lb...	3-10c. per lb...	50.48	37.86
Valued at 1 cent and not above 1 4-10 cents per pound ....lbs...	5-10 c. per lb...	4-10c. per lb...	39.06	31.25
Valued above 1 4-10 cents and not above 1 8-10 cents per pound, lbs.....................................	8-10 c. per lb...	6-10 c. per lb...	52.76	39.57
Valued above 1 8-10 cents and not above 2 2-10 cents per pound lbs.....................................	9-10 c. per lb...	7-10 c. per lb...	44.68	34.76
Valued above 2 2-10 cents and not above 3 cents per pound.....lbs...	1 2-10 c. per lb..	9-10 c. per lb...	43.11	32.33
Valued above 3 cents and not above 4 cents per pound.....lbs...	1 6-10 c. per lb..	1 2-10c. per lb..	41.54	31.16
Valued above 4 cents and not above 7 cents per pound.....lbs...	2 c. per lb.......	1 3-10c. per lb.	35.64	23.16
Valued above 7 cents and not above 10 cents per pound...lbs...	2 8-10c. per lb..	1 9-10 c. per lb,	30.36	20.60
Valued above 10 cents and not above 13 cents per pound...lbs...	3½ c. per lb...	2 4-10c. per lb,	30.07	20.62
Valued above 13 cents and not above 16 cents per pound...lbs...	4 2-10c. per lb..	2 8-10c. per lb..	29.38	19.58
Valued above 16 cents per pound, lbs.....................................	7 c. per lb.......	4 7-10c. per lb.	30.75	20.65

Sheets and plates and saw plates of steel, not specially provided for:

	McKinley law.	New law.	McKinley law.	New law.
Valued above 1 cent and not above 1 4-10 cents per pound, lbs.....................................	5-10 c. per lb...	4-10 c. per lb...	42.91	34.33
Valued above 1 4-10 cents and not above 1 8-10 cents per pound, lbs.....................................	8-10 c. per lb...	6-10 c. per lb...	48.11	36.08
Valued above 1 8-10 cents and not above 2 2-10 cents per pound, lbs.....................................	9-10 c. per lb...	7-10 c. per lb...	41.45	32.24
Valued above 2 2-10 cents and not above 3 cents per pound.....lbs...	1 2-10c. per lb..	9-10 c. per lb...	43.33	32.50
Valued above 3 cents and not above 4 cents per pound.....lbs...	1 6-10 c. per lb..	1 2-10c. per lb..	49.48	37.11

A comparison of rates of duties between McKinley act and new law.—Continued.

	Rates of duty under—		Average ad valorem under—	
	McKinley law.	New law.	McKinley law.	New law.
SCHEDULE C.—METALS AND MANUFACTURES OF—Continued.				
Sheets and plates and saw plates of steel, not specially provided for—Continued.			*Per ct.*	*Per ct.*
Valued above 4 cents and not above 7 cents per pound.....lbs...	2 c. per lb........	13-10 c. per lb..	31.71	20.61
Valued above 7 cents and not above 10 cents per pound...lbs...	2 8-10 c. per lb..	1 9-10 c. per lb.	33.26	22.57
Valued above 10 cents and not above 13 cents per pound...lbs...	3½ c. per lb....	2 4-10 c. per lb..·	31	21.30
Valued above 13 cents and not above 16 cents per pound...lbs...	4 2-10c. per lb..	2 8-10 c. per lb..	29.81	19.86
Valued above 16 cents per pound...........................lbs...	7 c. per lb.......	47-10 c. per lb..	24.78	16.62
Wire rods: (a)				
Rivet, screw, fence, and other iron or steel wire rods, whether round, oval, flat, square, in any other shape, in coils or otherwise, not smaller than No. 6 wire gauge, valued at 3½ cents or less per pound...............lbs...	6 1-10 c. per lb..	4-10 c. per lb...	34	22.67
Flat iron or steel with longitudinal ribs, for the manufacture of fencing, valued at 3 cents or less per pound....................lbs...	......do.............	4-10 c. per lb..	34.04	22.70
Wire cf iron or steel:				
Flat steel wire or sheet steel in strips of any width, whether drawn through dies or rolls, untempered or tempered, 25-1000th of an inch thick or thinner.......................................lbs...	50 per cent.......	40 per cent.......	50	40
Not smaller than No. 10 wire guage ....lbs...	1¼ c. per lb..	1¼ c. per lb ...	32.54	32.54
Smaller than No. 10 and not smaller than No. 16 wire guage, lbs	1¾ c. per lb...	1½ c. per lb....	48.77	41.80
Smaller than No. 16 and not smaller than No. 26 wire gauge lbs	2¼ c. per lb...	2 c. per lb......	45.95	30.63
Smaller than No. 26 wire gauge. lbs	3 c. per lb......	.........do.........	26.08	17.39
Coated with zinc or tin or any other metal (except fence wire and iron or steel, flat, with longitudinal ribs, for the manufacture of fencing)—				
Not smaller than No. 10 wire gauge ....lbs...	1¾ c. p r lb...	1¼ c. per lb....	47.88	34.28
Smaller than No. 10 and not smaller than No. 16 wire gauge.............................lbs...	2¼ c. per lb...	1½ c. per lb...	98.25	65.50
Smaller than No. 26 wire gauge..............................lbs...	3½ c. per lb...	40 per cent....	15.75	40
Wire of iron or steel, covered with cotton, silk, or other material, and wires or strip steel commonly known as crinoline, c rset and hat wire.....................................lbs...	5 c. per lb.......	40 per cent.....	16.66	40

Comparison of rates and duties between McKinley act and new law.—Continued.

	Rates of duty under—		Average ad valorem under—	
	McKinley law.	New law.	McKinley law.	New law.
SCHEDULE C.—METALS AND MANUFACTURES OF—Continued.				
Wire of iron or steel, valued at more than 4 cents per pound (on which the specific duty does not amount to 45 per cent) ....lbs...	45 per cent.....	.........do	*Per ct.* 45	*Per ct.* 40
Do., galvanized....lbs...	45 per cent + ½c. per lb.	.........do.........	54	40
Wire, card, for the manufacture of card clothing....lbs...	35 per cent.....	.........do	35	40
Wire rope and wire strand:				
Made of iron wire—				
Smaller than No. 10 and not smaller than No. 16 wire gauge....lbs...	2¾ c. per lb...	2¼ c per lb.....	73.94	60.49
Smaller than No. 16 and not smaller than No. 26 wire gauge....lbs...	3¼ c. per lb...	2½ c. per lb...	57.56	44.27
Smaller than No. 26 wire gauge....lbs...	4 c. per lb......	3 c. per lb......	26.50	19.87
Smaller than No 26 wire gauge....lbs...	45 per cent + 1 c. per lb	.........do.........	61.74	52.26
Galvanized—				
Smaller than No. 10 and not smaller than No. 16 wire gauge....lbs...	3¼ c. per lb...	2½ c. per lb...	88.85	68.35
Smaller than No. 16 and not smaller than No. 26 wire gauge....lbs...	3¾ c. per lb...	1 cent per lb. and 40 per ct.	53.60	55
Smaller than No. 26 wire gauge....lbs...	4½ c. per lb...	.........do	86.72	59.27
Smaller than No. 26 wire gauge....lbs...	45 per cent + 1½ c. per lb...	.........do	63.86	52.57
Made of steel wire—				
Not smaller than No. 10 wire gauge....lbs...	3¼ c. per lb...	1 cent per lb. and 40 per ct.	66.[illegible]8	60.61
Smaller than No. 10 and not smaller than No. 16 wire gauge....lbs...	3¾ c. per lb...	.........do	57.02	55.20
Smaller than No. 16 and not smaller than No. 26 wire gauge....lbs...	4¼ c. per lb...	.........do.........	47.66	51.21
Smaller than No. 26 wire gauge....lbs...	5 c. per lb......	.........do.........	13.67	42.79
Galvanized—				
Not smaller than No. 10 wire gauge....lbs...	3¾ c. per lb.....	.........do.........	80.65	61.51
Smaller than No. 10 and not smaller than No. 16 wire gauge....lbs...	4¼ c. per lb...	.........do.	109.25	65.71
Smaller than No. 16 and not smaller than No. 26 wire gauge....lbs...	4¾ c per lb.....	.........do.	77.40	56.29
Smaller than No. 26 wire gauge....lbs...	5½ c. per lb...	.........do.........	80.84	54.70

Comparison of rates of duty between McKinley act and the new law.—Continued.

	Rates of duty under—		Average advalorum under—	
	McKinley law.	New law.	McKinley law.	New law.
SCHEDULE C.—METALS AND MANUFACTURES OF—Continued.				
Wire rope and wire strand—Cont'd Not smaller than No. 5 wire gauge, cold-rolled, cold-hammered, or polished in addition to the ordinary process of hot rolling or hammering lbs......	45 p. c.—2 cts per pound.	40 per cent......	*Per ct.* 96.15	*Per ct.* 40
Wire cloths and wire nettings, made meshes of any form, from iron or steel wire— Not smaller than No. 10 wire gauge...............lbs...	3¼ c. per lb...	1 cent per lb. and 40 per ct.	79.30	64.40
Galvanized— Smaller than No. 10 and not smaller than No. 16 wire gauge lbs..............	4¼ cts.—1½ ct per pound.	..........do..........	24.84	44.97
Steel ingot, cogged ingots, blooms and slabs, by whatever process made; die blocks or blanks; billets and bars and tapered or beveled bars; steamer, crank and other shafts; shafting; wrist or crank pins; connecting rods and piston rods; pressed, sheared, or stamped shapes; hammer molds or swaged steel; gun-barrel molds, not in bars; alloys used as substitutes for steel tools; all descriptions and shapes of dry-sand, loam, or iron-molded steel castings; and steel in all forms and shapes not specially provided for, cold-rolled, cold-hammered, or polished in any way in addition to the ordinary process of hot-rolling or hammering:				
Valued above 7 cents and not above 10 cents per pound...lbs...	2 8-10 c.—¼ c. per pound.	1 9-10 c per lb.	36.63	22.75
Valued above 13 cents and not above 16 cents per pound...lbs...	4 2-10 c. per lb..	2 8-10 c. per lb.	29.41	18.51
Valued above 16 cents per pound lbs..............	7 c. per lb......	4 7-10c. per lb..	25.85	16.76
Boiler or other plate iron or steel (except saw plates), not thinner than No. 10 wire gauge, sheared or unsheared, and skelp iron or steel, sheared or rolled in grooves, cold-rolled, cold-hammered, or polished in addition to the ordinary process of hot rolling or hammering—				
Valued above 2 cents and not above 3 cents per pound.....lbs...	1 1-10 c.—½ c. per pound.	35 per cent.....	55.81	35
Valued above 3 cents and not above 4 cents per pound lbs	1 5-10 c. —¼c. per pound.	35 per cent......	48	35

Comparison of rates of duties between McKinley act and new law.—Continued.

	Rates of duty under—		Average ad valorem under—	
	McKinley law.	New law.	McKinley law.	New law.
SCHEDULE C—METALS AND MANUFACTURES OF—Continued.				
Sheets of iron or steel, common or black, including iron or steel known as common or black taggers' iron or steel, and skelp iron or steel, valued at 3 cents per pound or less, cold-rolled, cold-hammered, or polished in any way in addition to the ordinary process of hot rolling or hammering—				
Thinner than No. 10 and not thinner than No. 20 wire gauge ... lbs...	1¼ c. per lb...	.825 c. per lb...	*Per ct.* 41.70	*Per ct.* 27.52
Thinner than No. 20 and not thinner than No. 25 wire gauge ... lbs...	1.35 c. per lb...	.925 c. per lb...	55.61	38.10
Thinner than No. 25 wire gauge lbs ...	1.65 c. per lb...	1.225 c. per lb...	79.47	58.99
Sheets and plates and saw plates of steel, not specially provided for, cold-rolled, cold-hammered, or polished in any way in addition to the ordinary process of hot rolling or hammering—				
Valued above 16 cents per lb. lbs ...	7 c. + ¼ c. per pound.	4 7-10 c. per lb..	31.19	20.22
Sheets and plates and saw plates of steel, not specially provided for, cold-rolled, cold-hammered, blued, brightened, tempered, or polished by any proce s to such perfected surface finish or polish better than the grade of cold-rolled, smooth only, hereinbefore provided for—				
Valued above 4 cents and not above 7 cents per pound..lbs...	2 c. + 1¼ c. per pound.	1 3-10 c. per lb..	50.11	20.04
Valued above 7 cents and not above 10 cents per pound..lbs...	2 8-10 c. + 1¼ c. per pound.	1 9-10 c. per lb.	51.48	24.14
Valued above 10 cents and not above 13 cents per pound..lbs...	3½ c. + 1¼ c. per pound.	2 4-10 c. per lb..	42.34	21.39
Valued above 13 cents and not above 16 cents per pound..lbs...	4 2-10 c. + 1¼ c. per pound.	2 8-10 c. per lb..	35.05	18.00
Valued above 16 cents per pound lbs ...	7 c. + 1¼ c. per pound.	4 7-10 c. per lb..	15.33	8.74
Steel circular-saw plates—				
Valued above 4 cents and not above 7 cents per pound..lbs...	3 c. per lb ...	1 3-10 c. per lb..	50.81	22.01
Valued above 7 cents and not above 10 cents per pound..lbs...	3 8-10 c. per lb..	1 9-10 c. per lb..	39.48	19.74
Valued above 10 cents and not above 13 cents per pound..lbs...	4½ c. per lb ...	2 4-10 c. per lb..	35 99	19.20

Comparison of rates of duties between McKinley act and new law.—Continued.

	Rates of duty under—		Average ad valorem under—	
	McKinley law.	New law.	McKin-ley law.	New law.

SCHEDULE C.—METALS AND MANUFAC-TURES OF—Continued.

	McKinley law.	New law.	McKinley law.	New law.
			Per ct.	*Per ct.*
Anchors or parts thereof, mill irons and mill cranks, of wrought iron, and wrought iron for ships, and forgings of iron or steel, for vessels, steam engines, and locomotives, or parts thereof, weighing each 25 pounds or more............lbs...	1 8-10 c. per lb..	1 2-10 c. per lb.	32.95	21.89
Axles or parts thereof, axle bars, axle blanks, or forgings for axles, of iron or steel, without reference to the stage or state of manufacture (a) lbs ...	2 c. per lb	1½ c. per lb ...	27.35	20.51
Anvils ....lbs...	2¼ c. per lb ...	1¾ c. per lb ...	39.04	27.33
Hammers and sledges (blacksmiths'), track tools, wedges, and crowbars, of iron or steel.............lbs...	2¼ c. per lb ...	1½ c. per lb ...	36.50	24.33
Tubes, pipes, flues, or stays, boiler or other, of wrought iron or steel lbs ...	2½ c. per lb ...	25 per cent......	10.18	25
Bolts, with or without threads or nuts, or bolt blanks, and finished hinges or hinge blanks of iron or steel ....lbs...	2¼ c. per lb ...	1½ c. per lb ...	31.88	21.26
Nuts and washers of wrought iron or steel ....lbs...	......do	25 per cent......	26.35	25
Card clothing:				
Manufactured from tempered steel wire.....................sq. ft...	50c. per sq. ft...	40 c. p. sq. ft...	58.10	46.48
Other.........................sq. ft...	25c. per sq. ft..	20 c. p. sq. ft...	25.92	20.74
Castings:				
Cast-iron pipe of every description ....lbs...	9-10 c. per lb...	6-10 c. per lb...	19.81	13.21
Cast-iron vessels, plates, stove plates, andirons, sad irons, tailors' irons, and hatters' irons, and castings of iron not specially provided for...............lbs...	1 2-10c. per lb..	8-10 c. per lb ..	26.97	17.98
Malleable-iron castings, not specially provided for...............lbs...	1¾ c. per lb ...	9-10 c. per lb ..	31.83	16.37
Hollow ware, coated, glazed, or tinned ....lbs...	3 c. per lb	2 c. per lb	35.33	23.55
Chain or chains of all kinds, made of iron or steel:				
Not less than ¾ of 1 inch in diameter ....lbs...	1 6-10 c. per lb..	30 per cent......	77.93	30
Less than ¾ of 1 inch and not less than ⅜ of 1 inch in diameter ....lbs...	1 8-10 c. per lb..	......do..............	47.28	30
Less than ⅜ of 1 inch in diameter ....lbs...	2½ c. per lb ...	......do..............	51.84	30
Other ....lbs...	45 per cent......	......do..............	45	30
Cutlery:				
(a) Penknives or pocket knives of all kinds, or parts thereof, and erasers, or parts thereof, wholly or partly manufactured—				
Valued at not more than 50 cents per dozen ....doz...	12 c. per doz. and 50 p. ct.	{ 25 per cent ... 12 c. per doz. and 25 p.ct.	79.72	} 25(b) 54 72 (c)

Comparison of rates of duties between McKinley act and new law.—Continued.

	Rates of duty under—		Average adval-orem under—	
	McKinley law.	New law.	McKin-ley law.	New law.

SCHEDULE C METALS AND MANUFAC-
    TURES OF—Continued.

Valued at more ... ... dozen and ... ... ing $1.50 per dozen...doz...	50 c. per doz. and 50 p. ct.	25 c. per doz. and 25 p.ct.	96.17	(d) 61.94 (e)
Valued at more than $1.50 per dozen and not exceed-ing $3 per doz...........doz...	$1 per dozen and 50 p. ct.	40 c. per doz. and 25 p.ct. 75 c. per doz. and 25 p. ct.	94.47	58.36
Valued at more than $3 per doz...................doz...	$2 per dozen and 50 p. ct.	50 per cent......	86.95	50
Razors and razor blades, finished or unfinished—				
Valued at less than $4 per dozen ....doz...	$1 per dozen and 30 p. ct.	45 per cent......	67.07	45
Valued at $4 or more per dozen ....doz...	$1.75 per doz. and 30 p. ct.	......do..............	62.74	45
Swords, sword blades, and side arms..	35 per cent......	35 per cent......	35	35
Table knives, forks, steels, and all butchers', hunting, kitchen, bread, vegetable, fruit, cheese, plumbers', painters', palette, and artists' knives of all sizes, finished or unfinished:				
Valued at not more than $1 per dozen pieces ....doz...	10 c. per doz. and 30 p.ct.	......do..............	47.64	35
Valued at more than $1 and not more than $2 per dozen pieces doz...............	35 c. per doz. and 30 p. ct.	......do..............	52.99	35
Valued at more than $2 and not more than $3 per dozen pieces doz...............	40 c. per doz. and 30 p. ct.	......do..............	46.05	35
Valued at more than $3 and not more than $8 per dozen pieces doz	$1 per dozen and 30 p. ct.	45 per cent	51.89	45
Valued at more than $8 per dozen pieces...........doz...	$2 per dozen and 30 p. ct.	......do..............	48.73	45
All carving and cooks' knives and forks of all sizes, finished or unfinished—				
Valued at not more than $4 per dozen pieces ....doz...	$1 per dozen and 30 p. ct.	35 per cent......	74.46	35
Valued at more than $4 and not more than $8 per dozen pieces doz...............	$2 per dozen and 30 p. ct.	45 per cent......	60.97	45
Valued at more than $8 and not more than $12 per dozen pieces ....doz...	$3 per dozen and 30 p. ct.	......do..............	59.83	45
Valued at more than $12 per dozen pieces ....doz...	$5 per dozen and 30 p. ct.	......do..............	58.52	45
Files, file-blanks, rasps, and floats of all cuts and kinds:				
4 inches in length and under..doz...	35 c. per doz.	35 c. per doz...	67.08	67.08
Over 4 inches in length and un-der 9 inches...............doz...	75 c. per doz...	60 c. per doz...	65.48	52.39
Files, file-blanks, rasps, and floats of all cuts and kinds—Continued.				
9 inches in length and under 14 inches, ...doz...	$1.30 per doz..	$1 per doz......	50.97	39.20

Comparison of rates of duties between McKinley act and new law.—Continued.

	Rates of duty under—		Average ad valorem under—	
	McKinley law.	New law.	McKinley law.	New law.
Schedule C.—Metals and Manufactures of—Continued.				
Files, file-blanks, &c.—Continued.			Per ct.	Per ct.
14 inches in length and over, doz..	$2 per dozen...	$1 per doz......	49.76	24.88
Firearms:				
Muskets and sporting rifles............	25 per cent......	25 per cent......	25	25
Pistols, revolving—				
Valued at not more than $1.50 each number......................	40c. each and 35 per cent.	30 per cent......	64.03	30
Valued at more than $1.50 each, number......................	$1 each and 35 per cent.	......do............	68.43	30
Shotguns, double-barreled sporting, breech-loading—				
Valued at not more than $6. each................No...	$1.50 each and 35 per cent.	......do............	67.99	30
Valued at more than $6 and not more than $12 each..No...	$4 each and 35 per cent.	......do............	80.30	30
Valued at more than $12 each, No	$6 each and 35 per cent.	......do............	46.49	30
Shotguns, single barreled, breech-loading...............No...	$1 each and 35 per cent.	......do............	41.10	30
Sheets and plates, wares or articles, of iron and steel:				
Enameled or glazed with vitreous glasses ....,...	45 per cent.....	35 per cent......	45	35
Enameled or glazed with vitreous glasses with more than one color, or ornamented................	50 per cent.....	......do............	50	35
Nails, spikes and tacks:				
Nails and spikes, cut, of iron or steel, pounds............................	1 c. per lb......	22½ per cent...	23.58	22.5
Nails, horseshoe, hob, and all other wrought iron or steel nails, not specially provided for lbs	4 c. per lb......	30 per cent......	36.48	30
Nails, wire, made of wrought iron or steel—				
Shorter than 1 inch and lighter than No. 16 wire gauge. lbs	......do............	25 per cent.....	46.43	25
From 1 inch to 2 inches in length, and lighter than No. 12 and not lighter than No. 16 wire gauge................lbs...	2½ c. per lb.....	......do............	36.50	25
2 inches long and longer, not lighter than No. 12 wire gauge ....lbs...	2 c. per lb.......	......do............	30.91	25
Spikes of wrought iron or steel...lbs...	1 8-10 c. per lb.	......do............	107.15	25
Horse, mule or ox shoes of wrought iron or steel............................lbs...	......do............	......do............	19.66	25
Tacks, brads or sprigs, cut—				
Not exceeding 16 ounces to the M.....................................M...	2½ c. per M....	......do............		25
Needles:				
For knitting or sewing machines, crochet and tape needles, and bodkins of metal.......................	35 per cent......	......do............	35	25
Knitting and all others not specially provided for......................	25 per cent......	......do............	25	25

Comparison of rates of duties between McKinly act and the new law.—Continued.

	Rates of duty under—		Average ad valorem under—	
	McKinley law.	New law.	McKinley law.	New law.
SCHEDULE C.—METALS AND MANUFACTURES OF—Continued.			*Per ct.*	*Per ct.*
Engraved plates of steel	25 per cent	25 per cent	25	25
Stereotype plates and electrotype plates, and plates of other materials engraved or lithographed for printing	do	do	25	25
Railway fish plates or splice bars, of iron or steel...............lbs	1c. per lb	do	72.18	25
Rivets of iron or steel...............lbs	2½ c. per lb	do	20.78	25
Saws:				
Circular saws	30 per cent	do	30	25
Crosscut saws...........linear feet	8 c. p. lin. ft.	6 c. p. lin. ft.	16.98	12.74
Hand, back, and other saws not specially provided for	40 per cent	25 per cent	40	25
Mill, pit, and drag saws—(a)				
Not over 9 inches wide, linear feet	10 c. p. lin. ft.	10c.p.lin. ft. }	16.67	15
Over 9 inches wide, linear feet	15 c. p. lin. ft.	8c.p.lin. ft. }		
Screws, commonly called wood screws—				
½ inch and less in length......lbs	14 c. per lb	10 c. per lb	1.33	1
Over ½ inch and not more than 1 inch in length...............lbs	10 c. per lb	7 c. per lb	83.33	58.33
Over 1 inch and not more than 2 inches in length...............lbs	7 c. per lb	5 c. per lb	46.67	33.33
More than 2 inches in length..lbs	5 c. per lb	3 c. per lb	110.95	66.57
Umbrella and parasol ribs, stretcher frames, tips, runner handles, or parts thereof, made in whole or chief part of iron, steel or any other metal (no data)	45 per cent	50 per cent	45	50
Wheels or parts thereof, made of iron or steel, and steel-tired wheels for railway purposes, whether wholly or partly finished, and iron or steel locomotive, car, or other railway tires, or parts thereof, wholly or partly manufactured (a)...............lbs	2½ c. per lb	1¼ c. per lb	83.72	41.86
Ingots, cogged ingots, blooms, or blanks, for railway wheels and tires, without regard to the degree of manufacture...............lbs	1¾ c. per lb	do	55.61	39.72
Aluminum:				
In crude form, and alloys of any kind in which aluminum is the component material of chief value...............lbs	15 c. per lb	10 c. per lb	22.28	14.85
Argentine, albata or German silver, unmanufactured...............lbs	25 per cent	15 per cent	25	15
Brass:				
Bars or pigs...............lbs	1½ c. per lb	10 per cent	9.97	10
Old and clippings from brass, or Dutch metal, and old sheathing, or yellow metal, fit only for re-manufacture...............lbs	do	do	11.37	10
Bronze powder...............lbs	12 c. per lb	40 per cent	36.26	40
Bronze or Dutch metal, in leaf, in packages of 100 leaves...............pkgs	8 c. per pack	do	102.25	40

Comparison of rates of duties between McKinley act and new law—Continued.

	Rates of duty unde,—		Average ad valorem under—	
	McKinley law.	New law.	McKinley law.	New law.
Schedule C.—Metals and Manufactures of—Contined.				
			Per ct.	*Per ct.*
Aluminum—leaves in packages of 100 leaves..........................pkgs...	8 c per pack...	40 per cent	88.93	40
Plates, rolled, called brazier's copper, sheets, rods, pipes and copper bottoms................................lbs...	35 per cent......	20 per cent.....	35	20
Sheathing or yellow metal, of which copper is the component material of chief value, and not composed wholly or in part of iron ungalvanized..............................lbs...	......do............	......do............	35	20
Gold and silver, manufactures of :				
Bullions and metal thread of gold, silver, or other metals not specially provided for.........	30 per cent......	25 per cent......	30	25
Gold leaf, in packages of 500 leaves.............................pkgs...	$2 per pack.....	30 per cent.....	44.87	30
Silver leaf, in packages of 500 leaves.............................pkgs...	75 c. per pack..	......do............	77.78	30
Lead, and manufactures of : (b)				
Lead contained in silver ore, (b) lbs....................................	1½ c. per lb....	¾ c. per lb......	75.36	37.68
Lead contained in other ore and dross...............................lbs...	......do............	......do............	28.20	14.10
Pigs and bars, molten and old refuse lead, run into blocks and bars, and old scrap lead fit only to be remanufactured (c) ...lbs...	2 c. per lb......	1 c. per lb......	49.13	24.56
Sheets, pipes, shot, glaziers' lead, and lead wire.....................lbs...	2½ c. per lb...	1¼ c. per lb...	36.65	18.33
Metals unwrought, and metallic mineral substances in a crude state, not specially provided for....................	20 per cent	20 per cent.....	20	20
Mica...................................lbs...	35 per cent	......do............	35	20
Nickel, nickel oxide, alloy of any kind in which nickel is the material of chief value.......................lbs...	10 c. per lb.....	6 c. per lb......	23.77	14.26
Pens, metallic, except of gold..gross...	12c. per gross..	8. c. p. gross..	44.47	29.71
Gold pens..	30 per cent.....	25 per cent......	30	25
Penholder tips and penholders, or parts thereof..............................	30 per cent......	25 per cent......	30	25
Pins, solid head or other, including hair, safety, hat, bonnet, shawl, and belt pins.............................	......do............	......do............	30	25
Quicksilver..	10 c. per lb.....	7 c. per lb	24.79	17.35
Type metal	1½ c. per lb....	¾ c. per lb.....	47.66	23.83
Types, new.......................................	25 per cent.....	15 per cent......	25	15
Chronometers, box or ship's, and parts thereof	10 per cent......	10 per cent......	10	10
Watches, and parts of :				
Watches	25 per cent......	25 per cent......	25	25
Watch cases, movements, glasses, and parts of..............................	......do............	......do............	25	25
Zinc or spelter, and manufactures of :				
In blocks or pigs.....................lbs	1¾ c. per lb...	1 c. per lb......	32.32	18.47
In sheets..................................lbs	2¼ c. per lb...	1¼ c. per lb ...	29.19	14.59
Old and worn out, fit only to be remanufactured ....lbs	1¼ c. per lb...	¾ c. per lb.....	21.99	13.19

Comparison of rates of duties between McKinley act and new law—Continued.

	Rates of duty under—		Average ad valorem under—	
	McKinley law.	New law.	McKinley law.	New law.
SCHDEULE C.—METALS AND MANUF. CTURES OF—Continued.				
Manufactures, articles or wares not specially provided for:			*Per ct.*	*Per ct.*
Brass	45 per cent	35 per cent	45	35
Buttons, metal	do	do	45	35
Carriages, etc	do	do	45	35
Clocks	do	25 per cent	45	35
Copper	do	35 per cent	45	35
Gold and silver	do	do	45	35
Machinery	do	do	45	45
Iron and steel	do	do	45	35
Lead	do	do	45	35
Aluminum	do	do	45	35
Bronze	do	do	45	35
Metals, n. e. s	do	do	45	35
Nickel	do	do	45	35
Platinum	do	do	45	35
Zinc	do	do	45	35
Total Schedule C, metals			58.33	36.53
SCHEDULE D.—WOOD AND MANUFACTURES OF.				
Boards, planks, deal, and other sawed lumber:				
Of hemlock, whitewood, sycamore, white pine, and bass wood—				
Planed or finished on one side, M ft	$1.50 per M ft	Free	21.66	Free
Planed or finished on two sides, M ft	$2 per M ft	Free	15.26	Free
Planed on one side and tongued and grooved	do	Free	13.85	Free
Planed on two sides and tongued and grooved	$2.50 per M. ft	Free	13.20	Free
All sawed lumber not specially provided for:				
Planed or finished on one side, M ft	do	Free	26.35	Free
Planed or finished on two sides, M ft	$3 per M ft	Free	26.24	Free
Planed on one side and tongued and grooved	do	Free	24.16	Free
Planed on two sides and tongued and grooved	$3.50 per M ft	Free	30.99	Free
Sawed boards, planks, deals, and all forms of sawed cedar, lignum vitæ, lancewood, ebony, box, granadilla, mahogany, rosewood, satinwood, and all other cabinet woods not further manufactured than sawed, M ft	15 per cent	25 per cent	15	25
Shooks, sugar box, and packing boxes and packing-box shooks	30 per cent	20 per cent	30	20
Casks and barrels, empty	do	do	30	20
Tooth-picks of vegetable substance (no data)	35 per cent	25 per cent	35	25

Comparison of rates of duties between McKinley act and New Law.—Continued.

	Rates of duty under—		Average ad valorem under –	
	McKinley law.	New law.	McKinley law.	New law.
Schedule D.—Wood and Manufacture of—Continued.			*Per ct.*	*Per ct.*
Chair cane, or reeds wrought or manufactured from rattans or reeds.	10 per cent......	10 per cent......	10	10
Furniture, cabinet or house, wholly or partly finished...............	35 per cent......	25 per cent......	35	25
All other manufactures of wood,'or of which wood is the component material of chief value, not specially provided for............................	......do.............	......do............	35	25
Clocks, wood chief value..............	35 per cent......	25 per cent......	35	25
Carriages and parts of, wood chief value	......do.............	......do............	35	25
Total Schedule D, wood..........			31.79	23.62
Schedule E.—Sugar.				
Sugar and molasses :				
Molasses.........................galls...	Free...............	Above 40° and not above 56°, 2 c. per gal., above 56°, 4 c. per gall.	Free	15.54
Sugar all not above No. 16, Dutch standard in color, tank bottoms, sugar drainings, and sugar sweepings, sirups of cane juice, melada, concentrated melada, and concrete and concentrated mola ses ....lbs...	Free...............	40 per cent......	Free	40
Sugar, above No. 16, Dutch standard in color—				
Beet, cane, and other except maple............................lbs...	5-10 c. per lb...	40 per ct. and 1-8 c. per lb..	12.86	43.21
Beet, cane, and other, except maple (if export bounty is in excess of that paid on sugar of a lower grade)...lbs...	6-10 c. per lb...	40 per cent. and 1-8 cent plus 1-10 c. per lb.=40 per cent and 2½ mills per lb.	16.12	46.07
Maple........................... lbs...	5-10 c. per lb..	40 per cent and 1-8 c. per lb.	6.20	41.52
Sugar candy and confectionery, including chocolate confectionery, made wholly or in part of sugar—				
Valued at 12 cents or less per pound, and refined sugar, when tinctured, colored, or in any way adulterated-lbs...	5 c. per lb	35 per cent......	119.90	35
Other, not specially provided for............................	50 per cent......	......do.............	50	35
Glucose or grape sugar...............lbs...	¾ c. per lb...	15 per cent......	23.71	15
Saccharine (not enumerated)..............		25 per cent......		25
Total Schedule E, sugar..............			14.55	39.59

Note.—Hawaiian molasses and sugar, now free of duty, are excluded from the estimate. There was imported of the same during the fiscal year 1893, from Hawaii 67,324 gallons of molasses and 288,517,929 pounds of sugar.

Comparisons of rates of duties between the McKinley act and new law.

	Rates of duty under—		Average ad valorem under—	
	McKinley law.	New law.	McKinley law.	New law.
SCHEDULE F.—TOBACCO, AND MANUFACTURES OF.				
Tobacco, and manufacture of :			*Per ct.*	*Per ct.*
Leaf tobacco, suitable for cigar wrappers—				
Not stemmed ....lbs...	$2 per lb.........	$1.50 per lb.....	338.68	179.01
Stemmed ....lbs...	$2.75 per lb.....	$2.25 per lb.....	89.93	73.10
Leaf, other, unmanufactured and not stemmed...............lbs...	35 c. per lb.....	35 c. per lb.....	81.93	81.93
Leaf, other, stemmed.............lbs...	50 c. per lb.....	50 c. per lb.....	95.44	95.44
All other ....lbs...	40c. per lb......	40 c. per lb.....	198.59	198.59
Snuff and snuff flour, manufactured of tobacco, ground dry, or damp, and pickled, scented or otherwise...................lbs...	50 c. per lb.....	50 c. per lb.....	141.78	141.78
Cigars and cheroots of all kinds, lbs....................	$4.50 per lb. and 25 per c.	$4 per lb. and 25 per cent...	125.36	114.22
Cigarettes and paper cigars, including wrappers.............lbs...	......do.............	......do.............	155.44	140.95
Total Schedule F, tobacco.........			117.82	105.95
SCHEDULE G.—AGRICULTURAL PRODUCTS AND PROVISIONS.				
Animals, not elsewhere specified :				
Horses—				
Valued at less than $150 each, No.......................	$30 per head...	20 per cent......	31.55	20
Valued at $150 and over...No...	30 per cent.....	......do.	30	20
Mules......................No...	$30 per head...	......do.	93.26	20
Cattle—				
One year old or less.........No...	$2 per head.....	......do	43.53	20
More than 1 year old.......No...	$10 per head...	......do	63.22	20
Hogs......................No...	$1.50 per head.	......do , ...	12.03	20
Sheep—				
Less than 1 year old........No...	75c. per head..	......do	22.01	20
One year old or more......No...	$1.25 per head..	......do	25.35	20
All other....................	20 per cent.....	......do	20	20
Breadstuffs :				
Barley...................bush...	30c. per bu....	30 per cent.....	64.68	30
Barley malt............ ....bush...	45c. per bu.....	40 per cent......	36.30	40
Barley, pearled, patent, or hulled, lbs..	2c. per lb........	30 per cent......	15.95	30
Buckwheat,...............bush...	15c. per bu.....	20 per cent......	37	20
Corn or maize.............bush...	......do	......do.............	22.20	20
Corn meal...............bush...	20c. per bu......	......do.............	24.58	20
Macaroni, vermicelli, and similar preparations.....................lbs...	2c. per lb........	20 per cent......	39.26	20
Oats.....................bush...	15c. per bu......	......do.............	35.99	20
Oatmeal..................lbs...	1c. per lb........	15 per cent......	17.82	15
Rice :				
Cleaned..................lbs...	2c. per lb........	1½c. per lb....	111.85	83.89
Uncleaned................lbs...	1¼c. per lb....	8-10c. per lb...	64.19	41.08
Paddy...................lbs...	¾c. per lb......	¾c. per lb......	51.04	51.04
Rice flour, rice meal, and broken rice which will pass through a wire sieve known commercially as No. 12.................lbs...	¼c. per lb......	¼c. per lb.	14.08	14.08
Rye......................bush...	10c. per bu.....	20 per cent.....	4.94	20

Comparison of rates of duties between McKinley act and new law.—Continued.

	Rates of duty under—		Average ad valorem under—	
	McKinley law.	New law.	McKinley law.	New law.
SCHEDULE G.—AGRICULTURAL PRODUCTS AND PROVISIONS.—Continued.			*Per ct.*	*Per ct.*
Rye flour.....................lbs...	¼c. per lb......	20 per cent.....	....	20
Wheat.....................bush...	25c. per lb......	......do............	20.42	20
Wheat flour ....bbls...	25 per cent.....	......do	25	20
Dairy Products:				
Butter, and substitutes therefor, lbs......................	6c. per lb........	4c. per lb........	32.88	21.92
Cheese ....lbs...	......do	......do............	42.96	28.64
Milk, preserved or condensed, including weight of package..lbs...	3c. per lb........	2c. per lb........	33.92	22.62
Milk, sugar of......................lbs...	8c. per lb........	5c. per lb........	65.37	40.85
Vegetables:				
Beans ....bush...	40c. per bu.....	20 per cent.....	40.63	20
Prepared or preserved—				
Beans, pease, and mushrooms, in tins, jars, bottles, or otherwise..........................	40 per cent.....	30 per cent.....	40	30
Eggs..............................doz...	5c. per doz.....	3c. per doz.....	41.29	24.78
Hay..............................tons...	$4 per ton......	$2 per ton......	43.31	21.65
Honey..............................galls...	20c. per gall...	10c. per gall...	44.83	22.42
Hops..............................lbs...	15c. per lb......	8c. per lb......	36.21	19.28
Onions..............................bush...	40c. per bu.....	20c. per bu.....	51.48	25.74
Pease:				
Dried..............................bush...	20c. per bu.....	......do............	18.10	18.10
Split ....bush...	50c. per bu.....	50c. per bu.....	15.84	15.84
Others, in carton, papers, or small packages......................lbs...	1c. per lb.......	1c. per lb	....	....
Potatoes..............................bush...	25c. per bu.....	15c. per bu.....	51.96	31.18
Seeds, not elsewhere specified:				
Castor beans or seeds.........bush...	50c. per bu.....	25c. per bu.....	49.38	24.69
Linseed or flaxseed ....bush...	30c. per bu.....	20c. per bu......	23.31	15.54
Poppy and other oil seeds...bush...	......do	......do............	9.41	6.28
Garden seeds, agricultural and other seeds, n. s. p................	20 per cent.....	10 per cent.....	20	10
Pickles and sauces..........................	45 per cent.....	30 per cent......	45	30
All other, not specially provided for	......do	......do............	45	30
Vegetables, other in their natural state	25 per cent.....	10 per cent.....	25	10
Straw......................................tons...	30 per cent......	15 per cent.....	30	15
Teazles	......do	......do............	30	15
Fish:				
Anchovies and sardines, packed in oil or otherwise:				
In tin boxes—				
Whole boxes, measuring not more than 5 by 4 by 3½ inches..boxes....	10c. per box...	10c. per box ...	30.12	30.12
Half boxes, measuring not more than 5 by 4 by 1⅝ inches..boxes....	5c. per box......	5c. per box.....	22.43	22.43
Quarter boxes, measuring not more than 4¾ by 3½ by 1¼ inches. boxes..................	2½c. per box..	2½c. per box..	31.03	31.03
In any other form...............	40 per cent......	40c. per cent...	40	40
Cod, haddock, hake, etc., pickled in barrels..........................bbls...	1c. per lb......	¾c. per lb......	25.80	19.43

Comparison of rates of duties between McKinley act and new law—Continued.

	Rates of duty under—		Average ad valorem under—	
	McKinley law.	New law.	McKinley law.	New law.
SCHEDULE G.—AGRICULTURAL PRODUCTS AND PROVISIONS.—Continued.				
Fish—Continued.			*Per ct.*	*Per ct.*
Mackerel, pickled or salted..bbls...	1c. per lb.......	¾ c. per lb......	17.32	13.15
Salmon, pickled or salted.....lbs...	......do	......do..............	14.25	10.69
Other fish:				
Pickled or salted, in barrels bbls....................................	......do	......do..............	26.42	19.82
Cod, haddock, hake, and pollock:				
Dried, smoked, salted, or pickled otherwise than in barrels........................lbs...	¾c. per lb......	......do..............	19.12	19.12
Herring, dried or smoked......lbs...	......do, ...	......do..............	37.94	37.94
Other fish, dried or smoked....lbs...	......do	......do..............	17.90	17.90
Pickled or salted, not in barrels or half barrels....................lbs...	......do.	......do..............	17.17	17.17
Herring, pickled or salted...bbls...	½c. per lb......	½c. per lb......	14.16	14.16
In cans or packages made of tin or other material, except anchovies and sardines and fish packed in any other manner, not specially provided for—				
Herring....................................	30 per cent......	20 per cent......	30	20
Mackeral....................................	......do	......do..............	30	20
Salmon....................................	......do.	......do..............	30	20
Other....................................	......do	......do..............	30	20
Cans or packages, made of tin or other material, containing shellfish admitted free of duty, not exceeding 1 quart in contents doz....................................	8c. per doz......	....	....	....
Grapes....................................bbls...	60c. per bbl...	20 per cent......	19.62	20
Plums and prunes.......................lbs...	2c. per lb........	1½c. per lb.....	44.24	33.18
Figs...lbs...	2½c. per lb.....	....do..............	45.77	27.47
Oranges:				
In packages of capacity of 1¼ cubic feet or less.............pkgs...	13c. per pkg...	8c. per cu. ft..	15.86	12.20
In packages of capacity exceeding 1¼ cubic feet and not exceeding 2½ cubic feet.....pkgs...	25c. per pkg...	......do..............	19.18	15.34
In packages of capacity exceeding 2½ cubic feet and not exing 5 cubic feet..............pkgs...	50c. per pkg...	......do..............	24.41	19.53
In packages of capacity exceeding 5 cubic feet.............cu. ft...	10c. per cu ft..	......do..............	18.25	14.60
In bulk...M...	$1.50 per M....	$1.50 per M....	31.15	31.15
Lemons:				
In packages of capacity of 1¼ cubic feet or less..............pkgs...	13c. per pkg...	8c. per cu. ft...	12.56	9.66
In packages of capacity exceeding 1¼ cubic feet and not exceeding 2½ cubic feet......pkgs...	25c. per pkg...	......do..............	13.16	10.53
In packages of capacity exceeding 2½ cubic feet and not exceeding 5 cubic feet......pkgs...	50c. per pkg...	......do..............	18.71	14.97
In packages of capacity exceeding 5 cubic feet..............cu. ft...	10c. per cu. ft.	......do..............	19.09	15.27
In bulk...M...	$1.50 M..........	$1.50 per M....	11.63	11.63

Comparison of rates of duties between McKinley act and new law.—Continued.

	Rates of duty under—		Average ad valorem under—	
	McKinley law.	New law.	McKinley law.	New law.
			Per ct.	*Per ct.*
SCHEDULE G — AGRICULTURAL PRODUCTS AND PROVISIONS—Continued.				
Limes:				
In packages of capacity of 1¼ cubic feet or less............pkgs...	13c. per pkg...	8c. per cu. ft...	41.05	31.57
In packages of capacity exceeding 1¼ cubic feet and not exceeding 2½ cubic feet......pkgs...	25c. per pkg...	......do............	19	15.25
In packages of capacity exceeding 2½ cubic feet and not exceeding 5 cubic feet........cu. ft...	50c. per pkg...	......do..........	25.17	20.14
In packages of capacity exceeding 5 cubic feet.............cu. ft...	10c. per cu. ft.	......do............	21	17.75
In bulk......................................M...	$1.50 per M....	$1.50 per M....	26.59	26.59
Barrels or boxes containing oranges, lemons or limes, exclusive of contents (a) ....lbs...	30 per cent......	30 per cent......	30	30
Raisins ....lbs...	2½ c. per lb...	1¼ c. per lb...	52.42	31.44
Preserved—				
Comfits, sweetmeats and fruits preserved in sugar, sirup, molasses or spirits, not specially provided for, and jellies of all kinds	35 per cent......	30 per cent......	35	30
Ginger, preserved or pickled........	......do............	......do............	35	30
Cocoanut, dessicated...................	20 per cent......	30 per cent......	20	30
Fruits preserved in their own juices...	30 per cent......	20 per cent......	30	20
Orange and lemon peel, preserved or candied.................................lbs...	2 c. per lb......	30 per cent......	29.92	30
Nuts:				
Almonds:				
Not shelled......................lbs...	5 c. per lb......	3 c. per lb......	51.34	30.80
Shelled ....lbs...	7½ c. per lb...	5 c. per lb......	42.42	28.28
Filberts and walnuts:				
Not shelled......................lbs...	3 c. per lb......	2 c. per lb......	52.99	35.32
Shelled ....lbs...	6 c. per lb......	4 c. per lb......	49.04	32.68
Peanuts or ground beans:				
Unshelled ....lbs...	1 c. per lb......	20 per cent......	72.86	20
Shelled ....lbs...	1¼ c. per lb...	......do............	16.82	20
All other shelled or unshelled, not specially provided for..lbs...	......do............	......do............	39.22	20
Cocoanuts........................	Free....	......do............	Free ...	20
Apples :				
Green or ripe.....................bush...	25 c. per bu...	......do............	33.93	20
Dried, dessicated, evaporated, lbs...	2 c. per lb......	......do............	42.41	20
Currants, Zante ....lbs...	Free....	1½ c. per lb...	Free ...	41.97
Dates ....lbs...	......do............	20 per cent......	Free ...	20
Pineapples	......do............	......do............	Free ...	20
Olives, green or prepared	......do............	......do............	Free ...	20
Orchids, lily of the valley, azaleas, palms and other plants used for forcing under glass for cut flowers or decorative purposes	......do............	10 per cent......	Free ...	10
Bacon and hams.................lbs...	5 c. per lb......	20 per cent......	26.06	20
Beef......................lbs...	2 c. per lb......	......do............	26.05	20
Fresh Mutton ....lbs...	......do............	......do............	17.13	20
Pork..................lbs...	......do............	......do............	24.33	20

Comparison of rates of duties between McKinley act and new law—Continued.

	Rates of duty under—		Average ad valorem under—	
	McKinley law.	New law.	McKinley law.	New law.
SCHEDULE G.—AGRICULTURAL PRODUCTS AND PROVISIONS—Continued.				
			Per ct.	*Per ct.*
Meats, dressed or undressed, but not otherwise prepared	10 per cent	20 per cent	10	20
Meats of all kinds, prepared or preserved	25 per cent	......do	25	20
Extract of meat:				
Fluid extract.....lbs	15 c. per lb	15 per cent	18.01	15
All other not specially provided for.....lbs	35 c. per lb	15 per cent	17.95	15
Lard.....lbs	2 c. per lb	1 c. per lb	23.72	11.86
Poultry, live.....lbs	3 c. per lb	2 c. per lb	32.51	21.67
Poultry, dressed.....lbs	5 c. per lb	3 c. per lb	53.93	32.34
Chicory root, burnt or roasted, ground or granulated, or in rolls, or otherwise prepared.....lbs	2 c. per lb	2 c. per lb	54.40	54.40
Chocolate, other than confectionery, and sweetened chocolate (*b*).....lbs	......do	......do	9.21	9.21
Cocoa, prepared or manufactured, not specially provided for.....lbs	......do	......do	5.80	5.80
Cocoa butter or butterine.....lbs	3½ c. per lb	3½ c. per lb	13.75	13.75
Dandelion root and acorns prepared, and other articles used as coffee, or as substitutes for coffee, not specially provided for.....lbs	1½ c. per lb	1½ c. per lb	40.15	40.15
Starch, and all preparations for use as starch.....lbs	2 c. per lb	1½ c. per lb	84.38	63.28
Dextrin, burnt starch, gum substitute or British gum.....lbs	1½ c. per lb	1½ c. per lb	43.51	43.51
Mustard, ground or preserved, in bottles or otherwise.....lbs	10 c. per lb	25 per cent	38.09	25.00
Spices not elsewhere specified:				
Cayenne pepper, unground.....lbs	2½ c. per lb	2½ c. per lb	35.10	35.10
Sage.....lbs	3 c. per lb	1 c. per lb	171.10	57.03
All other, ground or powdered, not specially provided for.....lbs	4 c. per lb	3 c. per lb	57.94	43.46
Vinegar.....stand. galls	7½ c. per gall	7½ c. per gall	27.40	27.40
Total schedule G, agricultural products, etc			33.21	23.10
SCHEDULE H.—SPIRITS, WINES, ETC.				
Spirits distilled:				
Brandy.....prf. galls	$2.50 per prf. gallon.	$1.80 per prf. gallon.	91.67	65.98
Other, not specially provided for, manufactured or distilled—				
From grain.....prf. galls	......do	......do	293.26	211.14
From other materials, prf. galls	......do	......do	366.91	264.06
Compounds or preparations of which distilled spirits are a component part of chief value, not specially provided for, prf. galls	$2.50 per prf. gallon.	$1.80 per prf. gallon.	97.63	70.27
Cordials, liquors, arracks, absinthe, kirchwasser, ratafia and other spirituous beverages, or bitters containing spirits, and not specially provided for, prf. galls	......do	......do	115.05	82.83

Comparison of rates of duties between McKinley act and new law—Continued.

	Rates of duty under—		Average ad valorem under—	
	McKinley law.	New law.	McKinley law.	New law.
SCHEDULE H.—SPIRITS, WINES, ETC.— Continued.			Per ct.	Per ct.
Bay rum or bay water, whether distilled or compounded.....prf. galls...	$1.50 per prf. gallon.	$1 per proof gallon.	227.13	151.42
Wines containing not more than 24 per cent of alcohol:				
Champagne and all other sparkling, in bottles—				
Containing ½ pint each or less............doz...	$2 per dozen..	$2 per dozen..	53.82	53.82
Containing more than ½ pint each and not more than 1 pint............doz...	$4 per dozen..	$4 per dozen..	52.62	52.62
Containing more than 1 pint each and not more than 1 quart............doz...	$8 per dozen..	$8 per dozen..	55.22	55.22
Quantity in excess of 1 quart per bottle............galls...	$2.50 per gall.	$2.50 per gall.		
Still wines:				
In casks............galls...	50 c. per gall...	50 c. per gall...	69.39	69.39
In bottles or jugs—				
Containing each not more than 1 pint............doz...	80 c. per doz...	80 c. per doz...	26.25	26.25
Containing each more than 1 pint and not more than 1 quart............doz...	$1.60 per doz...	$1.60 per doz...	28.96	28.96
Quantity in excess of 1 quart or 1 pint per bottle......pts...	5 c. per pint...	5 c. per pint...		
Vermuth, including ginger wine and ginger cordial:				
In casks............galls...	50 c. per gall...	50 c. per gall...	50.49	50.49
In bottles or jugs—				
Containing each not more than 1 pint............doz...	80 c. per doz...	80 c. per doz...	30	30
Containing each more than 1 pint and not more than 1 quart............doz...	$1.60 per doz..	$1.60 per doz..	53.38	53.38
Bottles or jugs containing wines, cordials, brandy or other spirituous liquors............No...	3 c. each.........	40 per cent.....	a60	40
Malt liquors, viz, ale, beer and porter:				
In bottles or jugs............galls...	40 c. per gall...	30 c. per gall...	41.56	31.17
Not in bottles or jugs.........galls...	20 c. per gall...	15 c. per gall...	60.53	45.40
Malt extract:				
Fluid—				
In bottles or jugs.........galls...	40 c. per gall...	30 c. per gall...	43.35	32.51
In casks............galls...	20 c. per gall...	15 c. per gall...	38.87	29.15
Solid or condensed............	40 per cent......	30 per cent......	40	30
Beverages not elsewhere specified:				
Cherry juice and other fruit juice, not specially provided for—				
Containing not more than 18 per cent of alcohol ...galls...	60 c. per gall...	56 c. per gall...	156.41	130.34
Containing more than 18 per cent of alcohol.........galls...	$2.50 per prf. gallon.	$1.80 per prf. gallon.	150.86	108.54

Comparison of rates of duties between McKinly act and new law.—Continued.

	Rates of duty under—		Average ad valorem under—	
	McKinly law.	New law.	McKinley law.	New law.
SCHEDULE II.—SPIRITS, WINES, ETC.— Continued. Bever……as specified— Prune juice or prune wine—			*Per ct.*	*Per ct.*
Containing not more than 18 per cent of alcohol.....galls...	60 c. per gall...	50 c. per gall...	69.16	57.9
Containing more than 18 per cent of alcohol...........galls...	$2.50 per gall...	$1.80 per proof gallon.		
Ginger ale and ginger beer— In plain, green, or colored, molded, or pressed glass bottles— Containing each not more than ¾ of a pint ......doz...	13 c. per doz...	20 per cent......	17.25	20
Containing more than ¾ of a pint each and not more than 1⅓ pints ....doz...	26 c. per doz...	.......do	36.20	20
Otherwise than in such bottles, or in such bottles containing more than 1⅓ pints each..galls...	50 c. per gall...	.......do		20
Mineral waters, and all imitations of natural mineral waters, and all artificial mineral waters not specially provided for— In plain, green, or colored glass bottles— Containing not more than 1 pint........................doz...	16 c. per doz...	20 per cent......	22.59	20
Containing more than 1 pint and not more than 1 quart ....doz...	25 c. per doz...	.......do	19.52	20
Otherwise than in such bottles, or in bottles containing more than 1 quart............galls...	20 c. per gall...	.......do	24	20
Total Schedule II, spirits, wines, etc			69.90	61.01
SCHEDULE I.—COTTON MANUFAC- **TURES.** Cotton, manufactures of : Thread, yarn, warp, or warp yarn, whether single or advanced beyond the condition of single by grouping or twisting two or more single yarns together, whether on beams or in bundles, skeins, or cops, or in any other form—(a) Valued at not exceeding 25 cents per pound ....lbs...	10 c. per lb......	8 c. per lb	45.03	36.02
Valued at over 25 and not exceeding 40 cents per pound, pounds	18 c. per lb......	15 c. per lb......	51.12	42.60
Valued at over 40 and not exceeding 50 cents per pound, pounds	23 c. per lb......	45 per cent......	50.17	45
Valued at over 50 and not exceeding 60 cents per pound, pounds	28 c. per lb......	.......do	48.96	45

Comparison of rates of duties between McKinly act and new law.—Continued.

	Rates of duty under—		Average ad valorem under—	
	McKinly law.	New law.	McKinly law.	New law.

SCHEDULE I.—COTTON MANUFACTURES—Continued.

			Per ct.	Per ct.
Cotton manufactures of—Cont'd.				
Valued at over 60 and not exceeding 70 cents per pound, pounds	33 c. per lb	25 per cent	50.19	45
Valued at over 70 and not exceeding 80 cents per pound, pounds	38 c. per lb	do	49.95	45
Valued at over 80 cents and not exceeding $1 per pound...lbs...	48 c. per lb	do	53.55	45
Valued at over $1 per pound..lbs...	50 per cent	do	50	45
Thread on spools, 100 yards on each spool ....doz...	7 c. per doz	5½ c. per doz..	56.38	44.30
Cloth—				
Not exceeding 50 threads to the square inch, counting the warp and filling—				
Not bleached, dyed, colored, stained, painted, or printed, valued at 6½ cents or less per square yard ....sq. yds...	2 c. per sq. yd..	1 c. per sq. yd.	41.65	20.83
Bleached, valued at 9 cents or less per square yard.. sq. yards..................	2½ c. per sq. yd	1¼ c. per sq.yd	29.61	14.80
Dyed, colored, stained, painted, or printed, valued at 12 cents or less per square yard..sq. yds...	4 c. per sq. yd..	2 c. per sq. yd.	46.68	23.34
Exceeding 50 and not exceeding 100 threads to the square inch, counting the warp and filling—				
Not bleached, dyed, colored, stained, painted, or printed, valued at 6½ cents or less per square yard ....sq. yds...	2¼ c. per sq.yd	1¼,1½ and 1¾ c. per sq. yd. =1½ c. per. sq. yd.	40.83	27.22
Bleached, valued at 9 cents or less per square yard.. sq. yards..................	3 c. per sq. yd..	1¼,1¾,and 2 c. per sq. yd. =1¾ c. per sq. yd.	47.79	27.88
Dyed, colored, stained, painted, or printed, valued at 12 cents or less per square yard.........sq. yds...	4 c. per sq. yd..	2¾,3,and 3¼c. per sq. yd. =3 c. per sq. yd.	43.57	32.68
Not exceeding 100 threads to the square inch, counting the warp and filling—				
Not bleached, dyed, colored, stained, painted, or printed, valued at over 6½ cents per square yard.. sq. yards..................	35 per cent	25 per cent	35	25

Comparison of rates of duties between McKinley act and new law.—Continued.

	Rates of duty under—		Average ad valorem under—	
	McKinley law.	New law.	McKinley law.	New law.
SCHEDULE I.—COTTON MANUFACTURES—Continued.				
Cotton manufacturers of—Cont'd.				
Bleached, valued at over 9 cents per square yard.. square yards	25 per cent	25 per cent	*Per ct.* 35	*Per ct.* 25
Dyed, colored, stained, painted, or printed, valued at over 12 cents per sq. yard.........sq. yds	do	30 per cent	35	30
Exceeding 100 and not exceeding 150 threads to the square inch, counting the warp and filling—				
Not bleached, dyed, colored, stained, painted, or printed, valued at 7½ cents or less per square yard.........sq. yds	3 c. per sq. yd	1½, 1¾, 2, and 2¼, c. per sq. yd.=1⅞ c. p. sq. yd.	52.74	32.96
Valued at over 7½ cents per square yard..sq. yds	40 per cent	30 per cent	40	30
Bleached, valued at 10 cents or less per square yard.........sq. yds	4 c. per sq. yd.	2½, 2¾, 3, and 3¼ cts. p. sq. yd. = 2⅞ c. per sq yd.	49.59	35.65
Valued at over 10 cents per square yard......sq. yds	40 per cent	35 per cent	40	35
Dyed, colored, stained, painted, or printed, valued at 12½ cents or less per square yard..sq.yds	5 c. per sq. yd.	3½, 3¾, 4, and 4¼ c. p. sq. yd. = 3⅞ c. per sq. yd.	48.76	37.78
Valued at over 12½ cents per square yard..sq. yds	40 per cent	35 per cent	40	35
Exceeding 150 and not exceeding 200 threads to the square inch, counting the warp and filling—				
Not bleached, dyed, colored, stained, painted, or printed, valued at 8 cents or less per square yard.........sq. yds	3½ c. per sq. yd	2, 2¼, 2½, and 2¾ c. per sq. yd.=2⅝ c. per sq. yd.	67.35	45.71
Valued at over 8 c. per square yard.....sq. yds	45 per cent	35 per cent	45	35
Bleached, valued at 10 cents per square yard.....sq. yds	4½ c. per sq. yd	2¾, 3, 3¼, and 3½ cts. per sq. yd.=3⅛ cts. per sq. yd.	61.66	42.83

Comparison of rates of duties between McKinley act and new law.—Continued.

	Rates of duty under—		Average ad valorem under—	
	McKinley law.	New law.	McKinley law.	New law.
SCHEDULE I. COTTON MANUFACTURES.—Continued.				
Cotton, manufactures of—Continued.				
Cloth—Continued.				
Exceeding 150 and not exceeding 200 threads to the square inch, counting the warp and filling—Continued.				
Valued at over 10 cents per square yard..sq. yds..	45 per cent......	35 per cent.....	*Per ct.* 45	*Per ct.* 35
Dyed, colored, stained, painted, or printed, valued at 12 cents or less per square yard..sq. yds..	5½ c. per sq yd	4¼, 4½, 4¾, and 5 c. per sq. yd.=4⅝c. per sq. yd.	51.33	43.16
Valued at over 12 cents per square yard..sq. yds..	45 per cent.....	40 per cent.	45	40
Exceeding 200 threads to the square inch, counting the warp and filling—				
Not bleached, dyed, colored, stained, painted, or printed, valued at 10 cents or less per square yard.................sq. yds...	4½ c. per sq. yd	3, 3¼, 3½, and 3¾ c. per sq. yd.=3⅝ c. per sq. yd.	53.36	40.02
Valued at over 10 cents per square yard......sq. yds...	45 per cent......	40 per cent......	45	40
Bleached, valued at 12 cents or less per square yard.................sq. yds...	5½ c. per sq. yd	4, 4¼, 4½, and 4¾ c. per sq. yd.=4⅜ c. per sq. yd.	55.18	43.89
Valued at over 12 cents per sqvare yard..sq. yds..	45 per cent......	40 per cent.....	45	40
Dyed, colored, stained, painted, or printed, valued at 15 cents or less per square yard sq. yds.........................	6¾ c. per sq. yd	5¾ and 6 c. per sq. yd. =5⅞ c. per sq. yd	54.14	47.12
Valued at over 15 cents per square yard..sq. yds..	45 per cent.....	40 per cent.....	45	40
Bleached, dyed, colored, stained, painted, or printed, containing an admixture of silk, and not otherwise provided for...............sq. yds...	10 c. per sq. yd. and 35 per cent.	45 per cent......	61.57	45
Corsets not elsewhere specified doz..	50 per cent......	40 per cent......	50	40

Comparison of rates of duties between McKinley act and new law.—Continued.

	Rates of duty under—		Average ad valorem under—	
	McKinley law.	New law.	McKinley law.	New law.

SCHEDULE I. COTTON MANUFACTURES.—
Continued.

	McKinley law.	New law.	McKinley law. *Per ct.*	New law. *Per ct.*
Cotton, manufactures of—Continued. Other articles of wearing apparel and ready-made clothing— Of which India rubber is a component material.....lbs...	50 cents per pound and 50 per cent.	40 per cent......	89.44	40
All other not specially provided for........................	50 per cent......	.... do..........	50	40
Plushes, velvets, velveteens, corduroys, and all other pile fabrics composed of cotton or vegetable fibre— Plushes, velvets, and velveteens— Not bleached, dyed, colored, stained, painted, or printed........sq. yds...	10 c. per sq. yd. and 20 per cent.	...........do..........	72.65	40
Bleached.............sq. yds...	12 c. per sq. yd. and 20 per ct.	47½ per cent..	53.95	47.5
Dyed, colored, stained, painted, or printed sq. yds..............................	14 c. per sq. yd. and 20 per ct.	...........do..........	60.25	47.5
All other........ .....sq. yds...	40 per cent......	40 per cent......	40	40
Corduroys and other pile fabrics— Not bleached, dyed, colored, stained, painted or printed.. ....sq. yds...	10 c. p. sq. yd. and 20 p. ct.	40 per cent......	68.75	40
Bleached ....sq. yds...	12 c. p. sq. yd. and 20 p. ct.	47½ per cent...	62.42	47.5
Dyed, colored, stained, painted or printed, sq. yds..............................	14 c. p. sq. yd. and 20 p. ct.	......do...............	60.52	47.5
All other ....sq. yds...	40 per cent......	40 per cent......	40	40
Chenille curtains, table covers, and all goods manufactured of cotton chenille, or of which cotton chenille forms the component material of chief value...	60 per cent......	45 per cent......	60	45
Knit goods made on knitting machines or frames— Stockings, hose and half hose, other, valued at not more than $1.50 per dozen ....doz...	35 per cent......	30 per cent......	35	30
Shirts and drawers valued at not more than $1.50 per dozen ....doz...	....do.............	50 per cent......	35	50
Valued at more than $1.50 and not more than $3 per dozen...............doz...	$1 per dozen and 35 p. ct.	......do	74	50
Valued at more than $3 and not more than $5 per dozen...............doz...	$1.25 per doz. and 40 p. ct.	......do.............	72.86	60

Comparison of rates of duties between McKinley act and new law—Continued.

	Rates of duty under—		Average ad valorem under—	
	McKinley law.	New law.	McKinley law.	New law.
SCHEDULE I. COTTON MANUFACTURES —Continued. Other artcl's of wearing app'l—Cn'td. Valued at more than $5 and not more than $7 per dozen..............doz...	$1.50 per doz.	50 per cent......	*Per ct.* 65.59	*Per ct.* 50
Valued at more than $7 per dozen..............doz...	$2 per dozen and 40 p. ct.	......do..............	59.51	50
Stockings, hose and half hose— Selvedged, fashioned, narrowed, or shaped wholly or in part by knitting machines or frames, or knit by hand, including such as are commercially known as seamless stockings, hose or half hose, finished or unfinished— Valued at not more than 60 cents per dozen pairs......doz...	20 c. per doz. and 20 p. ct.	......do..............	54.19	50
Valued at more than 60 cents and not more than $2 per dozen pairs ....doz...	50 c. per doz. and 30 p. ct.	......do..............	71.97	50
Valued at more than $2 and not more than $4 per dozen pairs ....doz...	75 c. per doz. and 40 p. ct.	......do..............	67.54	50
Valued at more than $4 per dozen pairs, doz	$1 per doz. and 40 p. ct.	......do..............	56.74	50
Cords, braids, boot, shoe and corset lacings— On which duty computed at 35 cents per pound is less than 40 per cent ad valorem, lbs......................................	40 per cent......	45 per cent......	40	45
All other ....,.....lbs...	35 c. per lb.....	......do..............	56.85	45
Gimps, galloons, webbing, goring, suspenders and braces, elastic or non-elastic	40 per cent......	......do..............	40	45
Damask....................................	......do..............	35 per cent......	40	35
All other manufactures of cotton not specially provided for.........	......do........	......do..............	40	35
Total schedule I, cotton manufactures			55.25	43.54
SCHEDULE J.—FLAX, HEMP AND JUTE, AND MANUFACTURES OF. Flax and hemp, and manufactures of flax, hemp, jute and other vegetable fibers: Unmanufactured— Flax, hackled, known as "dressed line" ....tons...	3 c. per lb......	1½ c. per lb...	10.77	5.39

Comparison of rates of duties between McKinley act and new law—Continued.

	Rates of duty under—		Average ad valorem under—	
	McKinley.	New law.	McKinley law.	New law.
SCHEDULE J. FLAX, HEMP AND JUTE, AND MANUFACTURES OF -Continued.				
Flax, hemp, etc., unmanufactured— Continued.			*Per ct.*	*Per ct.*
Hemp, hackled, known as line of hemp......................tons...	$50 per ton	1 c. per lb......	23.35	10.46
Manufactures—				
Yarn, jute................................lbs...	35 per cent......	30 per cent	35	30
Cables, cordage and twine— Cables and cordage—				
Of hemp, untarred ...lbs...	2¼ c. per lb...	10 per cent	22.34	10
Other, untarred, composed in whole or in part of istle or Tampico fibre, manila, sisal grass, or sunn........................lbs...	1½ c. per lb ...	......do..............	16.86	10
Tarred........................lbs...	3 c. per lb	......do..............	31.23	10
All other..................lbs...	1½ c. per lb	......do..............	18.78	10
Hemp and jute carpets .....sq. yds...	6 c. per sq. yd.	20 per cent......	15.83	20
Burlaps, of flax, jute, or hemp, or of which flax, jute, or hemp, or either of them, shall be the component material of chief value (except such as may be suitable for bagging for cotton)—				
Not exceeding 60 inches in width........................lbs...	1¾ c. per lb ...	Free..............	29.23	Free.
Exceeding 60 inches in width lbs....................................	40 per cent	......do..............	40	Free.
Bags for grain made of burlaps..lbs...	2 c. per lb	......do..............	44.73	Free.
Bagging for cotton, gunny cloth, and all similar material for covering cotton, composed in whole or in part of hemp, flax, jute, or jute butts—				
Valued at 6 cents or less per square yard................sq. yds...	1 6-10 c. per sq. yd.	Free..............	32.52	Free.
Valued at more than 6 cents per square yard................sq. yds...	1 8-10 c. p. sq. yd.	......do..............	26.37	Free.
Gill netting, nets, webs, and seines of flax—				
Made of thread or twine from yarn of a number not higher than 20................................lbs...	15 c. lb. and 35 per cent.	40 per cent......	144.63	40
Made of thread or twine from yarn finer than No. 20......lbs...	20 c. lb. and 40 per cent.	......do..............	58.17	40
Hose, linen hydraulic, made in whole or in part of flax, hemp, or jute.......................................lbs...	20 c. per lb	......do..............	34.31	40
Oilcloths for floors, stamped, painted, or printed, including linoleum, corticene, cork carpets, figured or plain, and all other oilcloth (except silk oilcloth), and waterproof cloth, not specially provided for--				
Valued at 25 cents or less per square yard............sq. yds...	40 per cent......	25 per cent......	40	25

*Comparison of rates of duties between McKinley act and new law—*Continued.

	Rates of duty under—		Average ad valorem under—	
	McKinley law.	New law.	McKinley law.	New law.
SCHEDULE J.—FLAX, HEMP, AND JUTE, AND MANUFACTURES OF—Continued.				
Flax, and hemp, and manufactures of flax, hemp, jute, and other vegetable fibres—Continued.			*Per ct.*	*Per ct.*
Valued above 25 cents per square yard...........sq. yds...	15 c. per sq. yard and 30 per cent.	40 per cent......	57.17	40
Yarns or threads—				
Flax or hemp—				
Valued at 13 cents or less per pound ....lbs...	6 c. per lb......	35 per cent......	63.92	35
Valued at more than 13 cents per pound .....lbs...	45 per cent ....do..............		45	35
Manufactures of flax or hemp, or of which these substances, or either of them, is the component material of chief value	50 per cent ....do..............		50	35
Manufactures of flax containing more than 100 threads to the square inch, counting both warp and filling (until January 1, 1895)......................................	35 per cent ....do..............		35	35
Wearing apparel—				
Collars and cuffs entirely of cotton..................doz. pcs...	15 c. per doz. and 35 p. ct.	......do..............	68.26	35
Collars and cuffs, composed in whole or in part of linen doz	30 c. per doz. and 40 p. ct.	30 c. per doz. and 30 p. ct.	68.54	58.54
Shirts and all articles of wearing apparel of every description, not specially provided for, composed wholly or in part of linen	55 per cent......	50 per cent	55	50
Tapes composed of flax, woven with or without metal threads, on reels or spools, designed expressly for use in the manufacture of measuring tapes (no data)......................................	35 per cent	25 per cent	35	25
Laces, edgings, embroideries, insertings, neck rufflings, ruchings, trimmings, tuckings, lace window curtains, and other similar tamboured articles, and articles embroidered by hand or machinery, embroidered and hemstitched handkerchiefs, and articles made wholly or in part of lace, rufflings, tuckings, or ruchings, composed of flax, jute, or other vegetable fibre, except cotton, or of which either of these substances, except cotton, is the component material of chief value, not specially provided for......................................	60 per cent.....	50 per cent......	60	50

Comparison of rates and duties between McKinley act and new law.—Continued.

	Rates of duty under—		Average ad valorem under—	
	McKinley law.	New law.	McKinley law.	New law.

SCHEDULE J.—FLAX, HEMP, AND JUTE, AND MANUFACTURES OF—Continued.

	Rates of duty under McKinley law.	Rates of duty under New law.	Avg McKinley	Avg New
Flax and hemp, and manufactures of flax, etc.—Continued.				
Laces, edgings, embroideries, insertings, neck rufflings, ruchings, trimmings, tuckings, lace window curtains, and other similar tamboured articles, and articles embroidered by hand or machinery, embroidered and hemstitched handkerchiefs, and articles made wholly or in part of lace, rufflings, tuckings, or ruchings, composed of cotton, or of which cotton is the component material of chief value, not specially provided for	60 per cent.....	50 per cent......	*Per ct.* 60	*Per ct.* 50
All other manufactures not specially provided for—				
Manufactures of jute, or of which jute is the component material of chief value, not specially provided for—				
Valued at 5 cents per pound or less..........lbs...	2c. per lb.......	35 per cent......	55.37	35
Valued above 5 cents per pound.....................lbs...	40 per cent......	......do.........	40	35
Manufactures of other vegetable fibre, except flax, hemp, or cotton, or of which other vegetable fibre, except flax, hemp, or cotton, is the component material of chief value, not specially provided for—				
Valued at 5 cents per pound, or less.................lbs...	2c. per lb......	......do............	52.53	35
Valued above 5 cents per pound.........................lbs...	40 per cent......	......do............	40	35
Total Schedule J, flax, hemp, etc	....	....	45	41.05
SCHEDULE K.—WOOLEN GOODS. *a*				
Manufactures composed wholly or in part of wool, worsted, the hair of the camel, goat, alpaca, or other animals:				
Shoddy.....................lbs...	30c. per lb.......	15 per cent......	52.50	15
Yarns, woolen and worsted—				
Valued at not more than 30 cents per pound........lbs...	27½c. per lb. and 35 p. c.	30 per cent......	278.66	30
Valued at more than 30 and not more than 40 cents per pound.................lbs...	33c. per lb. and 35 p. c.	......do	118.79	30
Valued at more than 40 cents per pound.............•....lbs...	38½c. per lb. and 40 p. c.	40 per cent......	105.42	40

Comparison of rates of duties between McKinley act and new law,—Continued.

	Rates of duty under—		Average ad valorem under—	
	McKinley law.	New law.	McKinley law.	New law.

Schedule K—Woolen Goods—Cont'd.

			Per ct.	*Per ct.*
Cloths, woolen or worsted:				
Valued at not more than 30 cents per pound..............lbs...	33c. per lb. and 40 p. c.	40 per cent......	163.09	40
Valued at more than 30 and not more than 40 cents per pound lbs......................................	38½ c per lb. and 40 p. c.	40 per cent......	114.86	40
Valued above 40 cents per pound lbs.......................................	44 c. per lb. and 50 p.c.	50 per cent......	99.50	50
Shawls, woolen or worsted:				
Valued at not more than 30 cents per pound ....lbs...	33 c. per lb. and 40p. c.	35 per cent......	....	35
Valued at more than 30 and not more than 40 cents per pound lbs.....................................	38½ c. per lb. and 40 p. c.	......do..............	150.30	35
Valued at above 40 cents per pound ....lbs...	44 c. per lb. and 50 p. c.	40 per cent......	88.60	40
Knit fabrics, and all fabrics made on knitting machines or frames:				
Valued at not more than 30 cents per pound ....lbs...	33 c. per lb. and 40 p. c.	35 per cent......	....	35
Valued at more than 40 and not more than 40 cents per pound lbs.....................................	38½ c. per lb. and 40 p. c.	......do..............	136	35
Valued at above 40 cents per pound .. ..lbs...	44 c. per lb. and 50 p. c.	40 per cent......	82.25	40
All knit wearing apparal........lbs...	49½ c. per lb. and 60 p. c.	......do..............	94.09	40
All other manufactures, not specially provided for :				
Valued at not more than 30 cents per pound ....lbs...	33 c. per lb. and 40 p. c.	......do..............	159.60	40
Valued at more than 30 and not more than 40 cents per pound lbs.....................................	38½ c. per lb. and 40 p. c.	......do..............	142.59	40
Valued at above 40 cents per pound ....lbs...	44 c. per lb. and 50 p. c.	50 per cent......	87.03	50
Blankets:				
Valued at not more than 30 cents per pound ....lbs...	16½ c. per lb. and 35 p. c.	25 per cent......	88.22	25
Valued at more than 30 and not more than 40 cents per pound lbs	22 c. per lb. and 35 p. c.	30 per cent......	100	30
Valued at more than 40 and not more than 50 cents per pound lbs	33 c. per lb. and 35 p. c.	35 per cent......	103.90	35
Valued at more than 50 cents per pound ....lbs...	38½ c per lb. and 40 p. c.	......do..............	80.33	35
Hats of wool :				
Valued at not more than 30 cents per pound ....lbs...	16½ c. per lb. and 35 p. c.	25 per cent......	86	25
Valued at more than 30 and not more than 40 cents per pound lbs	22 c. per lb. and 35 p. c.	30 per cent......	106.38	30
Valued at more than 40 and not more than 50 cents per pound lbs	33 c. per lb. and 35 p. c.	35 per cent......	104.22	35
Valued at more than 50 cents per pound ....lbs...	38½ c. per lb. and 40 p.c.	......do	87.26	35

Comparison of rates of duties between McKinly act and new law.—Continued.

	Rates of duty under—		Average ad valorem under—	
	McKinley law.	New law.	McKinley law.	New law.

SCHEDULE K—WOOLEN GOODS—Cont'd.

Flannels for underwear :

			Per ct.	Per ct.
Valued at not more than 30 cents per pound ....lbs...	16½ c. per lb. and 35 p. c.	25 per cent......	84.90	25
Valued at more than 30 and not more than 40 cents per pound lbs.....................	22 c. per lb. and 35 p. c.	30 per cent......	103.51	30
Valued at more than 40 and not more than 50 cents per pound lbs.....................	33 c. per lb. and 35 p. c.	35 per cent......	103.22	35
Weighing over 4 ounces per square yard.....................lbs...	38½ c. per lb. and 40 p. c.	50 per cent......	96.54	50

Dress goods, women's and children's, coat linings, Italian cloths, and goods of similar description :

Of which the warp consists wholly of cotton or other vegetable materials, with the remainder of the fabric composed wholly or in part of wool, worsted, the hair of the camel, goat, alpaca, or other animals—

Valued at not exceeding 15 cts per square yard......sq. yds...	7 c. p. sq. yd. and 40 p. c.	......do............	93.93	50
Valued at above 15 cents per square yard.............sq. yds...	8 c. p. sq. yd. and 50. p. c.	......do............	89.60	50
Weighing over 4 ounces per square yard....................lbs...	44 c. per lb. and 50 p. c.	......do............	103.86	50

Composed wholly or in part of wool, worsted, the hair of the camel, goat, alpaca or other animals—

Weighing over 4 ounces per square yard...................lbs...

	44 c. per lb. and 50 per c.	50 per cent......	87.14	50
All other ....sq. yds...	12 c. p. sq. yd. and 50 per c.	......do............	109.09	50

Other clothing, ready-made, and articles of wearing apparel (except knit goods), made up or manufactured wholly or in part...................lbs...

	49½ c. per lb. and 60 per c.	...do............	80.32	50
Felts, not woven ....lbs...	......do............	45 per cent......	93.09	45
Plushes and other pile fabrics.....lbs...	......do............	50 per cent......	105.09	50

Cloaks, dolmans, jackets, talmas, ulsters, or other outside garments for ladies' and children's apparel, and goods of similar description, or used for like purposes.............lbs...

	......do............	..... do............	81.23	50

Webbing, gorings, suspenders, braces, beltings, bindings, braids, galloons, fringes, gimps, cords, cords and tassels, dress trimmings, laces and embroideries, head nets, buttons or barrel buttons, or buttons of other forms for tassels or ornamen's, wrought by hand, or braided by machinery, which are elastic or nonelastic ....lbs...

	60 c. per lb. and 60 p c.	......do............	93.82	50

Comparison of rates of duties between McKinley Act and new law.—Continued.

	Rates of duty under—		Average ad valorem under—	
	McKinley law.	New law.	McKinley law.	New law.

SCHEDULE K.—WOOLEN GOODS—Continued.

			Per ct.	Per ct.
Carpets and carpeting—				
Aubusson, Axminister, moquette, and chenille carpets, and carpets woven whole for rooms, and Oriental, Berlin and other similar rugs ....sq. yds...	60 c. p. sq. yd. and 40 per c.	40 per cent......	60.85	40
Saxony, Wilton and Tournay velvet carpets ....sq. yds...	.......do.............	......do.............	69.56	40
Brussels carpets...............sq. yds...	44 c. p. sq. yd. and 40 per c.	......do.............	81.56	40
Velvet and tapestry velvet carpets, printed on the warp or otherwise...............sq. yds...	40 c. p. sq. yd. and 40 p. c.	......do.............	71.86	40
Tapestry Brussels, printed on the warp or otherwise.. ......sq. yds...	28 c. p. sq. yd. and 40 p. c.	42½ per cent...	77.97	42.50
Treble ingrain, three-ply and all chain Venetian carpets..sq. yds...	19 c. p. sq. yd. and 40 p. c.	32½ per cent...	63.05	32.50
Wool, Dutch and two-ply ingrain carpets ....sq. yds...	14 c. p. sq. yd. and 40 p. c.	30 per cent......	64.74	30
Druggets and bockings, printed, colored or otherwise.....sq. yds...	22 c. p. sq. yd. and 40 p. c.	......do.............	82.57	30
Felt carpeting...............sq. yds...	11 c. p. sq. yd. and 40 p. c.	......do.............	62.57	30
Carpets of wool, or in part of, not specially provided for..sq. yds...	50 per cent......	......do.............	50	30
Carpets and carpetings of cotton..	......do.............	......do.............	50	30
Total, schedule K, wool, manufactures of...............			98.62	48.82

SCHEDULE L.—SILK AND SILK GOODS.

Silk, manufactures of:				
Silk, not raw—				
Partially manufactured from cocoons or from waste silk, and not further advanced or manufactured than carded or combed silk..lbs...	50 c. per lb	20 per cent......	60.50	20
Sewing silk and silk thread or yarns of every description...............lbs...	30 per cent......	30 per cent......	30	30
Spun silk, in skeins or cops or on beams...............lbs...	35 per cent......	......do.............	35	30
Thrown silk, not more advanced than singles, tram or organzine, twist and floss...............lbs...	30 per cent......	......do.............	30	30
Velvets, plushes, or other pile fabrics—(a)				
Containing, exclusive of selvedges, less 75 per cent in weight of silk............ ....lbs...	$1.50 per lb. and 15 p. c.	{ $1.50 per lb) { 1.00 per lb)	72.63	55.71
Containing, exclusive of selvedges, 75 per cent or more in weight of silk............lbs...	$3.50 per lb. and 15 p. c.	$1.50 per lb.....	56.21	17.66
Other...............	50 per cent......	50 per cent......	50	50

Comparison of rates of duty between McKinley act and the new law.—Continued.

	Rates of duty under—		Average ad valorum under—	
	McKinley law.	New law.	McKin-ley law.	New law.

SCHEDULE L.—SILK AND SILK GOODS—
Continued.

Silk, manufactures of—Continued.

	McKinley law	New law	McKinley law *Per ct.*	New law *Per ct.*
Webbings, gorings, suspenders, braces, beltings, braids, bindings, galloons, fringes, cords and tassels, elastic or nonelastic	50 per cent	45 per cent	50	45
Buttons	do	do	50	45
Handkerchiefs	60 per cent	50 per cent	60	50
Laces and embroideries, neck rufflings, and ruchings	do	do	60	50
Wearing apparel—Knit goods—Composed in part of India rubber.........ozs	8 cts. per oz. and 60 p. ct.	do	81.42	50
Other	60 per cent	do	60	50
Ready-made clothing and other—Composed in part of India rubber.........ozs	8 cts. per oz. and 60 p. ct.	do	77.79	50
Other	60 per cent	do	60	50
Dress and piece goods	50 per cent	45 per cent	50	45
Ribbons	do	do	50	45 •
All other, not specially provided for	do	do	50	45
Total Schedule L, silk and silk goods			53.56	46.39

SCHEDULE M.—PULP, PAPER, AND BOOKS.

	McKinley law	New law	McKinley law	New law
Pulp of wood:				
Mechanically ground.........tons	$2.50 per ton	10 per cent	14.44	10
Chemical, unbleached.........tons	$6 per ton	do	12.38	10
Chemical, bleached.........tons	$7 per ton	do	10.76	10
Paper sheathing	10 per cent	do	10	10
Sheathing, patent	20 per cent	do	20	10
Printing paper, suitable only for books and newspapers:				
Unsized.........lbs	15 per cent	15 per cent	15	15
Sized or glued.........lbs	20 per cent	do	20	15
Paper, albumenized or sensitized	35 per cent	30 per cent	35	30
Papers known commercially as copying paper, filtering paper, silver paper, and all tissue paper, white or colored, made up in copying books, reams, or in any other form.........lbs	8 cts. per lb. and 15 p. ct.	35 per cent	62.14	35

*Comparison of rates of duties between McKinley act and new law—*Continued.

	Rates of duty under—		Average ad valorem under—	
	McKinley law.	New law.	McKinley law.	New law.

SCHEDULE M.—PULP, PAPER AND BOOKS—Continued.

			Per ct.	Per ct.
Papers known commercially as surface-coated papers, and manufactures thereof, cardboards, lithographic prints from either stone or zinc, bound or unbound (except illustrations when forming a part of a periodical, newspaper, or in printed books accompanying the same), and all articles produced either in whole or in part by lithographic process, and photograph, autograph, and scrap albums wholly or partially manufactured (b)	35 per cent	30 per cent	35	30
Envelopes (c) M	25 cts. per M	20 per cent	20.98	20
Hangings, and paper for screens or fireboards	25 per cent	20 per cent	25	20
Book pamphlets, bound or unbound, maps, charts, and all printed matter not specially provided for	do	25 per cent	25	25
Engravings, bound or unbound, etchings, and photographs	do	do	25	25
Blank books, bound or unbound	do	20 per cent	25	20
Cards, playing packs	50 c. per pk	10 c. per pk. and 50 p. c.	286.70	107.24
Writing, drawing, and all other paper, not specially provided for	25 per cent	20 per cent	25	20
Other manufactures of paper, or of which paper is the component of chief value	do	do	25	20
Total Schedule M, pulp, paper, etc			23.85	20.53

SCHEDULE N.—SUNDRIES.

Bristles lbs	10 c. per lb	7½ c. per lb	10.67	8.10
Brooms of all kinds	40 per cent	20 per cent	40	20
Brushes of all kinds, including feather dusters and hair pencils in quills	do	35 per cent	40	35
Buttons and button forms:				
Button forms: Lastings, mohair cloth, silk, or other manufactures of cloth, woven or made in patterns of such size, shape, or form, or cut in such manner as to be fit for buttons exclusively	10 per cent	10 per cent	10	10
Agate buttons	25 per cent	25 per cent	25	25
Pearl and shell buttons line	2½ c. per line and 25 p. c.	1 c. per line and 15 p. c.	143.61	84.50
Ivory, vegetable ivory, bone or horn buttons	50 per cent	35 per cent	50	35
Glass buttons	60 per cent	do	60	35
Shoe buttons, made of paper board, papier mache, pulp, or similar material, not specially provided for, valued at not exceeding 3 cents per gross gross	1 c. per gross	25 per cent	65.03	25

Comparison of rates of duties between McKinley act and new law—Continued.

	Rates of duty under—		Average ad valorem under—	
	McKinley law.	New law.	McKinley law.	New law.
Schedule N.—Sundries—Continued.			*Per ct.*	*Per ct.*
Coal and coke:				
Bituminous coal and shale..tons...	75 c. per ton...	40 c. per ton...	22.72	12.12
Slack, or culm of coal, such as will pass through a half-inch screen ....tons...	30 c. per ton...	15 c. per ton...	28.68	14.34
Coke ....,.......tons...	20 per cent......	15 per cent......	20	15
Corks..lbs...	15 c. per lb....	10 c. per lb.....	30.55	20.37
Cork bark, cut into squares or cubes, lbs ,	10 c. per lb.....	25 per cent......	9.60	25
Dice, draughts, chessmen, chess balls, and billiard, pool, and bagatelle balls, of ivory, bone, or other material..	50 per cent......	50 per cent......	50	50
Dolls, doll heads, toy marbles of whatever material composed, and all other toys not composed of rubber, china, porcelain, parian, bisque, earthen or stone ware, and not specially provided for..............	35 per cent......	25 per cent......	35	25
Emery; Grains, and ground, pulverized, or refined.........................lbs...	1 c. per lb......	8-10 c. per lb...	25.19	20.15
Gunpowder, and all explosive substances:				
Firecrackers of all kinds......lbs...	8 c. per lb......	50 per cent......	147.32	50
Fulminates, fulminating powders, and all like articles, not especially provided for............	30 per cent......	30 per cent......	30	30
Gunpowder, and all explosive substances, used for mining, blasting, artillery, or sporting purposes—				
Valued at 20 cents or less per pound,.........................lbs...	5 c. per lb....*.	5 c. per lb......	25.80	25.80
Valued at above 20 cents per pound.......................lbs...	8 c. per lb......	8 c. per lb......	8.68	8.68
Matches, friction or lucifer, of all descriptions:				
In boxes containing not more than 100 matches per box, gross...................................	10 c. per gross	20 per cent......	33.93	20
Otherwise than in boxes containing not more than 100 matches each ....M...	1 c. per thousand.	......do............	21.19	20
Musical instruments :				
Metal, chief value...........................	45 per cent......	25 per cent......	45	25
Wood, chief value..........................	35 per cent......	......do	35	25
Percussion caps	40 per cent......	30 per cent. / $2.07 per M (caps).	40	30
Feathers, dressed, colored, or manufactured, including dressed and finished birds suitable for millinery ornaments :				
Ostrich feathers	50 per cent......	35 per cent......	50	35
All other...............................	......do	......do	50	35

A comparison of rates of duties between McKinley act and new law.—Continued.

	Rates of duty under—		Average ad valorem under—	
	McKinley law.	New law.	McKinley law.	New. law.

SCHEDULE N.—SUNDRIES—Continued.

			Per ct.	*Per ct.*
Feathers and flowers, artificial and ornamental, or parts thereof, of whatever material composed, not specially provided for	50 per cent	30 per cent	50	35
Furs dressed on the skin, but not made up into articles	20 per cent	20 per cent	20	20
Furs, not on the skin, prepared for hatters' use	do	do	20	20
Fans, of all kinds, except palm-leaf fans (no data)	According to material of chief value.	40 per cent		40
Beads of glass, loose, unthreaded or unstrung	10 per cent	10 per cent	10	10
Gun wads of all descriptions	35 per cent	do	35	10
Human hair, clean or drawn, but not manufactured	20 per cent	20 per cent	20	20
Haircloth, known as crinoline cloth, sq. yds	8 c. per sq. yd.	6 c. per sq. yd.	27.99	20.99
Haircloth, known as hair seating, sq. yds	30 c. per sq. yd.	20 c. per sq. yd.	23.22	15.48
Hair, curled, suitable for beds or mattresses	15 per cent	10 per cent	15	10
Hats, for men's, women's, and children's wear, composed of the fur of the rabbit, beaver, or other animals, or of which such fur is the component material of chief value, wholly or partially manufactured, including fur hat bodies	55 per cent	40 per cent	55	40
Jewelry and precious stones, not elsewhere specified :				
Jewelry : All articles not specially provided for, composed of precious metals or imitations thereof, whether set with coral, jet, or pearls, or with diamonds, rubies, cameos, or other precious stones or imitations thereof, or otherwise, and which shall be known commercially as "jewelry," and cameos in frames	50 per cent	35 per cent	50	35
Pearls	10 per cent	10 per cent	10	10
Precious stones, and imitations of—				
Cut, but not set	do	25 per cent	10	25
Set, and not specially provided for	25 per cent	30 per cent	25	30
Imitations of, not set, composed of paste or glass, not exceeding 1 inch in dimensions	10 per cent	10 per cent	10	10
Diamonds and other precious stones, rough or uncut	Free	10 per cent	Free...	10
Leather, and manufactures of :				
Bend or belting, and sole	10 per cent	10 per cent	10	10
Calf skins, japanned	30 per cent	20 per cent	30	20

Comparison of rates of duties between McKinley act and new law.—Continued.

	Rates of duty under—		Average ad valorem under—	
	McKinley law.	New law.	McKinley law.	New law.

SCHEDULE N.—SUNDRIES—Continued.

			Per ct.	*Per ct.*
Calf skins, tanned, or tanned and dressed	20 per cent	20 per cent	20	20.
Piano-forte and piano-forte action leather	35 per cent	....do	35	20
Skins for morocco—				
Finished	20 per cent	20 per cent	20	20
Tanned, but unfinished	10 per cent	10 per cent	10	10
Skins, chamois or other, not specially provided for; bookbinder's calf skins, kangaroo, sheep, and goat skins, including lamb and kid skins, dressed and finished	20 per cent	20 per cent	20	20
Upper leather, dressed, including patent, enameled, and japanned leather, dressed or undressed, and finished	....do	....do	20	20
All leather not specially provided for	10 per cent	10 per cent	10	10
Boots and shoes	25 per cent	20 per cent	25	20
Gloves, composed wholly or in part of kid or other leather, and whether wholly or partly manufactured—				
Ladies' and children's—		Ladies' or children's "glace" finish--Schmaschen--		
Fourteen inches and under in extreme length—				
Schmaschen--				
Plain...........doz	$1.75 per doz	Not over 14 in. $1 p. doz. prs—	52.70	40
Pique or prick seam, and embroidered with more than 3 single strands or cords...........doz	$2.25 per doz	Over 14 in. and not over 17 $1.50. p. doz. prs.	58.56	40
Lined ....doz	$2.75 per doz	Over 17 in.. $2 p. doz. prs.--	64.96	40
Lamb—				
Plain...........doz	$2.25 per doz	Men's $3 p. doz. prs. "glace" finish, lamb or sheep;	55.57	40
Pique or prick seam, and embroidered with more than three single strands or cords...........doz	$2.75 per doz	Not over 14 in. $1.75 per doz. prs.;	58.55	40
Lined ....doz	$3.25 per doz	Over 14 and not over 17, $2.75 p. doz. prs.	64.44	40
Kid—				
Plain...........doz	....do	Over 17 in. $3.75 per doz. prs.;	60.77	40
Pique or prick seam, and embroidered with more than 3 single strands or cords...........doz	$3.75 per doz	Men's $4 per doz, "glace" finish, goat, kid or other;	61.56	40
Lined ....doz	$4.25 per doz	Not over 14 in. $2.25 p. doz. prs.;	57.07	40

Comparison of rates of duties beeween McKinley act and new law—Continued.

	Rates of duty under—		Average ad valorem under—	
	McKinley law.	New law.	McKinley law.	New law.

SCHEDULE N.—SUNDRIES—Continued.

Gloves composed wholly or in part of kid or other leather, etc.—Cont'd.

	McKinley law.	New law.	McKin-ley law. Per ct.	New law. Per ct.
Suedes and other, whether more or less than 14 inches in extreme length—				
Plain ....doz	50 per cent......	Over 14 and not over 17, $3 p. doz. prs.;	50	40
Pique or prick seam, and embroidered with more than 3 single strands or cords..doz...	50c. per doz. and 50 p. ct.	Over 17 in. $4 p. doz. prs.; Men's $4 p. doz. prs. Ladies' or children's of sheep origin.	57.82	40
Lined ....doz...	$1 per doz. and 50 p. ct.	Not over 17 in., $1.75 p. doz.	73.13	40
Ladies' and children's, on which the above rates of duty do not equal a duty of 50 per cent..doz...	50 per cent......	........................».	50	40
Men's gloves—				
Fourteen inches and under in extreme length, plain .....doz...	50 per cent......	Over 17 in. $2.75 p. doz. prs.: Men's $4 p. doz. prs. Ladies', etc., kid, goat. etc.— Not over 14 in., $2.25 p. doz. prs.	50	40
Over 14 inches in extreme length—				
Plain............................doz...	$1 per doz. and 50 p. c.	Over 14 and not over 17, $3 per doz. prs.	70.29	40
Pique or prick seam, and embroidered with more than 3 single strands or cords doz	$1.50 per doz. and 50 p. c.	Over 17 in., $4 p. doz. prs.	73.52	40
Lined ....doz...	$2 per dozen and 50 per c.	Men's $4 per doz. prs.	79.36	40
Do ....doz...	$2.50 per doz. and 50 per c.	All leather gloves, when lined, $1 per dozen additional.	75.62	40
Do ....doz...	$3 per dozen and 50 per c.	NOTE: Owing to change in classification of sizes, no comparison can be given, (Estimated rate by proposed bill=40 p. c. on all.)	75	40
Miscellaneous manufactures:				
Alabaster and spar, manufactures of.....................	25 per cent......	45 per cent.....	25	45
Amber, manufactures of.................	.... do.............	25 per cent.....	25	25
Asbestos, manufactures of.............	.... do.............	.... do.............	25	25
Bladders, manufactures of.............	.... do.............	.... do.............	25	25

Comparison of rates of duties between McKinley act and new law—Continued.

	Rates of duty under—		Average ad valorem under—	
	McKinley law.	New law.	McKinley law.	New law.

SCHEDULE N.—SUNDRIES—Continued.

Miscellaneous manufactures—Cont'd.

			Per ct.	Per ct.
Coral, manufactures of	25 per cent	25 per cent	25	25
Catgut or whipgut or wormgut, manufactures of	do	do	25	25
Jet, manufactures of	do	do	25	25
Paste, manufactures of	do	do	25	25
Wax, manufactures of	do	do	25	25
Candles, and tapers of wax	do	do	25	25
Osier or willow, prepared for basket-makers' use	30 per cent	20 per cent	30	20
Osier or willow, manufactures of	40 per cent	25 per cent	40	25
Bone and horn, manufactures of	30 per cent	do	30	25
Chip, manufactures of (baskets)	do	do	30	25
Grass, manufactures of	do	do	30	25
India rubber, manufactures of	do	do	30	25
Palm leaf, manufactures of	do	do	30	25
Straw, manufacture of	do	do	30	25
Do for julips	do	do	30	25
Whalebone, manufactures of	do	do	30	25
Leather, manufactures of	35 per cent	30 per cent	35	30
Fur, manufactures of	do	do	35	30
India rubber, vulcanized, known as hard rubber	do	do	35	30
Gutta percha	do	do	35	30
Hair, manufactures of	do	do	35	30
Papier mache, manufactures of	do	do	35	30
Ivory and vegetable ivory, manufactures of	40 per cent	35 per cent	40	35
Shell and mother-of-pearl, manufactures of	do	do	40	35
Masks, composed of paper or pulp	35 per cent	25 per cent	35	25
Matting and mats made of cocoa fibre or rattan :				
Matting sq. yds	12 c. per sq. yd.	20 per cent	71.87	20
Mats sq. yds	8 c. per sq. ft.	do	41.46	20
Pencils :				
Wood filled with lead or other material and pencils of lead gross	50 c. per gross and 30 per c.	50 per cent	53.67	50
Slate pencils (a) gross	4 c. per gross	30 per cent	47.57	30
Pencil leads, not in wood	10 per cent	10 per cent	10	10
Pipes and smokers' articles :				
Common pipes of clay gross	15 c. per gross	do	50.11	10
Pipes, pipe bowls of all materials, and all smokers' articles, whatsoever, not specially provided for, including cigarette books, cigarette book-covers, pouches for smoking or chewing tobacco, and cigarette paper in all forms	70 per cent	50 per cent	70	50
Umbrellas, parasols, and sunshades, and sticks for :				
Umbrellas, parasols, and sunshades—				
Covered with silk or alpaca	55 per cent	45 per cent	55	45

Comparison of rates of duty between McKinley act and the new law.—Continued.

	Rates of duty under—		Average ad valorem under—	
	McKinley law.	New law.	McKinley law.	New law.
SCHEDULE N.—SUNDRIES—Continued.				
Umbrellas, parasols, and sunshades, and sticks for—Continued.				
Umbrellas, parasols and sunshades—Continued.			*Per ct.*	*Per ct.*
Covered with other materials	45 per cent	45 per cent	45	45
Sticks for umbrellas, parasols, and sunshades—				
Carved	50 per cent	30 per cent	50	30
Plain	35 per cent	......do	35	30
Waste, all not specially provided for	10 per cent	10 per cent	10	10
Total Schedule N, sundries			26.80	24.45
Section 4 (act of Oct. 1, 1890):				
Unmanufactured	10 per cent	10 per cent	10	10
Manufactured	20 per cent	20 per cent	20	20
Enfleurage grease	......do	Free	20	Free.
Repairs on vessels	50 per cent	50 per cent	50	50
Total sec. 4			18.98	18.73
Total schedules			49.58	38.68

Comparison of McKinley act, 1890, Wilson bill, and Senate bills of 1894..

	Schedules.	Importations of the fiscal year ending June 30, 1893.		Estimated duties by bill (H. R. 4864) as passed by the—		Senate increase over House bill	Average ad valorem under—				Per ct. of reduction by Senate bill over present law.
		Values.	Duty received.	House.	Senate (July 2).		Present law.	House bill.	Senate bill.	
							Per ct.	*Per ct.*	*Per ct.*	*Per ct.*
A	Chemicals, oils, and paints	$21,066,221.25	$6,284,555.13	$6,096,316.00	$4,860,370.05	*$235,945.95	31.61	25.09	24.44	22.68
B	Earths, earthenware, and glassware	23,646,698.85	12,118,239.41	8,080,370.31	8,383,152.65	252,782.34	51.20	34.13	35.21	31.23
C	Metals, and manufactures of	46,306,560.61	26,854,071.84	13,606,116.03	16,678,936.04	1,272,810.01	58.33	34.99	36.59	37.37
D	Wool, and manufactures of	2,247,265.40	711,518.62	488,688.36	4+1,931.17	*3,162.19	31.72	21.96	23.62	25.70
E	Sugar	109,817,948.14	183,234.48	16,832.14	43,478,957.57	43,462,126.13	11.55	Free	39.59	*172.10
F	Tobacco and manufactures	12,588,107.12	14,831,989.99	11,328,783.11	13,337,977.28	1,989,191.17	117.82	91.58	105.95	10.07
G	Agricultural products and provisions	11,528,276.00	12,421,203.69	7,983,441.78	9,594,583.51	1,611,141.75	33.21	21.59	23.10	30.44
H	Spirits, wines, and other beverages	13,874,921.06	9,698,336.91	8,421,347.54	8,465,396.86	44,089.32	69.90	60.69	61.01	12.75
I	Cotton manufactures	20,540,438.98	11,323,646.35	7,898,585.28	8,929,286.92	1,043,701.64	55.25	38.45	43.54	21.19
J	Flax, hemp, and jute, and manufactures of	41,706,792.44	18,767,353.37	12,724,279.49	13,848,060.04	1,123,780.55	45	30.51	41.05	8.76
K	Wool, and manufactures of	36,913,787.16	36,404,797.81	14,711,879.23	18,019,778.37	3,304,899.14	98.62	39.78	49.82	50.50
L	Silk and silk goods	37,919,948.92	20,310,258.74	17,113,647.62	17,589,653.77	476,006.15	53.56	45.18	46.39	13.38
M	Pulp, papers, and books	8,640,319.32	2,070,121.19	1,638,398.97	1,781,922.00	123,523.03	23.85	19.10	20.53	13.92
N	Sundries	51,975,796.63	14,773,886.16	13,100,352.45	13,444,152.56	343,800.11	26.80	26.33	21.45	8.02
	Unenumerated	1,361,192.47	258,951.01	258,951.01	203,973.33	*54,977.68	18.99	18.98	18.73	1.31
Sec. 4	Articles transferred to free list by both House and Senate									
		41,398,000.71	11,438,264.48				27.63			
		514,463,408.49	198,373,452.97	124,657,429.32	179,251,142.16	$54,593,712.84	49.84	35.51	39.68	21.99

*Schedule A, D, and section 4 are decreases.   †Increase   ‡Net increase over House bill.

NOTE.—The computations of the average ad valorem rates of duty are calculated upon the dutiable value only. The value of the articles that are free from duty by either the present law, House, or Senate bills are excluded.

	Dutiable value.	Duty.	Ad valorem rate.	Decrease of duty.
			Per cent.	
Under present law	$400,069,658.48	$199,373,152.97	49.58	
Under House bill	351,041,063.12	124,657,429.32	35.51	$73,716,023.65
Under Senate bill	463,447,163.11	179,251,142.16	38.68	19,129,310.81

Articles transferred from dutiable to free list by both House and Senate.

Articles	Importations of 1893.				Rates.		Equivalent ad valorem.	
	Quantities.	Value.	Duties.	Unit of value.	McKinley.	New Law.	McKin-ley.	New Law.
SCHEDULE A.—CHEMICALS, OILS, AND PAINTS.							*Per ct.*	
Acid, sulphuric or oil of vitriol, not otherwise specially provided for ....lbs.	634	$43 00	$1 59	$0.068	¼ c. per lb.....	Free ...	3.10	Free.
Copper, sulphate of or blue vitriol ....lbs.	8,941	363 00	178 82	.041	2 c. per lb......	do	49.26	Do.
Coal tar, all preparations of, not colors or dyes, not specially provided for.......lbs.	....	158,713 04	31,742 61	....	20 per cent.....	do	20	Do.
Oils, mineral—								
Naphtha, benzine, benzole, dead oil, and similar products of coal tar...........galls.	691,167	41,103 00	10,275 75	.039	25 per cent.....	do	25	Do.
All other.........galls.	454,312	18,423 10	3,684 60	.011	20 per cent.....	do	20	Do.
Iron, sulphate of, or copperas............lbs.	1,010,039	4,099 00	3,030 12	.004	3 10 c. per lb..	do	73.92	Do.
Indigo:								
Carmined...........lbs.	29,687	35,304 00	2,968 70	1.19	10 c. per lb.....	do	8.41	Do.
Extracts or pastes of.........lbs.	1,317,835	101,317 00	9,883 90	.077	¾ c. per lb......	do	9.75	Do.
Iodine, resublimed..........lbs.	6	25 00	1 80	4.17	30 c. per lb.....	do	7.20	Do.
Oils:								
Cotton seed...........galls.	5,104	1,858 00	510 40	.36	10 c. per gal....	do	27.47	Do.
Croton ....lbs.	....	....	....	....	30 c. per lb.....	do	....	Do.
Paints, colors, etc.:								
Baryta, sulphate of, or barytes, including baryta, unmanufactured............tons.	2,709.25	6,995 00	3,031 36	2.58	$1.12 per ton....	do	43.38	Do.
Ocher and ochery earths, dry............lbs.	7,367,817	71,286 00	17,919 64	.010	¼ c. per lb......	do	25.16	Do.
Sienna and sienna earths, dry............lbs.	1,297,870	29,538 00	3,214 70	.023	do	do	10.98	Do.
Umber and umber earths, dry............lbs.	1,399,075	15,494 00	3,497 69	.011	do	do	22.57	Do.
Potash, caustic or hydrate of, refined in sticks or rolls............lbs.	3,513	1,781 00	95 13	.19	1 c. per lb......	do.	5.34	Do.
Soda, sulphate of :								
Glauber salts ....tons.	218.66	4,012 53	273 34	18.85	$1.25 per ton....	do	6.81	Do.
Salt cake, or niter cake............tons.	19,724.37	221,846 00	21,654 24	11.25	do.....	do	11.11	Do.
Total Schedule A transferred to free list...........		712,180 57	114,967 29				16.14	
SCHEDULE B.—EARTH, EARTHENWARE, AND GLASSWARE.								
Stone:								
Burr stone, manufactured or bound up into mill-stones............		636 00	95 40		15 per cent.....	Free ...	15	Do.
Total Schedule B transferred to free list...........		636 00	95 40				15	

Articles transferred from dutiable to free list by both House and Senate.—Continued.

	Importations of 1893.				Rates.		Equivalent ad valorem.	
	Quantities.	Value.	Duties.	Unit of value.	McKinley.	New Law.	McKinley.	New Law.
SCHEDULE C.—METALS, AND MANUFACTURES OF.								
Iron ores:								
Chromate of iron, or chromic ore............tons.	6,000.34	$54,098 00	$8,304 70	$9.12	15 per cent	Free	15	Free.
Cotton ties of iron or steel:								
Not thinner than No. 10 wire gauge.........lbs.	1,017,586	30,505 00	12,211 02	.030	1 2-10 c. per lb.	...do	40.03	Do.
Thinner than No. 10 and not thinner than No. 20..lbs.	999 225	25,863 00	12,989 92	.026	1 3-10 c. per lb.	...do	50.23	Do.
Antimony, as regulus or metal............lbs.	3,802,153	352,831 00	29,516 13	.093	¾ c. per lb.	...do	8.09	Do.
COPPER, AND MANUFACTURES OF:								
Ores (fine copper contained therein)........lbs.	7,465,101	454,224 00	37,325 53	.061	½ c. per lb	...do	8.22	Do.
Regulus of, and black or coarse copper, and copper cement, fine copper contained therein......lbs.	2,109,847	189,080 00	21,098 47	.06	1 c. per lb	...do	15.17	Do.
old, fit only for remanufacture, and clippings from new copper.............lbs.	72,373	7,352 45	723 73	.10	......do	...do	9.84	Do.
Composition metal, of which copper is a component material of chief value, not specially provided for........lbs.	38,679	5,963 00	386 79	.15	......do	...do	6.49	Do.
Plates, not rolled, bars, ingots, Chile or other pigs, and in other forms, not manufactured, not specially provided for........lbs.	576,075	61,020 00	7,200 94	.11	1¼ c. per lb	...do	11.80	Do.
Total Schedule C transferred to free list....		1,131,240 45	128,657 23				11.37	
SCHEDULE D.—WOOD, AND MANUFACTURES OF.								
Timber:								
Used for spars and in building wharves........cu. ft.	78,452	9,431 85	943 19	.12	10 per cent	...do	10	Do.
Hewn and sawed.........cu. ft.	1,419,484	62,867 83	6,286 73	.044	...do	...do	10	Do.
Squared or sided, not specially provided for......cu. ft.	65,139	491 61	325 69	.008	½ c. per cu. ft.	...do	66.25	Do.
Lumber:								
Boards, planks, deals, and other sawed lumber—								
Of hemlock, white wood, sycamore, white pine, and basswood—								
Not planed or finished.........M ft.	514,989.12	6,183,030 36	514,930 12	12 01	$1 per M. feet	...do	8.33	Do.
All sawed lumber, not specially provided for—..M ft.	154,111.09	1,440,203 30	308,222 19	9.35	2 per M feet	...do	21.40	Do.
Paving posts, railroad ties, and telephone and telegraph poles of cedar......No.	1,815,949	271,235 91	54,247 19	.15	20 per c	...do	20	Do.
Unmanufactured, not specially provided for ..		25,952 20	5,190 44		...do	...do	20	Do.
Veneers of wool........		750.00	150.00		...do	...do	20	Do.

Article	Unit	Quantity	Value	Duty	Rate	%	Rate of duty			Do.
Clapboards—										
Pine	M	67.99	2,003.40	67.99	29.47	3.89	$1 per M	...do...		Do.
Spruce	M	6,997.44	111,985.00	10,496.19	16	9.37	$1.50 per M	...do...		Do.
Hubs for wheels, posts, last, wagon, oar, gun, and heading blocks, and all like blocks or sticks, rough hewn or sawed only	M									
Laths	M	327,411.88	28,227.30	5,645.46	1.41	20	20 per c	...do...		Do.
Pickets and palings	M	5,4~3.09	462,140.04	49 116.34	6.69	10.63	15 c. per c	...do...		Do.
			3,670.00	3,670.00		10	10 per c	...do...		Do.
Shingles—										
White pine	M	216,780.75	397,313.95	43,356.15	1.83	10.91	20 c. per M	...do		Do.
All other	M	258,220.70	519,445.00	73,966.25	2.06	14.62	30 c. per M	...do		Do.
Staves of all kinds			646,613.40	64,661 34		10	10 per c	...do		Do.
Total Schedule D transferred to free list			10,198,391.11	1,143,294.34		11.21				

Provided that all articles mentioned in Schedule D, when imported from any country which lays an export duty on any of them, shall be subject to the duties existing prior to the passage of this act.

SCHEDULE G.—AGRICULTURAL PRODUCTS ETC.

Article	Unit	Quantity	Value	Duty	Rate	%	Rate of duty			Do.
Milk, fresh	galls	6,265	1,429.75	313.25	.23	21.91	5 c. per gall	...do		Do.
Broom corn	tons	12.25	524.00	98.02	42.77	18.71	$8 per ton	...do		Do.
Cabbages	No	328,683	19,178.31	3,960.49	.040	71.82	3 c. each	...do		Do.
Cider	galls	13,146.50	3,549.00	657.25	.27	18.52	5 c. per gall	...do		Do.
Eggs, yolk of			12.00	8.00		25	25 per c	...do		Do.
Plants, trees, shrubs and vines			139,004.15	27,900.78		20	20 per c	...do		Do.
Pease, green, in bulk or packages	bush	345.19	568.39	138.07	1.65	24.29	40 c. per bush	...do		Do.
Fish, fresh:										
Herring	lbs	383,619	4,937.00	959 05	.013	19.43	¼ c. per lb	...do		Do.
Salmon	lbs	1,228,605	116,124.00	9,289.55	.094	8	¾ c. per lb	...d		Do.
All other	lbs	9,909,522	408,717.81	74,321.52	.041	18.18	...do	...do		Do.
Tallow	lbs	45,800	5,047.00	483.00	.11	9.49	1 c. per lb	...do		Do.
Grease of wool, known as degras	lbs	11,683,560	196,848.00	58,469.28	.017	29 70	½ c. per lb	...do		Do.
Salt:										
In bags, sacks, barrels, or other packages	lbs	130,676,356	446,273.93	156,813.97	.003	35 11	12 c. p. 100 lbs	...d		Do.
In bulk	lbs	181,443,328	176,820.94	145,158.63	.001	33.33	8 c. p. 100 lbs	...do		Do.
Total Schedule G transferred to free list			1,512,574.31	484,365.84		32.02				

SCHEDULE H.—SPIRITS, WINES, ETC.

Article	Unit	Quantity	Value	Duty	Rate	%	Rate of duty		Do.
Lemonade, soda water, and other similar waters:									
In plain, green, or colored, molded, or pressed, glass bottles—									
(Containing each not more than three-fourths of a pint	doz	44.794.50	31,240.00	5,828.39	.70	18.64	19 c. per doz	...do	Do.
(Containing more than three-fourths of a pint each and not more than one and one-half pints	doz	224	240.00	58.24	1.07	24.27	26 c. per doz	...do	Do.

Articles transferred from dutiable to free list—Continued.

	Importations of 1893.				Rates.		Equivalent ad valorem.	
	Quantities.	Value.	Duties.	Unit of value.	McKinley.	New law.	McKinley law.	New law.
							Per ct.	
SCHEDULE H.—SPIRITS, WINES, ETC.—Continued.								
Lemonade, soda water, and other similar waters—Cont'd. Otherwise than in such bottles, or in such bottles containing more than one and one-half pints each-gals.	30	$10 00	$15.00	$0.33	50 c. per gall...	Free ...	18.72	Free.
Total Schedule H transferred to the free list...		31,490.00	5,896.53					
SCHEDULE J.—FLAX, HEMP, JUTE, ETC.								
Flax:								
Straw ....tons.	152.19	4,091.00	765.52	26.77	$5 per ton	do ...	18.68	Do.
Not hackled or dressed ....tons.	3,260.70	759,421.00	73,029.79	232.90	$22.40 per ton...	do ...	10.77	Do.
Tow of ....tons.	1,921.81	291,387.60	21,567.81	151.36	$11.20 per ton...	do ...	7.40	Do.
Hemp, tow of ....tons.	524.84	64,189.00	5,878.25	122.21	do ...	do ...	9.16	Do.
Hemp, manufactured in whole or in part of istle or Tampico fiber, manila, sisal grass, or sunn: ....tons.	4,239.79	607,372.00	105,994.82	143.25	$25 per ton......	do ...	17.45	
Binding ....lbs.	35,684	3,863.00	249.79	.11	7-10 c. per lb....	do ...	6.47	Do.
Total Schedule J transferred to free list...		1,730,231.60	207,495.99				11.99	
SCHEDULE K.—WOOL.								
Wools, hair of the camel, goat, alpaca, and other like animals, and manufactures of:								
Unmanufactured—								
Class 1: Merino, mestiza metz, or metis wools, or other wools of merino blood. immediate or remote. Down clothing wools, and wools of like character with any of the preceding, including such as have been heretofore usually imported into the United States from Buenos Ayres, New Zealand, Australia, Cape of Good Hope, Russia, Great Britain, Canada, and elsewhere, and also including all wools not hereinafter described or designated in classes 2 and 3—								
Unwashed wool..........lbs.	85,329,611.50	6,516,121 92	3,885,487 27	.18	11 c. per lb......	do ...	59 63	Do.
Washed wool..........lbs.	6,123	2,757 00	1,347 06	.45	22 c. per lb......	do ...	48.86	Do.
Scoured wool..........lbs.	74,287	36,761 00	24,514 71	.49	33 c. per lb......	do ...	66.69	Do.

Article	Quantity	Value			Rate of duty		Ad val. equiv.	
Class 2: Leicester, Cotswold, Lincolnshire, Down combing wools, Canada long wools, or other like combing wools of English blood, and usually known by the terms herein used, and also all hair of the camel, goat, alpaca, and other like animals—								
Wool, unscoured............lbs.	5,740,629.37	1,225,165 00	688,875 53	.21	12 c. per lb.	do	56.23	Do.
Wool, scoured..............lbs.	304	231 00	109 44	.93	36 c. per lb.	do	43.60	Do.
Wool, sorted...............lbs.	15,322	4,011 00	3,677 28	.26	24 c. per lb.	do	91.68	Do.
Hair of the goat, alpaca, and other like animals, unscoured....lbs.	1,278,932	306,164 00	163,471 84	.24	do	do	50.13	Do.
Hair of the goat, alpaca, and other like animals, scoured....lbs.	252	221 00	90 72	.88	36 c per lb.	do	41.05	Do.
Class 3: Donskoi, native South American, Cordova, Valparaiso, native Smyrna, Russian camel's hair, and including all such wools of like character as have been heretofore usually imported into the United States from Turkey, Greece, Egypt, Syria, and elsewhere—								
Value 13 cents or less per pound—								
Wool....................lbs.	125,611,283	9,504,403 00	3,041,408 94	.076	32 per cent	do	32	Do.
Wool, sorted............lbs.	153,467	14,365 00	9,193 60	.094	64 per cent	do	64	Do.
Camel's hair, Russian...lbs.	4,850,714	325,550 00	104,176 00	.074	32 per cent	do	32	Do.
Value over 13 cents per pound—								
Wool....................lbs.	3,041,337	466,102 00	233 051 00	.15	50 per cent	do	50	Do.
Wool, sorted............lbs.	10,780	1,817 00	1,817 00	.17	100 per cent	do	100	Do.
Camel's hair, Russian...lbs.					50 per cent	do		
Manufactures composed wholly or in part of wool, worsted, the hair of the camel, goat, alpaca, or other animals—								
Rags, mungo, flocks, noils and waste—								
b Top, slubbing, roving, ring, yarn, garnetted, and other wastes....lbs.	93,477	23,561 10	28,063 10	.36	30 c. per lb	do	83.55	Do.
c Rags, mungo, and flocks....lbs.	158,265.50	46,108 00	15,888 55	.29	10 c. per lb.	do	34.32	Do.
Noils....................lbs.	40,777	13,193 00	12,255 10	.32	30 c. per lb.	do	92.72	Do.
Total Schedule K transferred to free list......		15,496,563 92	8,203,223 14				44.35	

SCHEDULE N.—SUNDRIES.

Article	Value			Rate of duty		Ad val. equiv.	
Feathers and downs, crude, not dressed:							
Ostrich feathers..........	745,437 00	54,543 70		do	do	10	Do.
All other..........	268,164 69	26,806 40		10 per cent.	do	10	Do.
Paintings, in oil or water colors..........	2,096,764 69	313,014 71		do	do	15	Do.
Statuary..........	175,002 16	26,250 32		do	do	15	Do.
Hatters' plush, black, composed of silk, or of silk and cotton..........	120,428 00	12,042 80		do	do	10	Do.
Total Schedule N transferred to free list......	3,195,695 85	432 657 93				13.54	

Articles transferred from dutiable to free list—Continued.

SCHEDULE N.—SUNDRIES—Continued.

		Importations of 1893.			Unit of value.	Ra'es.		Equivalent ad valorem.	
		Quantities.	Value.	Duties.		McKinley.	New law.	McKinley.	New law.
Articles under section 3, act of October ber 1, 1890:								*Per ct.*	
Coffee	lbs..	19,757,574	$3,365,105 00	$592,727 22	$0.17	3 c. per lb	Free....	17.93	Free.
Goatskins, raw	lbs..	1,825,621	398,614 00	27,384 34	.22	1½ c. per lb	...do ...	6.87	Do.
Hides, raw or uncured, whether dry, salted, or pickled, and other skins, except sheepskins with the wool on	lbs..	6,494,611	685,398 00	97,419 19	.11	...do ...	...do ...	14.22	Do.
Total (Sec. 3)			4,389,007 00	717,530 79				16.35	
Total transfers from dutiable to free list by both House and Senate			41,398,000 71	11,438,264 48				27.63	

STATEMENT BY GROUPS

OF THE

Reduction of Duty from McKinley Law Made by New Law.

ONE HUNDRED PER CENT.*

Paragraph of present law.	Articles.	Per cent reduction.
	SCHEDULE A.—CHEMICALS, OILS, AND PAINTS.	
5	Acid, sulphuric, or oil of vitrol, not otherwise specially provided for	100
13	Copper, sulphate of, or blue vitriol	100
19	Coal tar, all preparations of, not colors or dyes, not specially provided for	100
	Oils, mineral:	
	Naphtha, benzine, benzole, dead oil, and similar products of coal tar	100
	All other	100
23	Iron, sulphate of, copperas	100
29	Indigo:	
	Carmined	100
	Extracts or paste of	100
31	Iodine, resublimed	100
	Oils:	
39	Cotton seed	100
40	Croton	100
	Paints, colors, etc.:	
49	Baryta, sulphate of, barytes, including barytes earth, unmanufactured	100
54	Ocher and ochery earths, dry	100
	Sienna and sienna earths, dry	100
	Umber and umber earths, dry	100
70	Potash, caustic or hydrate of, refined in sticks or rolls	100
85	Soda, sulphate of:	
	Glauber salts	100
	Salt cake, or niter cake	100
	SCHEDULE B.—EARTH, EARTHENWARE, AND GLASSWARE.	
126	Stone:	
	Burr stone manufactured or bound up into millstones	100

*All articles in group of 100 per cent are made free of duty.

Statement by groups of the reductions of duty by present law, etc.—Continued.

ONE HUNDRED PER CENT.—Continued.

Paragraph of present law.	Articles.	Per cent reduction.
	SCHEDULE C.—METALS, AND MANUFACTURES OF.	
	Iron ores:	
132	Chromate of iron, or chromic ore...................................	100
140	Cotton ties of iron or steel:	
	Not thinner than No. 10 wire gague.................................	100
	Thinner than No. 10 and not thinner than No. 20...............	100
187	Antimony, as r gulus or metal..	100
	Copper, and manufactures of :	
	Ores (fine copper contained therein).............................	100
191 to 195	Regulus of, and black or coarse copper, and copper cement, fine copper contained therein....................................	100
	Ol l, fit only for remanufacture, and clippings from new copper.	100
	Composition metal, of which copper is a component material of chief value not specially provided for................	100
195	Plates, not rolled, bars, ingots, Chile or other pigs, and in other form, not manufactured, not specially provided for...	100
	SCHEDULE D.—WOOD, AND MANUFACTURES OF.	
	Timber:	
216	Used for spars and in building wharves...........................	100
217	Hewn and sawed...	100
217	Squared or sided, not specially provided for.....................	100
	Lumber:	
218	Boards, planks, deals, and other sawed lumber—	
	Of hemlock, white wood, sycamore, white pine and basswood—	
	Not planed or finished...	100
	Planed or finished on one side...................................	100
	Planed or finished on two sides..................................	100
	Planed on one side and tongued and grooved.............	100
	Planed on two sides and tongued and grooved...........	100
	All sawed lumber, not specially provided for—	
	Not planed or finished...	100
	Planed or finished on one side...................................	100
	Planed or finished on two sides..................................	100
	Planed on one side and tongued and grooved.............	100
	Planed on two sides and tongued and grooved...........	100
219	Paving posts, railroad ties, and telephone and telegraph poles of cedar..	100
	Unmanufactured, not specially provided for..................	100
	Veneers of wood..	100
	Clapboards:—	
221	Pine	100
222	Spruce...	100
223	Hubs for wheels, posts, last, wagon, oar, gun, and heading blocks, and all like blocks or sticks, rough hewn or sawed only..	100
224	Laths	100
225	Pickets and palings..	100

Statement by groups of the reductions of duty by present law, etc.—Continued.

ONE HUNDRED PER CENT.—Continued.

Paragraph of present law.	Articles.	Per cent reduction.
226	Shingles—	
	White pine	100
	All other	100
227	Staves of all kinds	100
	SCHEDULE G.—AGRICULTURAL PRODUCTS, ETC.	
268	Milk, fresh	100
272	Broom corn	100
273	Cabbage	100
274	Cider	100
276	Eggs, yolk of	100
282	Plants, trees, shrubs, and vines	100
281	Peas, green, in bulk or packages	100
	Fish, fresh:	
294	Herring	100
293	Salmon	100
293	All other	100
316	Tallow	100
	Grease of wool, known as degras	100
322	Salt:	
	In bags, sacks, barrels, or other packages	100
	In bulk	100
	SCHEDULE H.—SPIRITS WINES, ETC.	
340	Lemonade, soda water, and other similar waters:	
	In plain, green, or colored, molded, or pressed glass bottles—	
	Containing each not more than three-fourths of a pint	100
	Containing more than three-fourths of a pint each and not more than one and one-half pints	100
	Otherwise than in such bottles, or in such bottles containing more than one and one-half pints each	100
	SCHEDULE J.—FLAX, HEMP, JUTE, ETC.	
	Flax:	
356	Straw	100
357	Not hackled or dressed	100
359	Tow of	100
359	Hemp, tow of	100
360	Hemp	100
	Twine, manufactured in whole or in part of istle or Tampico fibre, manila, sisal grass, or sunn:	
362	Binding	100
	Burlaps, of flax, jute, or hemp, or of which flax, jute, or hemp, or either of them, shall be the component material of chief value (except such as may be suitable for bagging for cotton)—	
364	Not exceeding 60 inches in width	100
	Exceeding 60 inches in width	100

Statement by groups of the reductions of duty by present law, etc.—Continued.

ONE HUNDRED PER CENT.—Continued.

Para-graph of present law.	Articles.	Per cent reduction.
	SCHEDULE J.—FLAX, HEMP, JUTE, ETC.—Continued.	
365	Bags for grain made of burlaps..	100
366	Bagging for cotton, gunny cloth, and all similar material for covering cotton, composed in whole or in part of hemp, flax, jute, or jute butts—	
	Valued at 6 cents or less per square yard........	100
	Valued at more than 6 cents per square yard............	100
	SCHEDULE K.—WOOL.	
	Wools, hair of the camel, goat, alapaca, and other like animals, and manufactures of :	
	Unmanufactured—	
384	Class 1 : Merino, mestiza, metz, or metis wools, or other wools of merino blood, immediate or remote, Down clothing wools, and wools of like character with any of the preceding, including such as have been heretofore usually imported into the United States from Buenos Ayres, New Zealand, Australia, Cape of Good Hope, Russia, Great Britain, Canada and elsewhere, and also including all wools not hereinafter described, or designated in classes 2 and 3—	
	Unwashed wool.........	100
	Washed wool.........	100
	Scoured wool.........	100
	Class 2 : Leicester, Cotswold, Lincolnshire, Down combing wools. Canada long wools, or other like combing wools of English blood, and usually known by the terms herein used, and also all hair of the camel, goat, alapaca and other like animals—	
	Wool, unscoured.........'.......	100
	Wool, scoured.........	100
	Wool, sorted.........	100
	Hair of the goat, alapaca and other like animals, unscoured	100
	Hair of the goat, alapaca, and other like animals, scoured	100
	Class 3 : Donskoi, native South American, Cordova, Valparaiso, native Smyrna, Russian camel's hair, and including all such wools of like character as have been heretofore usually imported into the United States from Turkey, Greece, Egypt, Syria, and elsewhere—	
385	Value 13 cents or less per pound—	
	Wool.	100
	Wool, sorted......... ....:'	100
	Camel's hair, Russian.........	100

Statements by groups of the reduction of duty by present law, etc.—Continued.

ONE HUNDRED PER CENT—Continued.

Paragraph of present law.	Articles.	Per cent reduction.
	SCHEDULE K.—WOOL—Continued.	
386	Value over 13 cents per pound—	
	Wool.......	100
	Wool, sorted........	100
	Camel's hair, Russian........	100
	Manufactures, composed wholly or in part of wool, worsted, the hair of the camel, goat, alpaca, or other animals—	
	Rags, mungo, flocks, noils and waste—	
388	Top, slubbing, roving, ring, yarn, garnetted and other wastes......	100
389	Rags, mungo and flocks......	100
388	Noils......	100
	SCHEDULE N.—SUNDRIES.	
443	Feathers and downs, crude, not dressed :	
	Ostrich feathers......	100
	All other......	100
465	Paintings, in oil or water colors......	100
	Statuary......	100
469	Hatters, plush, black, composed of silk, or of silk and cotton.....	100
	Articles under section 3, act of Oct. 1, 1890 :	
	Coffee......	100
	Goatskins, raw......	100
	Hides, raw or uncured, whether dry, salted or pickled, and other skins, except sheepskins with the wool on......	100
	Unenumerated under section 4, act of Oct. 1, 1890 :	
	Enfleurage, pomades......	100

FROM SEVENTY-FIVE TO ONE HUNDRED PER CENT.

	136	Bar iron, all other, and slabs, blooms or loops......	76.31
C.	175	Spikes of wrought iron or steel......	76.67
G.	247	Mules......	78.55
K.	391	Yarns, woolens, etc., valued at not more than 30 cents per pound......	89.23
	392	Cloths, woolens, etc., valued at not more than 30 cents per pound......	75.47
	392	Shawls, woolen, etc., valued at more than 30 cents and not more than 40 cents per pound......	76.71
N.	468	Common pipes of clay......	80.04

FROM FIFTY TO SEVENTY-FIVE PER CENT.

14	Borax, refined......	60
26	Sumac, extract of......	56.97
37	Oil, castor......	56.28
	Opium :	
47	Aqueous, extract of......	50
48	Prepared for smoking......	50

Statement by groups of the reductions of duty by present law, etc.—Continued.

FROM FIFTY TO SEVENTY-FIVE PER CENT—Continued.

Para- graph of present law.	Articles.	Per cent reduc- tion.
49	Paints and colors: Baryta, sulphate of	55.36
59	Whiting and Paris white, dry	50
59	Whiting, ground in oil (putty)	50
	Lead:	
	Acetate of—	
62	White	50
63	Litharge	50
64	Nitrate of	50
65	Orange mineral	50
67	White	50
	Potash:	
71	Hydriodate, Iodide and iodate of	50
72	Nitrate of	50
78	Santonine	60
79	Soap, all other	50
	Soda:	
80	Bicarbonate of	50
81	Hydrate of	50
83	Sal	50
86	Sponges	50
B. 95	Cement, other	50
101	Clocks, China, chief value	58.33
125	Clocks, marble chief value	50
C. 148	Wire rope a d wire strand, made of steel wire galvanized, not smaller than No. 5 wire gauge, cold rolled, etc	58.40
152	Sheets and plates and saw plates of steel not specially provided for, cold r lled, better than the grade hereinbefore provided for:	
	Valued above 4 cents and not above 7 cents per pound	60.09
	Valued above 7 cents and not above 10 cents per pound	53.11
152	Steel circular saw plates valued above—	
	4 cents and not above 7 ce ts p r pound	56.68
	7 ce ts a d not above 10 cents per pound	50
164	Chains, not less than ⅜ of 1 inch in diameter	61.50
165	Penknives valued at not more than 50 cents per dozen	68.64
167	All carving or cooking knives, valued at not more than $4 per dozen pieces	52.99
168	Files, 14 inches in length and over	50
170	Pistols, revolvi g:	
	Valued at not more than $1.50 each	53.15
	Valued at more than $1.50 each	56.16
170	Shotguns, double-barreled, valued at—	
	Not more than $6 each	55.88
	More than $6 and not more than $12 each	62.64
181	Railway fish plates, etc	65.36
185	Wheels, or parts thereof, etc	50
190	Bronze or Dutch metal, etc	60.88
	aluminum leaves in packages of 100 leaves	55.02
198	Silver leaf	61.43

FROM FIFTY TO SEVENTY-FIVE PER CENT—Continued.

Statement by groups of the reductions of duty by present law, etc.—Continued.

Paragraph of present law.	Articles	Per cent. reduction.
	Lead :	
199	Contained in silver ore	50
199	Contained in other ore	50
200	Pigs and bars, etc	50
201	Sheets, pipes, shot, etc	50
208	Type metal	50
	Zinc :	
C. 213	In sheets	50
E. 238	Sugar candy and confectionery valued at 12c. or less per pound..	70.81
G. 248	Cattle :	
	One year old or less	54.05
	More than 1 year old	68.36
252	Barley	53.62
270	Beans	50.78
277	Hay	50.01
280	Onions	50
284	Seeds : Castor beans or seeds	50
286	Garden seeds, etc., n. s. p	50
288	Vegetables, other, in their natural state	60
289	Straw.	50
290	Teazles	50
308	Peanuts, unshelled	72.55
297	Apples, dried, etc	52.84
314	Lard	50
326	Sage	66.67
I.	Cloth, cotton :	
344	Bleached, not exceeding 50 threads to the square inch, valued at 9 cents or less per square yard	50
	Dyed, etc., valued at 12 cents or less per square yard	50
349	Other articles of wearing apparel, etc., of which India rubber is a component material	55.28
J. 358	Hemp, hackled	55.20
362	Cables, cordage and twine, of hemp, untarred	55.24
	tarred	67.98
367	Gill netting, made of thread or twine not higher than 20	72.34
K. 388	Shoddy	71.43
391	Yarns, woolens, etc., valued at more than :	
	Thirty cents and not more than 40 cents per pound	74.75
	Forty cents per pound	62.05
392	Cloths, woolen, etc., valued at :	
	More than 30 cents and not more than 40 cents pound	65.17
	Above 40 cents per pound	50.00
	Shawls, woolen, etc., valued at above 40 cents per pound	54.85
	Knit fabrics, etc., valued at :	
	More than 30 cents and not more than 40 cents per pound	74.27
	Above 40 cents per pound	51.37
	All knit wearing apparel	57.49
	All other manufactures :	
	N. S. P., valued at not more than 30 cents per pound	74.94

Statements by groups of the reductions of duty by present law, etc.—Continued.

FROM FIFTY TO SEVENTY-FIVE PER CENT—Continued.

Paragraph of present law.	Articles.	Per cent reduction.
	All other manufactures—Continued.	
	Valued at more than 30 cents and not more than 40 cents per pound. ..	71.95
393	Blankets, valued at :	
	Not more than 30 cents per pound	71.66
	More than 30 cents and not more than 40 cents per pound. ...	70
	More than 40 cents and not more than 50 cents per pound.....	66.31
	More than 50 cents per pound	56.43
	Hats, of wool, valued at :	
	Not more than 30 cents per pound	70.93
	More than 30 cents and not more than 40 cents per pound. ...	71.80
393	More than 40 cents and not more than 50 cents per pound....	66.42
	More than 50 cents per pound	59.89
	Flannels for underwear, valued at :	
	Not more than 30 cents per pound.	70.55
	More than 30 cents and not more than 40 cents per pound.....	71.02
	More than 40 cents and not more than 50 cents per pound...	66.09
394	Dress goods, of which the warp consists wholly of cotton, etc., valued at :	
	Weighing over 4 ounces per square yard	51.09
	All other.	54.17
395	Felts not woven.	51.66
	Plushes and other pile fabrics	52.42
	Carpets, etc.:	
401	Brussels	50.92
405	Wool, Dutch, etc.	53.66
406	Druggets and bockings, etc.	63.67
	Felt, carpeting	52.05
L. 409	Silk, not raw, partly manufactured, etc	66.94
411	Velvets, Plushes, and other pile fabrics containing, exclusive of selvedges, 75 per cent or more in weight of silk.	68.58
M. 416	Sheathing paper, patent	50
424	Cards, playing	62.60
N. 427	Brooms	50
431	Shoe buttons, etc.	61.56
N. 438	Firecrackers.	66.06
432	Slack or culm of coal.	50
446	Gun wads.	71.43
464	Mattings and mats made of cocoa fiber or rattan :	
	Matting	72.17
	Mats	52.22

FROM TWENTY-FIVE TO FIFTY PER CENT.

A. 2	Boracic acid.	40
3	Chromic acid.	33.31
7	Tartaric acid	39.23

Statement by groups of the reductions of duty by present law etc.—Continued.

FROM TWENTY-FIVE TO FIFTY PER CENT.—Continued.

Para-graph of present law.	Articles.	Per cent reduc-tion.
9	Alum, alumina, etc	33.23
10	Ammonia, muriate of	34 21
14	Borax, crude or borate of soda, or borate of lime	33.33
16	Chalk, prepared	37.54
18	Coal-tar, colors or dyes	28 57
28	Glycerine :	
	Crude not purified	39.79
	Refined	33.33
32	Iodoform	33.33
34	Magnesia :	
	Carbonate of	25
	Sulphate	33.46
	Oils :	
38	Cod-liver	30.19
41	Flax seed or linseed	37.50
41	Poppy-seed	37.50
45	Peppermint	46.89
46	Whale	26.25
51	Blanc fixe	47.41
53	Chrome yellow or chrome green, dry or ground in oil	33.33
55	Ultramarine	33.33
56	Spirit varnishes : All other, including gold size or Japan	28.57
57	Vermilion, red, containing quicksilver	25.29
60	Zinc, oxide of, ground in oil	42.80
66	Lead, red	49.99
68	Phosphorus	25
69	Potash—chromate and bichromate of	31.92
75	Calomel, etc	28.57
	So la :	
82	Bichromate and chromate of	45.16
84	Silicate of	25.01
87	Strychnia	25.00
88	Sulphur :	
	Sublimed	30.22
	Refined	41 57
89	Sumac, ground	49.52
91	Tartar—tartars and less crystals	35.63
92	Tartrate of soda and potassa or Rochelle salts	33.33
B. 93	Brick, fire—glazed, enameled, etc	33.33
94	Brick, other than fire—ornamented, glazed, etc	33.33
97	Plaster of Paris : Calcined	28.43
	Clays or earths :	
98	Unwrought	33.33
	China clay	33.33
	Wrought	33.33
	Earthenware and china :	
100	Painted, tinted, etc	41.67
101	Plain white	45.45
100	Lava tips	45.45

Statement by groups of the reductions of duty by present law, etc.—Continued.

FROM TWENTY-FIVE TO FIFTY PER CENT.—Continued.

Paragraph of present law.	Articles.	Per cent reduction.
103	Bottles and vials, flint and lime:	
	empty—holding	
	not more than 1 pint and not less than ⅓ pint............	25
	more than 1 pint............	25
	filled—holding	
	not more than 1 pint and not less than ⅓ pint............	25
	more than 1 pint............	25
	green and colored—	
	empty—holding	
	not more than 1 pint and not less than ⅓ pint.........	25
	more than 1 pint............	25
	filled—holding	
	not more than 1 pint and not less than ⅓ pint	25
	more than 1 pint............	25
	Demijohns and carboys, empty, holding more than 1 pint.........	25
B. 105	Flint and lime, pressed glassware, not cut, etc............	33.33
106	Articles of glass, cut, engraved, etc	33.33
108	Thin-blown glass............	33.33
108	All other manufactures of glass	41.67
108	Glass buttons............	41.67
109	Heavy-blown glass	33.33
110	Porcelain or opal glassware............	33.33
112	Cylinder, crown and common window-glass:	
	Not exceeding 10 by 15 inches square	27.36
	Above 10 by 15 inches, and not exceeding 16 by 24 inches..	33.33
	Above 16 by 24 inches, and not exceeding 24 by 30 inches..	26.32
	Above 24 by 30 inches, and not exceeding 24 by 36 inches..	30.44
	All above 24 by 36 inches	32.01
113	Cylinder and crown glass, polished, unsilvered:	
	Not exceeding 16 by 24 inches square	37.72
	Above 16 by 24 inches, and not exceeding 24 by 30 inches..	33.33
	Above 24 by 30 inches, and not exceeding 24 by 60 inches..	25
	Plate-glass:	
114	Fluted, rolled or rough—	
	Above 10 by 15 inches, and not exceeding 16 by 24 inches..	25
	Above 16 by 24 inches, and not exceeding 24 by 30 inches............	33.33
	All above 24 by 30 inches............	25
	Fluted, rolled or rough, ground smooth or otherwise obscured, all above 24 by 60 inches	30
115	Polished, finished, etc., all above 24 by 60 inches............	30
116	Cast, polished and silvered:	
	Above 24 by 30 inches and not exceeding 24 by 60 in...	34.30
	All above 24 by 60 inches............	36.67
116	Cylinder and crown glass, polished, silvered and looking-glass plates:	
	Above 24 by 30 inches and not exceeding 24 by 60 inches..	34.30
	All above 24 by 60 inches	36.67

Statement by groups of the reductions of duty by present law, etc.—Continued.

FROM TWENTY-FIVE TO FIFTY PER CENT—Continued.

Para-graph of present law.	Articles.	Per cent reduc-tion.
118	Cylinder, crown and common window glass, unpolished, when groun , obscured, etc.:	
	Above 10 by 15 inches and not exceeding 16 by 24 inches..	27.11
	Above 24 by 30 inches and not exceeding 24 by 36 inches..	26.28
	All above 24 by 36 inches	28.34
118	Cylinder and crown gla-s, polished, silvered when ground, ob-scured, etc.:	
	Above 24 by 30 inches and not exceeding 24 by 60 inches..	25.62
	All above 24 by 60 inches	27.50
118	Plate-glass, cast, polished, silvered, when ground, obscured, etc.:	
	All above 24 by 60 inches	27.38
119	Sp ctacles and eyeglasses	33.33
120	Lenses costing $1.50 per gross pairs, or less	41.67
121	Spectacle and eyeglass lenses, with edge- ground, etc.	41.67
127	Free-tone, sandsto e, granite, etc., except marble, undressed or unmanufactured	36.38
128	Freestone, sandstone, granite, etc., except marble, dressed	25
129	Stone, grindstone	27.22
130	Slate, slates, slate chimney pieces, etc	33.33
C. 133	Iron ores: All other ore	46.67
134	Iron in pigs, etc.:	
	Ferrosilicon	40.47
	Spiegeleisen	39.55
	All other	40.47
	Scrap iron, etc.:	
	Iron, wrought and cast	40.48
	Steel	40.49
	Bar iron, rolled or hammered flats:	
135	Less than 1 inch wide and less than ¾ of an inch thick, etc..	40
	Not less than 1 inch wide, etc.	25.01
	Round iron not less than ¾ inch, etc	33.33
136	Bars or shapes of rolled iron not specially provided for	27.25
	Bars, blooms, billets, etc.	45.46
137	Beams, girders, joists	33.33
138	Boiler or other plate iron or steel valued above:	
	1.4 cents and not above 2 cents per pound	44.80
	2 cents and not above 3 cents per pound	32.51
	3 cents and not above 4 cents per pound	26.07
	4 cents and not above 7 cent per pound	33.81
	13 cents per pound	44.44
139	Forgings of iron or steel.	34.82
140	Hoop, band or scroll, etc., valued at 3 cents per pound or less:	
	Not thinner than No. 10 wire gauge	34.35
	Thinner than No. 10 and not thinner than No 20 wire gauge.	27.55
	Thinner than No. 20 wire gauge..	39 42
141	Flat rails punched, iron or steel	41.69
	T-rails, etc., iron.	41.67
C. 142	Sheets of iron, etc, thinner than—	
	No. 10 and not thinner than No. 20 wire gauge	30
	No. 20 and not thinner than No. 25 wire gauge	27.29

Statement by groups of the reductions of duty by present law, etc.—Continued.

FROM TWENTY-FIVE TO FIFTY PER CENT.—Contnnued.

Paragraph of present law.	Articles.	Per cent reduction.
143	Sheets or plates of iron or steel, etc., thinner than—	
	No. 10 and not thinner than No. 20 wire gauge	45.73
	No. 20 and not thinner than No. 25 wire gauge	43.25
	No. 25 wire gauge	37.22
144	Sheets and plates, pickled etc., thinner than—	
	No. 10 and not thinner than No. 20 wire gaug	34.01
	No. 20 and not thinner than No. 25 wire gauge	31.51
	No. 25 wire gauge	25.66
144	Sheet iron or sheet steel, polished, etc.	30
145	Tin :	
	Plates, lighter than 63 pounds per 100 square feet	46.05
	All other.	45.55
	Manufactures of, not specially provided for.	36.36
	Foil	36.36
146	Steel ingots, cog ingots, etc. Valued :	
	At 1 cent per pound or less	25
	Above 1 4-10 cents and not above 1 8-10 cents per pound	25
	Above 2 2-10 cents and not above 3 cents per pound	25
	Above 3 cents and not above 4 cents per pound	25
	Above 4 cents and n t above 7 cents per pound	35.02
	Above 7 cents and not above 10 cents per pound	32.15
	Above 10 cents and not above 13 cents per pound	31.43
	A ove 13 cents and not above 16 cents per pound	33.33
	Above 16 cents per pound.	32.85
146	Sheets and plates and saw plates of steel not specially provided for, valued above—	
	1 4-10 cents and not above 1 8-10 cents per pound	25
	2 2-10 cents and not above 3 cents per pound	25
	3 cents and not above 4 cents per pound.	25
	4 cents an not above 7 cents per pound	35
	7 cents and not above 10 cents per pound	32.14
	10 cents and not above 13 cents per pound	31.29
	13 cents and not above 16 cents per pound	33.33
	16 cents per pound.	32.93
147	Wire rods :	
	Rivet, screw, fence, etc., valued at 3½ cents or less per pound	33.33
	Flatiron or steel, etc., valued at 3 cents or less per pound	33.33
148	Wire of iron or steel, etc.—	
	Flat steel wire or shee steel, etc.—	
	Smaller than No. 16 and not smaller than No. 26 wire gauge	33.33
	Smaller than No. 26 wire gauge	33.33
	Coated with zinc or tin or any other metal—	
	Not smaller than No. 10 wire gauge	28.40
	Smaller than No. 10 and not smaller than No. 16 wire gauge	33.33
	Smaller than No. 26 wire gauge	42.82
	Wire of iron and steel, galvanized, valued at more than 4 cents per pound	25.93

Statement by groups of the reductions of duty by present law, &c.—Continued.

FROM TWENTY-FIVE TO FIFTY PER CENT.—Continued.

Paragraph of present law.	Articles.	Per cent reduction.
	Wire rope and wire strand—	
	Made of iron wire, smaller than No. 26 wire gauge	25
	M de of iron wire, galvanized, smaller than No. 26 wire gauge	31.65
	Made of steel wire, galvanized—	
	Smaller than No. 10 and not smaller than No. 16 wire gauge.	39 85
	Smaller than No. 16 and not smaller than No. 26 wire gague	27.27
	Smaller than No. 26 wire gague	32.34
152	Steel ingots, cog ingots, blooms, and slabs :	
	Valued above 7 cents and not above 10 cents per pound	37.89
	Valued above 13 cents and not above 16 cents per pound	37.06
	Valued above 16 cents per pound	35.16
	Boiler or other plate iron or steel not thinner than No. 10 wi e gauge :	
	Valued above 2 cents and not above 3 cents per pound	37.29
	Valued above 3 cents and not above 4 cents per pound	27.08
	Sheets of iron and steel, etc., valued at 3 cents per pound or less, etc., thinner than—	
	No. 10 and not thinner than No. 20 wire gauge	34
	No. 20 and not thinner than No. 25 wire gauge.	31.49
	No. 25 wire gauge	25.77
	Sheets and plates, and saw plates of steel, not specially provided for, cold rolled, valued above 16 cents per pound.	35.17
	Sheets and plates, and saw plates of steel, not specially provided for, cold rolled, better than the grade hereinbefore provided for, valued above—	
	10 cents and not above 13 cents per pound	49.48
	13 cents and not above 16 cents per pound	48.64
	16 cents per pound	42.99
	Steel circular-saw plates, valued above 10 cents and not above 13 cents per pound	46.65
C. 153	Anchors, or parts thereof, etc	33.57
154	Axles, or parts thereof, etc	25
155	Anvils	30
156	Hammers and sledges, etc	33.33
158	Bolts, with or without threads, etc.	33.31
160	Cast-iron pipe	33.32
161	Cast-iron vessels, e c.	33.33
162	Malleable iron castings	48.57
163	Hollow ware	33.34
164	Chains:	
	Less than ¾ of 1 inch and not less than ⅜ of 1 inch in diameter	36.55
	Less than ⅜ of 1 inch in diameter	42.13
	Other	33.33
165	Penknives valued at not more than 50 cents per dozen	31.36
	Valued at more than 50 cents, and not exceeding $1.50 per dozen	35.59
	$1.50 and not exceeding $3 per dozen	38.22
	$3 per dozen	42.5

Statement by groups of the reductions of duty by present law, etc.—Continued.

FROM TWENTY-FIVE TO FIFTY PER CENT—Continued.

Paragraph of present law.	Articles.	Per cent reduction.
	Razors:	
	Valued at less than $4 per dozen	32.76
	Valued at $4 or more per dozen	28.27
167	Table knives, etc., valued at:	
	Not more than $1 per dozen pieces	26.53
	More than $1 and not more than $2 per dozen	33.95
	All carving and cook knives, etc., value at more than $4 and not more than $8 per dozen pieces	26.19
170	Shotguns:	
	Double-barreled, valued at more than $12 each	35.47
	Single-barreled	27.01
172	Sheets and plates, etc., enameled or glazed with vitreous glasses, with more than one color or ornamented	30
175	Nails, wire:	
	Shorter than 1 inch and lighter than No. 16 wire gauge	46.16
	From 1 to 2 inches in length and lighter than No. 12, and not lighter than No. 16 wire gauge	31.51
178	Needles for knitting or sewing machines	28 57
183	Saws:	
	Cross-cut	27.91
	Hand back	37.50
184	Screws:	
	Over ½ inch and not over 1 inch in length	30
	Over 1 inch and not more than 2 inches in length	28.58
	More than 2 inches in length	40
185	Ingots, cogged ingots, blooms, or blanks for railway wheels, etc.	28.57
186	Aluminum in crude form	33.35
188	Argentine, albata, etc	40
195	Plates, rolled, called brazier's copper, etc	42.86
	Sheathing or yellow metal, etc	42.86
197	Gold leaf	33.14
202	Mica	42.85
203	Nickel	40
204	Quicksilver	30
207	Pens, metallic, etc	33.19
208	Types, new	40
	Zinc:	
212	In pigs or blocks	42.85
214	Old and worn out	40
215	Manufactures, articles, or wares not specially provided for:	
	Clocks, and parts of	44.44
	Musical instruments	44.44
D. 228	Shooks, sugar box, etc	33.33
	Casks, and barrels, empty	33.33
230	Furniture, cabinet or house	28.57
	All other manufactures of wood, etc	28.57
	Musical instruments, wood chief value	28.57
	Clocks, wood chief value	28.57
	Carriages and parts of, wood chief value	28.57

Statement by groups of the reductions of duty by present law, etc.—Continued.

FROM TWENTY-FIVE TO FIFTY PER CENT—Continued.

Paragraph of present law.	Articles.	Per cent reduction.
E. 238	Sugar candy and confectionery, etc., other not specially provided for........	30
240	Glucose and grape sugar..........	36.74
F. 242	Leaf tobacco, not stemmed, for cigar wrappers	25
G. 247	Horses valued at less than $150 each........	36.61
	$150 and over........	33.33
255	Buckwheat........	45.95
258	Macaroni, etc........	49.06
259	Oats	44.43
261	Rice, cleaned........	25
266	Butter and substitutes therefor........	33.33
G. 267	Cheese........	33.33
269	Milk, preserved, etc........	33.31
	Milk, sugar of........	37.51
271	Prepared or preserved : Beans, peas, etc........	25
275	Eggs	40
278	Honey	49.99
279	Hops........	46.76
283	Potatoes........	39.99
285	Linseed or flaxseed........	33.33
	Poppy and other oil seeds........	33.26
287	Pickles and sauces........	33.33
	All other not specially provided for........	33.33
295	In cases or packages made of tin :	
	Herring........	33.33
	Mackarel	33.33
	Salmon	33.33
	Other	33.33
300	Figs........	39.98
302	Raisins	40.02
304	Fruits preserved in their own juices........	33.33
	Nuts :	
306	Almonds—	
	Not shelled........	40.01
	Shelled........	33.33
307	Filberts and walnuts—	
	Not shelled	33.35
	Shelled........	33.36
309	All other shelled or unshelled n. s. p.	49.60
297	Apples green or ripe........	41.06
311	Fresh beef........	28.70
315	Poultry, live........	33.34
	Dressed........	40.03
323	Starch........	25
325	Mustard	46.60
	Spirits, distilled—	
H. 329	Brandy........	28.02
	Grain	28.00
	Other materials........	28.03

Statement by groups of the reductions of duty by present law, etc.—Continued.

FROM TWENTY-FIVE TO FIFTY PER CENT.—Cont nued.

Paragraph of present law.	Articles.	Per cent reduction.
331	Compounds or preparations, etc............	28
332	Cordials, liquors, etc...........	28.01
334	Bay rum......	33.33
337	Malt liquors :	
	In bottles or jugs.....	25
	Not in bottles or jugs......	25
338	Malt extract :	
	In both bottles and jugs......	25
	In casks..	25
	Solid or condensed......	25
339	Cherry juice and other fruit juice containing more than 18 per cent of alcohol	28.05
340	Ginger ale, etc., containing more than ¾ of a pint each and not more than 1½ pints......	44.75
I. 344	Cloth, not bleached, dyed, etc, not exceeding 50 threads to the square inch, valued at 6½ cents or less, per square yard......	49.99
345	Cloth exceeding 50 threads and not exceeding 100 threads per square inch :	
	Not bleached, etc., valued at 6½ cents or less per square yard...	33.33
	Bleached, etc., valued at 9 cents or less per square yard........	41.66
	Cloth not exceeding 100 threads per square inch :	
	Not bleached, etc., valued at over 6½ cents per square yard..	28.57
	Bleached, valued at over 9 cents per square yard............	28.57
346	Cloth exceeding 100 threads and not exceeding 150 threads per square inch :	
	Not bleached, etc., valued at 7½ cents per square yard........	37.50
	Not bleached, etc., valued at over 7½ cents per square yard...	25
	Bleached, etc., valued at 10 cents or less per square yard......	28.11
347	Cloth exceeding 150 threads and not exceeding 200 threads per square inch :	
	Not bleached, etc., valued at 8 cents or less per square yard	32.13
	Not bleached, valued at 10 cents per square yard............	30.55
348	Cloth exceeding 200 threads per square inch :	
	Not bleached, valued at 10 cents or less per square yard......	25
	Bleached, etc., n. o. s.	26.91
350	Plushes, velvets, etc., not bleached............	44.94
	Corduroys, etc., not bleached, etc	41.82
351	Chenille, curtains, etc..	25
353	Shirts and drawers :	
	Valued at more than $1.50 and not more than $3 per dozen...	32.43
	Valued at more than $3 and not more than $5 per dozen......	31.37
	Stockings, etc., selvedged, etc :	
	Valued at more than 60 cents and not more than $2 per dozen pairs	30.52
	Valued at more than $2 and not more than $4 per dozen pairs...	25.97
J. 358	Flax, hackled............	49.95
362	Cables, cordage and twine—other untarred, etc......	40.69
	All other......	46.75
367	Gill netting made from thread or twine finer than 20............	31.24

Statement of groups of the reductions of duty by present law, etc.—Continued.

FROM TWENTY-FIVE TO FIFTY PER CENT.—Continued.

Paragraph of present law.	Articles.	Per cent reduction.
369	Oil cloths for floors, etc.:	
	Valued at 25 cents or less per square yard......................	37.50
	Valued above 25 cents per square yard...........................	30.03
370	Yarns or threads, flax or hemp, valued at less than 13 cents per pound...	45.24
371	Manufactures of flax or hemp, of which these substances or either of them is the component material of chief value.........	30
372	Collars and cuffs entirely of cotton....................................	48.73
374	Manufactures of jute, etc., valued at 5 cents per pound or less...	36.79
	Manufactures of other vegetable fibre, valued at 5 cents per pound or less..	33.37
K. 392	All other manufactures of wool, n. s. p., valued at above 40 cents per pound...	42.55
393	Flannels weighing over 4 ounces per square yard..................	48.21
394	Dress goods, composed wholly or in part of wool, etc., weighing over 4 ounces per square yard...	42.62
	Dress goods, not exceeding 15 cents per square yard............	46.77
	Dress goods, valued at above 15 cents per square yard..........	44.19
396	Other clothing, ready made, etc..	37.75
397	Cloaks, dolmans, etc..	38.45
398	Webbing, gorings, suspenders, etc.....................................	46.71
	Carpets, etc.	
399	Aubusson, Axminster, etc.:	34.26
400	Saxony, Wilton, etc..	42.49
402	Velvet and tapestry velvet..	44.33
403	Tapestry Brussels..	48.05
404	Treble ingrain, etc...	48.45
407	Carpets of wool, etc...	40
408	Carpets and carpeting of cotton..	40
413	Knit goods, composed in part of India rubber........................	38.59
	Ready-made clothing and other, composed in part of India rubber.	35.72
M. 415	Pulp of wood, mechanically ground....................................	30.75
418	Printing paper, etc., sized or glued....................................	25
419	Paper, known commercially as copying paper, etc..................	42.99
N. 426	Bristles...	25
429	Pearl and shell buttons..	41.16
430	Ivory, vegetable ivory, buttons..	30
434	Corks...	33.32
436	Dolls, dollheads, etc..	28.57
432	Bituminous coal and shale...	46.65
	Coke..	25
441	Matches, in boxes containing not more than 100 per box..........	41.06
442	Percussion caps..	25
443	Ostrich feathers, dressed.	30
	All other feathers, dressed..	30
	Feathers, and flowers, artificial, ornamental, etc..................	30
448	Haircloth, crinoline cloth..	25
449	Haircloth (seating)...	33.33
450	Hair curled, suitable for beds or mattresses........................	33.33
451	Hats, composed of rabbit fur, etc......................................	27.27
452	Jewelry, n. s. p..	30

Statement by groups of the reductions of duty by present law, etc.—Continued.

FROM TWENTY-FIVE TO FIFTY PER CENT.—Continued.

Paragraph of present law.	Articles.	Per cent reduction.
456	Calfskins, japanned..................	33.33
	Pianoforte and pianoforte action leather.	42.86
458	Ladies' and children's gloves :	
	Schmachen, pique or prick seam, etc..............................	31.69
	Schmachen, lined	38.42
	Lamb, plain...........	28.02
	Lamb, pique or prick seam, etc	31.68
	Lamb, lined.....	37.93
	Kid, plain..	34.18
	Kid, pique or prick seam	35.02
	Kid, lined..	29.91
	Pique or prick seam, etc..............................	30.82
	Pique or prick seam, lined.	45.30
	Gloves, men's, over 14 inches in extreme length :	
	Plain....	43.09
	Pique or prick seam, etc	45.59
	Lined, composed wholly or in part of kid........	49.60
	Do	47.10
	Do	46.67
459	Osier or willow........	33.33
	Osier or willow manufactures of.	37.50
463	Masks, composed of paper or pulp	28.57
466	Slate pencils	36.94
468	Pipes, pipe bowls, etc.......	28.57
471	Sticks for umbrellas, parasols, etc., carved..........	40

LESS THAN TWENTY-FIVE PER CENT.

A. 1	Acids: Acetic, specific gravity exceeding 1.047	10.55
4	Citric	12.98
6	Tannic	19.94
10	Ammonia:	
	Carbonate of.................	24.70
	Sulphate of.........	9.95
11	Blacking	20
13	Bone char	20
15	Camphor, refined	18.03
20	Cobalt, oxide of..	16.69
21	Collodion:	
	All compounds of pyroxylin.........	23.13
	Rolled or in sheets........	16.66
25	Ethers: Fruit ethers, oils, or essences..........	20
26	Logwood and other dyewoods........	12.51
27	Fish glue or isinglass:	
	Valued at not above 7 cents per pound......	.48
	Valued at above 30 cents per pound	16.67
	Gelatin, valued at above 30 cents per pound	16.67
	Glue: Valued at not above 7 cents per pound	4.34
	Valued at above 30 cents per pound........	16.67
30	Ink and ink powder.................	16.67

Statement by groups of the reductions of duty by present law, etc.—Continued.

LESS THAN TWENTY-FIVE PER CENT.—Continued.

Paragraph of present law.	Articles.	Per cent reduction.
33	Licorice	9.11
34	Magnesia, calcined	12.50
46	Oil, fish	22.17
52	Black made from bone, etc.	20
54	Ocher and ocher earths, ground in oil	16.66
	Sienna and sienna earths	16.66
	Um' er and umber earths	16.66
56	Spirit varnishes	14.38
60	Zinc, oxide of, dry	20
61	All other paints and colors, mixed or ground, etc.	16.67
73	Potash, prussiate of:	
	Red	13.91
	Yellow	1.57
77	Preparations used as applications to the hair, mouth, etc.	20
79	Soap, fancy	4.53
90	Tartar, cream of	6.76
93	Brick, fire, not glazed	.60
94	Tiles, ornamented, glazed, etc	11.11
96	Lime	16.67
99	Earthenware and china, brown	20
102	Gas retorts	1.09
103	Bottles and vials, flint and lime:	
	Empty, holding less than ½ pint	20
	Filled, holding less than ½ pint	20
	Bottles and vials, green, colored:	
	Empty, holding less than ½ pint	19.99
	Filled, holding less than ½ pint	20
107	Chemical glass-ware	11.11
114	Plate glass, fluted, rolled, or rough, ground smooth or otherwise obscured, above 24 by 30 inches and not exceeding 24 by 60 inches	20
115	Plate glass, polished, finished, etc., above 24 by 30 inches and not exceeding 24 by 60 inches, unsilvered	10
118	Cylinder, crown, and common glass, unpolished when ground, obscured, etc:	
	Not exceeding 10 by 15 inches square	13.56
	Above 16 by 24 and not above 24 by 30	23.70
	Cylinder and crown glass, polished unsilvered when ground, obscured, etc:	
	Not exceeding 16 by 24 inches square	22.53
	Above 16 by 24 inches and not exceeding 24 by 30 inches	22.62
	Above 24 by 30 inches and not exceeding 24 by 60 inches	20.94
	Plate glass, cast, polished, silvered when ground, obscured, etc., above 24 by 30 inches and not exceeding 24 by 60 inches	17 62
	Plate glass, cast, polished, unsilvered when ground, obscured, etc., above 24 by 30 and not exceeding 24 by 60 inches	6.78
	All above 24 by 60 inches	19.38
122	Stained or painted window glass, etc	22.22
	Lenses of glass or pebble wholly or partly manufactured, etc.	22.22

Statement by groups of the reductions of duty by the present law, etc,—Continued.

LESS THAN TWENTY-FIVE PER CENT—Continued.

Para-graph of present law.	Articles.	Per cent reduction
123	Marble:	
	In block, rough, or squared	23.
124	Veined marble, sawed, etc.	22.
125	All manufactures of	10
131	Slate, roofing	20
C. 138	Boiler or other plate iron or steel :	
	Valued above 1 cent and not above 1.4 cents per pound	7.
	Valued above 7 cents and not above 10 cents per pound	19.
	Valued above 10 cents and not above 13 cents per pound	21.
141	T-rails, etc., steel or in part of steel	24.
142	Sheets of iron, etc.:	
	Thinner than No. 25, wire gauge	21.
	Corrugated or crimped	21.
146	Steel ingots, cog ingots, etc.:	
	Valued at 1 cent and not above 1.4 cents per pound	20
	Valued above 1.8 cents and not above 2.2 cents per pound	22.
	Sheet and plates and saw plates of steel, not specially provided for :	
	Valued above 1 cent and not above 1.4 cents per pound	20
	Valued above 1.8 cents and not above 2.2 cents per pound	22.
148	Wire of iron or steel :	
	Flat steel wire or sheet steel, etc.	20
	Smaller than No. 10 and not smaller than No. 16 wire gauge	14.
	Wire of iron and steel valued at more than 4 cents per pound	11.
	Wire rope and wire strands, made of iron wire :	
	Smaller than No. 10 and not smaller than No. 16 wire gauge	18.
	Smaller than No. 16 and not smaller than No. 26 wire gauge	23.
	Smaller than No. 26 wire gauge	15.
	Wire rope and wire strand, made of iron wire galvanized :	
	Smaller than No. 10 and not smaller than No. 16 wire gauge	23.
	Smaller than No. 26 wire gauge	17.
	Wire rope and wire strand made of steel wire :	
	Not smaller than No. 10 wire gauge	9.
	Smaller than No. 10, and not smaller than No. 16 wire gauge	3.
	Wire rope and wire strand made of steel wire, galvanized, not smaller than No. 10 wire gauge	23.
	Wire cloths, etc., not smaller than No. 10 wire gauge	18.
158	Nuts or washers of wrought iron or steel	5.
159	Card clothing :	
	Manufactured from tempered steel wire	20
	Other	19.
167	Table knives, etc.:	
	Valued at more than $2, and not more than $3 per dozen pieces	23.

Statement by groups of the reductions of duty by present law, etc.—Continued.

LESS THAN TWENTY-FIVE PER CENT—Continued.

ra-ph f sent v.	Articles.	Per cent. reduc- tion.
	Table knives, etc.—Continued.	
	Valued at more than $3, and not more than $8 per dozen pieces	13.28
	Valued at more than $8 per dozen	7.65
	All carving and cook knives, etc.:	
	Valued at more than $8 and not more than $12 per dozen pieces	24.78
	Valued at more than $12 per dozen pieces	23.10
168	Files:	
	Over 4 inches in length and under 9 inches	19.99
	Nine inches in length and under 14 inches	23.09
171	Sheets and plates, etc., enameled or glazed with vitrious glass	22.22
173	Nails and spikes, cut	4.58
	Nails:	
174	Horseshoe, hob, etc.	17.76
175	Wire, 2 inches long and longer, not lighter than No. 12 wire gauge	19.12
183	Saws:	
	Circular	16.67
	Mill, pit, not over 9 inches wide	10.02
184	Screws, half inch or less in length	24.81
189	Brass, old and clippings from brass, etc.	12.05
196	Bullions and metal thread of gold, silver, etc.	16.67
205	Gold pens	16.67
	Penholder tips, etc.	16.67
206	Pins	16.67
215	Manufactures, articles or wares not specially provided for:	
	Brass	
	Buttons, metal	
	Carriages, etc.	
	Copper	
	Gold and silver	
	Machinery	
	Iron and steel	22.22
	Lead	
	Aluminum	
	Bronze	
	Metals, n. e. s	
	Nickel	
	Platinum	
	Zinc	
242	Leaf tobacco, stemmed, for cigar wrappers	18.71
246	Cigars and cheroots	8.89
	Cigarettes and paper cigars, etc.	9.32
250	Sheep:	
	Less than 1 year old	9.13
	One year old or more	21.10
256	Corn or maize	9.91
257	Corn meal	18.63

Statement by groups of the reductions of duty by present law, etc.—Continued.

LESS THAN TWENTY-FIVE PER CENT—Continued.

Paragraph of present law.	Articles.	Per cent reduction.
260	Oat meal	15.8?
261	Rice, uncleaned	20
264	Wheat	2.0?
265	Wheat flour	20
292	Fish :	
	Cod, haddock, etc., pickled, in barrels	24.91
	Mackerel pickled or salted	24.91
	Salmon pickled or salted	24.98
	Other fish pickled or salted	24.98
299	Plums and prunes	8.8?
301	Oranges, in packages :	
	Of capacity of 1¼ cubic feet or less	23.08
	Of capacity exceeding 1¼ and not exceeding 2½ cubic feet	20.0?
	Of capacity exceeding 2½ not exceeding 5 cubic feet	19.9?
	Of capacity exceeding 5 cubic feet	20
	Lemons, in packages :	
	Of capacity of 1¼ cubic feet or less	23.0?
	Of capacity exceeding 1¼ and not exceeding 2½ cubic feet	19.98
	Of capacity exceeding 2½ and not exceeding 5 cubic feet	19.9?
	Of capacity exceeding 5 cubic feet	20.01
	Limes :	
	Of capacity of 1¼ cubic feet or less	23.0?
	Of capacity exceeding 1¼ and not exceeding 2½ cubic feet	19.74
	Of capacity exceeding 2½ and not exceeding 5 cubic feet	19.98
	Of capacity exceeding 5 cubic feet	15.4?
303	Preserved comfits, sweetmeats, etc	14.2?
	Ginger preserved or pickled	14.2?
310	Bacon and hams	23.2?
311	Fresh pork	17.8?
312	Meats of all kinds prepared or preserved	20
313	Extract of meat :	
	Fluid extract	16.71
	All other	10.87
326	Spices, n. e. s., all other ground or powdered, n. s. p.	24.99
11. 339	Cherry juice and other fruit juice containing not more than 18 per cent of alcohol	16 67
	Prune juice or prune wine	16.1?
341	Mineral waters in bottles :	
	Containing not more than 1 pint	11.46
	Containing more than 1 quart	16.67
I. 342	Thread, yarn warp or warp yarn, etc , of cotton :	
	Valued at not exceeding 25 cents per pound	20
	Valued at over 25 cents and not exceeding 40 cents per pound	16.67
	Valued at over 40 cents and not exceeding 50 cents per pound	10.30
	Valued at over 50 cents and not exceeding 60 cents per pound	8.09
	Valued at over 60 cents and not exceeding 70 cents per pound	10.34

Statement by groups of the reductions of duty by present law, etc.—Continued.

LESS THAN TWENTY-FIVE PER CENT—Continued.

Paragraph of present law.	Articles.	Per cent reduction.
	Thread, warp yarn or yarn warp, etc., of cotton—Continued.	
	Valued at over 70 cents and not exceeding 80 cents per pound	9.91
	Valued at over 80 cents and not exceeding $1 per pound	15.97
	Valued at over $1 per pound	10
343	Thread on spools	21.43
345	Cotton cloth exceeding 50 and not exceeding 100 threads per square inch, dyed, etc., valued 12 cents or less per square yard	24.99
	Cloth not exceeding 100 threads per square inch, dyed, etc., valued at over 12 cents per square yard	14.28
346	Cloth exceeding 100 and not exceeding 150 threads per square inch:	
	Bleached, valued at over 10 cents per square yard	12.50
	Dyed, etc., valued at 12½ cents or less per square yard	22.52
	Dyed, etc., valued at over 12½ cents per square yard	12.50
	Not bleached, valued at over 8 cents per square yard	22.22
347	Cloth exceeding 150 and not exceeding 200 threads per square inch:	
	Not bleached, valued at over 8 cents per square yard	22.22
	Bleached, valued at over 10 cents per sq are yard	22.22
	Dyed, etc., valued at 12 cents or less per square yard	15.92
	Dyed, etc., valued at over 12 cents per square yard	11.11
348	Cloth exceeding 200 threads to the square inch:	
	Not bleached, etc., valued at over 10 cents per square yard	11.11
	Bleached, valued at 12 cents or less per square yard	20.46
	Bleached, valued at over 12 cents per square ya d	11.11
	Dyed, etc., valued at 15 cents or less per square yard	12.97
	Dyed, etc., valued at over 15 cents per square yard	11.11
349	Corsets, n. e. s	20
	Other articles of wearing apparel, etc. All others n. s. p	20
350	Plushes, velvets, etc.:	
	Bleached	11.95
	Dyed, etc	21.16
	Corduroys, etc.:	
	Bleached	23.90
	Dyed, etc	21.51
353	Stockings, etc., valued at not more than $1.50 per dozen	14.28
352	Shirts and drawers:	
	Valued at more than $5 and not more than $7 per dozen	23.77
	Valued at more than $7 per dozen	15.47
353	Stockings, etc., selvedged, etc.:	
	Valued at not more than 60 cents per dozen pairs	7.73
	Valued at not more than $4 per dozen pairs	11.88
354	Damask	12.50
	Cords, braids, etc., all other	20.84
355	All other manufactures of cotton, n. s. p	12.50
361	Yarn, jute	14.28
370	Yarn, or threads, of flax or hemp, valued at more than 13 cents per pound	22.22

Statement by groups of the reductions of duty by present law, etc.—Continued.

LESS THAN TWENTY-FIVE PER CENT—Continued.

Paragraph of present law.	Articles.	Percent reduction.
372	Collars and cuffs	14.59
	Shirts, etc	9.00
373	Laces, edgings, etc.:	
	Composed of flax, jute, or other fiber	16.67
	Composed of cotton	16.67
374	Manufactures of jute, etc., valued above 5 cents per pound	12.50
	Manufactures of other vegetable fiber valued above 5 cents per pound	12.50
L. 410	Spun silk	14.29
411	Velvets, plushes, or other pile fabrics, containing, exclusive of selvedges, less than 75 per cent in weight of silk	23.29
412	Webbings, gorings, suspenders, etc	10
	Buttons	10
413	Handkerchiefs	16.67
	Laces, embroideries, etc	16.67
	Knit goods, other	16.67
	Ready-made clothing and other	16.67
414	Dress and piece goods	10
	Ribbons	10
	All other, n. s. p	10
M. 415	Pulp of wood, chemical:	
	Unbleached	19.22
	Bleached	7.06
419	Paper albumenized, etc	14.29
420	Papers known commercially as surface-coated papers, etc	14.29
421	Envelopes	4.67
422	Hangings and paper for screens, etc	20
423	Blank books	20
425	Writing, drawing, etc., paper	20
	Other manufactures of paper	20
N. 427	Brushes of all kinds	12.50
437	Emory, grains and ground	20
441	Matches, otherwise than in boxes containing more than 100	5.62
456	Boots and shoes	20
	Ladies and children's—	
458	Gloves:	
	Schmaschen, plain	24.10
	Suedes and other, etc., plain	20
	Ladies and children's, on which the rates of duty do not equal a duty of 50 per cent	20
	Men's, 14 inches and under in extreme length, plain	20
460	Bone and horn, manufactures of	16.67
	Chip, manufactures of (baskets)	16.67
	Grass, manufactures of	16.67
	India rubber	16.67
	Palm leaf, manufactures of	16.67
	Straw:	
	Manufactures of	16.67
	For julips	16.67

Statement by groups of the reductions of duty by present law, etc.—Continued.

LESS THAN TWENTY-FIVE PER CENT—Continued.

Paragraph of present law.	Articles.	Per cent reduction.
	Whalebone, manufactures of...	16.67
461	Leather, manufactures of...	14.29
	Fur, manufactures of..	14.29
	India rubber, vulcanized..	14.29
	Gutta-percha...	14.29
	Hair, manufactures of	14.29
	Papier mache, manufactures of..	14.29
462	Ivory and vegetable ivory, manufactures of........................	12.50
	Shell and mother-of-pearl, manufactures of........................	12.50
466	Pencils, wood, filled with lead, etc..................................	6.84
470	Umbrellas and parasols, covered with silk or alpaca.............	18.18
471	Sticks for umbrellas, parasols, etc., plain	14.29

INCOME TAX PROVISIONS

As Contained in the New Revenue Law.—Mr. McMillin's Report in House.

Sec. 27. That from and after the first day of January, eighteen hundred and ninety-five, and until the first day of January, nineteen hundred, there shall be assessed, levied, collected, and paid annually upon the gains, profits, and income received in the preceding calendar year by every citizen of the United States, whether residing at home or abroad, and every person residing therein, whether said gains, profits, or income be derived from any kind of property, rents, interest, dividends, or salaries, or from any profession, trade, employment, or vocation carried on in the United States or elsewhere, or from any other source whatever, a tax of two per centum on the amount so derived over and above four thousand dollars, and a like tax shall be levied, collected, and paid annually upon the gains, profits, and income from all property owned and of every business, trade, or profession carried on in the United States by persons residing without the United States. And the tax herein provided for shall be assessed, by the Commissioner of Internal Revenue and collected, and paid upon the gains, profits, and income for the year ending the thirty-first day of December next preceding the time for levying, collecting, and paying said tax.

Sec. 28. That in estimating the gains, profits, and income of any person there shall be included all income derived from interest upon notes, bonds, and other securities, except such bonds of the United States the principal and interest of which are by the law of their issuance exempt from all Federal taxation; profits realized within the year from sales of real estate purchased within two years previous to the close of the year for which income is estimated; interest received or accrued upon all notes, bonds, mortgages, or other forms of indebtedness bearing interest, whether paid or not, if good and collectible, less the interest which has become due from said person or which has been paid by him during the year; the amount of all premium on bonds, notes, or coupons; the amount of sales of live stock, sugar, cotton, wool, butter, cheese, pork, beef, mutton, or other meats, hay, and grain or other vegetable or other productions, being the growth or produce of the estate of such person, less the amount expended in the purchase or production of said stock or produce, and not including any part thereof consumed directly by the family; money and the value of all personal property acquired by gift or inheritance; all other gains, profits, and income derived from any source whatever except that portion of the salary, compensation, or pay received for services in the civil, military, naval, or other service of the United States, including Senators, Representatives, and Delegates in Congress, from which the tax has been deducted, and except that portion of any salary upon which the employer is required by law to withhold, and does withhold the tax and pays the same to the officer authorized to receive it. In computing incomes the necessary expenses actually incurred in carrying on any business, occupation, or profession shall be deducted and also all interest due or paid within the year by such person on existing indebtedness. And all national, State, county, school, and municipal taxes, not including those assessed against local benefits, paid within the year shall be deducted from the gains, profits, or income of the person who has actually paid the same, whether such person be owner, tenant, or mortgagor; also losses actually sustained during the year, incurred in trade or arising from fires, storms, or shipwreck, and not compensated for by insurance or otherwise, and debts ascertained to be worthless, but excluding all estimated depreciation of values and losses within the year on sales of real estate purchased within two years previous to the year for which income is estimated: *Provided,* That no deduction shall be made for any amount paid out for new buildings, permanent improvements, or betterments, made to increase the value of any property or estate: *Provided further,* That only one deduction of four thousand dollars shall be made from the aggregate income of all the members of any family, composed of one or both parents, and one or more minor children, or husband and wife; that guardians shall be allowed to make a deduction in favor of each and every ward, except that in case where two or more wards are comprised in one family, and have joint property interests, the aggregate deduction in their favor shall not exceed four thousand dollars: *And provided further,* That in cases where the salary or other compensation. paid to any person in the employment or service of the United States shall not exceed the rate of four thousand dollars per annum, or shall be by fees, or uncertain or irregular in the amount or in the time during which the same shall have accrued or been ea ned, such sa ary or other comp. nsation shall be included in estimating the annual gains, profits or income of the person to whom the same shall have been paid, and shall include that portion of any income or salary upon which a tax has not been paid by the employer, where the employer is required by law to pay on the excess over four thousand dollars: *Provided also,* That in computing the income of any person, corporation, company or association there shall not be included the amount received from any corporation, company or association as dividends upon the stock of such corporation, company or association if the tax of two per centum has been paid upon its net profits by said corporation, company or association as required by this act.

Sec. 32. That there shall be assessed, levied, and collected, except as herein otherw se provided, a tax of two per centum annually on the net profits or income above actual operating and business expenses, including expenses for materials purchased for manufacture or bought for resale, losses, and interest on bonded and other indebtedness of all banks, banking institutions, trust companies, saving institutions, fire, marine, life, and other insurance companies, railroad, canal, turnpike, canal navigation, slack water, telephone, telegraph, express, electric light, gas, water, street railway companies, and all other corporations, companies, or associations doing business for profit in the United States, no matter how created and organized, but not including partnerships.

 * * * * * * * *

The net profits or income of all corporations, companies, or associations shall include the amounts paid to shareholders, or carried to the account of any fund, or used for construction, enlargement of plant, cr any other expenditure or investment paid from the net annual profits made or acquired by said corporations, companies, or associations.

That nothing he ein contained shall apply to States, counties or municipalities; nor to corporations, companies or associations organized and conducted solely for charitable, religious or educational purposes, including fraternal beneficiary societies, orders or associations operating upon the lodge system and p oviding for the payment of life, sick, accident and other benefits to the members of such societies, orders or associations and dependents of such members; nor to the stocks, shares, funds or securities held by any fiduciary or trustee for charitable, religious or educational purposes; nor to building and loan associations or companies which make loans only to their shareholders; nor to such savings banks, savings institutions or soci ties as shall, first, have no stockholders or members except depositors and no capital except deposits; secondly, shall not receive deposits to an aggregate amount, in any one year, of more than one thousand dollars from the same depositor; thirdly, shall not allow an accumulation or total of deposits, by any one depositor, exceeding ten thousand dollars; fourthly, shall actually divide and distribute to its depositors, ratably to deposits, all the earnings over the necessary and proper expenses of such bank, institution or society, except such as shall be applied to surplus; fifthly, shall not possess, in any form, a surplus fund exceeding ten per centum of its aggregate deposits; nor to such savings banks, savings institutions or societies composed of members who do not participate in the profits thereof and which pay interest or dividends only to their depositors; nor to that part of the business of any savings banks, institution or other similar association having a capital stock, that is conducted on the mutual plan solely for the benefit of its depositors on such plan, and which shall keep its accounts of its business conducted on such mutual plan separate and apart from its other accounts.

Nor to any insurance company or association which conducts all its business solely upon the mutual plan, and only for the benefit of its policy holders or members, and having no capital stock and no stock or shareholders, and holding all its property in trust and in reserve for its policy holders or members; nor to that part of the business of any insurance company having a capital stock and stock and shareholders, which is conducted on the mutual plan, separate from its stock plan of insurance, and solely for the benefit of the policy holders and members insured on said mutual plan, and holding all the property belonging to and derived from said mutual part of its business in trust and reserve for the benefit of its policy holders and members insured on said mutual plan.

That all State, county, municipal, and town taxes paid by corporations, companies, or associations, shall be included in the operating and business expenses of such corporations, companies, or associations.

Sec. 33. That there shall be levied, collected, and paid on all salaries of officers, or payments for services to persons in the civil, military, naval, or other employment or service of the United States, including Senators and Representatives and Delegates in Congress, when exceeding the rate of four thousand dollars per annum, a tax of two per centum on the excess above the said four thousand dollars; and it shall be the duty of all paymasters and all disbursing officers under the Government of the United States, or persons in the employ thereof, when making any payment to any officers or persons as aforesaid, whose compensation is determined by a fixed salary, or upon settling or adjusting the accounts of such officers or persons, to deduct and withhold the aforesaid tax of two per centum; and the pay roll, receipts, or account of officers or persons paying such taxes as aforesaid shall be made to exhibit the fact of such payment. And it shall be the duty of the accounting officers of the Treasury Department, when auditing the accounts of any paymaster or disbursing officer, or any officer withholding his salary from moneys received by him, or when settling or adjusting the accounts of any such officer, to require evidence that the taxes mentioned in this section have been deducted and paid over to the Treasurer of the United States, or other officer authorized to receive the same. Every corporation which pays to any employee a salary or compensation exceeding four thousand dollars per annum shall report the same to the collector or deputy collector of his district and said employee shall pay thereon, subject to the exemptions herein provided for, the tax of two per centum on the excess of his salary over four thousand dollars : *Provided*, That salaries due to State, county, or municipal officers shall be exempt from the income tax herein levied.

    *   *   *   *   *   *   *

Sec. 3167. That it shall be unlawful for any collector, deputy collector, agent, clerk, or other officer or employee of the United States, to divulge or to make known in any manner whatever not provided by law to any person the operations, style of work or apparatus of any manufacturer or producer visited by him in his official duties, or the amount or source of income, profits, losses, expenditures, or any particular thereof, set forth or disclosed in any income return by any person or corporation, or to permit any income return or copy thereof or any book containing any abstract or particulars thereof, to be seen or examined by any person except as provided by law; and it shall be unlawful for any person to print or publish in any manner whatever not provided by law, any income or part thereof or the amount or source of income, profits, losses, or expenditures appearing in any income return ; and any offense against the foregoing provision shall be a misdemeanor and be punished by a fine not exceeding one thousand dollars or by imprisonment not exceeding one year, or both, at the discretion of the court; and if the offender be an officer or employee of the United States he shall be dismissed from office and be incapable thereafter of holding any office under the Government

PLAYING CARDS.

Sec. 38. That on and after the first day of August, eighteen hundred and ninety-four; there shall be levied, collected, and paid, by adhesive stamps, a tax of two cents for and upon every pack of playing cards containing not more than fifty-four cards, manufactured and sold or removed, and also upon every pack in the stock of any dealer on and after that date: and the Commissioner of Internal Revenue, with the approval of the Secretary of the Treasury, shall make regulations as to dies and adhesive stamps.

Report on the Income Tax.

Mr. McMillin, from the Committee on Ways and Means, submitted the following report on the income tax :

The wealth of this country amounts to more than $65,000,000,000, and the question arises whether it is not just and fair that a portion of this money should be raised by a tax on the earnings of wealth instead of imposing it all or nearly all on consumption. The committee believe that it is eminently just and proper that the amount proposed by this bill should be collected from a tax on incomes instead of placing all of it on the necessities of life, which are consumed by all but are not used in proportion to their ability to pay taxes, but according to the necessities of existence.

What just complaint can there be against placing thirty millions of this burden on wealth rather than all of it upon consumption? It is not proposed to raise all of it by an income tax. It is not even proposed to raise half, or one-fourth, or one-tenth of it that way; but only a small per cent by an imposition of 2 per cent tax on the incomes over $4,000 of all individuals and the net incomes of all corporations. The committee see no hardship in requiring those who have incomes of more than $4,000 a year to pay 2 per cent of all in excess of that amount to carry on the Government under which it has been accumulated and by which it is protected.

Corporations are by law given special privileges and advantages. Their stock-holders in the main are freed from personal liability by the laws of their creation. They have almost perpetual life; they may sue or be sued as individuals. Through the courts of the country they are protected and enabled to carry on their operations. It has therefore been deemed by the committee not unjust to place a tax of 2 per cent on their net earnings. * * *

It is said that this tax cannot be collected. Against this assertion we place the facts of history. The following table shows the collections under the income-tax law in existence from 1862 to 1870, and the committee place this collection of $346,-000,000 against the assertion that it is impossible to collect this. Had this tax been retained, even at the reduced rates imposed in 1867, the public debt could have been extinguished from this source alone years ago.

Internal revenue receipts from income tax.

Receipts by fiscal years.			Receipts under each act.			
In fiscal Year.	Amount.	For calendar year.	Date of act.	Amount.	Rate of tax.	How estimated.
1863.........	$2,741,858.25	1862	July 1, 1862	$2,741,858.25	3 per cent and 5 per cent.	3 per cent on incomes over $600 and n t over $10,000; over $10,000, 5 per cent
1864.........	20,294,731.74	1863	July 1 1862, and J. R. July 4, 1864	20,294,731.74	...... do	Same as above for act of 1862, and under joint resolution 5 per cent on incomes over $600.
1865.........	32,050,017.44	1864 }	Mar. 3, 1865	105,032,176.17	{ 5 per cent and 10 per cent.	5 per cent on incomes over $600 and not over $5,000; over $5,000, 10 per cent.
1866.........	72,982,159.03	1865 }				
1867.........	66,014,429.34	1866 }	Mar. 2, 1867	189,037,757.16	5 per cent	On incomes over $1,000.
1868.........	41,155,598.36	1867				
1869.........	34,791,855.84	1868 }				
1870.........	37,775,873.62	1869				
1871.........	19,162,650 75	1870				
1872.........	14 436 861 78	1871	July 14, 1870	34,661,824 15	2½ per cent	On incomes over $2 000.
1873.........	5,062 311.62	1872				
1874.........	139,472 09	1862-'71				
1875.........	232 64	1862-'71				
1876.........	588.27	1862-'71	Under repealed laws. }	199,040 35	{ Various rates.	On incomes over $600 as above.
1877.........	97 79	1862-'71				
1881.........	3 021.92	1862-'71				
1884.........	55,627.64	1862-'71 }				
Total...	346,967,388.12		....	346,967,388.12		

Note.—After the year 1862 the collections during any given fiscal year were not confined to the previous calendar year, but naturally include amounts due and unpaid for any previous year.

Treasury Department, *Internal Revenue Office, August 23, 1893.*

The effort to carry on the administration of Government by taxing consumption alone has be n tried in other countries and proven as unequal in its burd ns and unsatisfactory in its result- as here. Great Britai n tried the experiment for many years of encouraging and protecting manufacturers b the imposition of tariff duties. There, as here, it proved inadequate. In 1798 an income tax was imposed to supplement failing revenues. It was maintained until 1816, then the old system was returned to in the hope that it would be sufficient in times of peace But in 1842 Sir Robert Peel was forced to resort to an income tax. He b lieved that to equalize the burdens of taxation a greater share s ould b placed on we lth and less on things t at had to be bought and consumed daily.

It was predict d then, as it is now, that the tax would be unsatisfactory; that it wa inquis itorial, and would b ., therefore, unpopular. But the courageous premier was willing to risk his party and his administration on the intrinsic justice of the measure. He succeeded in having it adopted. Notwithstanding a half a century has elapsed, and m ny political revolutions have swept over the country, carrying down the ministry with th m, there has been no power strong enough even in t! at great monarchy to break it down and put all of taxation back on cons umption.

This, under peculiar institutions, favoring the accumulation of re l estate, and where their possession, in the hands of the ruling classes, is encouraged and thought to contribute to the stability of the governments.

Under that law only £150 ($750) is exempted from taxation. Great Britain derived from this source £13,290,000—about $66,500,000—last year. The rate imposed is 7 pence a pound.

P us ia, the greate t of the states composing the German Empire, imposed an income tax as far back as 1851, and has had that form of taxation for many years. There is only $225 income exempt. It is graduated from le s than 1 to 4 per cent. For the year 1892-'93 there was derived from this sour e 124,842,848 marks—about $30,210.712. Almost all the twenty odd states of the German Union have imposed an income tax very similar to that of Prussia.

An income tax has existed in Austria since the beginning of the nineteenth century, except the period between 1829 and 1849. In 1892 it yielded $10,000,000.

In 1892 there was collected from incomes by the Italian Government $45,000,000. The rate is 12 per cent, and in addition thereto 1½ per cent is levied for war purposes.

Other governments have followed this tendency.

THE INCOME TAX.

Extract From the Speech of Scott Wike, of Illinois.

Hon. Mr. Wike said :

In my judgment a very heavy graduated income tax should be levied, not on incomes simply, but on incomes of fortunes, to stay the insatiable hands of fortune-seeking adventurers who aim really more to gratify a vaulting ambition to belong to the aristocracy of gigantic wealth, with the attendant fascination of power, than from any rational desire or hope to enjoy or make useful these unreasonable and unholy amassments.   *   *   *

When these colossal fortunes were unknown in this country, pauperism, too, was in a measure unknown ; but now destitution, poverty, and want prevail in a ratio of geometrical proportion as the property of the country is concentrated in the hands of a few. Already the unsightly piles of wealth look down with ever increasing menace to the perpetuity of the simple and popular government that was devised to secure the blessings of liberty and prosperity to the masses.

Figures give no adequate idea of the common understanding of the immensity of hundreds and thousands of these fortunes, or the rapidity with which they are amassed. For example, if Adam, created in the beginning, and which was recently popularly supposed to be five thousand years ago, had been endowed with what seventy-five years ago would have been considered a large fortune—$50,000—and had doubled it the first year, and had lived and added to it a like amount annually from that day to the present time, saving it all, he would not yet have accumulated the princely fortune that at least one family possesses, or which, perhaps, is possessed by several separate families and individuals in this country to-day.

Incomes, both in numbers and amounts, in the United States far exceed those in Great Britain, and the increase in wealth has been infinitely more rapid here than in that country. Since the adoption of the present revenue system and bounty policy, the concentration of wealth in the hands of the few is unprecedented in any country. The extent to which this concentration has been going on since the war is not only alarming, but in the light of the ultimate consequences is absolutely appalling. It is now maintained that one-half of the wealth of the country is already concentrated in the hands of 25,000 persons, and three-fourths or four-fifths of it in the hands of 250,000 people.

The question of the concentration of wealth and the extent of such concentration becomes a very important one in c nsidering the utility and desirableness of the income tax.

Let us see, therefore, if we can, whether these statements as to the extent of such concentration are true or not. In the absence of official information we must examine the most reliable data at hand, and to this end attention is invited, in the first place to the statements and statistics published in the Forum Magazine for September and November, 1889, by Mr. Thomas G. Shearman, one of the foremo t economists of this country, as furnishing perhaps the clearest and most convincing analysis and exposition of the question that has been written.

STATISTICS SHOWING CONCENTRATION OF WEALTH.

Your attention is first called to the following statemen ts, made in the September magazine article alluded to:

"The St. Louis *Globe* recently published a list of seventy-two persons who were worth, collectively, the whole amount of our national debt, averaging $18,000,000 each. The wealthiest railroad manager in America in 1865 was worth $40,000,000, but not more. His heir died recently, leaving an estate of nearly $200,000,000; and there are several gentlemen now living who are worth $100,000,000 each. Within a short period a number of quiet, unobtrusive men, of no national fame, have died in Pennsylvania, leaving estates of over $20,000,000 each. Twenty living persons in the oil business are reputed to be as rich. Forty persons could be easily named none of them worth less than $20,000,000, and averaging $40,000,000 each.

"At the lowest reasonable estimate there must now be more than two hundred and fifty persons in this country whose wealth averages over $20,000,000 for each. But let us call the number only two hundred. Income-tax returns in Great Britain and in the United S ates show that in general the number of incomes, when arranged in large cl sses, multiplies by from three to five fold for every reduction in the amount of one-half. For extreme caution, however, we estimate the increase in the number of incomes at a very much low r rate than this. At this reduced rate the amount of wealth in the hands of persons worth over $500,000 each in the United States would be about as follows:

200 persons at $20,000,000	....	$4,000,000,000
400 persons at 10,000,000	....	4,000,000,000
1,000 persons at 5,000,000	....	5,000,000,000
2,000 persons at 2,500,000	....	5,000,000,000
6,000 persons at 1,000,000	....	6,000,000,000
15,000 persons at 500,000	....	7,500,000,000
Total	....	31,500,000,000

"This estimate is very far below the actual truth. Yet, even upon this basis, we are confronted with the startling result that 25,000 pers ns now possess more than half of the whole national wealth, real and personal, according to the highest estimate ($60,000,000,000) which any one has yet ventured to make of the aggregate amount."

In the November article mentioned a statement is made of the wealthiest estates in England, showing the richest of the Rothschilds and the world-renowned banker, Baron Overstone, each left about $17,000,000. Earl Dudley, the owner of the rich st iron mines, left $20,000,000.

The Duke of Buccleuch (who carried half of Scotland in his pocket) left about $30,000,000. The Marquis of Bute was worth, in 1872, $28,000,000 in land, and he may now be worth $4,000,000 in all. The Duke of Norfolk may be worth $40,000,000, and the Duke of Westminster perhaps $50,000,000.

The table of incomes derived from the profits of business, exclusive of railways, mines, etc., in Great Britain, is also given, as follows:

Persons.	Incomes.	Average income.
104	£50,000 and over.	£91,783
1,192	10,000 to £50,000	17,644
1,871	5,000 to 10,000	6,553
1,117	4,000 to 5,000	4,270
1,947	3,000 to 4,000	3,266
4,202	2,000 to 3,000	2,282
13,268	1,000 to 2,000	1,277
52,765	400 to 1,000	541
159,198	200 to 400	282
235,664		

Then follows this statement:

"Th great law of average may be relied upon as confidently in America as in Europe. We need only find a starting point, then we may safely proceed to calculations based upon general experience as to the average increase in the number of persons owning wealth, in proportion to the decrease of the amount owned by each individual. To find this starting point it will be necessary to give a list of Americans whose wealth is approximately known."

After which are given the names of seventy individuals, with an estimate of the wealth of each, aggregating $2,700,000,000, and averaging over $38,500,000. Mr. Gould, the Vanderbilts, and Rockefeller are put down as worth $100,000,000 each, and Drexel, Morgan, and Marshall Field $25,000,000 each, while I have no doubt that popular opinion and the facts place them at a much higher figure, if in fact not doubt these amounts.

In discussing the moderation of his own estimates, Mr. Shearman says:

"Making the largest allowance for exaggerated reports, there can be no doubt that these seventy names represent an aggregate wealth of $2,700,000,000, or an average of over $37,500,000 each. The writer has not especially sought for information concerning anyone worth less than $20,000,000, but has incidentally learned of fifty other persons worth over $10,000,000, of whom thirty are valued in all at $450,000,000, making together one hundred persons worth over $3,000,000,000. Yet this list includes very few names from New England and none from the South. Evidently, it would be easy for any specially well-informed person to make up a list of one hundred persons averaging $25,000,000 each, in addition to ten averaging $100,000,000 each. No such list of concentrated wealth could be given in any other country in the world. The richest dukes in England fall below the average wealth of a dozen American citizens, while the greatest bankers, merchants, and railway magnates of England cannot compare in wealth with many Americans."

According to the facts as here stated, one hundred and ten persons own $3,500,-000,000 of the national wealth, or nearly one-seventeenth of the whole, leaving out of the calculation public property.

The writer then goes on to say that lists were lately published of sixty seven millionaires residing in Pittsburg, of sixty-three residents of Cleveland possessing in the aggregate $300,000,000, and sixty persons residing in three villages near New York city whose wealth is said to aggregate $500,000,000, and in fact $750,000,000, and that the Goelet estate in New York city paid taxes on $25,000,000 real estate. The mayor of Chicago is given as authority that four gentlemen in that city are worth over $20,000,000 each.

MR. T. E. WILSON'S ESTIMATES.

Confirmatory of the accuracy of the estimates here placed upon individual fortunes, and of the statements relative to the rapidity with which vast wealth is concentrating in the hands of the few, I beg to submit and call your attention to two lists of names furnished me by Mr. T. E. Wilson, the very able statistician and economic writer of the New York *World*. One of these lists shows the names of one hundred and twenty-five individuals in the city of New York whose incomes each amount to $250,000 and over, and the other contains the names of three hundred business houses in that city, and including none from Brooklyn, that are each rated by the commercial agencies at $1,000,000 and over. These lists, which I hold in my hand, were publish d in the New York *World*, and so far as I know the accuracy of the ratings has never been questioned, while the source from which they emanate entitles them to implicit confidence.

Of course many of the incomes alluded to must exceed by very many times the amount stated, $250,000, some of them rising, no doubt, to a half score of millions. If these incomes were accumulated by interest on bonds or money loaned, dividends on stocks, and net rentals of real estate, then the recipient of a $250,000 income, it is fair to presume, would be worth anywhere from five to ten million dollars, while numbers of the millionaires in New York are estimated to be worth from $40,000,000 to $250,000,000—forty women alone being worth in that city an average of several million dollars each.

It is evident, therefore, that there must be a very large number of millionaires in the city who are not included in the list of individuals mentioned. And it is apparent also that the wealth of many of the business houses given must be greatly in excess of $1,000,000. So that it would be very interesting and profitable, indeed, to know just how much the wealth of all the millionaires and millionaire establishments in New York city aggregates, and Mr. Wilson will have a most valuable contribution to the cause of revenue reform he so ably advocates wh n his researches in this prolific field of inquiry shall be completed.

The probability is, if the facts could b a curately ascertained, that the individuals, companies, corporations, and trusts worth $1,000,000 and over throughout the United States would aggregate from one-fourth to one-third of the entire wealth outside of public property.

MR. SHEARMAN'S STATEMENT CONTINUED.

Mr. Shearman, proceeding with his argument, declares that the official tax list of Boston shows that more than fifty families pay taxes on over $1,000,000 each, and that two hundred pay taxes on amounts clearly indicating that they really are millionaires, and says :

The facts already stated conclusively demonstrate that the wealthiest class in the United States is vastly richer than the wealthiest class in Great Britain. The average annual income of the richest hundred Englishmen is about $450,000; but the average annual income of the richest hundred Americans cannot be less than $1,200,000, and probably exceeds $1,500,000. It follows inevitably that wealth must be far more concentrated in the United States than in Great Britain ; because where enormous amounts of wealth are placed in a few hands, this necessarily implies that the great mass of the people have very small possessions.

The writer then observes that in 1877 two hundred and twenty-two thousand British capitalists possessed over $25,000 each, while the number of persons deriving profits of over $1,000 per annum each was nearly two hundred thousand, while these two classes of people are not at all the same, not more than one-fifth to one-third of either class being included in the other, but that in the absence of detailed information the classification of the distribution of wealth must be taken with much reserve. He then proceeds to say :

But incomes, in their very nature, are much more equally distributed than wealth. Millions have incomes who have practically no wealth. Therefore, a computation on this basis will greatly underestimate the concentration of wealth in the higher

gures while it will lead to such an overestimate of wealth in the lower figures as
to make it gradually quite misleading. Such a computation is indeed of no use
whatever outside of the first two hundred and fifty thousand families, and must be
greatly modified long before reaching that number.

Bearing these considerations in mind, we proceed to estimate the distribution of
American wealth.

* * * * * * *

Taking the number of British incomes exceeding £200 as a basis for comparative
classification, starting on the basis of known facts concerning American wealth and
modifying the figures gradually, for the reason already stated, we arrive at the following conclusions:

Distribution of American wealth on the basis of British income returns.

Families.	Average wealth in thousands.	Total in millions.
10........	$100,000	$1,000
100........	25,000	2,500
1,200........	6,000	7,200
2,000........	2,200	4,400
1,000........	1,400	1,400
2,000........	1,000	2,000
4,000........	700	2,800
13,000........	400	5,200
52,000........	150	7,800
160,000........	60	9,600
200,000........	20	4,000
1,000,000........	3½	3,500
2,000,000........	2	4,000
9,565,000........	¾	7,175
13,000,310........		62,575
Public property, churches, etc........		2,500
Total........		65,075

From this table it will be seen that by adding together the possessions of fifty
thousand of the richest families they own one-half of the wealth of the country,
not taking into account the public property.

Considering the above table so as to arrange it in three great classes, we arrive at
this result:

Class.	Families.	Wealth, in millions.	Average per family.
Rich........	235,310	$43,900	$186,567
Middle........	1,200,000	7,500	6,250
Working........	11,565,000	11,175	968
Total........	13,000,310	62,575	4,813

In considering the foregoing table Mr. Shearman states that the number of the
very largest millionaires has been kept down to nearly the limit of his personal information, while in his judgment there must be at least as many more of whom he
has never heard, and says:

"If this surmise is correct, it would add at once $2,500,000,000 to the share of wealth
belonging to the millionaire class, and would confirm the writer's rough estimate
in the Forum for September, that 25,000 persons own just about one-half of all the
wealth of the United States."

UNTAXING THE RICH.

Taxes on Luxuries and Wealth Repealed at Different Times by the Republican Party.

Statement showing the date of repeal of the several classes of articles and occupations that have been taxed under the internal revenue laws of the United States and the amount of revenue derived therefrom during the last entire year before their repeal.

1ST, MANUFACTURES AND PRODUCTS.

This class, exclusive of distilled spirits, manufactured tobacco and fermented liquors, contained the largest number of different articles on which an internal tax has been imposed and yielded during the fiscal year ended June 30, 1866, a revenue amounting to $127,230,6 18.66, but by reductions in the rates of tax and additions to the free list under act of July 13, 1866, this sum was reduced to $91,531,331.31 in the next fiscal year, which was the last full year before the repeal of the tax on this class of articles (illuminating gas excepted) by acts of February 3, 1868, March 31, 1868, and July 20, 1868.

2ND, GROSS RECEIPTS.

This class included, when taxation under it was at its maximum, the tax on the gross receipts of advertisements, bridges and toll roads, canals, ships, barges, etc., stage coaches, steamboats and railroads for transportation of passengers and freights, of express, insurance and telegraph companies, etc. The largest receipts were during the fiscal year 1866, when they amounted to $11,262,429.82. All taxes under this class not before reduced or abolished were repealed by act of July 14, 1870. The receipts from this source for the fiscal year 1870, the last year before its repeal, were $6,894,799.99.

3D, SALES.

The principal sales included in this class were auction sales, brokers' sales of merchandise, stocks, bonds, gold and silver bullion and coin, foreign exchange, etc., and manufacturers' sales. The tax on sales, except those of spirits, tobacco and beer, was repealed by act of July 14, 1870. Receipts during the fiscal year ended June 30, 1870, $8,837,394.97.

4TH, SPECIAL TAXES NOT RELATING TO SPIRITS, TOBACCO AND FERMENTED LIQUORS.

This class included the annual special or license tax that was levied on nearly every trade, profession or occupation, and the amount of tax varied from five (5) dollars on butchers whose annual sales did not exceed $1,000 to five hundred (500) dollars on assayers when their assays amounted to over $500,000 per annum. The tax on this class was repealed May 1, 1871, by act of July 14, 1870. The receipts from this source during the last full year before its repeal in 1870, were $11,020,-787.78.

5TH, INCOME.

The tax on income of individuals, as finally amended by act of July 14, 1870, proided that on all taxable incomes over $2,000 (income less than that amount being xempt from tax) there should be levied and collected a tax of 2½ per cent, and a ke tax on bank and insurance companies, dividends, and additions to surplus unds, and on canal, turnpike, and railroad companies' dividends and additions to urplus and interest on bonds. This tax expired by limitation December 31, 1871. 'he income tax collected from individuals during the fiscal year 1872, assessed on he incomes of the calendar year 1891, was $8,416,688.87, and from banks, railroad ompanies, and other corporations, and from salaries of United States officers, 6,020,175.91, making a total of $14.436,861.78.

6TH, LEGACIES AND SUCCESSIONS.

The tax on legacies and successions was repealed by act of July 14, 1870. The mount of revenue derived from the same during the fiscal year ended June 3d, 870, was $3,091,825.50.

7TH, ARTICLES OF LUXURY KEPT FOR USE.

The tax on such articles in this class, as billiard tables, carriages, plates of gold nd silver, gold watches, piano-fortes, and yachts, that had not before been re-ealed, was abolished by act of July 14, 1870. The receipts from this source during he fiscal year 1870 were $907,442.09.

8TH, SLAUGHTERED ANIMALS.

The tax imposed on slaughtered cattle, sheep and swine was repealed by act of uly 13, 1866. The receipts from this source for the fiscal year ended June 3, 1866, rere $1,291,570.51.

9TH, PASSPORTS.

The tax imposed on passports by the internal revenue laws, was repealed by ct of July 14, 1870, and the receipts from the same during the fiscal year 1870 mounted to $22,756.00.

10TH, STAMP TAXES.

Stamp taxes, so-called, did not include stamps used to pay the tax on distilled pirits, fermented liquors,, cigars, cigarettes, snuff, chewing and smoking tobacco. 'hey were taxes imposed on nearly every form of legal instrument, on bank hecks, patent medicines, perfumery, cosmetics, friction matches, playing cards, tc., and yielded a revenue during the fiscal year 1870 of $16,544,043.06. This ax was reduced by acts of July 14, 1870, and June 6, 1872, so that during the ast year before its repeal on July 1, 1883, by act of March 3, 1883, the receipts rom this source were $8,139,217.96

11TH, ILLUMINATING GAS.

The only tax remaining on manufactures not repealed by acts of March 31, .868, and July 20, 1868, was that on illuminating gas, which was abolished Au-ust 1, 1872, by act of June 6, 1872. The receipts from this source during the fiscal 'ear ended June 30, 1872, were $2,831,718.56.

12TH, BANK CAPITAL AND DEPOSITS.

The tax on the capital and deposits of all banks, private, state and national, was repealed by act of March 3, 1883. The amount of revenue collected on the capital and deposits of banks and bankers other than national banks during the fiscal year ended June 30, 1882, the last full year the tax was in force before its repeal was $5,249,172.70, and of national banks $5,959,702.37, making a total of $11,208,875.07

The above statement includes all classes of internal taxes that have been entirely abolished and shows the amount of revenue derived from them during the last entire fiscal year that those taxes were in force.

SUGAR DUTIES.

Action of Republican Senators Increasing Duties in Favor of the Trust.

The Republican members of Congress and the Republican press have had much to say against the Democratic party and especially the Democratic Senators, for having given undue protection to the refining industry, commonly known as the "sugar trust." These accusations appear supremely hypocritical in the face of the fact that this gigantic monopoly grew up under the protecting care of the Republican party.

That the protection given to the sugar refiners, over and above the 40 per cent ad valorem on raw and refined, is more than is necessary, is probably true ; but the question is n t how much should have been given the "trust" but how much could be taken away from it. The Republican party has always been the staunch friend of "trusts" and at all times, when in power, favored the "sugar trust." That their advocacy of free sugar in the Senate, during the consideration of the tariff bill, was a sham, and only done for the purpose of creating a division in the ranks of the Democratic members, in the endeavor to defeat all the tariff l gislation and thereby save the sugar and all the other great trusts from harm, was apparent from the fact that when a separate bill, abolishing the differential duty on refined sugar, was tendered to them, they either voted against its consideration or refrained from voting, thereby breaking a quorum. Under the act of 1883, a Republican measure, the duty on sugar under No. 13, Dutch standard in color, was 2 cents a pound; over No. 13 and not above No. 16, 2¾ cents per pound; above No. 16, and not above No. 20, 3 cents per pound, and above No. 20, 3½ cents per pound. The sugar refiners under this act had a protection of 1½ cents per pound against sugars below No. 13; ¾ of a cent a pound against sugars between Nos. 13 and 16, and ½ cent a pound against all below No. 20, Dutch standard.

The McKinley bill, as originally drafted, provided for an ad valorem duty of 35 per cent on raw and 40 per cent on refined. At the dictation of the "Trust" raws were made free and a specific duty of 4-10 of a cent per pound placed on refined, and a bounty of 2 cents per pound provided for the sugar planters.

When the bill reached the Senate the agents of the "Trust" were again on hand and the Finance Committee of the Senate, a majority of whom were Republicans, were induced to report an amendment, increasing the specific rate of 4-10 on sugars above No. 16, Dutch standard, to 6-10 of a cent per pound.

Upon the adoption of this amendment the yeas and nays were as follows :

YEAS 29.—Aldrich, Allen, Butler, Cameron, Casey, Chandler, Dawes, Dixon, Dolph, Eustis, Evarts, Frye, Gibson, Hale, Hawley, Hoar, McMillan, Manderson, Paddock, Pasco, Platt, Plumb, Quay, Reagan, Sawyer, Stewart, Stockbridge, Teller, Washburn.

NAYS 23.—Allison, Barbour, Bate, Berry, Blackburn, Carlisle, Cockrell, Colquitt,

Cullom, Edmunds, Faulkner, Gorman, Mitchell, Morgan, Pugh, Ransom, Sherman, Spooner, Vance, Vest, Walthall, Wilson of Iowa, Wilson of Md.

ABSENT 32.—Blair, Blodgett, Brown, Call, Coke, Daniel, Davis, Farwell, George, Gray, Hampton, Harris, Hearst, Higgins, Hiscock, Ingalls, Jones of Arkansas, Jones of Nevada, Kenna, McPherson, Moody, Morrill, Payne, Pettigrew, Pierce, Powers, Sanders, Squire, Sanford, Turpie, Voorhees, Wolcott.

Of the yeas, five, Butler, Eustis, Gibson, Pasco, and Reagan were Democrats and the balance 24 Republicans; and of the nays one, Allison, was a Republican, and the balance 22, were Democrats.

The increase of 1-5 of a cent per pound over the rate proposed in the McKinley bill was made upon the recommendation of a Republican committee and adopted by Republican votes.

After the adoption of this amendment, Senator Quay offered the following amendment :

All sugars above No. 13, Dutch standard in color, shall be classified by the Dutch standard of color, and shall pay duty as follows, namely : All sugars above No. 13 and not above No. 16, Dutch standard of color, three-tenths of 1 cent per pound. All sugars above No. 16 and not above No. 20, Dutch standard in color, shall pay a duty of six-tenths of 1 cent per pound. All sugars above No. 20, Dutch standard in color, shall pay a duty of eight-tenths of 1 cent per pound : *Provided*, That if an export duty shall hereafter be laid upon sugar or molasses by any country from whence the same may be imported, such sugar or molasses so imported shall be subject to duty as provided by law prior to the passage of this act.

This amendment proposed an increase on sugars between Nos. 13 and 16, of 3-10, and in sugars above No. 20, Dutch standard, of 4-10 of 1 cent per pound. Senator Manderson proposed an amendment to the amendment, striking out "one cent," and inserting in lieu thereof "eight-tenths of a cent," and upon this proposition said :

Now, Mr. President, it seems to me that there is abundant reason in these suggestions for establishing the distinction suggested by the amendment of the Senator from Pennsylvania.   That amendment, making this graded rate of duty on all sugars above No. 13, will have not only the effect of encouraging this sugar industry, but, as I have suggested, it permits manufacturers of sugar from factories which they expect to establish in this country to refine their own products without shipping to the large refiners of sugar in the East   I believe the duty of 1 per cent per pound, as proposed by the amendment of the Senator from Pennsylvania, is probably higher than we need to go.   I think that eight tenths of a cent per pound will amply reach every element of protection, and I hope that amendment may be made.

In opposition to the amendment of Senator Quay and the amendment to the same by Senator Manderson, Senator Gorman said :

Mr Gorman.   Mr. President, this amendment is not only an increase on the bill as it came to this body from the other House, but the Senate has already made a very large increase in favor of the interest of refining by the change from 16 and 13, Dutch standard, and from four-tenths to six-tenths of a cent per pound on all sugars above No. 16.   It is now proposed by this amendment to o beyond even the recommen ations of the Committee on Finance and to impose this duty upon all sugars above No. 20, which would simply give the sugar refiners an absolute monopoly of all the refined article and would add to their profit, in my judgment, from the best information I can g t, beyond the point where the present law exists, and would simply be an imposition upon the people of the country.   As the bill is amended it is doubtful whether the people will get any very considerable benefit from it.

Senator Vest also vigorously opposed the amendment. He said :

Mr. Vest. Mr. President, practically this amendment amounts to very little. I shall vote against it, as I have voted against the increase from four to six-tenths of a cent above No. 16, and imposing a duty of three-tenths of a cent between No. 13 and No. 16. The refiners have now all they want. The votes that have been taken here to-day have put into the pockets of the refiners millions upon millions of dollars.

The first report that was made by the McKinley committee in the House put the grade at No. 16 in color under the Dutch standard. When the Mills bill was considered in the House the first report was in favor of No. 16 and in behalf of the consumers of the country. Then, by some sort of manipulation, it was reduced to No. 13, which has been the standard that the refiners have demanded all the time.

The very same thing which was made the subject of attack against the Democratic committee in 1888 has occurred now in the House of Representatives, and again in the Senate. The refiners have triumphed again, and have put this down to No. 13, Dutch standard. There has never been any test as to sugars below No. 13, because they must all be refined, and that is the sugar which is the raw material to the refiners. But the test has always been, as every Senator who knows anything about the tariff is well aware, upon the grades between 13 and 16.

There are two grades between 13 and 16 which can be used when imported into this country without being refined. They are the light beet sugars that come from Germany and a dark sugar which is used largely in the northwest. Over these two grades the battle has raged all the time, the refiners always claiming that the standard should be down to No. 13 in color, whilst the friends of the consumers of the country, as I regard the question, have insisted upon No. 16.

By the vote here to-day to put three-tenths of a cent a pound duty upon the grades between 13 and 16, and then above 16, we have increased the duty in the bill as it came from the House from four-tenths to six-tenths of a cent, which makes it absolutely exclusive. So the refiners, as this bill now stands, without voting upon the present amendment, get their raw material free when it is under No. 13, get a duty which amounts almost to exclusion upon the two grades between 13 and 16, and get an absolutely exclusive duty on all grades above 16.

Now, the Senator from Pennsylvania simply wants to make—

> Assurance double sure,
> And take a bond of fate—

By putting all above 20 at $1. Mr. President, since the Senate has put the rate at three-tenths of a cent between 13 and 16 and six-tenths of a cent above No. 16, the refiners have secured all they want, and it is a matter of indifference to me whether or not you add one more outrage, in my judgment, and put it at 1 cent under the amendment. But in any event I shall vote against it, as I have voted against all the rest of this legislation.

Upon the conclusion of Senator Vest's remarks, the demand for the yeas and nays was withdrawn and the amendments rejected.

ANTI-TRUST PROVISIONS.

Sections of the New Tariff Law Against Trusts, Combinations and Companies.

Sec. 73. That every combination, conspiracy, trust, agreement, or contra t is hereby declared to be contrary to public policy, illegal, and void, when the same is made by or l etween two or more persons or corporations either of whom is engaged in importing any article from any foreign country into the United States, and when such combination, conspiracy, trust, agreement, or contract is intended to operate in restraint of lawful trade, or free competition in lawful trade or commerce, or to increase the market price in any part of the United States of any article or articles imported or intended to be import d into the United State-, or of any manufacture into which such imported article enters or is intended to enter. Every person who is or shall hereafter be engaged in the importation of goods or any commodity from any foreign country in violation of this section of this act, or who shall combine or conspire with another to violate the same, is guilty of a misdemeanor, and, on conviction thereof in any court of the United States, such person shall be fined in a sum not less than one hundred dollars and not exceeding five thousand dollars, and shall be further punished by imprisonment, in the discretion of the court, for a term not less than th ee months nor exceeding twelve months.

Sec. 74. That the several circuit courts of the United States are hereby invested with jurisdiction to prevent and restrain violations of section seventy-three of this act; and it shall be the duty of the several district attorneys of the United States, in their respective districts, under the direction of the Attorney-General, to institute proceedings in equity to prevent a d restrain such violations. Such proceedings may be by way of petitions setting forth the case and praying that such violations shall be enjoined or otherwise prohibited. When the parties complained of shall have been duly notified of such petition the court shall proceed, as soon as may be, to the hearing and determination of he case; and pending such petition and before final decree, tue court may at any time make such temporary restraining order or prohibition as shall be deemed just in the p emises.

Sec. 75. That whenever it shall appear to the court before which any proceeding under the seventy-fourth section of this act may be pending, that the ends of justice require that other parties should b brought before the court, the court may cause them to be summoned, whether they reside in the district in which the court is held or not; and subpœnas to that end may be served in any district by the marshal thereof.

Sec. 76. That any property owned under any contract or by any combination, or pursuant to any conspiracy (and being the subject thereof) mentioned in section seventy-three of this act, and being in the course of transportation from one State to another, or to or from a Territory, or the District of Columbia, shall be forfeited to the United States, and may be seized and condemned by like proceedings as those provided by law for the forfeiture, seizure and condemnation of property imported into the United States contrary to law.

Sec. 77. That any person who shall be injured in his business or property by any other person or corporation by reason of anything forbid 'en or declared to be unlawful by this act may sue therefor in any circuit court of the United States in the district in which the defendant resides or is found, without respect to the amount in controversy, and shall recover three-fold the damages by him sustained, and the costs of suit, including a reasonable attorney's fee.

SUGAR, COAL, IRON AND WIRE.

Secretary Carlisle's Letter to Senator Harris, August 15 1894, as to Receipts and Expenditures.

TREASURY DEPARTMENT, OFFICE OF THE SECRETARY,
Washington, D. C., August 15, 1894.

DEAR SIR: Your letter advising me that the House of Representatives had passed and sent to the Senate bills putting sugar, coal, iron ore and barbed wire on the free list, and requesting "an official statement from you (me) as to the effect that the passage of these bills, or either of them, would have upon the revenues of the Government," is received, and in response I have the honor to say that, according to the most careful estimates that can be made, if no change is made in the proposed revenue legislation which has recently passed through Congress, the total receipts into the Treasury during the current fiscal year will be as follows:

Estimated revenues for fiscal year ending June 30, 1895.

From duties on imports:
    Senate bill, including $43,000,000 on sugar........................ ..... $179,000,000
From internal taxes:

Whisky	$95,000,000
Tobacco	33,000,000
Fermented liquors	33,000,000
Income	15,000,000
Oleomargarine	1,800,000
Playing cards	1,000,000
Miscellaneous	200,000

                                    179,000,000
From sales of land and other miscellaneous sources........................ 20,000,000

    Total estimated revenue 378,000,000

The estimated receipts for the present year from the proposed tax on incomes and playing cards, and the proposed additional tax of 20 cents per gallon on distilled spirits, are, it will be observed, much less than is stated in the various tabulated statements which have heretofore been used in the discussion of these subjects, but I am satisfied the amounts here given are approximately correct.

The proposed income tax will not become payable, by the terms of the bill recently passed, until "on or before July 1, 1895," which is the close of the fiscal year; and it is estimated by the Commissioner of Internal Revenue that by reason of the large stock on hand the receipts from the tax on playing cards will not amount to more than $1,000,000 during this year.

The estimated increase of receipts on account of the additional tax on distilled spirits during the present year has already been prevented to a great extent by the withdrawal of large quantities of goods from the bonded warehouses and the payment of the tax thereon at 90 cents per gallon, and this process is still going on.

The total expenditures during the current fiscal year will be as follows:

Civil and miscellaneous, including deficiency in postal revenues	$90,000,000
War, including rivers and harbors	56,000,000
Navy, including new vessels and armament	33,000,000
Indians	10,000,000
Pensions	143,500,000
Interest	30,500,000
Total estimated expenditures	$363,000,000
Estimated surplus for year	15,000,000

The duty on sugar proposed in the recent bill will, according to importations of that article during the fiscal year 1893, yield an annual revenue of $43,478,958, and the duties on the other articles mentioned in your communication would yield, under that bill, about $1,000,000; that is to say, iron ore, $270,920; coal, $436,149; and barbed wire, fencing wire, and wire rods, of iron or steel, when imported for the manufacture of barbed-wire fencing, about $300,000.

It will be seen, therefore, that if sugar alone is placed on the free list, the expenditures during the present fiscal year will exceed the receipts to the amount of $28,478,058, and if the duties are removed from all the articles specified in your letter the deficit will be $29,478,058, not including any expenditure on account of the sinking fund, or the payment of $2,363,000 of Pacific Railroad bonds which will mature during this fiscal year.

In view of the existing and prospective requirements of the public service, I am of the opinion that it would not be safe to place all the articles enumerated in your letter, or even sugar alone, upon the free list, without imposing taxation upon other articles or subjects sufficient to raise an annual revenue of about $30,000,000.

I have the honor to be, very respectfully yours,

J. G. CARLISLE, *Secretary.*

Hon. ISHAM G. HARRIS,
    Acting Chairman Senate Finance Committee.

NOTE.—The bonds of the Pacific Railroad guaranteed by the Government, to the amount of $2,362,000, mature during the present fiscal year; and this amount is not included in the above estimate of expenditures.

Tariff Reform.

SPEECH

OF

HON. ROGER Q. MILLS,

OF TEXAS.

IN THE SENATE OF THE UNITED STATES,

Tuesday, April 24, 1894.

The Senate, as in Committee of the Whole, having under consideration the bill (H. R. 4864) to reduce taxation, to provide revenue for the Government, and for other, purposes—

Mr. MILLS said:

Mr. President, we have the cheapest labor on the globe. We have the poorest paid labor in proportion to the work our laborers do that is to be fo und on earth Why so? Because we work by machinery, and one laborer in this country produces in some cases five, ten, and even over ten times more than is performed by the man who is doing the same work in other countries. Great Britain approaches more closely to us than any other country in the world, but she is behind us. We can produce the things we are producing cheaper than anybody else on earth can do it, if they can do it at all.

I have a statement here to which I want to call the attention of the Senate and of the country and especially of the wage-workers. Some time ago, looking over Mulhall's Dictionary of Statistics, I came across a statement in which he gives the number of persons employed in manufactures in all the different countries of the world that are manufacturing to any considerable extent. He gives the total value of the product made in each country and the number of persons employed. By dividing the number of hands by the value of the product we get precisely the amount of value turned out by each hand. This statement shows that for 1888 the United Kingdom had 5,189,000 persons employed in manufacture; that they turned out a product worth $4,100,000, 000, and the product per hand was $790. France had 4,443,000 persons employed. They turned out a product valued at $2,425,000,000, or $545 per hand. Germany had 5,350,000 persons employed. They turned out a produc valued at $2 915,000,000, or $545 per head. Russia had 4,760,000 employed. She turned out a product valued $1,815,000,000, or $381 per head. I will print this table and will not go over it all. The United States had 3,837,000 persons employed, who turned out a product valued at $7,215,000,000, or $1,880 per head.

DEPARTMENT OF LABOR, *Washington, D. C., February* 6, 1894.

MY DEAR SIR: In response to yours of January 18 and January 26, I have the honor to state that from the very best sources which I have been able to consult,

I estimate the average annual earnings in all manufacturing industries in the countries named by you to be as follows:

1. United States, $347; 2, Great Britain, $204; 3, France, $175; 4, Belgium, $165; 5, Germany, $155; 6, Austria, $150; 7, Switzerland, $150; 8, Italy, $130; 9, Spain, $120; 10, Russia. $120.

The above estimates have been made, so far as the United States is concerned, from the actual number of persons employed and the total wages paid to them as shown by the census of 1880; for Great Britain they have been made largely from British figures, and for the other countries the estimates have been made from statements originating with foreign authorities and verified by facts collected by agents of this Department. While the actual figures given in the above estimates may not be more than approximately correct, the proportions, I feel sure, are fair.

    I am, very respectfully.

CARROLL D. WRIGHT,
Commissioner.

Hon. Roger Q. Mills,
   United States Senate.

The average annual rate of wages is for 1880. The number of hands and value of product is for 1888. The relative comparison is the same. The wages in all countries would be higher in 1888 than in 1880. But the relative differences would be substantially the same.

  *   *   *   *   *   *   *   *   *

I am now making a comparison based on the wage rate of 1880. I am not talking about 1890. I am taking the annual average wages paid in 1880 and comparing it with the product of 1888. It makes no difference, as I said before, that the wages are of 1880 and the product of 1888, for relatively they are the same thing. The wages for 1888 would have been a little larger in all the countries, but it is amply sufficient for the purposes which I have in view. Now, let us apply this. Seven hundred and ninety dollars' worth of product per hand in Great Britain cost in wages $204. In France $545 worth of product cost $175 for wages. In Germany $545 cost $155 for wages, and on going down I will print this table, so that all can read it.

Table showing number of employees, total value of product, value of product per employee, annual average wages paid per employee in manufacturing industries in the countries named below in 1880.

Countries.	Total value of product.	Number of employees.	Product per hand.	Annual wages paid.
United Kingdom	$4,100,000,000	5,189,000	$790	$204
France	2,425,000,000	4,443,000	545	175
Germany	2,915,000,000	5,350,000	545	155
Russia	1,815,000,000	4,760,000	381	120
Austria	1,265,000,000	3,000,000	409	150
Italy	605,000,000	2,281,000	265	130
Spain	425,000,000	1,167,000	364	120
Belgium	510,000,000	953,000	545	165
Switzerland	160,000,000	370,000	433	150
United States	7,215,000,000	3,837,000	1,880	347

In the United States $1,880 worth of product cost $347 for wages. Now, our friends point to the fact that the workman in the United States gets $347 for his annual work; in Great Britain he gets $204; in France he gets $175; in Germany $155. Ours is the high-priced workman, and these are paupers, but when we come to look at the fact, that our people are paid less than the foreigner for the amount of work they turn out, the boot is found on the other foot.

Now, let us carry this this thing out. Let us take the labor cost in other countries of $1,880 worth of product and compare it with ours. The $1,880 worth of goods imported into the United States is the thing that is to test the condition of our workmen. When the goods come here then the labor cost of a given amount of goods is compared with the labor cost of the same amount of goods in a foreign country. One thousand eight hundred and eighty dollars' worth of goods cost in this country $347 for labor.

Now, then, we imported from England last year $1,880 of cotton yarns that cost for labor in England $485, and in the United States $347. The labor cost in England was $138 more than in the United States, but our tariff taxes it $935 to protect our labor against competition with the Englishman. We imported $1,880 worth of kid gloves from France that cost for labor in France $604; in the United States $347. The labor cost in France was $257 more than in the United States, but they were taxed $1,165 to protect our workmen against competition with the Frenchman. We imported from Germany $1,880 worth of woolen goods, the labor cost of which in Germany was $535, which was $188 more than in the United States, but they were taxed $1,985 to protect our workmen against competition with the German. We imported from Russia cables, cordage, and twine valued at $1,880, the labor cost of which in Russia was $593, which was $246 more than in the United States, but it was taxed $487 to protect our workmen against competition with the poorly paid Russian.

We imported $1,880 worth of buttons from Austria, the labor cost of which was $689, or $342 more than in the United States, but these buttons were taxed $2,699 to protect our workmen against competition with the Austrian. We imported $1,880 worth of silk piece goods from Italy, the labor cost of which in Italy was $922, or $575 more than in the United States, but they were taxed $940 to protect our workmen against competition with the Italian. We imported $1,880 worth of iron ore from Spain, that cost for labor $620, or $455 more than in the United States, but it was taxed $802 to protect our workmen against competition with the Spaniard. We imported from Belgium $1,880 worth of window glass which cost for labor in Belgium $569; or $222 more than in the United States, but it was taxed $1,936 to protect our workmen against competition with the Belgian, and we imported from Switzerland $1,880 worth of laces and embroideries which cost for labor in Switzerland $651, or $304 more than in the United States, but they were taxed $1,128 to protect our workmen against competition with the Switzer.

*   *   *   *   *   *   *

Germany imports cotton yarns from Great Britian and weaves those yarns and sends them back and sells to Great Britain the cloth that is made from them. France imports cotton yarns from Great Britain. We import cottons yarn from Great Britian. There are certain things we cannot compete with; there are certain things England cannot compete with; and there are certain things that other countries cannot. I submit here the table I have prepared, that Senators and others may examine it:

Countries whence imported.	Labor cost of $1,880 worth of product.	Articles produced in the foreign countries named and imported into the United States.	Labor cost less in United States than exporting country.	Amount of tariff tax on $1,880 worth of articles imported.
United Kingdom.....	$485	Cotton yarns....................	$138	$935
France.................	604	Kid Gloves	257	1,165
Germany	535	Woolen goods............	188	1,985
Russia..................	593	Cables, cordage ahd twine.	246	487
Austria....................	689	Buttons	342	2,699
Italy......................	922	Silk piece goods	575	940
Spain.....................	620	Ir n ore................	455	802
Belgium	569	Window glass	222	1,936
Switzerland............	651	Lace and embroideries.....	304	1,128
United States	347			

Notwithstanding the fact that our labor is cheaper than that of other countries, our people are paying enormous duties to manufacturers to protect their workmen, not one dollar of which ever finds its way to the workman's pocket. Was not the Democratic national convention barking on the right trail when they denounced protection as a fraud? In the face of all these facts Congress is levying taxes to protect American workmen against competition with pauper labor!

The reports which I have read to you show that $100 worth of manufactures cost for labor in Great Britain $25.82; in France, $32.11; in Germany, $28.44, in Russia, $31.49; in Austria, $36.63; in Italy, $49.05; in Spain, $32.93; in Belgium, $30.27, in Switzerland, $34.64; and in the United States, $18.45. Now, who has the cheapest labor?

* * * * * * *

One of the most distinguished leaders of the Republican party, returning from Europe in 1888, started the campaign of that year in a speech at New York, an extract from which I take from the New York *Tribune* of August 11, 1888. In that speech Mr. Blaine said:

I am glad that this meeting is called in the name of the laboring men, because this question from first to last, from beginning to end, f om skin to core, and from core back to skin again, it a question of labor.

In this canvass, in which I shall take greater or less part, I shall hold this question from the beginning to the end as a question that interests every man, woman, and child in this country that depends upon daily labor for daily bread.

There is no need of making any law to protect capital. Capital always takes care of itself and gets a full share.

Truthful are those words as though they were written in Holy Writ. Capital takes care of itself and it takes care of the laborer, too. "It gets its full share" and never gets left. The only labor that it performs is in getting this immense bounty out of the pockets of the people in the name of labor and putting it in its own pocket. They toil not, neither do they spin. They talk and labor with their mouths to get Congress to give them higher prices for their goods, in trust for their laborers and then never give a farthing to the workman.

Mr. President, I will give some more figures to show how protective tariffs affect labor. In Consul Shaw's report, a very intelligent consul under a Republican Administration, made to this Government in 1882, in reporting on cotton goods, he says that in 1882 Great Britain had 486,000 hands employed in cotton manufacture. They made a product valued at $474,916,363. They were paid as wages $121,662,500. The value of the product of each hand was $977. The average wages of each, $250. The labor cost of the goods was 25.61 per cent.

Now let us compare that with the cotton product of the United States two years before.

In the United States, in 1880, our census returns show that we had 172,544 employees engaged in the manufacture of cotton goods. The value of these products was $192,090,110. They received as wages $42,040,510. The value of the product of each was $1,113. The average wages of each was $243. The labor cost of the goods was 21.6 per cent. The Englishman made for his employer $977 worth of goods. The American made for his employer $1,113 worth of goods. The Englishman got $25.61 for $100 worth of work. The American got $21.60 for $100 worth of work. Our workman turned out for his employer $136 more product than the Englishman and got $7 less pay. But the owners of the cotton goods got the protective tariff benefits all the same. And in 1890 his benefits were enlarged for the sole purpose of helping the workingman. Capital takes care of itself.

To produce in Great Britain the $1,113 worth of product turned out by our workmen it would have cost for labor $284, which was $41 more than was paid to our workmen in the United States.

Mr. Mulhall gives us another statement of cotton manufacture in Great Britain in 1888. He says for that year there were 504.000 operatives employed in cotton manufacture. The value of the product turned out by them was $507,000,000. For which they were paid in wages $147,000,000. The average value of the product turned out by each was $1,006. The average annual wages of each, $291. Labor cost of product 29 per cent. Now, let us compare this with 1890 in the United States, as shown by our census returns. We had in cotton manufacture 218,876 operatives. They turned out for their employers a product valued at $267,-981,724. Value of the product of each employee, $1,224. Average annual wages of each, $301. Labor cost, 24.64 per cent.

The Englishman got $29 for $100 worth of work, and the American got $24.64. To have manufactured the $1,224 in England that was made in the United States would have cost for labor $354.96 or $53.96 more than it did in the United States. And if the whole $267,981,724 worth of our product had been made in Great Britain at their wage rate it would have cost for labor $11,000,000 more than it did in the United States; and yet we have a tariff of $57 on each $100 worth to protect our labor against the cheap pauper labor of England! Indeed, it is a question of labor "from skin to core." If the $507,000,000 of cotton goods that were produced in England had been produced in the United States at our wage rate our work people would have gotten $125,000,000 where the Englishman got $147,000,000.

We imported last year $33,343,553 worth of cotton goods, the labor cost of which in Great Britain would have been $9,669,661, and in the United States $8,335,888. Notwithstanding the foreigner was paid for wages more than a million over the wages paid to our workmen, the people paid a tariff tax of $19,031,638 to protect our poor workmen against pauper competition. No one can deny that it is a question of labor "from skin to core and from core back to skin again." Did not the Democratic convention at Chicago hit the nail on the head when they branded protection as a fraud? In the name of the working people, thousands of whom they have turned out of employment and into the streets, they have plundered the country to build up a plutocracy; and now and here in the midst of the wide spread distress which they have sown from their hands they have the effrontry to still defend the monumental robbery in the name of the poor workingman. The American people understood the question in 1892 and took the skin from the party that made the McKinley law, and they will take the core when they come again. * * * I give here a list of articles which show from the census returns what wages are paid and from the tariff what protection is voted for our workmen. I hope some one who may be able to do so will explain why it is that the tariff takes the skin off the wrong man.

In 1 ton of steel rails the labor cost is $3; the tariff is $13.44.

In $100 worth of cutlery the labor cost is $44.24; the tariff is $89.11.

In $100 worth of mats and matting the labor cost is $34.90; the tariff is $68.59

In $100 worth of silk piece goods the labor cost is $22.54; the tariff is $60.

In $100 worth of cigars and cigarettes the labor cost is $34.51; the tariff is $125.36.

In $100 worth of woolen or worsted cloths the labor cost is $20.85; the tariff is $100.02.

In $100 worth of pottery the labor cost is $45.96; the tariff is $60.

In $100 worth of pearl buttons the labor cost is $39.69; the tariff is $143.61.

In $100 worth of tannin the labor cost is $16.34; the tariff is $119.47.

In a ton of coal the labor cost is from 40 to 50 cents; the tariff is 75 cents.

In $100 worth of cotton goods the labor cost is $24.24; the tariff $57.08.

In $100 worth of linen the labor cost is $32.92; the tariff is $50.

In $100 worth of common window glass the labor cost is $53.09; the tariff is $98.39.

In 1 ton of pig iron the labor cost is $1.59; the tariff is $6.72.

In 1 ton of bar iron the labor cost is $1.57; the tariff is $52.98. * * *

Mr. President, the only way that the laborer can receive any benefit is by the law of nature that gives him employment, that gives him constant employment, that gives him employment with a constantly increasing demand for his work. That is only done when we increase the consumption of the things upon which labor is expended, and we increase the consumption of the products of labor when we reduce the cost of making them—the labor cost and every other. Now, machinery does that, and so does the reduction of taxes. Then we must reduce the cost of reaching market and remove all obstructions out of the way so that we may get there. We must increase the demand for employment, and as the demand for the employment of labor increases by the increased consumption of the things that his labor makes, so wages will increase and employment will be constant. * * *

Mr. President, our friends contend that because prices have been falling here in the United States since they have had a tariff, that the tariff is the cause of the lowering of prices, and they are constantly pointing to us the fact that the price of a certain thing was so much thirty years ago, and it is so much less now. My distinguished and venerable friend across the way [Mr. MORRILL] told us the other day in his speech that two-ply ingrain carpet was worth $1 per yard thirty years ago, and that it is now worth 50 cents a yard. Behold the tariff! The tariff did all this thing! He did not tell us that the labor cost of that yard of ingrain carpet is now 6 cents a yard and the tariff on it is over 60 per cent to protect it against competition, when the labor cost of that amount of goods in Great Britain is 7 cents. How does my friend or how does any other man account for the fact that prices have been falling in free-trade England as well as in the United States for the last thirty years? I have a list here of articles which I have taken from the export prices of Great Britain, commencing with 1873, comparing 1873, 1877, and 1891, and it shows a constant downward tendency of prices all along the line :

Export prices of English products for the years named.

English products.	1873.	1877.	1891.
Butter........................per cwt...	$29.53	$33.04	$28.87
Candles ....per dozen pounds...	2.01	1.90	1.18
Cement...........................per cwt...	.76	.64	.49
Cordage ....do......	14.92	13.87	11.48
Wheat ....do......	3.37	3.25	2.35
Wheat flour ....do	4.74	4.35	3.02
Cotton yarn...................per pound...	.3552	.2575	.2188
Cotton piece goods plain............per yard...	.069	.0566	.0461
Cotton piece goods, printed...............do...	.0956	.0861	.0630
Cotton stockings.............per dozen pairs...	1.80	1.5575	1.50
Plate glass, rough ....per square foot...	.75	.555	.32
Flint glass.......................per cwt...	14.47	13.94	11.09
Common bottles ....do...	2.54	2.74	2.34
Hats of all sorts...................per dozen...	7.36	6.22	4.71
Boots and shoes......... .....per dozen pairs...	16.18	15.32	13.51
Linen yarn.....................per pound...	.3302	.3226	.2904
Jute yarn............................do...	.0808	.0696	.0494
White linen, plain.................per yard...	.1524	.1386	.1084
White linen, printed...................do...	.1526	.1572	.1224
Sail cloth............................do...	.2794	.2742	.2142
Pig iron....................per ton...	31.16	14.33	13.12
Bar, angle, bolt and rod iron.................do...	65.45	38.85	33.70
Sheet iron............................do...	89.75	63.95	42.05
Hoop iron............................do...	72.90	42.75	36.40
Tinned plates........................do...	163.85	99.00	79.90
Steel bars.........................do...	185.55	167.70	80.30
Manufactures of steel ....do...	347.55	316.70	173.85
Copper ingots....................per cwt...	23.40	18.90	13.90
Yellow metal........................do...	21.45	17.70	14.00
Pig, sheet and pipe lead.................per ton...	118.75	107.45	70.75
Paper..........................per cwt...	15.20	14.00	8.30
Silk piece goods..................per yard...	.88	.80	.57
Refined sugar....................per cwt...	7.50	6.89	3.59
Wool.......................per pound...	.4236	.3546	.2022
Woolen and worsted yarn ....do...	.7450	.6424	.4530
Carpets........................per yard...	.7725	.6204	.4968
Flannels............................do...	.37	.36	.25
Oxide of Cobalt.............per pound...	3.54	.306	2.07
Nickel..........................do...	2.67	1.15	.48

It will not do to say that the tariff reduces prices in the United States and free trade reduces prices in Great Britain. The same cause, under the same circumstances, ought to produce the same result. They tell us it will ; but here we have prices brought down by free trade in Great Britain and under a protective tariff in the United States. Sir, prices have been brought down by improved production, by machinery, by invention, increasing the amount of product in a given time, and lowering the cost of the product. I have here some figures that will give an illustration of that fact.

A long time ago when we were boys, when our mothers were spinning with the old hand wheel—

One thousand persons in one week spun 3,000 pounds of cotton yarn, No. 10, at $1.50 each $1,500
One person now spins 3,000 pounds of cotton yarn, No. 10, and receives for wages 6

Reduction in labor cost... 1,494

Our friends point to it and say a protective tariff did that, not the spinning jenny—not the skill and genius of the man who worked the machine and the man who invented it, but a protective tariff; and you levy 50 per cent duty on cotton yarn and say the duty did that.

Let us follow that up a little further:

The cost price of 3,000 pounds of yarn then, at 75 cents per pound $2,250
The cost price of 3,000 pounds of No. 10 cotton yarn now, at 15 cents per pound... 450

Reduction 1,800

By a protective tariff!

Labor cost of 247 hand weavers required to weave 3,000 pounds of yarn into 11,100 yards of sheeting, each weaving 45 yards per week and receiving $3 per week as wages, was... 741
Labor cost now of 8 weavers who weave that amount in one week and receive $6 per week as wages.. 48

Reduction in weaving... 693
Cost of cloth made by hand spinning and weaving, at 40 cents per yard... 4,440
Cost of cloth now, at 7 cents per yard, by machinery...................................... 777

Reduction in cost 3,663

And they say a protective tariff did it—not the spinning jenny and the power loom, but the protective tariff that levies 50 per cent duty on cotton yarn and 57 per cent on cotton goods.

Adam Smith tells of the immense benefits that come by the division of labor in making pins, from which I have gathered these figures:

Labor cost of 521 persons required to make 2,500,000 pins in one day, at 1 cent per hundred, was.. $250
Labor cost of 1 person, who now makes 2,500,000 pins in one day, and receives as wages $1.. 1

Reduction.. 249

That is done by a pin machine. Yet our friends stand here and tell us that is done by a protective tariff, and put on more duty in the interest of the poor workingman, and get him to believe that a protective tariff reduces prices and benefits him. Adam Smith stuck pins in the protective tariff in Great Britain till it was dead, and the common shoolhouse and the schoolmaster in this country are sticking pins in it now, and will continue to stick pins in it until it is as dead in this country as it is in Great Britain.

It would have required 58 persons, working one week, each making 12,000 eight-penny nails to make 704,000, now made by 1, and the wages of the 58, at $6 each, was $348
They are now made by one hand, at $5 per day, six days 30

Reduction 318

Mr. President, it is not taxing that reduces the price of a thing. Adding to the cost never reduces the price. That cannot be done. Adding to the cost of a thing increases the price of a thing, or mathematics is a lie. It is taking from the cost of a thing that reduces the price of it. That is what machinery does, what a revenue tariff does, and that is what free trade does still better. There can be no justification on earth, either in politics or common justice, to tax the products of human labor except to support the administration of government. When this Government was first founded, a hundred years ago, our old fathers advocated moderate protection, for what? Because they were involved in war all the time. They began in war; they continued in war, and for a generation and more they were struggling with the powers of all the world, it seemed. During Jefferson's administration the question was whether we would fall into the arms of Great Britain and the allied powers of the continent of Europe or France.

Finally, we became involved in war with Great Britain. We needed manufactured products; we needed them every hour and every day, but the honest men of those days said they were in favor of protective duties to build up the infants. They never claimed that it was a permanent policy. They claimed that it was for the purpose of building up infant industries in this country which would eventually come to maturity. One of the most distinguished leaders of the Republican party, Gen. Garfield, twenty-five years ago or less, in voicing the sentiment of the modern protectionist of that day in his own party said that he was in favor of that kind of protection that led to free trade. That was the kind of protection that clay advocated; that was the kind that was contended for by the early protectionists. It was not changed until about the time of George M. Dallas, when standing where you are sitting now, Mr. President, he gave the casting vote in 1846 for the Walker tariff. He said then that the infant had its growth; it must now stand upon its own feet; it must depend upon itself. The policy after that time was not infant manufactures, but it changed them to protection of American workmen against the pauper labor of Europe. * * *

We must take the tax off those materials that are wrought into manufactures. We must do that as far as we can. We must start in the good work, whether we can accomplish it all now or not. We must start, not protecting our manufactures and making them so high that our people cannot consume them, but making them low enough so that their consumption will be universal and to the largest possible extent. To do that we will have to reduce the revenues we are taking from manufactured goods and take something from the accumulated wealth of the nation.

Appropriations and Expenditures.—Reductions and Reforms.

Expenses Reduced $28,835,989.70.
No Contrats Authorized to Burden Future Congresses.
Six Hundred Offices Abolished.

REMARKS

OF

HON. JOSEPH D. SAYERS,

OF TEXAS,

IN THE HOUSE OF REPRESENTATIVES,

Thursday, August 16, 1894.

On the subject of appropriations.

Mr. SAYERS said:

Mr. SPEAKER: The appropriations made during the extraordinary session and the first regular session of the present Congress, including permanent appropriations, show a reduction of $28,835,989.70 under the appropriations made at the last session of the last Congress; and, deducting the amount of the river and harbor bill, $11,473,180, which should be done for the purpose of comparison, inasmuch as no river and harbor bill was passed by the last Congress at its last session, the reduction is $40,309,169.70.

A tabular history of the appropriation bills, showing also the estimates submitted to this Congress and the appropriations made at the last session of the last Congress, will be found in Table A, which I shall submit as a part of my remarks.

The thirteen regular annual appropriation bills, including the river and harbor bill, are grouped in the table so as to show the aggregates of the whole in the several stages through which they passed in the processes of legislation, from the estimates submitted until their final enactment. The table shows—

(1) That the bills, including deficiencies, as passed by the House, made a reduction under the estimates submitted to Congress of $32,571,188.62.

(2) That they were increased, as reported from committee to the Senate, $13,872,977.34.

(3) That they were increased, as passed by the Senate, $16,225,997.62; and

(4) That as they became laws, including miscellaneous, they appropriated less than the estimates, $29,994,471.20; more than as they passed the House, $9,370,-

140.89 ; less than as they passed the Senate, $6,855,856.73 ; and less than the laws for 1894, including permanent appropriations, $28,835,989.70.

As compared with the laws passed at the last session of the last Congress, the following reductions are shown in the table :

By the agricultural bill	$101,476.94
By the army bill	632,755.10
By the legislative, etc., bill, which carries, in the main the great salary list of the Government	557,507.02
By the Military Academy bill	26,033.04
By the pension appropriation bill	14,949,780.00
By the sundry civil bill	7,506,535.10
On account of deficiencies	10,456,440.60
On account of permanent appropriations (including $11,000,000 for sugar bounty, which is abolished, and $450,000 expenses under election laws that are repealed)	14,393,593.92
Total reduction	$48,624,221.72

The bills showing increases over the last laws are as follows :

The diplomatic and consular bill	$6,473.76
The District of Columbia bill	131,369.66
The fortification bill	216,949.00
The Indian bill	1,475,408.11
The naval bill	3,223,065.34
Postoffice bill	3,232,285.33
The river and harbor bill (total)	11,473,180.00
Miscellaneous	29,500.82
Total increase	$19,788,232.02

Net reduction by all of the bills, including deficiencies and permanent appropriations, $28,835,989.70.

*   *   *   *   *   *   *

THE NEW NAVY.

The reconstruction of the Navy was begun a little more than eleven years ago. During the period since March 3, 1883, fifty modern vessels of all classes, now built or being built, have been authorized by acts of Congress. Toward their construction, equipment, and armament there has been appropriated, including $9,955,025 in the naval bill at this session, the sum of $88,981,188.80. To finally complete, equip, and arm them it is estimated that there will yet have to be appropriated the further sum of $23,080,974.84, making a total of $112,062,163.64, which the new Navy, as now authorized, will cost. Of these fifty new naval vessels, only three were authorized by the present Congress, and the their total cost is limited to $450,000.

PUBLIC BUILDINGS.

The Fifty-first Congress authorized the construction of sixty-nine new public buildings, including three United States prisons, and extended the limit of cost of twenty-three buildings previously authorized to be constructed. The expense of these new buildings was fixed at $16,946,639.54. Of this sum the Fifty-first Congress appropriated only $8,886,639.54, leaving $8,060,000 to be provided by subsequent Congresses.

The present Congress and the last Congress authorized the construction of no new public buildings.

COMPARISON OF APPROPRIATIONS.

The appropriations made at the present and extraordinary session of Congress, as shown in the statement marked "Table B," and which I shall submit as part of my remarks, are :

Less than the appropriations made at the last session of the last Congress by.. $28,835,989.70

Less than the appropriations made at the first session of the last Congress by.. 16,931,819.20

Less than the appropriations made at the last session of the Fifty-first Congress by... 50,555,491.78

Less than the appropriations made at the first session of the Fifty-first Congress by... 3,787,879.14

And less than the estimates submitted by.. 29,994,471.20

The table referred to is compiled from the official records, including therein, for the Fifty-first Congress, expenditures under indefinite appropriations made by that Congress and under permanent appropriations authorized by said Congress after the estimates for permanent appropriations were submitted by the Secretary of the Treasury, all of which are fully explained in foot notes to the table.

APPROPRIATIONS ENTAILED BY THE FIFTY-FIRST CONGRESS.

In the statement marked "Table C" and submitted herewith there are shown appropriations made at this session and also by the Fifty-second Congress and by the Fifty-first Congress, pursuant to laws enacted during the Fifty-first Congress:

This statement shows that of the appropriation made at this session, $65,723,- 441.92 were required under laws passed during the Fifty-first Congress ; that only $34,574,191.01 were appropriated by the first session of the Fifty-first Congress under those laws ; that of the appropriations made during the two sessions of the last Congress $175,736,618.79 were the result of those laws, and that only $127,309,- 111.68 were appropriated at both sessions of the Fifty-first Congress under those laws which it passed entailing such enormous obligations upon its successors.

OFFICES ABOLISHED—SALARIES REDUCED.

During the present session of Congress the salaried list of the Government has been reduced by more than 600 in number and over $700,000 in annual cost, and more salaries have been reduced than increased.

The Fifty-first Congress specifically added, net, to the salaried list of the Government 1,705 new offices, at a total annual cost of $2,048,350.82, and specifically increased, net, 1,214 salaries, at a total annual cost of $247,724.82.

The Fifty-second Congress, exclusive of the authority to increase the enlistment of apprentice boys in the Navy by 750, added, net, to the salaried list of the Government, 158 new officers, at a total annual cost of $134,790. The latter Congress, exclusive of the nominal increase which it authorized in the monthly pay of the station-keepers and surfmen of the Life-Saving Service, and of the sergeants in the Army, reduced, net, 177 salaries, at an annual saving of $36,105.

The revenue of the Government from all sources, exclusive of postal receipts, which are dedicated solely to the postal service, have been, since and including the fiscal year ending June 30, 1890, as follows:

'or fiscal year 1890 ....$403,080,982.63
'or fiscal year 1891 .... 392,612,447.31
'or fiscal year 1892 .... 354,937,784.24
'or fiscal year 1893 .... 385,818,628.78
'or fiscal year 1894 .... 296,960,336.00

The net ordinary expenditures of the Government, including interest on the public debt, and exclusive of requirements of the sinking fund for the fiscal years 886, 1887, and 1888, they constituting the three full years of Mr. Cleveland's former administration, were as follows:

886 ....$267,932,179.97
887 .... 267,924,801.13
888 .... 290,288,978.25

And for the fiscal years 1890, 1891, and 1892, they being the three full years of Ir. Harrison's administration, such expenditures were as follows:

890 ....$318,040,710.66
891 .... 365,773,905.35
892 .... 345,023,330.58

This vast difference in the increase of expenditures of the three years last named over those first given can only be attributed to a recklessness of appropriation and expenditure by the then dominant party. It is true that the regular annual appropriations at the first session of the Fifty-first Congress for the fiscal year 1891 amounted to but $363,132,116.95, but when the amount of the permanent annual appropriations at the first session of that Congress, $131,324,131.70, being $32,448,-24.41 greater than for the year 1890, is considered, it may be readily seen in what the appropriations were made and the expenditures swollen by the Republican administration. From a constantly increasing expenditure and continual decreasing revenues unquestionably resulted the serious and embarrassing condition of the public Treasury when the present administration assumed control of the Govern-

TABLE A.—*Tabular history of appropriation bills, first and second sessions of the Fifty-third Congress; estimates and appropriations for the fiscal year 1894–'95; and appropriations for the fiscal year 1893–'94, passed at the last session of the Fifty-second Congress.*

Title.	Estimates, 1895.	Reported to the House. Amount.	Passed the House. Amount.	Reported to the Senate. Amount.	Passed the Senate. Amount.	Law, 1894–'95. Amount.	Law, 1893–'94. Amount.
Agriculture	$2,253,843.06	$3,180,643.06	$3,215,643.06	$3,204,183.06	$4,225,183.06	$3,222,023.06	$3,323,500.00
Army	25,332,918.52	23,569,204.68	23,586,924.68	23,606,384.68	23,611,384.68	23,592,884.68	24,225,639.78
Diplomatic and consular	1,612,638.76	1,511,738.76	1,500,738.76	1,580,438.76	1,591,218.27	1,563,918.76	1,557,445.00
District of Columbia *a*	5,391,473.91	5,157,573.57	5,206,473.57	5,454,598.57	5,887,088.57	5,544,593.57	5,413,223.91
Fortifications	7,438,413.00	2,219,654.00	2,224,654.00	2,779,104.00	2,836,604.00	2,427,604.00	2,210,055.00
Indian	6,931,156.61	6,611,260.79	6,735,518.90	9,327,386.69	9,404,249.49	9,329,648.49	7,854,240.38
Legislative, etc	22,310,510.33	21,086,923.29	21,105,787.29	21,344,739.79	21,378,315.79	21,308,295.79	21,865,802.81
Military Academy	463,183.58	401,283.08	401,283.08	410,263.04	410,263.04	406,523.08	432,556.12
Navy	27,875,914.02	25,290,930.27	25,389,580.27	25,215,060.27	25,437,105.30	25,327,126.72	22,104,061.38
Pension	162,631,570.00	151,581,570.00	151,581,570.00	151,581,570.00	151,581,570.00	151,581,570.00	166,531,350.00
Post Office *b*	90,399,485.33	87,470,599.55	87,240,599.55	87,236,599.55	87,236,599.55	87,236,599.55	84,004,814.22
River and harbor	*c* 7,625,000.00	9,458,689.56	9,538,689.56	12,771,140.00	12,946,680.00	11,413,180.00	(*d*)
Sundry civil	34,966,002.81	32,308,612.90	32,523,383.80	35,061,685.70	36,202,166.70	34,309,776.05	*e* 41,716,311.15
Total	395,232,109.93	369,837,793.40	370,209,846.52	379,981,094.15	382,748,367.49	377,223,143.75	381,238,499.75
Urgent deficiency, receiving silver, etc		300,000.00	300,000.00	306,000.00	306,000.00	306,000.00	
Further urgent deficiency, assistant custodians, etc		338,000.00	338,000.00	370,588.33	370,588.33	370,588.33	
Further urgent deficiency, customs, census, etc		1,651,896.31	1,889,455.86	1,989,455.86	1,989,455.86	1,968,470.86	
Further urgent deficiency, U. S. courts, etc	*f* 17,012,627.31	338,958.00	388,958.00	453,278.00	453,278.00	768,278.00	*g* 22,277,086.36
Further urgent deficiency, engraving and printing, courts, etc		1,237,255.66	1,242,255.66	1,785,889.66	2,842,304.66	1,854,304.66	
Further urgent deficiency, printing and customs		350,000.00	350,000.00	350,000.00	350,000.00	350,000.00	
Deficiency, 1894, and prior years		4,880,583.78	5,005,032.58	7,910,219.96	7,939,551.41	6,202,903.91	
Total	412,244,737.24	378,944,497.15	379,673,548.62	393,046,525.96	395,899,546.24	389,043,689.51	403,515,586.11
Miscellaneous	7,343,429.47					550,000.00	520,499.18

a One-half of the amounts for the District of Columbia payable by the United States, except amounts for the water department (estimated for 1895 at $265,083.93) which are payable from the revenues of the water department.

b Includes all expenses of the postal service payable from postal revenues and out of the Treasury.

c This is the amount estimated for rivers and harbors for 1895, exclusive of $4,885,000 required to meet contracts authorized by law included in the sundry civil service estimates. "The amount that can be profitably expended" in that fiscal year, as reported by the Chief of Engineers, is $43,760,611. [Book of Estimates for 1895, pages 192-97.]

d No river and harbor bill was passed for 1894, but the sum of $14,166,153 was included in the sundry civil act to carry out contracts authorized by law for river and harbor improvements.

e This amount includes $14,166,153 to carry out contracts authorized by law for river and harbor improvements, and for improvements under the Mississippi River and the Missouri River Commission.

f This amount includes $3,974,646.14 judgments and claims audited and certified as due several Pacific Railroad companies.

g This amount includes $14,149,724.85 deficiency for pensions for the fiscal year 1893.

h No amount is included in the estimates of permanent annual appropriations for 1895 for bounty on sugar, for the reason stated in the following note on page 267, Book of Estimates for 1895: "NOTE.—The Secretary of the Treasury having recommended the repeal of the sugar-bounty law, no estimate is submitted for the fiscal year 1895. In case the law is not repealed, $11,000,000 will be required for the purpose, which should be added to the sum total of the estimate for 1895."

i This is the amount submitted by the Secretary of the Treasury in the annual estimates for the fiscal year 1894, the exact amount appropriated not being ascertainable until two years after the close of the fiscal year.

TABLE B.—*Appropriations made by the Fifty-first and Fifty-second Congresses, and by extra and first regular sessions of the Fifty-third Congress, fiscal years 1891 to 1895, inclusive.*

Title.	Fifty-first Congress.		Fifty-second Congress.		Fifty-third Congress.
	First session, 1891.	Second session, 1892.	First session, 1893.	Second session, 1894.	Extra and first regular sessions, 1895.
Agriculture	$1,799,100.00	$3,028,163.50	$3,232,995.50	$3,323,500.00	$3,222,023.06
Army	24,206,471.79	24,613,529.19	24,309,499.82	24,225,639.78	23,592,884.68
Diplomatic and consular	1,710,815.00	1,656,925.00	1,604,015.00	1,557,445.00	1,563,918.76
District of Columbia	5,769,344.15	5,597,125.17	5,317,973.27	5,413,228.91	5,344,598.57
Fortifications	4,232,935.00	3,774,903.00	2,734,276.00	2,210,055.00	2,427,004.00
Indian	7,262,016.02	16,396,284.86	7,664,047.84	7,854,240.38	9,329,648.49
Legislative, etc.	21,030,752.75	22,027,674.75	21,900,132.95	21,965,802.81	21,308,295.79
Military Academy	435,296.11	402,064.64	424,917.33	432,556.12	406,523.08
Navy	24,136,085.53	31,541,654.78	23,543,385.00	22,104,061.38	25,327,126.72
Pension, including deficiencies *a*	123,779,368.35	164,550,383.34	154,411,662.00	180,681,074.85	151,581,570.00
Post Office	72,226,698.99	77,907,222.61	80,331,276.73	84,004,314.22	87,286,599.55
River and Harbor	25,136,295.00		21,154,218.00		11,473,180.00
Sundry civil	*b*31,100,341.38	*d*38,388,552.73	27,665,074.93	41,716,311.15	34,209,776.05
Deficiencies, except for pensions	13,295,541.61	9,364,148.62	8,280,859.50	8,127,361.51	11,820,545.76
Total	$356,121,211.68	399,238,522.19	282,527,985.89	403,515,586.11	389,043,689.51
Miscellaneous	7,010,905.27	*d*19,438,531.10	3,208,922.82	520,499.18	550,000.00
Total regular annual appropriations	*b*363,132,116.95	418,737,053.29	385,736,308.71	404,036,085.29	389,593,689.51
Permanent annual appropriations	*c*131,324,131.70	*e*122,486,308.00	*e*121,863,880.00	*e*115,468,273.92	*c*101,074,680.00
Total	494,456,248.65	541,223,361.29	507,600,188.71	519,504,359.21	490,668,369.51

a Deficiencies included as follows: 1891, on account of 1890, $25,321,907.25; 1892, on account of 1891, $29,385,598.34; 1893, on account of 1892, $7,674,332; 1894, on account of 1893, $14,119,724.85.

b This amount includes $1,362,059.16 actual expenditures under indefinite appropriations for pay and bounty claims.

c This amount includes $978,188.74 actual expenditures under indefinite appropriations for pay and bounty claims.

d This amount includes $15,227,000 for refund of direct taxes in addition to the specific sum of $500,000 appropriated for that purpose.

e This is the amount originally submitted to Congress by the Secretary of the Treasury as estimated to be necessary under permanent specific and permanent indefinite appropriations, except that to the amount thus submitted for 1894, $101,628,454, there are added expenditures under permanent appropriations made by the Fifty-first Congress subsequent to said estimate, as follows: Salaries diplomatic and consular service, $27,756.79; redemption national-bank notes, $29,558,208.50; expenses of Treasury notes, $918,362.60; coinage of silver bullion, $210,893.14; rebate tobacco tax, $770,082.39, and repayments to importers and for debentures and drawbacks, customs service,

Object.	Statutes.	Fifty-third Congress, first session, appropriated 1895.	Fifty-second Congress. First session, appropriated 1892.	Fifty-second Congress. Second ses'n, appropriated 1893.	Fifty-first Congress. First session, appropriated 1891.	Fifty-first Congress. Second ses'n, appropriated 1892.
Coinage of silver bullion, act July 14, 1890 (permanent)..	26,289	$125,000.00	$126,000.00	$150,000.00	$210,893.14	$10,000.00
Expenses of Treasury notes, act July 14, 1890 (permanent)..	26,289	100,000.00	816,315.65	210,000.00	218,362.60	310,000.00
Refund of direct tax, act March 2, 1891 (permanent)..	26,822			130,000.00		15,727,000.00
Bounty on sugar, act October 1 (permanent)..	26,583		10,000,000.00	10,000,000.00		7,000,000.00
Colleges for agriculture and mechanic arts, October 30, 1890 (permanent)..	26,417	960,000.00	833,000.00	531,000.00	1,364,000.00	833,000.00
Additional internal revenue appropriations on account of tariff, act of October 1, 1890..			211,990.00	211,990.00		
Increase in salaries of United States judges, act February 24, 1891..	26, 783	100,500.00	93,500.00	100,500.00		93,500.00
Circuit court of appeals, act March 3, 1891..	26, 836	81,000.00	81,000.00	81,000.00		60,000.00
Court of Private Land Claims, act March 3, 1891..	26, 854	59,500.00	33,500.00	33,500.00		55,000.00
Additional clerks for pension cases, act August 29, 1890..	26, 370	666,620.00	666,620.00	666,620.00		
Inspection of meats, etc., acts August 30, 1890, and March 3, 1891..	26, 414 / 26,1089	200,000.00	350,000.00	350,000.00		150,000.00
Interest on Cheyennes and Arapahos in Oklahoma fund, act March 3, 1891..	26,1025	50,000.00	50,000.00	50,000.00		66,335.60
Interest on Sisseton and Wahpeton fund, act March 3, 1891..	26,1038	84,990.00	84,990.00	84,990.00		112,757.23
Interest on Sacs and Foxes of the Mississippi in Oklahoma fund, act February 13, 1891..	26, 758	15,000.00	15,000.00	15,000.00		20,681.52
Indian depredation claims, acts March 3, 1891, and July 28, 1892..	26, 851	175,000.00	478,252.62	958,065.00		
World's Columbian Exposition, act April 25, 1890..	26, 62		3,291,250.00		320,000.00	768,000.00
National bank redemption fund, act July 14, 1890 (permanent)..	26, 289	5,000,000.00	9,500,000.00	7,000,000.00	23,553,298.50	16,000,000.00
Dependent pension act, act June 27, 1890..	26, 182	57,890,021.92	68,259,537.18	57,890,021.92	8,907,636.77	51,407,971.32
Ocean mail service, act March 3, 1891..	26, 830	215,810.00	498,563.67	363,372.75		120,675.00
Mint at Philadelphia, act March 3, 1891..	26, 838		870,500.00	250,000.00		
Total, by sessions..		65,723,441.92	96,260,019.12	79,476,589.67	34,574,191.01	92,734,920.67
Total, by Congresses..		65,723,441.92	175,736,618.79		127,309,111.68	

ECONOMY AND EFFICIENCY.

Reorganization of the Executive Departments and Improvement of Business Methods Therein.

After the election of Mr. Cleveland a law was passed by the last Congress at its last session, at the instance of Hon. A. M. Dockery, a Representative from Missouri, creating a joint commission of Congress to improve the methods of business in the Executive Departments at Washington and to reduce expenditures therein.

The commission as constituted consisted of Representative A. M. Dockery, J. D. Richardson, and Nelson Dingley, Jr., on the part of the House of Representatives, and Senators F. M. Cockrell, J. K. Jones, and S. M. Cullom. They set about their labors immediately after their appointment and the inauguration of Mr. Cleveland.

The first result of their work was the preparation, by competent persons, of a compilation of references to laws creating the Executive Departments and the several Bureaus and offices thereof, and other Government establishments at the National Capital; the creation of all officers therein, and their salaries as fixed from time to time. This work was the first of its character ever attempted—it was printed both as a House and a Senate report of Congress, and has already proved of inestimable value.

Next followed from the commission a comprehensive census of all the officers and employees of the Government at Washington.

A general summary of this report discloses the fact that the Executive Departments and other establishments at the National Capital are divided into 136 offices or bureaus and 498 divisions; that there are 17,599 persons employed therein, 11,667 males and 5,637 females; that of this number employed in the Executive Departments, the Department of Labor, Civil Service Commission, and Fish Commission, which are under the civil service law, 8,027 are in the class subject to competitive civil service examination preliminary to appointment, and 3,265 of that number entered the service after such examination; the residue, 4,762, were employed in the departments at the time they were classified and placed under the civil service law by executive order; that the ages of those employed, stated in multiples of five years, range from 20 years to 90 years, and the length of service of all employees ranges from one year to sixty years each; and that of the whole number employed, 5,610 have from one to nine relatives each in the Government service at Washington.

One of the great evils which for years had attracted public attention was the costly errors occuring more or less at every session of Congress in the enrollment of bills, enacted by that body; the system in vogue, of writing, by hand, every bill after final enactment had been handed down since the foundation of the Government. The commission corresponded with all of the leading foreign governments and after a careful study of their several systems recommended and Congress adopted a method by which every act of Congress is required to be printed in clear type before presenting to the President for approval. This facilitates the careful examination of all acts and reduces to a minimum the possibility of making the mistakes which in the past have cost the country millions in revenue and expenditures.

The first of the seven laws enacted thus far on the recommendation of the commission was approved January 22, 1894. It regulates the methods of making returns of money deposited by postmasters, and will save at least a month in the hitherto slow process of settling postmasters' accounts and holding them accountable for public funds.

The next law enacted on the recommendation of the commission prescribes a uniform method of advertising for and purchasing supplies for the Government service in Washington. Under the old system each department purchased in its own way, according to its needs, and without reference to prices paid for, or quality of articles procured by other departments. Under the new law each department will be advised of the prices and quality of all articles offered to the others, and business men are afforded an opportunity of making at one time offers for supplying articles for all of the departments instead of to only one as heretofore. Already the first letting of contracts under the new law shows large reductions on all supplies, and the indications are that the saving to the Government will amount to at least $100,000 during the year.

On the 27th of January, 1894, another law was passed at the instance of the commission to improve the methods of accounting in the Post Office Department. It makes a direct annual reduction of $52,515.00 in expenditures, abolishes the postal note, established a new money order system, and reduces the cost of money orders to the people from 2 to 15 cents on each order above $15 00.

This law also provides for turning into the Treasury the amount of all unpaid money orders and postal notes more than one year old. This provision of the law will cover into the Treasury for use as current revenue possibly $2,500,000, now lying idly in the sub-treasury at New York.

On March 29, 1894, another bill prepared by the commission became a law abolishing a useless report required from the Treasurer costing annually not less than $8,500.

On the same day another of their bills was enacted into law regulating the making of property returns by Government officers at an annual saving of $15,000.

On the Post Office appropriation act, a provision was enacted on the recommendation of the commission for the disposition of old money orders, and will save to the country annually in expenses of storage and handling $10,000.

On the great salary appropriation act of the Government for the next fiscal year, approved July 31, 1894, there is enacted provisions of law, recommended by the commission, completely reorganizing the methods of accounting in the Treasury Department. This new law brings to the service of the Government the best devices and methods known to the modern business world, for the protection of its interests in the settlement each year of accounts for the hundreds of millions of its revenue and disbursements. The new system provided by this law will be operated with 185 less officials and clerks and at an annual reduction of cost of $235,000 under the old methods.

On the recommendation of the commission new regulations have been adopted in the Treasury Department changing the old form of the Treasury warrant which will result in an annual saving of $6,000.

The Treasury and Post Office Departments have also taken action, at the request of the commission, discontinuing certain useless statistics relating to international money orders that will save annually $10,000.

The work already accomplished by the commission, to say nothing of that which it has under advisement and in course of preparation for presentation at the next session of Congress for legislative action, will save annually to the Government not less than $437,015.00.

SAVING IN THE WAR DEPARTMENT.

Under the business methods adopted by the Secretary of War the number of clerks in that department has been reduced from 1,348 to 965. The aggregate of the salaries of the clerks whose services were dispensed with was $452,800. This reduction in the clerical force permitted reductions in other items of expenditure directly connected with the business of the department. A reduction of nearly 10 per cent in the number of commissioned officers of the Army on duty in Washington a year ago has been made.

It is safe to say that the total savings in this department alone from the reform inaugurated will exceed a half million of dollars.

DIPLOMATIC RELATIONS.

The Foreign Policies of Republican and Democratic Administrations Compared.

The administration of our foreign relations during Mr. Harrison's incumbency forms a record in which no true American can take a just pride. From the earliest days of our history as a nation the policy of non-entangling alliances and non-interference with the affairs of foreign powers has been accepted by all parties as essential, not only to the preservation of our system of Government, but, as an example to other nations of the lofty principles which should animate and control the civilized people of the world in their relations towards each other.

To the maintenance of this principle and the fidelity with which it has been adhered to, in the face of great temptation, we are largely indebted for the preservation, the growth and the grandeur of our institutions, and it will be a sad day for the American people when they abandon it for the "jingoism" which characterized the acts of the last Republican administration.

SAMOAN ISLANDS.

The treaty entered into by our Government with Germany and Great Britain in 1889 relative to the government of the Samoan Islands was such a palpable departure from the accepted policies that should control our relations with foreign powers as to merit the severest rebuke from all parties.

In a recent report to the Senate (see Ex. doc. 93) Mr. Gresham, Secretary of State, in discussing the provisions of this treaty, said:

A period of almost five years having elapsed since the conclusion of the general act of Berlin, the present occasion is not inappropriate for a review of its results. Such a review, however, would hardly be intelligible without some consideration of the events that preceded the treaty. In order that the subject may be fully comprehended, it will be necessary to present a general survey of our relations to Samoa, both before and since the conclusion of the general act, and to exhibit the policy we have pursued toward the islands, both in respect of its character and its results.

This duty is especially important, since it is in our relations to Samoa that we have made the first departure from our traditional and well-established policy of avoiding entangling alliances with foreign powers in relation to objects remote from this hemisphere. Like all other human transactions, the wisdom of that departure must be tested by its fruits. If the departure was justified there must be some evidence of detriment suffered before its adoption, or of advantage since gained, to demonstrate the fact. If no such evidence can be found we are confronted with the serious responsibility of having without sufficient grounds, imperiled a policy which is not only coeval with our Government, but to which may, in great measure, be ascribed the peace, the prosperity, and the moral influence of the United States. Every nation, and especially every strong nation, must sometimes be conscious of an impulse to rush into difficulties that do not concern it, except in a highly imaginary way. To restrain the indulgence of such a propensity is not only the part of wisdom, but a duty we owe to the world as an example of the strength, the moderation, and the beneficence of popular government.

That our citizens had no material interests in jeopardy in Samoa, and that the assumption, financial or otherwise, of any obligations upon the part of our Government to assist in supporting and sustaining any form of government there was wholly gratuitous and liable to involve us in needless complications no one can gainsay. By the treaty the three parties recognized the independence and neutrality of the islands and stipulated for the provisional recognition of Malietoa Laupepa as King, and provided for the establishment of a government, the chief feature of which was a Supreme Court, composed of one judge, to be nominated by the treaty powers, and styled Chief Justice of Samoa. The Chief Justice was clothed with both appellate and original jurisdiction and his decisions made final. His salary was fixed at $6,000 a year in gold, to be paid the first year in equal proportions by the treaty powers and afterwards out of the revenues of the Samoan Government, with a proviso that if any deficiency should occur the same should be made good by the treaty powers. After the Supreme Court, was provided a local government for the municipal district of Apia. Of this government the principal organ was a municipal council composed of six members and a President; the President to be selected through the instrumentality of the treaty powers and receive an annual compensation of $5,000, to be paid the first year, in equal shares, by the treaty powers, and afterwards out of the Samoan revenues assigned to the use of the municipality. Many other provisions and stipulations are contained in the treaty, but these are sufficient to show the nature of the same and the obligations that our Government entered into to restore a semi-barbarous King to his throne and to set up a government over a semi-civilized people in a distant and insignificant island in which we had no interest.

The complications in which we are likely to become involved by this extraordinary treaty is strikingly illustrated by the Secretary in his report. He says:

As early as 1891 some of the natives, under the lead of Mataafa, began to betray rebellious symptoms of even a more pronounced character. In a dispatch of December 6, 1892, Mr. Blacklock, the consul of the United States at Apia, in reporting upon the condition of affairs that had prevailed in the islands for a year prior to that date, said:

"Ever since Mataafa's establishment at Malie he has endeavored to gather strength and there is not the slightest doubt had he been successful in getting sufficient following he would have made war upon Malietoa; he has done everything in opposing the Government except making war; he has defied its courts, obstructed its officials in the execution of their duties, harbored refugees from justice, succored and supported prisoners escaped from prison, and at the present moment is living in open defiance of the king and government and all the laws of the country, keeping up an armed force and plundering foreigners' plantations for subsistence. Time and again have white officials who went to Malie with warrants for the arrest of offenders been driven away by Mataafa's soldiers and warned against attempting any arrest under penalty of death."

This condition of things continued with increasing aggravation till July, 1893, when war actually broke out. The treaty powers were now compelled actively to intervene with their naval forces in order to keep Malietoa on the throne. In the end it became necessary to disperse the insurgents and to deport Mataafa and eleven other chiefs to another island, where they have since been kept at the joint expense of the three powers.

It appears, therefore, that we have by this treaty assumed not only a share of the expenses in maintaining the government provided by its provisions, but are obligated to aid in defending the same against the insurrections of its rebellious subjects. What interest we had in the people of Samoa, or what benefits were to accrue to us from the arrangement, we are left to conjecture, as none have ever become visible. Only recently the governments of Great Britain and Germany have been forced to send a naval force to Samoa to subdue the rebellious M taafa and his followers. It is a matter of supreme satisfaction that our Government did not assume to carry out her part of th agreement, but has abandoned the same.

OUR RELATIONS WITH CHILI.

The eff rts of Mr. Harrison's administration to precepitate a war with the Chilian people and the underlying causes which led to the bitter hostility manifested by them towa ds our representatives and sailors was one of the most disreputable transactions in which our Government was forced to take part. The true history of this controversy has never been fully disclosed. A comprehensive statement of the troubles which arose in Chili in 1891 and 1892 is necessary to a perfect understanding of the question. The power of the president of Chili was very great. His patronage was enormous, embracing not only the general civil service but local offices, except in the municipalities, and all appointments to the army and navy and in the telegraph and railroad service and the giving out of contracts. He was always able to dictate his successor. The only check to his nfluence and power was the custom which required him to choose his ministers from the dominant element in Congress and to dismiss them after a vote of censure. Congress could withhold supplies and had the power to fix, in the annual bill, the forces on land and sea. These res raints compelled the President to act in harmony with the majority in Congress. Balmaceda was exceedingly popular at the time of his election as President, but later broke with the majority and selected a cabinet of his own choice regardless of the sentiments of Congress. The breach began to widen and continued to become more antagonistic until finally Congress held an extraordinary session, at which the members sign d an act declaring the President unworthy of his post and no longer chief of the State or President of the Republic, because he had violated the Constitution and was guilty of treason. Balmaceda attempted to forestall the action of Congress by issuing a manifesto and assuming virtual dictatorship. The congressional party was backed by the land-holders, the wealth, the clergy and the foreign elements and had secured the co-op ration of the fleet. The President had command of the standing army and charge of th funds in the treasury. Balmaceda having assumed a military dictatorship, declared the whole country under martial law. The most rigorous measures were pursued by him. The farms and estates of the Congressionalists were pillaged, their crops burned and their houses sacked. Newspapers were uppressed; men of social position were bastinadoed to compel them to reveal the hiding places of political refugees; pris ns were choked with persons prominent in social, professional and comme cial circles. Mr. Patrick Egan, then our Minister to Chili, and Mr W. B. McCreery, our Consul at Valparaiso, instead of maintaining a strict neutrality in such a delicate situation, became ardent sympathizers with and strong supporters of Balmaceda. Why it was that our representatives studiously misrepresented the true situati n and labored to mislead our own as well as the people of other governments as to the final resu t, is perfectly clear when their real purposes and objects are understood. The true inwardness of their conduct was partially given through the columns of the public press, but nothing like a full exposition of their schemes and machinations has been given to the people of this country. From a private letter written by Mr. John Trumbull, a citizen of Chili (born of American parentage), of unquestioned character, standing and reputation, and filed in the Department of State, the following is taken. He said :

I firmly believe that pecuniary interests are at the bottom of all the trouble between Chili and the United States. To show that these existed enclosed you will find some photographs, which conclusively prove that Consul McCreery has been engaged in exchange speculations. He has been doing this throughout our troubles here, employing several brokers to make his purchases and sales. I have affirmed, and can prove, that his partial transactions with one broker in ten weeks amounted to £252,000. Allowing for transactions for quick delivery, which are not included, and supposing the same rate to have continued, as it undoubtedly has, and these cannot fail during the past year to have aggregated at least £2,000,000. My impression is that twice that sum is nearer correct, yet this will give you an idea of the extent to which the U. S. Consul has engaged in speculative ventures.

* * * * * *

At first he seems to have felt so sure that Balmaceda would ultimately win that he used to sign the broker's slips and received checks in payment of gains made, and so some positive proof has been obtainable ; but you will understand how averse people are to helping one collect such data. For some time back Consul McCreery has sought to keep in the background, though any number of business men and brokers can witness to his persistent continuance in the same exchange business. On May 27, 1891, through the failure of a Dr. Manuel Ramco, a bill for £5,000 sold to him by a Mr. Neckelman on the Consul's account, came back on the last named and made him lose over $7,000 in consequence. It is said the Consul recognized, promised to, but never did pay this. After that Mr. N. made transactions for him, as one of the slips will prove, but you will notice that as he no longer trusted the Consul's word he got him to sign and leave the notification in his possession as a guarantee. This transaction when closed netted a gain of $1,870, which Mr. N. concluded to keep as against the $7,400, and so handed in a statement to that effect. This called forth the letter reproduced, yet Consul McCreery has never made good his threat. He probably intends to wait until he leaves, when he will make out a power of attorney to some one authorizing him to present the claim. Meanwhile Mr. N.'s books conclusively show the truth of his statement, but he has no redress at law, since then he did not think it necessary to secure Mr. McCreery's signature, which legally is the only evidence of such transactions.

* * * * * * *

However, were this merely a question of exchange transactions and complications I wou'd never have touched it. In fact only on February 11, 1892, did this come to my knowledge ; whereas, on December 7, 1891, when war threatened, I cabled about these speculations in order to throw discredit on the reliability of officials whose course was manifestly intended to bring a rupture between the two countries. It is because I believe that self-interest prompted the course of Minister Egan and Consul McCreery, and because the attitude of the United States Government was, in consequence of their misrepresentations, one of great injustice to Chili and thoroughly discreditable to the traditions and impulses of your great country and people that I have taken up the matter so earnestly. The magnitude of the Consul's transactions make it unlikely that he went into them alone. Besides it is undeniable that he was in constant communication with Mr. Egan by letter and telephone; that he was our best source of information during the revolution; that activity on his part betokened news favorable or unfavorable to the Congress'anal arms which was sure to come out shortly after news of heavy exchange transactions. There are other things which tend to implicate Mr. Egan in these exchange deals, though I frankly own that his shrewdness has made it impossible for me to get any proof against him. On the other hand his family interest in Balmaceda's success is undeniable, and further on I will refer to facts which prove his bad faith throughout and since the revolution.

I return to exchange. During the early months of the uprising Mr. Egan's news to Consul McCreery was invaluable to him and a basis for sure operations. At any rate he then made gains right along for every mail.   I have furnished proof that his profits were on

February 18, 1891	$11,735.93
March 4, 1891	2,014.70
March 18, 1891	12,240.19
April 1, 1891	2,808.95
April 18, 1891	1,864.04
April 29, 1891	5,767.44
Total	$36,431.25

After the definite occupation of Tarapaca by the Revolutionary forces, and the sinking of the Blanco Encalado, things did not pay so well. During May the Consul was losing heavily.   For the European mail of May 13, 1891, he had bought £31,000 in various amounts and rates for $463,797.44, and had been compelled to sell for only $453,834.80.   Loss $9,963.64, making a total loss through Mr. Neckelman alone of $21,644.49.

When the May 13th losses were looming up, the Itata appeared in San Diego.   The Consul might effectively prevent her sailing with or for the arms.   On May 7, he went to the Intendencia (Governor's office) heard a few questions propounded to the Directors of the South American S. S. Co., and then and there in ink signed a dispatch drawn up in lead pencil addressed to Secretary Blaine, aiming at the seizure of the Itata by the United States Government.   Further, that cable, not in his handwriting, was sent to the State telegraph office by Intendente Viel. From there it was transferred to the Transandine Telegraph Co., to be forwarded ; but mark you "at the expense of the Intendente Viel."   An official message of the United States Government written probably by interested parties, not by the Consul ; emanating not from the Consulate, but from the Governor's dispatching ; sent not by the United States Consul, but by the Dictator's satellite ; paid for with money stolen from the people of Chili.   This is true, and yet it is not the only instance when an official cable to your Government was paid for by other than the proper parties.

The object of the Itata cable was to assist Balmaceda and also because the Consul knew that failure to secure arms would drive exchange down.   Other interest in the Dictator's success he may also have had.   Mr. Egan's son certainly had ; and hence one is not surprised to find that the Hon. Patrick Egan sought to give Balmaceda a cable line to Callao to further his ends ; that he cabled his urgent request for the sale of a cruiser, that he repeatedly asserts the perfect order maintained through terrorism, flogging, incarceration and assassination ; that he sought by silence to lead the U. S. Government to believe in the legality of a Congress designated by the farce of an election ; that he heralds the unanimity with which the would-be Presidential candidate was designated ; that he is careful to correct false assertions sent by cable only by letter, etc.

Minister Egan and Consul McCreery, whose motives you may gather from the foregoing, succeed admirably in making Admirals McCann and Brown, Capts. Schley and Evans, and others of the Navy take their cue from them.

A gentleman from Santiago told me that Mr. Egan, when they were cut off from Valparaiso, assured him the U. S. Government would get the first news of effective movements because he had advised Admiral Brown to watch the fleet and report. He certainly did.   On the afternoon of August 20th he ran out to Quinteros and came back flying.   He at once sent an officer to cable his cipher message to Washington.   That officer, H. G. L. Dyer, at the same time handed in to the Central & South American Telegraph Co., a dispatch for the N. Y. Herald (which must have been read by the Intendente, since it bears his signature "O. Viel" as a countersign to allow of its being forwarded), giving in plain English, which he thoroughly understood, the results of the San Francisco's observations.   *   *   *   On the strength of that news troops were hurried out of Concon, a bloody battle followed, but owing to its severity could not be followed up by the Congressionalists, and so a second great sacrifice was made necessary in Placilla.   This second carnage would have been avoided had the attacking party been able to reach the railroad line to prevent the incoming of troops from San Iago and the South, as but for the San Francisco's news would have happened.   The 1,400 men killed in Placilla directly owe their death to the interference of the U. S. Navy; indirectly, I believe, to the presence of such unworthy representatives as you have had here in Minister Egan and Consul McCreery.

After reading the foregoing no one will be surprised that the people of Chili felt sorely aggrieved at our representatives and our people, and in their excitement made an unwarranted assault upon the crew of the Baltimore at Valparaiso. Attorney General Miller, in obedience to the dictates of Egan and McCreery ordered the seizure of the Itata in San Deigo harbor when he knew or ought to have known that she had in nowise violated our laws of neutrality. It was done to prevent her from carrying the arms and ammunition which were on board the Robert and Minnie, to the Congressional forces.

This disgraceful record, however, did not end here. The final action of President Harrison was a fitting conclusion and ample proof that he was anxious to uphold the Dictator if he could only find an excuse that would give him the popular support of the people. His share in this transaction was clearly set forth in the Democratic text book of 1892, as follows :

HARRISON'S "JUST-IN-TIME" MESSAGE.

The closing chapter in the story of the Baltimore episode must be read by every American with a feeling of shame that the Chief Executive of this Great Republic could have been induced for the furtherance of his own political ambition to resort to such measures for the humiliation of a weak and almost defenseless neighboring power.

President Harrison and his advisers were fully informed as to the difficulties in the way of overcoming popular prejudice with which the new government of Chili was laboring in the effort to bring about a satisfactory termination of the controversy. President Montt's friendly attitude had been demonstrated in a hundred different ways and there was no possible doubt as to the outcome of the incident. Secretary Blaine was confident that the affair would be amicably settled within a few days, and in justice to him it should be said he took no part in urging upon the President the necessity for immediate action.

In this situation of affairs, the President, on January 21, forwarded to the Chilian Government through Minister Egan his famous " ultimatum," in which he declared that unless the offensive parts of the dispatch of December 11, embracing Chili's defense of her attitude, were not "at once withdrawn and a suitable apology offered," he would have no other course open to him " except to terminate diplomatic relations with the government of Chili." Various other vague threats were conveyed in this document, which was cabled entire to Minister Egan, with instructions to " furnish to the Minister of Foreign Affairs a full copy of this note." Minister Egan did not deliver the ultimatum at the foreign office in Santiago until the 23d. Answer was at once made asking for two days' delay in replying—i. e., until Monday—as President Montt was absent in the mountains.

President Harrison did not wait even for the Chilian authorities to read the ultimatum. He at once set to work upon an incendiary message to Congress, to be accompanied by such correspondence as he saw fit to make public at the time. The message has been well described as "an Indianapolis brief in a suit for damages, rather than a diplomatic state paper." It was studiously insulting to the Chilians from first to last. It insisted that the attack on the sailors' of the Baltimore was an expression of general Chilian hostility to the United States, in spite of the solemn disavowals of the Chilian Government. It treated the findings of the Chilian courts as unworthy of credit, and the assertions of the Chilian officials as unworthy of belief. It declared the President's conviction that the Chilian Government did not intend to take any steps toward making proper reparation for the assault upon the sailors and the insult to the American flag.

This message was sent to Congress early Monday morning, just four days after the ultimatum had been dispatched to Minister Egan. It was read in both Houses of Congress amid absolute silence, and was followed with the closest attention by Senators and Representatives and by thousands of citizens who crowded the galleries, to learn from the President's own words the exact measure of the peril to the country's peace. When the reading had been concluded, both Houses adjourned, in order to give time for proper consideration of the matter before taking action in compliance with the President's recommendations. In the hours that followed, leading men of both parties expressed their willingness to stand by the President in any measures necessary to preserve the honor of the nation. The newspapers throughout the country the next morning printed the President's message in full and copious extracts from the correspondence. The situation was generally believed to be very grave.

Then came the crash. It became known that before noon of Monday a full and ample apology had been received from the Chilian Government, including an offer to leave the question of reparation to the Supreme Court of the United States; and, in addition, the shameful fact was made public that this communication had been received at the State Department even before the President's Message was read in Congress. A semi-official explanation of the facts in connection with the receipt of the apology was made at the White House, and was to the effect that the message was received "too late to have a translation made" before the convening of Congress.

But these statements and other similar explanations subsequently offered deceived no one. The facts stood clearly revealed. In general public estimation, the President's action in deliberately suggesting to Congress the making war on a weak antagonist, without asking, up to the latest moment, whether an apology had been received, constituted a fitting close to a controversy carried on by the Administration in such a manner as to place the United States in an unenviable attitude before the public opinion of the the world.

What a record is here presented. The Government of the United States attempting to defeat the efforts of the people of a sister republic to overthrow a cruel despot, recover their liberties and restore their government, at the instigation of a minister, whose son had large government contracts at stake and a consul whose profits on exchange were dependent upon the result.

HAWAIIAN ISLANDS.

The record of the Republican administration in its relation with the government of Hawaii was still more reprehensible.

The facts relative to our diplomatic dealings with this government were tersely and clearly stated by the Hon. James B. McCreary of Kentucky, chairman of the Committee on Foreign Relations, in a speech in the House of Representatives on February 1, 1894. He said:

Saturday, the 14th of January, 1893, the queen of the Hawaiian Islands announced her intention to proclaim a new constitution, as King Kamehameha did in 1864, and as King Kalakaua did in 1887; but on the same day, in deference to the earnest objections of her cabinet, she abandoned her purpose and caused a printed proclamation to be issued saying she had abandoned it, and declaring that the new constitution would be sought only according to the methods in the existing constitution, and her minister of foreign affairs so informed Minister Stevens, in writing, early Monday morning, the 16th of January, before any public meeting had been held.

    *   *   *   *   *   *

About fifty friends of annexation, mostly foreigners, used this relinquished purpose of the queen as a pretext, and met in a private office on Saturday and appointed a committee of safety, consisting of thirteen persons, seven of whom were aliens—four being Americans, two Englishmen, and one German. And under the management of this committee of safety, a mass meeting of citizens was held on Monday, the 16th of January, which simply protested against the queen's illegal purpose and denounced her effort to proclaim a new constitution, without saying anything with regard to the establishment of a provisional government and the overthrow of the existing government.

At the same time this meeting was being held another meeting was in session, which was largely attended, and which passed resolutions expressing gratification as to the queen's conduct in abandoning her purpose to proclaim a new constitution and declaring she would seek a new constitution only according to the methods prescribed in the existing instrument.   Immediately after the public meeting held under the auspices of the committee of safety on Monday evening had adjourned, that committee held a meeting and resolved that "a provisional government be created to exist until terms of union with the United States had been negotiated and agreed upon," and at the same time addressed a letter to Minister Stevens, in which they said: "We are unable to protect ourselves without aid, and therefore pray for the protection of the United States forces."

    *   *   *   *   *   *

Mr. Speaker, after the letter appealing for the protection of the United States forces was sent by the committee of safety to Minister Stevens, that committee became so panic-stricken because of their action that they sent three of the committee to see Minister Stevens and requested him not to land the United States forces until the next morning, but he told them the troops had been ordered to land and whether the committee is ready or not they shall land this evening.

    *   *   *   *   *   *

It appears that on Monday, the 16th of January, 1893, between 4 and 5 o'clock in the afternoon, by request of Minister Stevens, when the peace and quiet of Honolulu were undisturbed, and no riot had occurred, nor was imminent, and the people were attending to their usual avocations, and the lives and property of Americans were not threatened nor in jeopardy, and not an armed man was seen on the streets, the commander of the United States ship Boston landed a force of armed soldiers, with two Gatling guns, and stationed the main body of his soldiers in a hall previously secured by Minister Stevens across the street and only 76 yards from the Government buildings, and in plain view of the Queen's palace.

A British war ship and a Japanese war ship were anchored in the harbor near Honolulu, and although there were 12,000 Japanese and 1,300 English people on the islands, these ships did not land a soldier, and there was no request either by the British minister or the Japanese minister for soldiers to be landed.

At the time the naval force was used by Minister Stevens to overthrow the constitutional government of a friendly power, the United States Congress was in session, but no authority to use force was asked and none was granted.

    *   *   *   *   *   *

I submit also at this point the evidence of Mr. W. F. Wunderburg, who was offered the position of collector-general of customs under the Provisional Government:

The committee of safety met at the office of W. O. Smith in Fort street, Honolulu, at about 4 o'clock in the afternoon of Monday, the 16th day of January, 1893, for the purpose of discussing the necessary steps to be taken in forming a new government.

Shortly after the committee met it was decided that they were not ready for the landing of the American troops, and a committee of three, with Thurston as the chairman, was immediately dispatched to the American legation to prevail upon

Ir. Stevens to delay the landing of the Boston's men. The committee returned nortly and reported that Mr. Stevens had said to them: "Gentlemen, the troops f the Boston land this afternoon at 5 o'clock, whether you are ready or not."

The foregoing report of Mr. Stevens's reply to the committee is as near literal as an be remembered, and gives a correct idea of the meaning conveyed. The committee of safety adjourned to meet the same evening, at 7:30 o'clock, at the house f Henry Waterhouse, in Nuuanu Valley. The American troops landed at 5 o'clock, s Mr. Stevens had told the committee they would, and marched up Fort street to Ierchant, and along Merchant street, halting in King street, between the palace nd Government building.

At the time the men landed the town was perfectly quiet, business hours were bout over, and the people—men, women, and children—were in the streets, and othing unusual was to be seen except the landing of a formidable armed force with atling guns, evidently fully prepared to remain on shore for an indefinite length f time, as the men were supplied with double cartridge belts filled with ammunion, also haversacks and canteens, and were attended by a hospital corps with tretchers and medical supplies. The curiosity of the people on the streets was roused, and the youngsters, more particularly, followed the troops to see what it as all about. Nobody seemed to know, so when the troops found quarters the opulace dispersed, the most of them going to the band concert at the hotel, which ras very fully attended, as it was a beautiful moonlight evening, all who were not a the secret still wondering at the military demonstration,

Mr. Speaker, the next act in the annexation scheme was easily and quickly resented. The United States soldiers being favorably stationed, on the next ay, Tuesday, the 17th day of January, the committee of safety selected ten f their number to attend to the business. They, by different routes, between and 2 o'clock in the afternoon, proceeded to the government building, which ras unoccupied, to proclaim the new government; and an American citien, who had only been in Honolulu nine months, read the proclamation from he steps of the government building, almost without hearers; but the United tates marines, with rifles and artillery, were only 76 yards away. Within an our after the proclamation was read United States Minister Stevens recognized the 'rovisional Government, although the barracks and the police station were still in ossession of the Queen's forces.

The Queen, on being informed by one of the leaders and by members of her cabiet of what had been done in the presence of United States soldiers, yielded to the uperior forces, and sent her protest to the Provisional Government and appealed o the United States Government for justice, as follows:

"I, Liliuokalani, by the grace of God and under the Constitution of the Hawaii n Kingdom, Queen, do hereby solemnly protest against any and all acts done gainst myself and the constitutional Government of the Hawaiian Kingdom by ertain persons claiming to have established a Provisional Government of and for his kingdom.

"That I yield to the superior force of the United States of America, whose minster plenipotentiary, His Excellency John L. Stevens, has caused United States roops to be landed at Honolulu and declared that he would support the said Pro-'isional Government.

"Now, to avoid any collision of armed forces and perhaps the loss of life, I do nder this protest, and impelled by said force, yield my authority until such time s the Government of the United States shall, upon the facts being presented to it, ndo the action of its representatives and reinstate me in the authority which I laim as the constitutional sovereign of the Hawaiian Islands.

"Done at Honolulu this 17th day of January, A. D. 1893.

"LILIUOKALANI, R.
"SAMUEL PARKER,
"*Minister of Foreign Affairs.*
"WM. H. CORNWELL,
"*Minister of Finance.*
"JNO. F. COLBURN,
"*Minister of the Interior.*
"A. P. PETERSON,
"*Attorney-General.*"

A protectorate was declared by Minister Stevens of the islands in the name of the United States, and the flag of the United States was hoisted over the Government building, and in two days after the Provisional Government was declared, annexation commissioners sailed from Honolulu to Washington.

If there was ever a transaction that in all its attending circumstances was suspicious, illegal, and indicative of intrigue it was this annexation scheme. If there was ever a just and proper executive act it was the withdrawal from the Senate of the proposed annexation treaty by President Cleveland for further examination and consideration.

    *   *   *   *   *   *

It has never been the practice of our Government to recognize revolutionary governments until they were supported by the people. For illustration of this practice, I need only refer to two recent cases. When the revolution in Brazil occurr d in 1889, our Minister was instructed to recognize the Republic, "so soon as a majority of the people of Brazil should have signified their assent to its establishment and maintenance;" and during the revolution in Chili in 1891, our Minister was directed to "recognize the new government if it was accepted by the people." Even in Europe, when it was proposed that the provinces of Savoy and Nice, which had for years belonged to the Italian Kingdom, should be ceded to France, it was expressly provided that the assent of the people should be obtained before annexation to France should occur, and under a plebescite a very full vote was polled, and a very large majority of the electors voted in each of the two province s for annexation, before it was consummated.

When the constitutional government of Hawaiia was overthrown the citizens of Honolulu did not know what was transpiring, and the thousands of people who inhabit the other islands did not hear what had occurred until several days afterward; and it is known beyond doubt that a very large majority of the people of the Hawaiian Islands, having the right to vote under the constitution of 1887, never avored and do not now favor the Provisional Government or the proposed annexation ot the United States, nor to any other country.

This extraordinary summary makes conspicuous not a revolution, but a conspiracy. There was no evidence of a wide-spread discontent or dissatisfaction with the existing government, and there was no popular uprising against the head of the government. The people did not seem to be in the movement, and the public meeting which was held on the 16th of January was not to declare in favor of the provisional gov rnment, but to oppose the promulgation of the new constitution. In its inception, progress, and consummation the entire affair seems to have been a conspiracy on the part of a few for. igners, against the people as well as the government of Hawaii, and in their work they were aided and supported by the American Minister and the naval forces of the United States, their object being to get possession of the government, and to annex the islands to the United States.

The conduct of Minister Stevens shows conspicuously that nearly one year before the eventful period when he hoisted the flag of the United States at Honolulu and proclaimed a protectorate, he was studying annexation quite as closely as he was diplomatic duty. As far back as the 8th day of March, 1892, in a letter addressed to the Secretary of State, after referring to the possibility that the existing Government of Hawaii might be overturned by an orderly and peaceful revolution, he said: "I desire to know how far the present Minister and naval commander may deviate from established i ternational rules and prece !ents in the contingency indicated in the first part of this dispatch."

On the 19th day of November, 1892, about two months before the movement looking to the subversion of the Hawaiian Government was made, and annexation to the United States attempted, in a long letter to the Secretary of State he refers to the loss of the owners of sugar plantations and mills in the Hawaiian Islands, and the depreciation of other property caused by the passage of the McKinley bill, and declared as follows:

"Unless some positive measure of relief be granted, the depreciation of 'sugar property here will continue to go on. Wise, bold action of the United States will rescue the property holders from great loss. * * * One of two courses seems absolutely necessary to be followed: Either bold and vigorous measures for annexation, or a 'customs union' and an ocean cable from the California coast to Honolulu or Pearl Harbor, properly ceded to the United States, with an implied but not necessarily stipulated American protectorate over the islands."

He reached his climax on the 1st day of February, 1893, when he wrote to the State Department:

"The Hawaiian pear is now fully ripe, and this is the golden hour for the United States to pluck it."

When Mr. Cleveland assumed for the second time his high office, he at once withdrew the proposed treaty of annexation and dispatched an able and trusted agent to Hawaii to ascertain and report the true history of the affair. Commissioner Blount was not slow in discovering the conspiracy by which the government of the Queen had been overthrown and the treacherous part taken by Minister Stevens· He ordered down the American flag, under the protection of which the conspirators were masquerading. Our national emblem does not stand for piracy, but for right and justice, and the act of Commissioner Blount in ordering it down when it had been raised for the first time in support of a conspiracy against a friendly but helpless power, was not only an act of patriotism but an example to the people of the civilized nations of the world of the greatness and grandeur of our republican institutions.

No more patriotic message was ever sent to Congress than that which President Cleveland, delivered when informing the two Houses of his action and the motives which influenced the same.   He said :

"By an act of war, committed with the participation of a diplomatic representative of the United States and without authority of Congress, the Government of a feeble but friendly and confiding people has been overthrown. A substantial wrong has thus been done which a due regard for our national character as well as the rights of the injured people requires we should endeavor to repair. The provisional government has not assumed a republican or other constitutional form, but has remained a mere executive council or oligarchy, set up without the assent of the people. It has not sought to find a permanent basis of popular support and has given no evidence of an intention to do so. Indeed, the representatives of that government assert that the people of Hawaii are unfit for popular government and frankly avow that they can be best ruled by arbitrary or despotic power.

"The law of nations is founded upon reason and justice, and the rules of conduct governing individual relations between citizens or subjects of a civilized state are equally applicable as between enlightened nations. The considerations that international law is without a court for its enforcement, and that obedience to its commands practically depends upon good faith, instead of upon the mandate of a superior tribunal, only give additional sanction to the law itself and brand any deliberate infraction of it not merely as a wrong but as a disgrace. A man of true honor protects the unwritten word which binds his conscience more scrupulously, if possible, than he does the bond a breach of which subjects him to legal liabilities ; and the United States, in aiming to maintain itself as one of the most enlightened of nations, would do its citizens gross injustice if it applied to its international relations any other than a high standard of honor and morality, on that ground the United States can not properly be put in the position of countenancing a wrong after its commission any more than in that of consenting to it in advance. On that ground it can not allow itself to refuse to redress an injury inflicted through an abuse of power by officers clothed with its authority and wearing its uniform ; and on the same ground, if a feeble but friendly state is in danger of being robbed of its independence and its sovereignty by a misuse of the name and power of the

United States, the United States can not fail to vindicate its honor and its sense of justice by an earnest effort to make all possible reparation.

"These principles apply to the present case with irresistible force when the spe - cial conditions of the Queen's surrender of her sovereignty are recalled. She surrendered not to the provisional government, but to the United States. She surrendered not absolutely and permanently, but temporarily and conditionally, until such time as the facts could be considered by the United States. Furthermore, the provisional government acquiesced in her surrender in that manner and on those terms, not only by tacit consent, but through the positive acts of some members of that government who urged her peaceable submission, not merely to avoid bloodshed, but because she could place implicit reliance upon the justice of the United States, and that the whole subject would be finally considered at Washington."

Contrast the uses to which our naval forces were put by Mr. Harrison's Administration and the policy which has been pursued since Mr. Cleveland was returned to power. During Mr. Harrison's they were pledged to defend and uphold the throne of a half savage King in a far off island ; they were used to bolster up the waning cause of a Dictator, over a free people ; and to overthrow a weak and defenseless government and set up an oligarchy in its stead.

Under the latter, in the harbors of Brazil, they were used to protect the commerce of the United States from interference and to preserve to the tradesmen of the civilized world the right to secure food and drink without molestation or harm Never was such homage paid to the Stars and Stripes as when the tradespeople of all nations sought its shelter and welcomed, with joy, its approach, when those of their own Government were within hailing distance and easy reach. At this time and in this work it ceased to be the flag of a nation and became, what it really is, the emblem of civilization and humanity.

INDIAN SCHOOLS.

Appropriations for Same not Sectarian.

The efforts of the Republican party to rekindle the fires of religious fanaticism and make political capital out of the appropriations for the education of the Indian children at private schools upon reservations where no Government schools have been established, merits, and should receive, the rebuke of all fair minded citizens. A more praiseworthy work was never undertaken. The Republican party in the Fifty-first Congress made the same appropriations for which they now seek to prejudice certain elements against the Democratic party. The same appropriations were made in the Fifty-second Congress, not only without the opposition of Republicans, but with their hearty approval. In fact, no one ever thought of raising any opposition to the appropriations for contract schools until it was thought that some political capital might be made out of it. The reappearance of that religious intolerance and fanaticism which rises like a ghost every few years to haunt the fears of a few narrow and weak-minded persons, was seized by the Republican members of Congress as a favorable time to blow their demagogical horns, in the hopes of capturing a few votes. The effort to induce the people to believe that Congress made large appropriations for the support of sectarian schools is a deliberate falsehood. Not a single appropriation has ever been made to any sectarian institution. The items which it is sought to torture into such appropriations were simply appropriations of certain sums to enable the Secretary of the Interior and the Commissioner of Indian Affairs to contract with certain private individuals for the yearly schooling of a certain number of Indian children.

The following is the form of all the appropriations complained of:

"For education and support of one hundred Chippewa boys and girls at Saint John's University and at Saint Benedict's Academy, in Stearns County, State of Minnesota, at one hundred and fifty dollars each per annum, and for the education and support of one hundred Indian pupils at St. Paul's Industrial School at Clontarf, in the State of Minnesota, thirty thousand dollars."

The Indians are the wards of the Nation, and the policy of educating their children so that they may be prepared for citizenship, which they soon must inevitably assume, is not only wise but should be highly commended. The policy of taking the Indian children away from their homes in the far West and sending them to the East has not proven humane or beneficial. The establishment of schools at or near the reservations was much to be preferred because it puts an end to the fraudulent practices that were indulged in by the agents of Eastern schools in getting possession of the children, and because of the civilizing influence upon the parents.

Mr. Holman touchingly pictured the cruel practice of tearing the Indian children from their parents and the benefits that would accrue by patronizing the schools that were nearest to their homes. He said:

"My friend from Pennsylvania [Mr. Mahon] says there has been no complaint of late years about children being taken away from the Indian reservation and sent to remote schools in the East. The gentleman labors under a misapprehension. If there is anything that creates dissatisfaction and wretchedness on your Indian reservations, it is this snatching away of the Indian children from their homes and their parents. You hear that complaint all along the line in the Indian reservations. The Indian is devoted to his children.

"Parental affection is a universal instinct, and a strong one among the Indian tribes. I was told a few years ago by a Mennonite teacher (the Mennonites are great missionaries and eager to benefit mankind) that he had been sent out by his people, living in Kansas, to establish a school at an old abandoned fort called Cantonment, in the old Indian territory, and he had gathered around him quite a large number of children of the Arapahoes and Cheyennes, neither of which tribes, as gentlemen know, are very highly civilized yet.

"He told me there never was a day that he could not look up at the windows of his school room without seeing some mother or father or some other relative of the children looking in for the purpose of seeing that their children were safe. And when I was at Rosebud, S. Dak., an old lady came, as the agent, Mr. Wright, told me, a distance of 90 miles, footsore and weary, for the purpose of seeing her little girl. He told me that she made this weary journey twice a year for this purpose of seeing her little girl at the school at Rosebud.

"This old lady came to the door of the school room, and her little girl came out to her. They went out upon the prairie and sat down. They did not seem to talk much to each other; but after they had sat there together for half an hour the child returned to the school room and the old mother got up and started homeward on her weary journey. Now, gentlemen, consider the agony of the old mother if her little girl was taken away by the agent of some Eastern institution in the name of philanthropy, when the little one would even, if in after years she returned to her, be lost to her. Is there any philanthropy in this? [Applause.] I venture to say that no well-authenticated case can be found throughout all your Eastern Indian school system where any Indian father or mother has voluntarily surrendered a child. In the name of common humanity let the Indian children be educated among their people, elevating at once the whole tribe."

It was this feeling of humanity that prompted many charitably-disposed persons to found schools near the homes of the Indians. The Government, instead of building houses and employing teachers at all points, simply availed itself of schools established by individuals and paid to the proprietors of the same an amount much less than it would have cost to have established Government schools.

It is no more an appropriation for the maintenance of a sectarian school than if a parent should send his child to a Presbyterian, to a Baptist, or to a Catholic school and pay the regular tuition, &c., therefor.

It may be asked why the Government does not build school houses, employ teachers and conduct its own schools, instead of patronizing private ones. The answer is very simple; it would not be wise or economical to do so. These schools at no distant day must all give way before the advancing column of civilization and settlements, and it is best that the Government should not, by an extravagant expenditure of money, prepare permanently for a thing which in its nature will only be temporary.

The fraud that is attempted to be practiced upon the voters of the country by publishing what, it is pretended, was a vote for and against the appropriations for the support of sectarian institutions, is a shameful and bare-faced one. We have shown that no such appropriations were incorporated in the bill, but even if it should be claimed that the appropriation of money to enable the officials of the department, to patronize such institutions was such, still the vote published had no connection whatever with such appropriations, but was upon a motion to lay an appeal from the decision of the Chair, upon a question of order, upon the table.

Mr. Geary of Iowa, after the bill had been reported by the Committee of the Whole House, moved to recommit the same with the following instructions:

Resolved, That the bill (H. R. 6913) "making appropriations for current and contingent expenses of the Indian Department and fulfilling treaty stipulations with various Indian tribes for the fiscal year ending June 30, 1895, and for other purposes," be recommitted to the Committee on Indian Affairs, with instructions to report the same back to the House forthwith, amended as follows:

Striking out all of the bill relating to the Indian school, beginning with line 8, on page 50, and all of pages 51, 52, 53, 54, 55, 56, 57, and 58, and inserting in lieu thereof the following:

For support of Government Indian day and industrial schools, and the erection and repair of Government school buildings on Indian reservations and at places where the Government has established and is now maintaining Government Indian schools, and for each and every purpose necessary in the judgment of the Secretary of the Interior for the establishment and proper conduct of such schools, $2,225,000 : *Provided*, That pending the establishment of such schools on Indian reservations, the Secretary of the Interior may in his discretion, during the fiscal year 1895, authorize contracts to be made with established schools not conducted by the Government, for the education and support of Indian pupils and to pay therefor from this appropriation; and the Secretary of the Interior shall report to the first regular session of the Fifty-fourth Congress, in detail, all expenditures made and authorized by him under this appropriation : *Provided further*, That nothing herein shall be construed to prevent the sending of Indian children, at no expense to the United States, to schools not conducted by the Government.

Mr. O'Neil of Massachusetts made a point of order against the proposed instructions. The following proceedings then took place:

Mr. O'Neil of Massachusetts. I make the point of order, Mr. Speaker, that this amendment is out of order for the reason that such an amendment is new legislation, and would therefore not be in order as an amendment to the bill while being considered in Committee of the Whole House on the state of the Union. That being so according to the uniform rulings of this House, a motion to recommit, with instructions to report a certain amendment, is not in order if the proposed amendment would not be in order as an amendment to the bill. That has been held uniformly by Speaker Carlisle and other Speakers.

The Speaker. There is no question of that.

Mr. Burrows. If it was not in order in committee, of course it would not be in order now.

Mr. O'Neil of Massachusetts. I make the point that it is new legislation and not in order ; that it changes existing law and does not retrench expenditures.

* * * * * * *

The Speaker. It seems to the Chair that this is new legislation on the subject of Indian schools. Does the gentleman know of any provision by which such legislation may go on an appropriation bill except when it reduces expenditures ?

Mr. Cannon of Illinois. Wherein does it legislate ?

The Speaker. It provides——

Mr. Cannon of Illinois. It appropriates.

The Speaker (continuing):

For the support of Government Indian day and industrial schools and the erection and repair of Government school buildings on Indian reservations and at places where the Government has established and is now maintaining Government Indian schools, and for each and every purpose necessary, in the judgment of the Secretary of the Interior, for the establishment and proper conduct of such schools, $2,250,000.

Mr. Cannon of Illinois. Then I just want to call the attention of the Chair——

The Speaker. And then it says :

That pending the establishment of such schools on Indian reservations the Secretary of the Interior may, in his discretion, during the fiscal year 1895, authorize contract to be made with established schools.

That authorizes him to make temporary contracts for the establishment of schools.

Mr. Cannon of Illinois. Yes, sir. May I call the attention of the Chair to one thing. because I think the Chair has not examined it or the bill itself. This resolution provides for all the Government schools that the bill provides for and for a part of the contract schools temporarily that the bill provides for, the Chair will find; and if there is legislation in one there is legislation in the other. And the Chair will find, further, that there is only appropriation in either.

Mr. Burrows. These contract schools are already provided for by law.

The Speaker. These are contract schools; but this proposes to give permission to make contracts from other schools.

Mr. Cannon of Illinois. Ah, but this provides for contract schools in any degree if no Government school be near.

The Speaker. Then you propose legislation to go beyond this appropriation?

Mr. Cannon of Illinois. Oh, no.

The Speaker. It must be one or the other.

Mr. Cannon of Illinois. We do not legislate at all in that resolution within the meaning of Rule XXI. We only provide in that instruction for the expenditure of the money appropriated here for the coming fiscal year, nothing more or less, and no broader in that respect than the bill itself.

The Speaker. As the Chair understands it, under the present law, under provisions contained in appropriation bills, the Government is engaged in supporting the education of Indians by contracts with existing schools.

Mr. Cannon of Illinois. And by Government schools and contract boarding schools.

The Speaker. Does the proposition contemplate abandoning the making of contracts.

Mr. Cannon of Illinois. So far as this particular affair provided for in the resolution is concerned, I will say to the Chair no, because then it provides an appropriation of money for Government schools, and provides that while school houses are being built that the Secretary of the Interior may contract for the education of the children with established schools not owned by the Government. Even if the permanent law did provide for contract schools it is in the discretion of Congress, in whole or in part, to withhold appropriations, although the law might be an inch thick. But this resolution does utilize for the coming fiscal year a portion of this money for contract schools. But suppose it did not utilize any of it, it would merely be a failure to appropriate for an object that the Government has heretofore appropriated for.

The Speaker. The Chair thinks so. The Chair thinks that the scope and intent of this is to get away from the contract schools and establish schools by the Government. Therefore the Chair holds that it would not be in order as an amendment, and not being in order as an amendment, it is not in · rder by way of indirection, b cause that which cannot be done directly cannot be done indirectly.

Mr. Cannon of Illinois. I respectfully appeal from the decision of the Chair.

The Speaker. The question is, Shall the decision of the Chair stand as the judgment of the House?

Mr. Springer. I move to lay the appeal on the table.

Mr. Burrows. The gentleman has moved that the appeal be laid on the table, and of course that is not debatable.

The Speaker. It is not debatable. The previous question has been ordered, and all collateral questions must be decided without debate after the previous question is ordered.

The Speaker. The question is on laying the appeal on the table.

The House divided; and there were—ayes 171, noes 35.

Mr. Cannon of Illinois. I ask for the yeas and nays.

The question was taken on ordering the yeas and nays, and 35 members voted in favor thereof; not a sufficient number.

Mr. Burrows. I ask for tellers on ordering the yeas and nays.

Tellers were ordered, 40 members voting therefor; and the Speaker appointed Mr. Cannon of Illinois and Mr. Holman.

The tellers reported—ayes 47, a sufficient number; so the yeas and nays were ordered.

The Speaker appointed to act as tellers at the desk Mr. Houk and Mr. Holman.

The question was taken; and there were—yeas 158, nays 58, answered "present" 1, not voting 135 ; as follows :

YEAS, 158.—Abbot, Alexander, Allen, Apsley, Arnold, Bailey, Baker Kans., Bankhead, Barwig, Bell Colo., Bell Tex., Berry, Black Ill., Black Ill., Branch, Bretz, Broderick, Brookshire, Bryan, Bunn, Bynum, Cabaniss, Campbell, Cannon Cal., Capehart, Catchings, Causey, Childs, Clarke Mo., Clarke Ala., Cobb Ala., Cobb Mo., Cockrell, Colleen, Cogswell Conn, Coombs, Cooper Fla., Cooper Ind., Cooper Tex., Cox, Crain, Crawford, Davis, DeArmond, DeForest, Denson, Dinsmore, Dockery, Donovan, Draper, Dunn, Dunphy, Durborrow, Edmunds, English Cal., Enloe, Epes, Everett, Fithian, Forman, Fyan, Geary, Goldzier, Gorman, Grady, Graham, Griffin, Hall Minn., Hall Mo., Hammond, Hare, Harris, Harter, Heard, Henderson N. C., Hermann, Holman, Hooker Miss., Hunter, Hutcheson, Ikirt, Izlar, Kem, Kyle, Lane, Lapham, Latimer, Lawson, Layton, Lester, Livingston, Lynch, Maddox, Martin Ind., McCulloch, McDannold, McDearmon, McEttrick, McGann, McKaig, McKeighan, McLaurin, McMillin, McRae, Meyer, Money, Montgomery, Morgan, Neil, Oates, Ogden, Outhwaite, Page, Patterson, Pearson, Pendleton Tex., Pendleton W. Va., Pickler, Pigott, Price, Reilly, Richards Ohio, Richardson Mich., Richardson Tenn., Ritchie, Robbins, Russell Ga., Ryan, Sayers, Shell, Sibley, Snodgrass, Somers, Sperry, Springer, Stallings, Stevens, Stockdale, Strait, Straus, Swanson, Talbert S. C., Tarsney, Tate, Taylor Ind., Terry, Tracey, Turner Ga., Tyler, Walker, Warner, Weadlock, Wheeler Ala., Williams Ill., Williams Miss., Wise, Woodard.

NAYS, 58.—Adams Ky., Aldrich, Baker N. H., Bingham, Blair, Boen, Bowers Cal., Burrows, Cannon Ill., Cooper Wis., Cousins, Curtis Kans., Dolliver, Dolittle, Ellis Oregon, Funk, Gardner, Gear, Hager, Haugen, Henderson Ill., Hepburn, Hopkins Pa., Hudson, Hulick, Hull, Johnson Ind., Johnson N. Dak., Kiefer, Lacy, Linton, Loud, Loudenslager, Mahon, Marsh, Marvin N. Y., Northway, Paynter, Pence, Perkins, Post, Ray, Robinson Pa., Settle, Shaw, Smith, Stephenson, Stone, C. W., Stone, W. A., Storer, Strong, Sweet, Tawney, Thomas, Updegraff, Van Voorhis Ohio, Waugh, Wilson Wash.

ANSWERED "PRESENT," 1.—McCleary, Minn.

This vote upon a question of order has been falsely published as a vote in favor of appropriating Government funds for the support of sectarian institutions. The campaign liar has certainly started out early and with renewed strength and courage.

THE FRIEND OF THE SOLDIER.

The Democratic Party and its Relations to the Union Soldiers and Sailors and the Pension System.

From forum, tribune, and in legislative halls the enemies of honest administrative methods have hurled at the Democratic party the accusation that it always was and is now the enemy of the old soldier, and that the very existence of the pension system in the future depends upon the restoration of the Republican party to power, thus perennially insulting the intelligence of the great public conscience for political advantage solely, as each campaign approaches, and striving to befog the public judgment in the consideration of a simple question of the honest administration of the law.

To the charge that the present administration is unfriendly and ungenerous to the Federal soldiery, let us address ourselves. With alacrity can the Democratic party take up the gauge of battle on these lines and go before the country upon the record with supreme confidence in that sense of fair play, love of justice and genius for the right inherent in the generous and intelligent manhood of the nation, that will not be swerved by the howling dervishes of misrule from its approbation of honest public servants who exemplify in the proper administration of the laws of the country that "a public office is a public trust."

The attitude of the Democratic party is best voiced by the sentiments contained in the National Democratic platforms from 1864 to 1892 and the several State platforms which urge liberal pensions to be granted as a right in accordance with the law and not in violation of it ; and also in the friendly and generous sentiments of President Cleveland, expressed towards the deserving volunteer soldiers, which abound in the many messages that from time to time he has sent to Congress :

CLEVELAND AND PENSIONS AND THE DEMOCRATIC RECORD IN CONGRESS.

Actions speak louder than words. What have the Democratic President and party done since the war to make good their promises, to show a sincere sense of the sacred debt due the defenders of the Union and merit the confidence of a grateful, generous country? The United States statutes furnish the proper answer.

(1). Cleveland approved the act of Aug. 4, 1886, increasing the pensions of 10,030 cripples, armless and legless veterans, from $24 to $30; $30 to $36, and from $37.50 to $45 per month.

(2). Act of March 19, 1886, considering the past alone, increased from $8 to $12 per month the pensions of 79,989 widows and dependents on the rolls at that time, as well as the tens of thousands who have since been placed there. These 79,989 certificates were issued by a Democratic Commissioner of Pensions without one cent of expense or a moment's unnecessary delay to these deserving beneficiaries, and with no hindrance to other just claims pending before the office.

(3). Act of May 15, 1886, granting certificates of discharge to members of the Missouri Home Guards, whose claims were adjudicated by the Hawkins-Taylor Commission.

(4). Act of May 17, 1886, amending the reports of the War Department, which discriminated against a large and worthy class of soldiers, relieving thousands of unfortunate veterans of the hardships, worked by the resting of charges against them, based upon technical errors in the records.

(5). Act of January 29, 1887, benefiting about 30,000 survivors and widows of the Mexican War, to whom more than $15,000,000 have been disbursed.

(6). Act of June 7, 1888, granting arrears to widows from the date of death of the husband, and providing that all United States officers authorized to administer oaths should administer all oaths required to be made in pension cases in the execution of vouchers for pensions free of charge—a just and humane act. This act in the past alone benefited more than 200,000 soldiers' widows, and was inspired by that universal regard for the decencies of life, which urged that this worthy class should suffer no discrimination in refraining from an unseemly scramble for pensions, ere ceased the last strains of the requiem over the dead soldier-husband's remains.

(7). Act of August 14, 1888, for the relief of certain appointed or enlisted men in the navy or marine corps from technical charges against them in the records, which stood between them and pensions to which they were justly entitled.

(8). Act of August 27, 1888, increasing pensions on account of deafness.

(9). Act of February 12, 1889, granting an increase in pension from $72 to $100 per month to all persons who in the line of duty, in the naval or military service of the United States, lost both hands. More than thirty of this extremely unfortunate class were benefited by this act immediately on the date of its passage.

(10). Act of March 1, 1889, relating to the payment of pensions to the widows or dependent heirs where subsequent to the issuance of the check the pensioner dies.

(11). Act of March 2, 1889, removing certain technical charges in the record, and relieving a large and meritorious class of volunteer and regular soldiers of the late war and the war with Mexico, placing them in an honorable light before posterity and the comrades with whom they fought side by side; and

(12). Act of December 21, 1893, making a pension a vested right.

During the four years of the last Republican administration President Harrison approved only seven acts which may, by any stretch, be characterized as general pension bills, and one, the Army Nurse Bill, was passed by a Democratic House.

Since 1875, the year of Democratic accession to power in the House of Representatives, in addition to the foregoing general acts, all of which were approved by a Democratic President, Democratic Houses of Representatives have initiated every pension law now upon the statute books, save during the brief period of the notorious (47th) Keifer Congress, and the equally notorious Billion Dollar (51st) Reed Congress. Democratic Houses passed:

(1). Act of August 15, 1876, issuing artificial limbs or commutation therefor to disabled soldiers and seamen, and providing transportation for the purpose of having the same properly fitted.

(2). Act of February 28, 1877, increasing the pension of those who lost both an arm and a leg.

(3). Act of March 9, 1878, granting pensions on account of service in the war of

1812 and the Revolutionary war, requiring a service of but 14 instead of 60 days on the part of survivors of the war of 1812, and granting pensions to widows regardless of date of marriage to soldiers of this war. It also granted pensions to widows of soldiers of the Revolutionary war on a service of 14 days. Former laws required marriage prior to the treaty of peace in the case of widows of the war of 1812.

(4). Act of June 17, 1878, increasing to $72 per month the pensions of those who lost both hands, both feet, or the sight of both eyes incident to the service, and two years later.

(5). Act of June 16, 1880, giving $72 per month to the totally helpless from any cause incident to the service.

(6). Act of March 3, 1879, increasing to·$37.50, hip-joint amputations. This sum was afterwards increased to $45 per month by a Democratic House.

(7). A Democratic Congress passed the arrears of pension acts January 25 and March 3, 1879, generous measures which benefited more than 225,000 pensioners and at a single bound caused the annual pension roll to leap from $33,780,526.19 to $57,240,540.14. The Republican party had control of both Houses of Congress for more than ten years after the close of the war, but passed no legislation of this character. Both Houses became Democratic in 1879, and on the 21st of June of that year they passed the following amendment for the protection of pensioners and abolishing biennial medical examinations.

(8). Sec. 3 act of June 21, 1879. That sections 4771, 4772, and 4773, providing for biennial examinations of pensioners are hereby repealed: *Provided*, That the Commissioner of Pensions shall have the same power as heretofore to order a special examination whenever in his judgment the same may be necessary, but in no case shall a pension be withdrawn or reduced except upon notice to the pensioner and a hearing upon sworn testimony. * * * In order to provide for the speedy payment of arrearages of pension, the Secretary of the Treasury is hereby authorized and directed to issue immediately in payment thereof, as may be adopted, the legal tender currency now in the United States Treasury held as a special fund for the redemption of fractional currency, etc., etc. This statute was passed not only to provide for the large payment of arrears that would soon fall due, but to protect the pensioners against Republican Commissioners of Pensions who were then suspending pensions without notice or hearing, and in many instances upon malicious anonymous letters and unsworn statements of vindictive and malevolent persons, and reducing or dropping the names of pensioners from the rolls upon the mere verbal *ex parte* reports of secret agents.

(9). Act of December 21, 1893, making a pension a vested right.

(10). Act of February 26, 1881, for the protection of pensioners in soldiers' homes.

(11). Act of July 14, 1892, establishing an intermediate rate of pension between $30 and $72 per month, and fixing the rate at $50 for all who required frequent and periodical though not regular and constant personal aid and attendance.

(12). Act of August 5, 1892, granting pensions to army nurses and forbidding the demanding of a fee by claim agents for prosecuting this class of cases. This was a generous recognition of the noble heroism who, leaving home and loved ones behind, in self-sacrifice braved pestilence and hardship in every form to minister to the stricken in hospitals of the army, with danger for their constant fare and death their never absent companion.

(13). Act of July 4, 1884, which established the proper relations which should exist between attorneys and clients, and fixed by law the fees to be allowed in

ension cases. By this act a Democratic Congress placed the strong arm of the
.w between the helpless applicant for pension and the unblushing rapacity of the
orde of pension pettifoggers that op rated up to th s time.

Some idea may be gathered of the state of affairs when we reflect that in the
even years alone prior to the passage of the above act, 584 claim agents were prose -
ited for violations of one form or another of the penal statutes relating to pen-
ons, 355 were suspended, 248 disbarred, 138 dropped from the roster of attorneys.
id 64 convicted. This Democratic measure smoke l them out.

CLEVELAND'S VETOES OF PRIVATE PENSION ACTS.

During the twenty-four (24) years of uninterrupted Republican administration—
861 to 1885—2,001 private pension acts passed by Congress became laws, an aver-
ge of about 83 a year. During Lincoln's administration, 41 ; Johnson's, 431 ;
rant's, 490 ; Hayes's, 303 ; Garfield and Arthur's, 736. In the first three years of
resident Cleveland's former administration—1885 to 1888—out of 1,560 submitted
i him, 1,369 became laws, more than thirty-three times as many as during Lincoln's
iur years ; more than three times as many as Johnson's four years ; nearly three
mes as many as Grant's eight years ; four-and-a-half times as many as Hayes's
iur years ; and nearly twice as many as Garfield and Arthur's four years. The
verage yearly number of these private pension acts which became laws under
leveland's former administration was 456, five-and-a-half times the average annual
imber during the preceding Republican administrations.

PENSION STATISTIC.

The pension estimates for the current fiscal year, capitalized at 3 per cent, would
e the interest on about $5,500,000,000, a sum greater than the national debt of any
iuntry on earth, and nearly twice the debt of the United States at the close of
ie war.

$85,292,931.08 have been paid for pensions under the general law during the last
scal year. For the same time $68,259,537.18 were paid under the act of June 27,
890, while from 1871 to the present time the total disbursements on account of
ie war of 1812, Indian wars, and the Mexican war were but $55,896,433.38. The
isults of these wars increased the territory of the United States from less than
000,000 to 3,603,884 square miles. The Mexican service pension bill was not
issed until thirty-nine years after the close of that war. This recognition was
ven to the survivors of 1812 fifty-seven years after, and the Revolution fifty-nine
ears after the close of these respective wars.

Pensions thus far paid exceed the entire appropriations from the foundation
i the Government up to 1861. The pension appropriation for the current fiscal
ear is equal to the entire cost of the army, navy and pension establishments of
razil, China, Mexico, Norway, and Sweden and Spain combined ; or Germany,
lexico and Spain ; it exceeds that of Germany and Spain combined, and is almost
jual to that of Russia and Brazil. It is fifty million dollars more than the entire
xpenditures for the military and naval establishments of Germany ; twenty
iillion dollars more than that of Russia ; and equals three-fourths of the entire
xpenditure of Great Britain in maintaining its naval, military, pension and civil
st establishments. Twelve States in the Union receive 50 per cent more in pen-
on money than the cost of their entire school establishments. Maine and Ver-
iont received two-and-a-half times as much in pensions as they pay for schools.

The estimates for the payment of pensions for the coming fiscal year exceed the total assessed valuation of the real and personal property of twenty-five (25) States in the Union. There are 76,661 pensioners in the six States of Washington, Kansas, Nebraska, North and South Dakota, and Oregon, nearly three times as many pensioners as these States furnished soldiers (26,286) to the army. In the ten States that formed the Southern Confederacy there are 48,639 pensioners, and in the six border States 128,936, making in all 177,575 pensioners, receiving an aggregate of $28,428,759.42 in the old slave States. In the aggregate the 30th of June, 1894, 2,114,908 original pension claims have been filed since 1861. 1,438,134 of these have been allowed. Upwards of two billions of dollars have been paid in pensions, local bounties, and private patriotic centributions for the relief of the families of the soldiers since the war.

At the close of the year, June 30, 1894, there were 969,544 persons upon the pension rolls, a greater number than were mustered out of the service 29 years ago, and 300,000 more than there were troops actively engaged in the army at any one time during the war. At the close of this year there were 737,358 invalids on the pension rolls, 89,000 more than the number of soldiers reported present for active duty by Provost Marshal General Frye March 31, 1865, the number enrolled being 980,086 and the number absent 332,339. During the last year (1893) $1,872,178.53 were paid in attorneys' fees ALONE, and upwards of $20,000,000 went to these claim agents since 1865. Only three States in the Union (New York, Pennsylvania, and Ohio) had a total population in 1860 greater than the number of pension claims filed since the war; only five States (New York, Pennsylvania, Ohio, Illinois, and Virginia) at the beginning of the war had a total population greater than the number of pension claims allowed since the war; only nine States have now a total population greater than the total number of pension claims filed, and twenty-one States and Territories of the Union have a total population less than the number of unsettled claims still pending 29 years after the close of the rebellion.

NUMBER OF PENSIONERS AND AMOUNTS PAID PER CONGRESSIONAL DISTRICT.

In Indiana the average is 5,300 pensioners, receiving $900,264 per Congressional district.

In Ohio, 4,904, receiving $825,080 per district.

In Iowa, 3,464, receiving $561,437.

Pennsylvania, 3,193, receiving $505,911.

Illinois, 3,124, receiving $500,906.

Massachusetts, 3,100, receiving $529,326.

Wisconsin, 2,761, receiving $437,885.

Rhode Island, 2,111, receiving $234,400.

Minnesota, 2,329, receiving $372,205.

The average number of pensioners in each Congressional district in the United States is 2,711, and the average amount of pension paid in each Congressional district is $440,282.

Illinois furnished 1½ times the number of troops Indiana did, but has only 58 per cent of the number of pensioners, receiving only 56 per cent of the amount of money per district as that State. She sent 83 per cent of the number of troops Ohio did, but has only 64 per cent of the number of pensioners, receiving 61 per cent as much pension per district as this State.

Pennsylvania sent 1¾ times the number of troops Indiana did, and has only 60 per

ent of the number of pensioners, receiving 56 per cent of the amount of pension per
istrict as this State. She sent 108 per cent of the number of troops Ohio did, and
as only 65 per cent of the number of pensioners, receiving 61 per cent of the
mount per district as this State.

Iowa, Massachusetts, Wisconsin, Minnesota, and Rhode Island, respectively, receive 62, 59, 49, 41, and 26 per cent as much pension per Congressional district as
ndiana, and 68, 64, 53, 45, and 28 per cent, respectively, as Ohio.

Again, take the two Northern States which, since the war, have almost invariably
ast their electoral vote for the Democratic ticket (New Jersey and Connecticut).
n the former 2,563 pensioners receive $410,021 per Congressional district; in the
atter, 2,904 pensioners receive $335,088 per district.

The pensioners in the State of Indiana are receiving average annual pensions
equal to $169.87. In Ohio it is $168.25; in Iowa, $162.10; Illinois, $160.34; Minnesota, $159.81; Wisconsin, $158.60; Pennsylvania, $158.44, and in Rhode Island,
$111.04.

THE DEMOCRATIC RECORD IN THE PENSION OFFICE.

During the four years of Democratic administration—from 1885 to 1889—a little
over 80 per cent of all the claims filed were allowed. During the preceding Repub-
ican administration the average was but 78 per cent, and during the last Repub-
ican administration (Tanner and Raum) only 67 per cent of the claims filed were
allowed, notwithstanding the addition to the clerical force of the bureau of more
than 400 persons.

During the four years of Democratic administration—from 1885 to 1889—$296,-
458,741.25 were paid for pensions, fifteen and one-half millions more than were
paid during the fifteen years of Republican administration from 1861 to 1875, inclusive; and, including the estimates for the current fiscal year, Democratic administrations under Judge Lochren and General Black, have, in five years, disbursed
$5,750,000 more than all the Republican administrations in the twenty years
from 1861 to 1880 inclusive.

The total disbursements for pensions since 1861 were, in round numbers, $1,730,-
500,000. During sixteen (16) years of that time, counting the present Congress,
the Democratic party in the House of Representatives, under the leadership of
Randall, Carlisle and Crisp, originated appropriation bills for 64 per cent of this
amount, in round numbers $1,109,000,000; while during eighteen (18) years under
the control of the Republican party, but 36 per cent, in round numbers $621,000,000
were disbursed, or a net ratio of nearly 200 per cent in favor of the Democratic party.

Soldiers of the republic, does this show the Democratic party has been ungenerous to the heroic men who saved the flag from tarnish, or to their dependents?
Wherein have Democratic administrations been inimical to the pensioners of the
nation? Partisan Republicans in their cheeping criticisms strive for political effect
solely. How plain a tale will put the prevaricator down?

ACT OF JUNE 27, 1890.

The enormous increase in the annual pension roll, due to the lax construction of
the act of June 27, 1890, which caused the amount yearly expended to leap from
$89,000,000 in 1889 to $158,000,000 at a bound in 1893, is mainly responsible for the
criticisms of the patient tax-payers of the nation, who gravely question whether
this enormous sum was properly disbursed by a Republican administration.

The amount paid, $158,000,000, in the third year since the passage of this act almost equals in a single year the total amount paid under all existing laws during the eleven years of Republican rule, from 1861 to 1871 inclusive.

This law was passed in recognition of the difficulties in the way of tracing disabilities to service origin after a long lapse of time, and the fact that deserving soldiers who, in their advancing years, were suffering from affliction not of service origin, but which unfitted them to earn a support by manual labor, were deemed proper objects of the national beneficence, and in obedience to this generous impulse the act was passed. But it had its requirements and limitations. Section 2d of the act, which is as follows, determines these :

"Section 2. That all persons who served ninety days or more in the military or naval service of the United States during the late war of the rebellion, and who have been honorably discharged therefrom, and who are now or who may hereafter be suffering from a mental or physical disability of a permanent character, not the result of their own vicious habits, which incapacitates them for the performance of manual labor in such a degree as to render them unable to earn a support, shall, upon making due proof of the fact according to such rules and regulations as the Secretary of the Interior may provide, be placed upon the list of invalid pensioners of the United States, and be entitled to receive a pension not exceeding twelve dollars per month and not less than six dollars per month, proportioned to the degree of inability to earn a support," etc., etc.

It will be perceived that it is imperative that there shall have been a service of at least ninety days, an honorable discharge, and in the case of invalids it must be shown by competent evidence that the applicant for pension under this act must be disabled for the performance of manual labor by reason of mental or physical disability not due to his own vicious habits, rendering him unable in greater or less degree to earn a support by manual labor.

How has the Republican party accounted for its stewardship to the people of the nation in the execution of this law? Has it been the faithful custodian of the trust imposed upon it? While providing with prodigality for the deserving beneficiaries has it buttressed the entrance to the public treasury against the strain of the rapacious claim agents and the unworthy pretender? It is the purpose of this to show that the Republican Commissioners of Pensions let down all the bars of the national pasture field, enabling the bounty-jumpers and others equally unworthy to enter with impunity. Names were put upon the pension rolls regardless of the requirement of at least ninety days' service; the dishonorably discharged who tarnished the blue were pensioned; able-bodied applicants, rich in worldly store, but protesting mendicancy, were fed at the public table ; and those who by vice were reduced to the relics of a misspent life, were allowed to partake of the Nation's bounty that of right belonged alone to the worthy pensioners of the Republic. A Republican Commissioner of Pensions declared it his intention to raid the public treasury with steam-shovel and gravel-train, and "God help the surplus when he got up steam enough!"

Under the act of June 27, 1890, aside from the requisite service and honorable discharge, there is but one condition that can give any right to a pension, namely, "a mental or physical disability of a permanent character, not the result of their own vicious habits, which incapacitates them for the performance of manual labor in such a degree as to render them unable to earn a support."

Scarcely was the ink dry on the approval of the act when in open violation of both the spirit and the letter of the law, a Republican Secretary of the Interior, by rder No. 164, issued October 15, 1890, directed the Commis-ioner of Pensions that isabilities rendering claimants unable to earn a support in such a degree as would e rated under former laws at or above $6 and less than $12 should be rated the ame as like disabilities of service origi , and that all cases showing a pensionable isability which, if of service origin, would be rated at or above $12, shall be rated t $12 per month. And to show conclusively that the inability of the applicant to erform manual labor was not taken into consideration at all in the rating of cases nder this law, let us read the circular of the then Republican Medical Referee, ated December 10, 1890, to the Medical Division of the Pension Office, and ap-roved by the Commissioner of Pensions:

" The ratings recommended should be the same as if the disability or disabilities ere incurred in t e service, rating each disability separately." In a letter to the ommissioner of Pensions, dated May 23, 1893, this same Medical Referee, in aswer to inquiry as to the practice in rating act of June 27 cas s under the Repub-can administration, stated that " the inability of the applicant to perform manual bor was not taken into consideration."

Within three years from the promulgation of this Order 164, more than three-uarters of a million claims were filed under the act of June 27, 1890, and 459,155 ensioners were placed upon the rolls under it. Order 164 established a practice in 1e bureau which disregarded the basic requirements of the law, and put hundreds f thousands of pensioners upon the rolls whom Congress never intended to re-ard. The gratitude of the nation to its defenders was preyed upon, and the reasury robbed in the soldier's name.

Under laws prior to June 27, 1890, rates of pension were fixed without regard to 1e capacity of the pensioner to earn a support by manual labor, while under the ct of June 27, 1890,the condition was imperative that there must be a disability inca-acitating for the performance of manual labor to obtain a support. There are 21 isabi'ities not specified by law but fixed by the Commissioner of Pensions es-ablishing rates of pension under laws prior to June 27, 1890, which are rated at 12 and upwards; and by Order 164 were rated under the law of 1890 by the Re-ublican Commissioner at $12 per month. To illustrate:

The loss of an eye ; nearly total deafness of one ear and slight of other ; loss of 1umb and index finger ; or the loss of a thumb, finger and toe was rated at $12 er month or more ; then the mandate of the order and the practice under it was 1at a claimant under the act of 1890 should be rated at $12 per month, although ongress designed that no man should receive $12 per month except for disabilities hich render him wholly unable to earn a support by manual labor. Stiffness of a 1oulder, elbow, knee, ankle or wrist joint—do these render a man wholly unable perform manual labor ? Does the loss of an eye or the deafness of anear wholly 1capacitate one ? Such has been the practice of the bureau under Republican ad-inistrations, and millions of dollars of the people's money wrongfully paid out.

Loss of little toe and little finger and small varicocele, without complications, in-irred 20 years or longer after the close of the war, entitled the applicant, accord-g to Raum's practice, to the minimum rating under the act of June 27, 1890 1d men were pensioned for baldness, bunions, and corns. So flagrantly at vari-1ce with the requirements of the law of June 27, 1890, were the practices of the epublican Commissioner that the Republican Secretary of the Interior, just two 1onths after the rebuke administered by the Republican reverses of 1892, issued 1e decision of January 7, 1893, and sought to restore to something like a just basis the practice of the department under the act of June 27, 1890. This is known as the Weike decision, rescinding Order No. 164, and establishing the principle :

(1) That the basis of rates under the act of June 27, 1890, is inability to earn a support by reason of incapacity for manual labor due to disability not the result of vicious habits.

(2) Schedule of nominal rates will not be added together to make up a rate under said act, but the rate will be based on the combined effect of all the causes involved upon the applicant's capacity for manual labor. (Assistant Secretary Bussey to Commissioner Raum.)

Previous to the Weike decision the Bureau had been allowing 78 2-10 per cent of all claims examined, but immediately after this decision allowances fell to 33½ per cent of the claims examined, less than half the rate at which pensions were allowed immediately prior thereto.

During the six months previous to this decision 43,683, or an average of 7,280, army and navy original invalid certificates weekly were issued under the act of June 27, 1890, by the Republican Commissioner (Raum); during the six subsequent months (three of which were under the Republicans and three under the new Democratic administration) 18,608, or a weekly average of 3,101—only 42 6-10 per cent of this class of certificates, the only kind affected by this decision—were issued. On this basis fully 170,000 of the 311,300 pensioners of this class placed upon the rolls under the act of June 27, 1890, by the Republican administration in two and a half years have no just right to be there, and more than $68,000,000 paid to them was absolutely given away without authority of law.

When a single decision like that had the effect of reducing allowances more than one-half, was it not high time to raise the question as to whether the act of June 27, 1890, was being honestly and properly administered? So great was the reduction of allowances under this decision that ex-Commissioner Tanner, in an interview in a Washington paper, demanded that President Harrison require the decision to be abrogated, or it would depopulate the pension rolls.

BENNETT DECISION.

The principle of procedure under the act of June 27, 1890, as laid down in the Weike decision was made more forcible on the accession of the Democratic party to power by the decision of Assistant Secretary Reynolds, May 27, 1893, in the case of Charles T. Bennett, wherein it was affirmed "that the basis of pension under section 2 of the act o June 27, 1890, is incapacity due to any permanent mental or physical disability not the result of vicious habits to such a degree as renders the claimant unable to earn a support by manual labor. * * * Neither the Secretary of the Interior nor the Commissioner of Pensions can, by order or by practice, supersede an act of Congress. The power of the Department, so far as its orders and practice are concerned, is limited to an execution of the law; it ceases when an effort is made to supersede the law.

THE BOARD OF REVISION AND AUTHORITY FOR SUSPENSIONS.

The showing that made it appear certain that under Order 164 many pensions were illegally granted caused the Commissioner of Pensions under the foregoing decision (Bennett) of May 27, 1893, to organize a board of revision composed of the best men in the Bureau regardless of political complexion. They were required to examine cases allowed under the act of June 27, 1890, and pick out such as had no legal or equitable basis to rest upon, "but with instructions to disturb no case where by the most liberal construction of the evidence the right to the pension could be sustained under any law. In cases where it was believed that pension could not be sustained and another medical examination was thought necessary, the payment of the pension was ordered to be suspended pending investigation, according to the practice of the Bureau from the beginning, and at the proper time the usual sixty days notice was given to the pensioner within which he could ask for a medical examination or supply further evidence to his right to pension."

This Board of Revision, up to December 21, 1893, when the act was passed declaring a pension to be a vested right, and requiring thirty days notice before suspension, took the blankets off 12,548 cases issued under Order 164. After a careful re-examination, guided by Order No. 240 of Commissioner Lochren, it was found that 8,461, or 67 per cent of them, were entitled to the pension originally allowed and the payment of pension was immediately ordered to be resumed; 568 were reduced to smaller rates than those wrongfully given; 701 were dropped from the rolls, as it was shown they were not entitled to pensions under any law, and 2,818 were still suspended and undergoing further investigation at the date of the passage of the act of December 21, 1893, since which time payment has been resumed in these cases under the terms of this act.

POWER TO SUSPEND.

The power to suspend current payments of pension, and upon satisfactory proof to drop the names of pensioners from the rolls, lies in the Secretary of the Interior and the Commissioner of Pensions. This view finds approval and confirmation in the following: Kellogg *vs.* Waite and trustee, 12 Allen, Mass., 530; United States *vs.* Hall, 98 U. S., 357; sections 4692 and 4693, R. S. U. S., and prior and subsequent acts, which prescribe the nature of the conditions precedent to title. Being conditions precedent nothing can defeat them and they must co exist before the title is perfected. If through fraud or mistake the Government is deceived or imposed upon and a pension certificate issues, no legal title arises because the necessary conditions of proof and fact do not exist, and the Government has the right to withhold or vacate every muniment of title that lacks the fundamental legal elements.

The practice of suspension has been the practice of the Bureau, followed since as far back as 1819, and has prevailed without interruption through all administrations. It is in line with the assertion of the right by successive Secretaries, and was asserted in the case of certificate numbered 70,032, by Secretary Delano, who held that if there was an improper allowance either through fraud or error suspensions were warranted; in certificate number 107,574, by Secretary Schurz, and by Secretary Zach. Chandler, the soldier's friend, who was Secretary of the Interior in 1875, and who by telegraph directed H. G. Sickel, United States Pension Agent at Philadelphia, to suspend payment of pension in every case which had been prosecuted by the following attorneys: Joseph E. Devitt & Co., E. B. Jackson, Francis Register, Matthews, Poulson & Co., *et al.*

This suspension order, just prior to the September, 1875, payment, must have affected nearly every pensioner residing in the city and county of Philadelphia, as well as those of the surrounding forty-six counties in Pennsylvania and all the State of Delaware, which comprised the district paid at the Philadelphia agency that year. 3,447,254 26 were paid to the 27,740 pensioners on the rolls in Pennsylvania and Delaware during the year ending June 30, 1875. As the Philadelphia agency com-

prised more than half the State of Pennsylvania and all of Delaware, it will be
perceived that the number of suspensions must have been many thousands.

It has been heralded thorughout the country that nearly 13,000 pensions had
been suspended by the Democratic administration, but these patriots who love the
soldier so well that they do not hesitate to alarm and harass him by lying reports,
do not state that out of th· exact number suspended (12,548) 4,095 of that number are foreign residents, whose pensions terminated July 1, 1893, by act of Congress passed March 1, 1893, and approved by Benjamin Harrison.

STATEMENTS OF FORMER REPUBLICAN COMMISSIONERS RELATIVE TO FRAUDS, DROP-PINGS, ETC.

When the urgent deficiency bill was before Congress last March, and Democratic
Representatives were asking for sufficient money for the payment of special examiners to purge the pension roll of frauds, they were confronted by Republicans with
such remarks as these: "The whole object and purpose is to pay the 'spies' and
'secret agents' to be put upon the track of the old soldier, to shadow him in his
outgoings and incomings."

Suspension was referred to as if it were a new trick on the part of the Democrats,
and frauds were said to exist only in the imagination of Southern Brigadiers. They
are unmindful of the fact that the whole special examination system was of their
own creation, as may be seen by a scrutiny of the annual reports of the earlier Republican Commissioners urging in unequivocal terms that the pension system under
the old *ex parte* methods were reeking with fraud, and each annual report is burdened with the clamors of these Republican Commissioners for an enlargement of
the powers conferred upon special agents by section 4744, R. S. So thoroughly has
the work gone on since then that now substantially every United States court in
the country has its calendar from the Pension Bureau of crimes in the procuring or
efforts to procure fraudulent pensions. From April 1, 1893, to June 2, 1894, in the
past year alone, the small force of 182 special examiners in the field, made 237
arrests, procured 531 indictments, 215 convictions, and 93 sentences of persons
charged with criminal violations of the penal statutes in relation to pensions, and
74 attorneys were suspended and disbarred for complicity in these crimes, saving to
the Government in first payments alone the enormous sum of $2,702,760.88, that
would have gone to these fraudulent claimants.

In the Month of May, 1894, alone, $398,992.87 was saved to the Government
from this source, and from April 1, 1893, to June 1, 1894, $29,538.79 of money im-
properly and illegally received as pensions was collected and refunded to the Government.

For the nine years from 1874 to 1882, inclusive, 3,283 names were dropped from
the rolls, over 18,000 were suspended pending investigation, thousands of pensions
were reduced, and the sum of $4,344,954.36 was saved to the Treasury. Upwards
of 600 persons were prosecuted, indicted, convicted or sentenced for criminal violations of the penal statutes in pension claims.

Thus it will be seen that pension frauds held high carnival in the golden age of
Republican supremacy as in later days when President Harrison's Attorney-General
(W. H. H. Miller) was led to say: "*I have never before had my eyes opened to the
enormity of the frauds which are being practiced upon the General Government by applicants for pension, and I am free to admit that I have not before appreciated the degree
of ease with which applications for pension may be prosecuted in the Pension Office at*

Washington, and pensions granted upon affidavits which have no grounding in the common principles of truth. It was a revelation to me."

Droppings of large numbers of names from the pension rolls for various causes is not a recent practice peculiar to the present administration, but has been occasioned every year through all administrations, Republican and Democratic alike. During the year ending June 30, 1881, Commissioner Dudley dropped from the rolls for all causes including deaths, 10,712 names when the pension roll was only $50,000,000 annually. In 1882, he dropped 11,446, when the roll was $54,000,000. In 1883, he dropped 20,997, when the roll was $60,000,000.

In 1889, Commissioner Raum dropped 16,507, when the roll was $89,000,000. In 1890, he dropped 20,319, when the roll was $106,000,000. In 1891 he dropped 20,525, when the roll was $118,000,000. In 1892 he dropped 25,303, when the roll was $141,000,000. In 1893, Commissioner Lochren dropped from the rolls on account of death, remarriage, legal limitation of minors, failure to claim pension, and for all other causes 33,690, 4,095 of whom were foreigners dropped under the act of March 1, 1893, (approved by a Republican President,) leaving 29,595 as the total number otherwise dropped, 2,296 of whom were dropped mainly for fraud and excessive rating under Order 164, when the roll contained the names of 966,012 pensioners, who received $158,800,437.35.

DISCRIMINATIONS IN FAVOR OF NEW LAW AND AGAINST OLD LAW CLAIMANTS.

Three hundred and seventy-even thousand two hundred and three invalid received pension under the act of June 27, 1890, and only 365,403 under former laws. 82,132 invalids and 72,482 widows receive $8 per month under the act of June 27, 1890, while only 63,790 of these two classes (invalids and widows) receive this amount under the general law. 214,379 receive $12 per month under the act of June 27, 1890, while only 151,660 receive this amount under the general law. A contemplation of these and foregoing facts shows that if the justice and usefulnes s of any system for the bestowal of pensions depend upon the uniformity of its operation that the Republican administration has fallen woefully short of a proper a preciation of the beneficent design underlying the pension system in discriminating against particular localities, for partisan ends, and against the wounded or invalid soldiers whose disabilities were incurred in the service and line of duty, or are directly traceable thereto, and in favor of a less worthy class.

UNEQUAL AND UNFAIR RATINGS RESULTING FROM LAX PRACTICES OF REPUBLICAN AD-MINISTRATIONS.

Prior to December 4, 1891, the rate for loss of sight of an eye was $8 per month. Those placed on the rolls prior to this time, under the act of June 27, 1890 for loss of sight of an eye are receiving $8 per month while those placed on the rolls since that date were given $8 per month to December 4, 1891, and $12 thereafter.

The same incongruities prevail in the ratings in regard to hernias, deafness, etc. There are, therefore, now on the pension roll two sets of pensioners under both the new and the old law, the former reciving one rate of pension and the latter a different rate for the same disability.

Under ruling 249 (November 2, 1892), when the change of time of reduction of rates for some degrees of deafness was made, there were added to the schedule several minor degrees of deafness, so that now it is possible for all who heretofore (prior to the issuing of Order 257, February 28, 1894,) had their pensions for deafness allowed from the date when first shown in a ratable degree under the then existing schedule to get a rerating and arrearages of from $1 to $2 per month from date of discharge, if claim was filed prior to July 1, 1880, or from date of filing in those filed on or subsequent to July 1, 1880, to the date when under the former schedule and practice of the office the disability was shown in a ratable degree by a medical examination.

These glaring inequalities and discriminations, due to the mischievous practices of the Republican administration, have been corrected by the Democratic Secretary and Commissioner as far as possible in the brief period they have been in power by Order 257, above referred to. Another vicious practice, which seems to have been devised for the benefit of pension attorneys exclusively, was the issuance of a certain kind of certificate called "supplementary certificate," which often had the effect of giving the attorney two fees when the amount allowed the claimant was scarcely sufficient to pay these fees.

And another was the allowance of certain restorations for disabilities shown to have long since ceased to exist, and still another, the Bureau informing the claimant that the disability for which he claims did not exist, but others did, for which he was required to send up an application, upon which pension was promptly allowed.

"SYMPATHETIC AFFIDAVITS."

Sympathetic affidavits are responsible for much of the evil that has arisen in the administration of the pension laws. These machine affidavits, written by the claimant or his attorney, have been placed before comrades or neighbors who oftentimes, without reading them, signed them and they were filed in pension claims. This evil has been corrected by Commissioner Lochren's Order No. 229, which requires that affiants shall have personal knowledge of the matters to which they testify in accordance with law.

LARGE APPROPRIATIONS FOR PENSIONS.

The Appropriations Committee of the Fifty-second Congress appropriated in all $323,800,437. During the fiscal year ending June 30, 1894, 76,946 claims were filed under all laws, and 80,213 claims were allowed. At the close of business June 30, 1894, 619,027 claims of all classes were pending, and the total number of pensioners on the rolls was 969,544. Of these 375,084 are invalids under the new law, and 362,274 under the old.

In 1891, the first year after the passage of the act of June 27, 1890, under Order 164, 138,216 names were added to the rolls; the next year there was an increase of 61,692; the next year there was a remarkable falling off, and only 89,944, less than half the number of the preceding year, were added to the rolls. If this ratio were continued it is apparent that the number added to the rolls will in a short while not greatly exceed the number dropped on account of death and other causes. As has been heretofore stated, after the rescinding of Order 164 by the Weike decision of January 7, 1893, under the Republican administration, allowances fell from 78 3-10 per cent of all claims examined to 33½ per cent, less than half the rate at which they were allowed immediately prior thereto.

During the last administration, after the passage of the act of June 27, 1890, word was passed round that at least 1,000 certificates a day must be turned out, leaving out of consideration a large number of other cases which must be handled—rejected or otherwise passed upon.

Some idea may be gleaned of the manner in which medical and legal opinions and decisions were rendered in cases which in some instances involve thousands of dollars, from the fact that a single examiner passed upon 2,400 cases in a single month, giving an average of less than four minutes to each case. The impossibility of rendering intelligent decisions at such a rate is evident, when it is reflected that the examiner is supposed to carefully read the application for pension, the evidence bearing upon it, closely scrutinize the certificate of physical examination, and after carefully weighing the testimony make up his judgment and endorse the same upon the face brief.

When Commissioner Lochren assumed charge of the Pension Bureau, it was soon apparent to him that under this "thousand-a-day" pressure, the requirements of the law were being ignored, and thousands of cases allowed which, when they were being considered, contained but three papers—claimant's application, his own statement of the case; what is known in office nomenclature as the "canary-slip," containing the date of his entering the service and leaving it merely, not saying anything about whether he was honorably or dishonorably discharged, either by sentence of court-martial or desertion ; and the certificate of physical examination. Upon these three papers alone tens of thousands of names were put upon the rolls with no right to be there, and under pretense of law the revenues of the Government were given away.

An idea of the mischief wrought by these skeleton "canary-slips" may be obtained from an examination of the case of certificate No. 680,869. The first "canary-slip" report in this case gave 95 days' service. The second, a full report, gave 30 days' service only. The soldier was pensioned on the first report at $12 per month, and this is but one of a large number of the same character. The first "canary-slip" reports of the War Department indicated that the fifth and sixth Delaware regiments served from November, 1862, to August, 1863. Quite a large number of claims were allowed to these persons. April 8, 1891, the War Department, however, informed thi bureau, in a general letter, that none of the men of the fifth and sixth Delaware volunteers served 90 days during the war of the rebellion, inasmuch as General Schenk did not call them into actual service prior to June, 1863.

SPECIAL CASES.

One of the most crying abuses of the Tanner-Raum regime was the making of claims "special" at the behest of claim agents and politicians. It meant the taking up of a case out of its turn, regardless of the date of filing, discriminating against all other cases, delaying meritorious claims, and very often it meant allowing them upon very meagre evidence if the pressure behind them was strong enough. It was a notorious fact that during the Republican administration a claim agent, who had placed the Commissioner of Pensions under financial obligations, had no less than 50 of such cases called up and made special in a single day, and the private secretary of this Commissioner had a rubber special stamp made, the better to accommodate this obliging attorney. When this private secretary was turned out of office there were found in his desk no less than 2,000 reference slips of the pension attorney heretofore referred to, all of which had been marked "special," the intention being to rush those 2,000 cases through the office in an irregular and unlawful manner,

From July 1, 1890, to July 1, 1892, during which a record of these cases was kept, Raum had 13,578 of these cases made special. The feeling was general that certain persons could get pensions by irregular means, while others with meritorious claims had to wait. So bold had they become that the Republican pension agent at Topeka, Kansas, said in a campaign speech, at a meeting of old soldiers in the fall of 1892, that "if they (the soldiers) voted the Populist ticket they would lose their pensions, and they ought to do so."

PENSION OFFICE CLERKS RERATING THEIR OWN PENSIONS.

Pension office clerks rerated their own pensions, and Commissioner Lochren, on assuming the duties of his position, discovered that many of the employees of the bureau, whose pensions were increased and rerated by their fellow-clerks during Corporal Tanner's regime, and without any warrant of law, had never had their pensions reduced, and the orders requiring such reduction were pigeon-holed by Tanner and Raum.

So great was the scandal caused by this collusion that many of the clerks who had no political "pull" were dismissed "upon consideration appertaining to a correct public service," and Hiram Smith, Jr., Republican first deputy commissioner, who had his own pension rerated in violation of law, resigned "in compliance with request."

WHOLESALE FRAUDS.

(*Vide Statement's of Former Republican Commissioners Relative to Frauds, etc., p. 12.*)

First in point of numbers come what are known as the W. Bowen Moore cases, Buffalo, New York. It has been shown that many of the affidavits filed by him were not sworn to and others were materially added to. About 6,000 of his cases have been submitted for investigation. Out of 229 of these cases 137 declarations were filed which are entirely invalid; 87 affidavits were found false in fact; 456 false in execution and in fact; 527 false in execution, making a total of 1,070 false and fraudulent papers. $10,498 would be due up to date on the invalid declarations in pending claims. $19,415 have been paid out to date on illegal declarations, and $13,169 paid out in claims shown to be wholly without merit. $22,495 have been saved from claims which would have been allowed, had not the investigation been instituted, and $2,263 in illegal fees have been collected by Moore in claims in which he was the attorney. This gives a total of $66,577, which has been illegally paid out in consequence of these frauds.

Second, New Mexico cases. About 1,700 of these cases are under investigation. One Marcellino, notary public and pension attorney, manufactured claimants as well as evidence to support claims. He forged signatures and endorsements to checks and vouchers, converted the money to his own use, plead guilty on 27 counts, and is now undergoing a seven years' sentence. Out of 240 of these New Mexico claims, ten were found to be deserters, 44 were never on the muster rolls, eight had no service, two were never discharged, one was cashiered, making 65 in all, and 43 per cent showed treatment in the service for venereal disease. The amount of actual saving in these New Mexican cases is $1,130,259.06, and the future annual saving will exceed another million.

Third, Indian Territory cases. About 1,400 have been referred for investigation. In these cases an untutored child of the forest (a Creek Indian) Thomas Deer, by manufacturing declarations and affidavits by the wholesale, defrauded the Government of the United States out of tens of thousands of dollars.

Fourth, Van Leuven of Iowa cases. About 1,200 in number. It was part of

Van Leuven's plan to corrupt boards of examining surgeons, and he was able to have such examinations and ratings as he desired, and even had the original certificates of the examining board submitted to him before they were sent to the Pension Bureau.

Fifth, Norfolk, Va., cases, of which there are about 550, filed mostly by W. R. Drury, at present serving a term of imprisonment, and who manufactured alike claimants, declarations and evidence. In 167 of his cases recommended to be dropped from the roll there were paid to the pensioners under the act of June 27, 1890, the sum of $54,074.43, and the future saving will be about $343,260.39. Including all cases in which Drury figured it is estimated that the Government has been robbed to the extent of at least $650,000.

In addition to the foregoing, to show the universality of these fraudulent practices, there have been referred for investigation about 300 cases, in which one C. W. Lewis, of Tennessee, has violated many of the pension laws, and who is now serving an extended term in the penitentiary.

About 100 claims filed by T. A. Dunlap, of Nashville, Tenn., in which many frauds have been found, and nearly 800 claims of persons residing in various portions of Louisiana, in which frauds have been discovered. Scarcely a day passes but that the name of some person is reported to the Bureau as having been guilty of a violation of the penal statutes.

THE REPUBLICAN RECORD.

Under the act of Jun · 27, 1890—

Numbe less names were put upon the pension roll regardless of the requirement of at least 90 days' service.

Dishonorably discharged soldiers and bounty-jumpers were pensioned.

Many who draw the maximum amount ($12 per month) are earning a living at manual labor as they have always done, and some are ra ed the richest men in the towns in which they live.

Pension jumpers of both sexes have been allowed two or more pensions.

Under Order 164, inability to perform manual labor was never taken into consideration, and in consequence more than 100,000 pensioners, with no legal right, were put upon the rolls, and the Treasury depl ted in the soldier's name.

Many of the le ist meritorious claims under this act of those who were soldiers only in name were preferred to the crippled heroes whose claims under the general laws re ained unsettled. Though only three years in operation more pensioners are receiving $8 or $12 per month under this law than under all former laws. In some cities the number of pen ioners und r this act is as large as the number who draw under all acts enacted during the previous twenty-five years.

Under the last Administration—

Republican clerks and officials high in the Pension Bureau rerated their own pensions, filching thousands of dollars from the Treasury.

A Republican Commissioner (Tanner) declared it to be his intention to raid the public Treasury with "steam-shovel and gravel-tra n," and "God help the surplus when he got up steam enough."

Public pla e in the Pension Office was given for bribe.

Orders 149 and 151, known as the "Completed Files" orders, it was openly charged, were issued at the instance of George E. Lemon, a millionaire Washington claim agent.

All sorts of incongruous ratings grew out of lax procedure and those with like disabilities received different ratings.

Machinery was made accessible to pension attorneys for procuring discharges for men who left their companies and went to Canada during the war.

The Pension Office was used for partisan purposes. It was called upon to help the Republican party to power by granting pensions as fast as possible in doubtful States and districts.

Pensions were promised for votes, and pensioners threatened if they did not vote the Republican ticket.

Cases by the thousand were made special for certain pension attorneys, and often allowed upon insufficient testimony, while no attention was paid to the poor soldiers who were getting small pensions for woun 's or diseases actually incurred in the service. Because they had no "pull" they could not get a hearing under Tanner or Raum. In open violation of the law employees of the Pension Office were put upon the track of certain Democratic members of Congress, in ord r, if possible, to encompass their defeat at the polls.

This is the Republican record.

CONCLUSION.

When the Democratic administration took charge of the Bureau of Pensions it was resolved to inaugurate an era of administrative reform to the end that (1) there shall be equality and not discrimination as to the meritorious soldiers in the measure of the nation's bounty; that their cases, long in the pigeon-holes of the Pension Office under the Republican party's control, shall have been disposed of and the least expensive and most expeditious mode to obtain a certificate vouchsafed them; (2) that the name of every pensioner on the pension roll to whom pensions should not be granted who have been placed thereon because of fraud, crime, error, or laxity, shall, without hazar ing the just rights of others, be stricken therefrom.

The pension roll was purged, and distinction made between brave men who loyally served their country and those who skulked.

Corrupt examining boards and attorneys were punished, machine affidavits were put an end to. There will be no more wholesale making of claims special in the interest of a favored pension attorney. Peculation in every form will be put a stop to. The "completed files" was discontinued. Claim agents frequently reported cases complete where the necessary evidence had not been filed, retarding the work of the Bureau—one of two things had to be done, either settle claims finally when the agents said they were complete, rejecting those where evidence was lacking, as would be done in a case at law called for tri l, or abolish the system altogether; the latter course was considered more favorable to the claimant—a salutary reform.

The making out of "statistic l cards" has been dis continued, and fifty- wo clerks, formerly employed upon this unnecessary work, were put upon the legitimate work of the office—adjudicating claims.

The "canary-slip" form of report from the War Department has been done away with, and in its stead a proper military history of the soldier must be given. Precedence is no longer given to cases under the act of June 27, 1890, but claims for pension under all laws are settled in their order in accordance with the law and the evidence.

A majority of the cases where the claim has been rejected since the advent of the Democratic administration are cases which were in the office before its advent, and had been neglected by the preceding administration in the hurry and skurry of skinning out the files, selecting cases easiest adjudicated before the Democratic administration came in.

This in brief is the Democratic record, upon which it is proposed to appeal to the duty soldier, who fought the battles of his country, has a record to be proud of, and courts investigation, that it might go down to future generations of his countrymen that he was a REAL so d er.

Fraudulent pensioners can be relied upon to support the party that would shield them from investigation and exposure, and above all from the danger of losing the gains of their perfidy.

It is believed that the time has come when the real soldiers and taxpayers of the land will sustain the men whose courage and honesty impelled them to the patriotic effort *to save the pension roll from dishonor and the taxpayer from pillage.*

The Dangers of Populism.

SPEECH
OF
HON. JAMES P. PIGOTT,
OF CONNECTICUT,
IN THE HOUSE OF REPRESENTATIVES,

Monday, August 13, 1894.

Mr. Speaker, the high-water mark of profligacy was reached by the Republican party during the last Administration, when Government appropriations exceeded a billion of dollars for a Congress, when a tariff bill was passed upon the avowed principle of revenue for monopolies only, and a desperate attempt was made to perpetuate the spoilers in power through the instrumentality of a Federal election law and a Congressional returning board. In the last year of its existence the Fifty-first Congress appropriated an amount exceeding $520,000,000, and the registrar of the decrees of the trust and monopolies, whose name was properly given to the McKinley bill, vauntingly exclaimed that expenditures would increase, for this was a "billion-dollar country."

Now, notwithstanding the large increase for pensions, postal deficiencies, and other necessary expenditures, including a very large amount for rivers and harbors, the appropriations made by the present Congress are some $40,000,000 less than those of the last year of the late Republican Congress, $29,000,000 below those of the last session of the Fifty-second Congress, and by legislative reforms having the sanction and active co-operation of the Executive Departments, once more in the hands of Democratic officials, still further reductions will be made, while at the same time the public service will be improved.

* * * * * * *

We have returned once more, as I have shown, to the good old Democratic policy of economy in expenditures, a policy enunciated in the first Democratic platform adopted in a national convention, and adhered to under all circumstances. It is, indeed, a fundamental Democratic principle, as much so as home rule, taxation for revenue, strict construction of the powers granted in the Constitution, or any of the great pillars upon which Jefferson founded the only political party that was born with the Constitution and continued its existence to the present time, renewing its youth in the fountain of the people's welfare as new problems are proposed for solution.

Sir, as we reflect upon the history of our country since the close of the civil war we have good reason for concluding that the people have pronounced finally against the kind of paternal government that culminated in the McKinley tariff and the fraud and force bill. But, sir, we are now confronted with paternalism in a more insidious form.

Taking opportunity of the distressed condition into which Republican policy has plunged the country, the attempt is made to drive the people from the support of the only people's party—the Democratic party—and array them under the banners of paternalism, under a new name and under a new form. What do the people want? Is it economy in Government expenditures? They will secure that under he banner of the Democratic party. Is it low taxes? That, too, is one of the proudest purposes of the Democracy. Is it home rule? Where else will they find t except under Democratic government? Is it sound money? The Democratic party has always stood for sound money—gold and silver coin—since the day of its birth. These are really what the people want, but the leaders who have inaugurated the so-called Populist party propose to conduct them into no such pastures. Their idea of government is paternalism of the worst kind. Every public ill, imaginary or real, is to be cured by some patent legislation. Money is to be printed, not coined, and distributed, not earned.

Government, which is supposed to have been instituted under our system to attend to public affairs and leave the people free to attend to their own, is to be called upon to meddle with private rights, and we are to be forced into an unwilling partnership between the individuals and the Government, which would end in bankruptcy before the close of a brief session of the American Congress. To show that I do not exaggerate, Mr. Speaker, let me call attention to some of the many measures introduced into Congress by Populist Senators and Representatives, some of which, if enacted, would change our Constitutional Government into a social despotism, and others would require the expenditure of more than four times the sum of the coined money of the world.

Herewith I present a synopsis of some of the schemes proposed in the Senate or the House by Populist members:

NEW WAY TO PAY OLD DEBTS.

Representative Davis of Kansas, in his bill No. 3436, has devised a plan which amounts to a new way to pay old debts. Under its provisions, any defaulting mortgage debtor is declared a bankrupt and his creditor cannot collect the debt due him, except from the United States, in the following manner: The mortgage debtor is to procure on abstract of title and certificate of value of land and improvements from the register of deeds of the county, upon presentation of which to the county treasurer, the latter official is to draw on the Treasurer of the United States for the amount due, including official fees, and when paid shall constitute a lien upon the property, the county record to be marked "Settled by the United States Government," and the debtor to be allowed twenty years to pay, the annual interest charge being but 1 per cent.

To provide the funds necessary for the purposes of the act, legal tenders are to be printed and issued from time to time as required. The above to be the only method by which a mortgagee can collect his debt, until such time as the aggregate circulation of lawful money of the United States shall reach, and as long as it shall continue at $50 per capita of population (say at the present time three and a third billions of dollars) not counting lawful reserves in banks and other fixed and noncirculating deposits required by law.

LOANS TO STATES.

To provide the several States with money to make improvements, loan money to counties, municipalities, and needy individuals, Representative Clover of Kansas proposed in his bill 6254 (Fifty-second Congress) to issue legal tenders to any State filing bonds with the Treasurer, payable at the option of the State, bearing interest at 2½ per cent, and in any sum not exceeding 50 per cent of the assessed value of the taxable property of the State making application.

MUNICIPAL LOAN BILL.

Ex-Representative Clover of Kansas believes the United States Government should help all cities, and to do this proposed in House bill 3999, Fifty-second Congress, to loan money to all cities and municipalities not exceeding $50,000 to any one municipality, and provided no issue shall be made to any one municipality in excess of 20 per cent of the assessed value of its taxable property, for not exceeding a period of 50 years, and at 2½ per cent per annum.

To provide money to make these loans legal-tender Treasury notes are to be printed by the Treasury Department.

LOAN BUREAU.

Senator PEFFER, Populist Senator from Kansas, introduced into the Senate a bill (S. 976) "to establish a bureau of loans," with a central agency in each State, Territory, and district, and local agents wherever required, with discretion to loan to each individual offering real estate security not exceeding 160 acres, and who has a house thereon which is mortgaged, or who not having such house desires to build one, not exceeding $2,500 to any one individual, for not exceeding ten years with stays of foreclosure proceedings that extend the period to fifteen years ; also establishes loan agencies in places having public store-houses, to loan to individuals having store-house certificates not exceeding two-thirds of the face value of the same.

To provide immediate means to carry out this law about $700,000,000 of paper money, full legal tender, is to be issued at once, and when that is disposed of the balance of the money in the Treasury not otherwise appropriated is to be used from time to time.

Somewhat similar is the loan bill of Representative SIMPSON (H. R. 5073, Fifty-second Congress), which provides for loans upon land in tracts of not less than 10 nor more than 320 acres, of not exceeding ten years at 2 per cent per annum. A bureau of loans is constituted, with an agency in each State and a sub-agent in each Congressional district. Legal tenders are to be issued fast enough to meet the demands.

LOAN BANK.

Representative KEM of Nebraska introduced into the House a bill (H. R. 5446) to establish a system of Government banking, under which there can be one Government bank in each county, managed by directors varying in salary from $2,000 to $4,000 per annum, at whose direction money may be loaned to individuals in sums not exceeding $3,000, and if on real estate security for a term not exceeding twenty years ; if on note for not exceeding on · y ar. To procure money to make the loans, the United States is to issue legal tenders, variously estimated in amount. at from one billion to one billion and a quarter of dollars ; also deposits to be received on which interest of 3 per cent is to be paid, and said deposits to be loaned out as above. All gold and silver certificates are to be redeemed in legal tenders.

In his three bills (H. R. 6660, 10000, and 10495), Fifty-second Congress, Representative WATSON shows the capabilities of the Government to manage all the affairs of the people and manufacture many billions of dollars of paper money to float both crops and mortgages. House bill 6660 provides for the establishment of a sub-treasury in every county, and the construction of subtreasury buildings upon county sites to be chosen by the citizens of the respective counties, who shall also elect the manager of such subtreasury, who shall receive a salary of $1,500 per year. The owner of any cotton, wheat, corn, or oats, or tobacco can deposit his produce in the nearest subtreasury for safe keeping and receive in greenbacks 80 per cent of the value the local county manager shall place upon it, and also a negotiable warehouse certificate bearing 1 per cent per annum interest, upon the surrender of which and paying loan, the holder receives back produce of the same kind and value. To start the wheels of this many-million-dollar project, fifty millions of greenbacks are to be printed at once.

By bill 10099 Mr. WATSON proposed the appointment of a national grain inspector with a salary of $10,000 a year who shall appoint an inspector for each State at a salary of $5,000 per year, who in turn shall appoint local inspectors for each county, or parish, or district of each State, there being no limit fixed to the number of such deputies, who are to provide warehouses or elevators for the storage of cotton and wheat, and give certificate of quantities and value to the person storing the same. The postmaster at the nearest post office is to receive such certificate and issue to the holder thereof a postal money order for two-thirds the certified value thereof. To carry out the act the Secretary of the Treasury is to start up the printing presses and issue such amount of greenbacks to the Postmaster General as may be required from time to time, not to exceed $100,000,000.

In House bill 10495 Mr. WATSON proposed the appointment of a "special auditor of the Treasury," salary $10,000 per year, and a deputy for each State, who shall appoint one land inspector in each Congressional district in his State. Any person owning land in city or country upon which is his home, or which he will swear he intends to make a home, who desires to borrow money from the United States, may do so upon the approved certificate of the deputy auditor, after going through certain forms, receiving two-thirds of the estimated value of the land, upon giving a mortgage to the United States, to be payable in five years, at the rate of 1 per cent per annum. The amount of greenbacks to be printed under this bill is limited to one hundred millions.

SPECIMEN PENSION BILLS.

Representative HUDSON of Kansas, in his bill (H. R. 3186) proposes to settle all pensions by the payment at once to each one now borne on the rolls, or that may be hereafter placed upon them, a lump sum ten times the annual amount of such pension. This would require the immediate expenditure, as fast as the money could be printed, of $1,500,000,000, and is to be made in Treasury notes or greenbacks "substantially in the same form as the greenbacks issued by the Government during the late war," except they shall be legal tender for all debts, public and private.

OTHER PENSION BILLS.

Representative DAVIS proposes in bill 4339 to pension every person who served in the war more than ninety days and less than a year at the rate of $10 per month; who served one year and less than two years, $15 per month; who served two years and less than three years, $20 per month, and to all who served three years or more, $25 per month. The Commissioner of Pensions, to whom the bill was referred, estimated that if this bill became law, the sum required for pensions this year alone would exceed $460,000,000. Under the bill, legal tenders are to be issued in payment.

Senator ALLEN's service pension bill (S. 2124) would require the first year an expenditure of $350,000,000.

Senator PEFFER's pension bill, known as the "cent-a-day" bill (Senate 358, Fifty-second Co gress), is a trifle as compared with Representative HUDSON's lump-sum bill. It places every soldier, sailor, and marine on the pension rolls, and requires the issue of a curious currency in denominations from 5 cents to $10, to be rectangular in form, the larger notes to be 6½ inches long by 2¾ inches wide, the smaller notes to be marked across the face, "service pension money." To start the ball $105,000,000 are to be issued at once.

INDUSTRIAL ARMY.

In his bill (H. R. 6767) Mr. DAVIS of Kansas, with a preamble declaring that "Whereas the wisdom of our forefathers in the preamble of the Constitution of the United States made ample provision in the phrase 'to promote the general welfare' for such enlarged governmental functions and progressive economic measures as the growing needs and the emergencies of the country might require," provides for the enlistment "a fast as practicable" of 500,000 men in an industrial volunteer army, to be clothed. fed, and paid as are recruits in the regular Army.

As it costs our government a thousand dollars a year for each soldier, the annual expenditure called for by this bill would be not less than half a billion of dollars. Mr. DAVIS provides for an additional issue of $300,000,000 of legal tenders at once, and $100,000,000 a year thereafter, "to create and pre erve an increasing and equitable volume of currency hereafter."

CHARITY FUNDS.

To provide for the immediate relief of the destitute, Senator PEFFER proposes in Senate bill 1300 to appropriate $6,300,000, to be expended by State boards of commissioners at the rate of $1 per each ten inhabitants in any county.

In joint resolution 166, Representative BOEN instructs the Secretary of War to provide camping grounds and tents for all "organized bodies of laboring people who may come within the said District" of Columbia, and the War Office is "to see to it" that their "rights as citizens, organizations, and individuals are respected and protected."

INTERNAL IMPROVEMENTS.

Representative BOEN of Minnesota introduced a bill in the House (7908) which provides for the issue of $1,000,000,000 in legal-tender notes, of which amount five hundred millions is to be expended in five years in building or purchasing railroads, two hundred and fifty millions for improving rivers, and not less than two hundred and fifty millions for purchasing sites and building post offices "in each village or city containing 1.000 or more inhabitants." To carry out the law would require, as variously estimated, from one and a half billions to two and a half billions, but only the issue of one billion of extra notes is provided for.

INCREASE OF CURRENCY.

In addition to other means of increasing the volume of the currency, Representative Simpson proposes in his bill 4412 to have the Government purchase all the gold and silver that is offered, issuing silver or gold certificates to the sellers at the rate of $1 for each 371.25 grains of silver. Then the Secretary is to coin all the gold and silver now in the Treasury or that may be thereafter purchased, and to issue Treasury certificates—$2 in Treasury notes for each dollar in coin. It is estimated this would soon give a total circulation of $3,000,000,000.

In his tax bill (H. R. 5448) Representative Davis proposes to substitute the tariff act of 1883 for the McKinley act, with horizontal reductions, one-fourth in 1894, one-third of the remainder in 1885, and one-fourth of the remainder in 1896, with certain additions to the free list ; to provide revenue, incomes and land are to be taxed, and three hundred and fifty millions of greenbacks are to be issued the first year, and annually thereafter $100,000,000.

Senator KYLE, in Senate bill 2531 (Fifty-second Congress), proposes an unlimited issue of fractional currency, to be paid out to persons applying therefor to any postmaster ; and Representative McKEIGHAN, in House bill 6010, proposes the same, limiting the legal-tender qualities of the currency, however ; and Representative Davis, in House bill 6003, concurs with Senator KYLE restricting the issue to $50,000,000.

Representative Davis, in House bill 5386, proposes "that if at any time the current revenue s of the Government shall be insufficient to meet the current expenses the Secretary of the Treasury shall issue non-interest-bearing Treasury notes," full legal tender. He is also required not to pay in gold more than one-half of any coin obligation, and is required to coin at once all the silver in the Treasury, to issue silver certificates "all uncoined silver," "to pay out 66⅔ per cent of all silver now in the Treasury, and never hereafter to retain in the Treasury in silver an amount exceeding one-third of silver coin for the redemption of outstanding silver certificates."

SALSOLI KALI TRAGUS.

Mr. BOEN, Representative from Minnesota, proposes to begin the destruction of the salsoli kali tragus wherever found on public or private property, and his bill would appropriate $1,000,000 (House bill 5745) to inaugurate the process.

RAIN WATER AND IRRIGATION.

Various bills have been introduced by Populist Senators and Representatives to authorize "the control of water for agricultural purposes," "to provide means for gathering and storing rain water," "to establish a bureau of irrigation," and so on, of which the following specimens are quoted :

Representative Davis proposes (House bill 7896) the immediate issue of $20,000,000 in greenbacks to be issued by the Secretary of Agriculture merely "to inaugurate a systematic control of water in the interest of agriculture."

Representative BAKER of Kansas asks a modest sum to enable the Secretary of Agriculture to provide means for gathering and storing rain water. House bill 7887.

Senator PEFFER has introduced Mr. DAVIS's bill into the Senate (Senate bill 2279). But he proposes more radical measures in his bill (S. 1168), which provides for a bureau of irrigation which is to dig for water, dam water, or ditch water, the appropriation for the purpose not being limited in amount, provided it does not exceed the amount of money in the Treasury not otherwise appropriated.

SOME OTHER THEORIES.

According to the Populist theory Congress is omnipotent, and the people in the States, counties, and municipalities are to have no voice in managing their local affairs, provided Congress wills otherwise. As examples of this overtopping power the following Populist measures are quoted :

In Senate bill 1182 (Fifty-third Congress) Senator PEFFER provides not only that no whiskies, beers, wines, or other intoxicants shall be imported into the United States, but also that no whiskies, beers, wines, or other intoxicants (domestic or imported) shall be sold in the United States "except what may be necessary for medicinal, scientific, and sacramental purposes." Of course every one knows that such legislation would be waste paper, as Congress has not been granted by the people any such police power.

Railways are to be managed according to act of Congress. If Representative BOEN has his way every railway must carry the mails, but Representative BOEN, in House bill 7638, insists that no passenger coach shall be attached to mail trains, but shall consist solely of an engine, tender, caboose, and postal cars. The Government, which in this bill is the Postmaster General, is to fix the schedule time of this train and is to pay as much or as little as that official agrees with himself to pay, but the railways may haul mail cars with passenger trains when their traffic is not interrupted "by strikes or other labor disturbances."

Senator KYLE proposes in Senate joint resolution 73, that Congress shall have "exclusive jurisdiction to regulate marriage and divorce in the several States and Territories," and Representative BELL of Colorado, insists in House joint resolution 124 that the women of the country shall vote at all elections, present local laws to the contrary notwithstanding, while Representative PENCE does not consider it necessary to take the trouble to amend the Constitution, as that instrument requires, to prescribe qualifications for voters, but proposes in House bill 5748 that women shall vote for members of the House of Representatives.

LIGHTS AND RAILROADS.

Senator PEFFER, in Senate bill 1972, provides that in certain contingencies the United States shall purchase a railroad system and manage it.

In Senate bill 1179 the same Senator proposes that the United States shall go into the lighting business in the District of Columbia; said light to be supplied to citizens at 10 per cent above cost; and $1,000,000 is appropriated.

A COMPREHENSIVE COMMITTEE.

Representative BELL provides in joint resolution 169 for the appointment of a committee to "devise means for the employment of the idle men of the country, restrict immigration, start up mines, increase the currency, and for other purposes." Therefore, etc., the committee in "thirty days" is to report a plan "by which our idle men may be re-employed n our mines and in building canals for the reclamation of the arid lands, or upon transportation, telegraph, or telephone lines of the United States, or in some other public or private works."

Legal tenders are to be issued "commensurate with our increasing population;" laws are to be passed to protect and preserve such labor for our own workmen; interest-bearing bonds are to be no longer issued by the United States, but means to be devised whereby States and municipalities may "secure an issue of money on such bonded securities as cheaply as national banks secure notes on Government bonds," and means to be pointed out whereby money "instead of bonds held exclusively for hire and investment" may be used in developing industries and enterprises.

RECAPITULATION.

Without duplicating the amounts carried in the bills quoted where their modes or purposes are similar, the following recapitulation will show the sum total of appropriations required to meet the bills named:

Representative DAVIS's bill (No. 3436) providing for the loan to certain mortgage debtors is estimated to require not less than the sum of $10,000,000,000

Representative Clover's bill (No. 6254, Fifty-second Congress) to loan to States, etc., 50 per cent of assessed valuation of property is estimated to require exceeding.. 12,000,000,000

Representative Clover's bill (No. 3999, Fifty-second Congress) is variously estimated to require the sum of from $8,000,000,000 to $15,000,000,000, say 10,000,000,000

Senator PEFFER's bill (No. 976) to loan not exceeding $2,500 to any individual applying having real estate security provides for an immediate issue of not less than $700,000,000, and an ultimate issue of much more, but is not estimated in the total, being similar in principle to House bill 3436, above quoted.

Representative KEM's bill (No. 5446), where not included in previous estimates, would require an issue of not less than..................... 1,000,000,000
Mr. Watson's various bills are not estimated, being included in their princip es in previous estimates.

Representative HUDSON's pension bill (H. R. 3186) would require the immediate issue of 1,500,000,000
R presentative DAVIS's industrial army bill (H. R. 6767) would require an annual expenditure of.............................. 500,000,000
Senator PEFFER's charity bill (S. 1300) appropriates..................... 6,300,000
Representative BOEN's bill (H. R. 7908), for internal improvements, app opriates 500,000,000

With an annual appropriation in addition.

Representative BOEN's bill (H. R. 5745) to exterminate the Russian thistle, appropriates.. 1,000,000
Senator PEFFER's rain water bill (No. 7896) makes an appropriation of...................... 20,000,000
                                                                              _____
     Total................ 35,507,300,000

These estimates do not include any duplication nor many items of expenditure proposed in the bills named, nor do they include salaries of the thousands upon thousands of officials to be appointed under their provisions. As the total estimated money of the world, including paper, gold, silver, copper, brass and iron tokens does not exceed $10,100,000,000, it appears that the amount of money called for by the bills named is nearly five times the volume of the currency of the world. What our paper money would be worth under such circumstances anyone of ordinary intelligence knows. It would be worth nothing at all.

On July 9, 1894, Senator PEFFER submitted a resolution, of which the following is a copy:

"In view of existing social and business conditions, and by way of suggesting subjects for remedial legislation; be it

"*Resolved by the Senate of the United States,* First. That all public functions ought to be exercised by and through public agencies. ·

"Second. That all railroads employed in interstate commerce ought to be brought into one organization under control and supervision of public officers; that charges for transportation of persons and property ought to be uniform throughout the country; that wages of employees ought to be regulated by law and paid promptly in money.

" Third. That all coal beds ought to be owned and worked by the States or by the Federal Government, and the wages of all persons who work in the mines ought to be provided by law and paid in money when due.

" Fourth. That all money used by the people ought to be supplied only by the Government of the United States; that the rate of interest ought to be uniform in all the States, not exceeding the net average increase of the permanent wealth of the people.

"Fifth. That all revenues of the Government ought to be raised by taxes on real estate."

To carry out the provisions of this resolution would require, at a very moderate estimate, some fifteen billions of dollars, making the total proposed expenditures upwards of fifty billions of dollars.

Among the other things that would follow such legislation it will be seen that the enormous amount of money necessary to carry on the Government is to be raised wholly and alone upon real estate.

Are the farmers of the country now ready to add to the burdens they have by a, still further tax to carry out these plans?

Sham Civil Service Reform.

EXTRACT FROM SPEECH

OF

HON. W. D. BYNUM,

OF INDIANA,

IN THE HOUSE OF REPRESENTATIVES,

July 31, 1894.

Mr. BYNUM said:

Mr. SPEAKER: At no time in the history of the country was the clamor for office so insatiate as upon the accession of the last Republican Administration to power. The old-timers, who had spent most of their lives in office and had become imbued with the idea that the Government positions belonged to them, reenforced by the younger element, who had been almost entirely excluded from the public stalls, came rushing to the Capitol by the thousands, eager to receive a crumb from the table supposed to be so plentifully supplied.

Rich and bountiful, however, as was the feast, it only served to sharpen the appetites of the hungry horde that swarmed through the lobbies, invaded the White House, filled the Departments and drove the members of the Cabinet to seek refuge in their private rooms. The endeavors to appease this inordinate demand resulted in the most brutal assaults that were ever committed upon the civil service of the Government. Amongst the many open, flagrant, willful, and corrupt violataions of the principles of the civil service during this period was the dismissal from the Railway Mail Service of nearly 3,000 efficient Democratic clerks and the appointment in their stead of inexperienced Republicans.

The facts, briefly stated, were as follows: On the 1st day of December, 1888, President Cleveland issued an order placing the Railway Mail Service under the classified service, to take effect on the 15th day of March, 1889.

Mr. Harrison became President on the 4th day of March, 1889, and within one week after his inauguration issued an order extending the time when the order of Mr. Cleveland was to take effect from the 15th day of March to the 1st day of May, 1889. That this extention was made for the sole purpose of enabling the Administration to make a raid upon the service in the interest of its partisans is as clear as the noonday's sun. From the 4th day of March, 1889, the day on which Mr. Harrison became President, to the 15th day of May, a period of less than two months, seventeen hundred Democratic clerks, with records for efficiency and integrity theretofore unequaled, were summarily dismissed, and their places filled with virulent Republican partisans without experience.

The fact, however, that the service became classified on May 1, did not deter such reformers as Wanamaker and Lyman from completing the work they had begun. They had gotten rid of 2,000 Democratic clerks, the other 1,000 must go, and after that date, when the service became fully classified, 927 more clerks were dismissed and 1,212 were appointed by the disgraceful and fraudulent practice of antedating the notices of removals and apppointments.

At the time I first introduced the measure I had but a faint conception of the extent to which this abuse had been carried. As soon, however, as the contents of the bill became known, I began to receive letters from every part of the country, giving information as to the ruthless manner in which Democrats had been discharged and the indecent haste in which Republicans had been rushed into their places. While I am not at liberty to give the names, I cannot refrain from publishing extracts from a few of these letters, as they convey more forcibly than I can express, the manner in which the work was accomplished:

TURKEY, N. C., *October 2, 1893.*

DEAR SIR: Having seen in the New York *World* that you had introduced a bill with reference to the restoration to service of ex-Democratic railway postal clerks, and being one of the number myself for whose purpose your bill is intended to secure justice, I herewith beg leave to thank as well as congratulate you for the position thus manifested in our behalf.

During Mr. Cleveland's first administration I received an appointment as railway postal clerk on one of the trunk lines of the country from Washington D. C., to Wilmington N. C., passed my examination on all the postoffices in Virginia, North Carolina and South Carolina, with a general average about 95 per cent; was always prompt and attentive in the discharge of my duty; had my absolute appointment, and was actually under the civil service, but was removed May 21, 1889, to gratify a Republican that wanted my place. All the Democrats on mine and connecting roads were removed in like manner.

I am yours,

————— ————.

Hon. WM. D. BYNUM,
  Washington, D. C.

The most striking illustration, however, of the haste to get rid of Democrats and restore Republicans comes from the State of Maine. I am conscious that the living of that State are always willing to sacrifice themselves in the public service, but I was not aware that in their eagerness to get rid of Democrats they were willing to make requisition upon the sextons of the cemeteries. Such, however, seems to be a fact.

WATERVILE, ME., *October 16, 1893.*

DEAR SIR: I received a copy of the bill you introduced in the House a short time since, and I wish to say to you that the ex-postal clerks are very much pleased with your undertaking and trust the bill may pass.

In their haste to remove us from the service they appointed one man who had been dead for more than one year, another who was nearly dead and who told the superintendent that he could not go back, he was too sick; but they made him go on, as they said, till they could straighten things out. He went on, and after a few months he resigned, went home, and died.

Yours respectfully,

————— ————.

Hon. WILLIAM D. BYNUM,
  Congressman, Washington, D. C.

[Laughter and applause.]

APPENDIX.

In reply to the fourth inquiry I have to state that the number of clerks appointed, reappointed, or reinstated to said service and who commenced service subquent to the 1st day of May, 1889, though appointed, reappointed, or reinstated pon orders bearing date prior thereto, was 1,212, and the dates upon which said erks entered upon their duties were as follows :

			Number of clerks.				Number of clerks.
ay	1,	1889	145	June	10,	1889	7
ay	2,	1889	36	June	11,	1889	3
ay	3,	1889	44	June	12,	1889	5
ay	4,	1889	40	June	13,	1889	4
a.(	5,	1889	17	June	15,	1889	4
ay	6,	1889	47	June	16,	1889	2
ay	7,	1889	39	June	17,	1889	3
ay	8,	1889	25	June	18,	1889	3
ay	9,	1889	38	June	19,	1889	6
ay	10,	1889	31	June	20,	1889	4
ay	11,	1889	27	June	21,	1889	3
ay	12,	1889	20	June	22,	1889	4
ay	13,	1889	38	June	23,	1889	3
ay	14,	1889	48	June	24,	1889	2
ay	15,	1889	56	June	26,	1889	3
ay	16,	1889	49	June	29,	1889	1
ay	17,	1889	26	June	30,	1889	1
ay	18,	1889	29	July	1,	1889	7
ay	19,	1889	15	July	3,	1889	1
ay	20,	1889	59	July	4,	1889	2
ay	21,	1889	44	July	7,	1889	1
ay	22,	1889	32	July	10,	1889	2
ay	23,	1889	20	July	15,	1889	1
ay	24,	1889	18	July	16,	1889	2
ay	25,	1889	8	July	17,	1889	1
ay	26,	1889	7	July	23,	1889	1
ay	27,	1889	21	July	24,	1889	1
ay	28,	1889	15	Aug.	1,	1889	1
ay	29,	1889	15	Aug.	3,	1889	1
ay	30,	1889	6	Aug.	23,	1889	1
ay	31,	1889	7	Aug.	25,	1889	1
ine	1,	1889	51	Sept.	25,	1889	1
ine	2,	1889	6				
ine	3,	1889	7	Total for the month of—			
ine	4,	1889	8		May		1,032
ine	5,	1889	11		June		156
ine	6,	1889	4		July		19
ine	7,	1889	2		August		4
ine	8,	1889	3		September		1
ine	9,	1899	6				

I have the honor to be, sir, very respectively,

W. S. BISSELL,
Postmaster-General.

HON. CHARLES F. CRISP,
Speaker of the House of Representatives,
Washington, D. C.

Mr. Speaker: In the palmiest days of Congressional spoils, I venture that a record ore replete with a debauchery of the public service cannot be found. It has been id by way of excuse that during Mr. Cleveland's administration a large number experienced and efficient clerks were dismissed from the service to make room for Democrats, and that the great number of changes made during that period had impaired the efficiency of the service, and that it was necessary to restore the old clerks to improve its standard.

This assertion is unqualifiedly false. It is a well known fact, and the official records support me in this statement, that the service had never before attained the standard of efficiency it did during the administration of Mr. Cleveland. From the very beginning the service began to improve. From the annual report of the Superintendent of the Railway Mail Service for the year 1893, I take the following figures :

Table of pieces of mail distributed, etc., annually since July 1, 1883.

Year ending June 30—	Number of pieces distributed.	Increase.	Number of errors.	Increase of errors.	Decrease of errors.	Number correct to each error.
1884........	4,519,661,900	538,145.620	1,167,223	208,745	....	3,872
1885..	4,948,058,400	428,397,500	887,704	....	279,519	5,575
1886........	5,329,521,475	381,462,075	1,260,443	372,739	....	4,228
1887........	5,834,690,875	505,479,393	1,734,617	474,174	....	3,364
1888........	6,528,772,030	694,081,185	1,755,821	31,204	....	3,694
1889........	8,026,837,130	498,065,070	1,777,295	11,474	....	3,954
1890........	7,847,723,600	820,886,470	2,769,245	991,950	....	2,834

It will be seen from the foregoing table that in 1885, the first year of Mr. Cleveland's administration, there was an increase of nearly five hundred millions o pieces distributed, and a decrease in the number of errors of nearly three hundred thousand. In 1884 there were 3,872 pieces correctly handled to each error, while in 1885 there were 5,575 pieces correctly handled to each error. During the year 1888, the last wholly under Democratic administration, 7,026,837,130 pieces were handled, with a total of 1,777,295 errors.   •

To each 3,954 pieces correctly handled there was one error, while during the first year, wholly under Republican Administration, from July 1, 1889, to July 1, 1890, 7,847,723,600 pieces were handled, with a total of 2,769,245 errors. The increase of errors was 991,950. The first year under the reforms inaugurated by the Republicans, the number of pieces correctly handled to each error fell from 3,954 to 2,834. It thus appears from the official records that in the first year of Mr. Harrison's Administration the standard of efficiency was reduced nearly 28 per cent.

REMARKS

OF

HON. GEO. W. COOPER,

OF INDIANA,

IN THE HOUSE OF REPRESENTATIVES.

Mr. COOPER of Indiana. I stated, as one of the reasons why the checking division of the Sixth Auditor's Office was behind, that the chief of that division had occupied much of his time and the time of the clerks in that service in preparing and publishing a life of ex-President Harrison.

While I was absent temporarily from the Hall of the House on yesterday, the gentleman from Ohio, after having, I will say in justice to him, endeavored to ascertain my presence, had read from the Clerk's desk a letter from this ex-chief of the checking division, in which he substantially contradicts the statement made by me. He said, in substance, that that division was about three years behind when he took charge of it, and that the prior Administration of the present President was to blame for that fact, and that during his incumbency the work was brought up something like a year in advance of what it was when he undertook it.

Now, Mr. Chairman, I wish to send to the Clerk's desk and have read a letter from one of the employees of that division, who is still in that service, upon that point.

The Clerk read as follows :

TREASURY DEPARTMENT,
OFFICE OF THE AUDITOR OF THE TREASURY
FOR THE POSTOFFICE DEPARTMENT,
Washington, D. C., May 25, 1894.

SIR: In reply to your request of this date, as to any facts I may know relative to Mr. Charles Hedges, late chief of the checking division, Sixth Auditor's Office, having during his term of office devoted his time, or caused clerks and other employees to have devoted their time during office hours to the preparation of a biographical sketch and compilation of speeches of ex-President Benjamin Harrison, I have this to state: That I have seen Mr. Hedges very busily engaged at his official desk, and during office hours, preparing writings, which turned out to be "Life and speeches of Hon. Benj. Harrison, President." Mr. Hall, one of his clerks, was at work in his room, using the typewriter, which seemed strange to me, as there is no work in that division which requires correspondence.

Sometime thereafter I noticed the room adjoining the chief's used as a storeroom for books, and upon inspecting them found they were the aforesaid mentioned books. Mr. Glendenning, one of his clerks, was engaged in addressing these books to subscribers and postmasters during office hours, and whilst his name was carried on the rolls. Shortly after, this clerk, a substitute, was appointed to a $1,000 position over a Miss Pettigrew, who stood at the top of the list in a competitive examination for promotion, notwithstanding that THOMAS B. REED had interested himself in her behalf.

It is the impression of the office that the appointment of Mr. Glendenning was the result of his labor for Mr. Hedges.

Very respectfully,

CHARLES A. GIVEN,
Clerk Sixth Auditor's Office.

Hon. GEORGE W. COOPER,
House of Representatives.

Mr. COOPER of Indiana. Now, I send forward a letter from another clerk, which I wish to have read.

The Clerk read as follows:

OFFICE OF THE AUDITOR OF THE TREASURY
FOR THE POSTOFFICE DEPARTMENT,
Washington, D. C., May 25, 1894.

SIR: In reply to your request of this date for information that I may possess relative to Charles Hedges, late chief of the checking division of the Sixth Auditor's Office, having used the Government's time for his own purposes by working himself, and, as chief of his division, causing Government employees under him to devote their time during office hours to the preparation of a book containing a biographical sketch and speeches of Benjamin Harrison, ex-president of the United States, I have this to say:

It is a matter openly talked that Judge Thomas, now chief clerk, Postoffice Department and late superintendent and disbursing clerk of the Postoffice Department, complained to the chief clerk of the Sixth Auditor's Office about one of the rooms of the Busch Building being occupied by some two wagonloads of mail sacks filled with the speeches of Benjamin Harrison, compiled by Charles Hedges, and that they were not removed until after complaint had been made.

It was a matter of common discussion in the division at that time that messengers, laborers, and clerks were used by Mr. Hedges during office hours, in violation of the rules and regulations of the Treasury Department, to prepare letters and circulars to promote the sale of said book, to unpack and store away in the Busch Building these books as they were received from the publishers, and wrap up singly or otherwise to deliver or mail to purchasers.

It was stated that Thornton Chesley, an employee of the office, was instructed by Mr. Hedges to make a canvass of the office for the sale of said book and that he did so during office hours, which is a violation of the rules and regulations of the Treasury Department prohibiting all canvassing whatever.

I know that clerks bought the book who could not afford to, to prevent incurring the displeasure of Mr. Hedges, and that clerks who did not buy the book felt that they were oppressed for not having done so.

As to the condition of the work on Mr. Hedge's division at the time of his retirement, I have this to say:

Chaos pervaded the entire division. New York postal notes were lost; not an official or clerk in the building could tell where to find them. The 9,000 books used in checking were everywhere but where they were wanted. It required three month's work of the assistant chief to catalogue and reduce to business system these books alone.

The division under Mr. Hedges had run itself. The clerks had checked as they choosed, or if they did not choose had turned in their weekly averages as checked when they were not, and sent the work to the files for this administration to take out of the files by the thousands and do over properly. In the basement were huge basketfuls of 1889, 1890 and 1891 work that clerks had left laying around loose and reported as done.

There was no uniformity in the work. As an illustration: Colorado not checked since 1889; Minnesota postal notes not checked since 1888; Washington, D. C., not checked since 1888; New York postal notes not checked since 1890.

Checking when done had been so badly done that more time of clerks was wasted erasing mischecks than would have been required to do the whole correctly in the beginning. The work is all reviewed now, and perfect business system followed in everything.

Respectfully,

CYNTHIA E. CLEVELAND,
Clerk Sixth Auditor's Office.

Hon. GEORGE W. COOPER,
House of Representatives.

Mr. COOPER of Indiana. Now, there is another letter at the desk. I ask to have it read. It is a short letter.

The Clerk read as follows:

WASHINGTON, D. C., *May* 25, 1894.

SIR: In reply to your request of this date for any information that I may have relative to the clerks or other employees in the Sixth Auditor's Office having devoted their time during office hours to the work of preparing a book containing a biographical sketch and speeches of ex-President Harrison, I have this to state:

The statements made by you are substantially correct. I was his private messenger and was employed during office hours, when my office work was done, in doing up for mailing from the office copies of the book in question. I did this under instructions from my chief, Mr. Hedges.

Very respectfully,

PATRICK DOOLAN,
Messenger Sixth Auditor's Office.

Hon. GEORGE W. COOPER,
House of Representatives.

DEMOCRATIC PLATFORM.

Adopted by the National Democratic Convention at Chicago, Ill., June 22, 1892.

"Section 1. The representatives of the Democratic party of the United States, in National Convention assembled, do reaffirm their allegiance to the principles of the party as formulated by Jefferson and exemplified by the long and illustrious line of his successors in Democratic leadership from Madison to Cleveland; we believe the public welfare demands that these principles be applied to the conduct of the Federal Government through the accession to power of the party that advocates them. and we solemnly declare that the need of a return to these fundamental principles of a free popular government, based on home rule and individual liberty, was never more urgent than now, when the tendency to centralize all power at the Federal Capital has become a menace to the reserved rights of the States that strikes at the very roots of our Government under the Constitution as framed by the fathers of the Republic.

AGAINST POLICY OF FORCE AND FRAUD.

"Section 2. We warn the people of our common country, jealous for the preservation of their free institutions, that the policy of Federal control of elections, to which the Republican party has committed itself, is fraught with the gravest dangers scarcely less momentous than would result from a revolution practically establishing monarchy on the ruins of the Republic. It strikes at the North as well as the South, and injures the colored citizens even more than the white; it means a horde of deputy marshals at every polling place armed with Federal power, returning boards appointed and controlled by Federal authority, the outrage of the electoral rights of the people in the several States, subjugation of the colored people to the control of the party in power and the reviving of race antagonisms now happily abated, of the tmost peril to the safety and happiness of all, a measure deliberately and ustly described by a leading Republican Senator as 'the most infamous bill that ever crossed the threshold of the Senate.' Such a policy, if sanctioned by law, would mean the dominance of a self perpetuating oligarchy of office-holders, and the party first intrusted with its machinery could be dislodged from power only by an appeal to the reserved rights of the people to resist oppression, which is inherent in all self-governing communities. Two years ago this revolutionary policy was emphatically condemned by the people at the polls, but in contempt of that verdict the Republican party has defiantly declared in its latest authoritative utterance that its success in the coming elections will mean the enactment of the force bill and the usurpation of despotic control over elections in all the States.

" Believing that the preservation of republican government in the United States is dependent upon the defeat of this policy of legalized force and fraud, we invite the support of all citizens who desire to see the Constitution maintained in its integrity with the laws pursuant thereto which have given our country a hundred years of unexampled prosperity; and we pledge the Democratic party, if it be intrusted with power, not only to the defeat of the force bill, but also to relentless opposition to the Republican policy of profligate expenditures which, in the short space of two years, has squandered an enormous surplus, emptied an overflowing Treasury, after piling new burdens of taxation upon the already overtaxed labor of the country.

REVENUE TARIFF.

"Section 3. We denounce Republican protection as a fraud—a robbery of the great majority of the American people for the benefit of the few. We declare it to be a fundamental principle of the Democratic party that the Federal Government has no constitutional power to impose and collect tariff duties, except for the purpose of revenue only, and we demand that the collection of such taxes shall be limited to the necessities of the Government when honestly and economically administered.

" We denounce the McKinley tariff law enacted by the Fifty-first Congress as the culminating atrocity of class legislation; we indorse the efforts made by the Democrats of the present Congress to modify its most oppressive feature in the direction of free raw materials and cheaper manufactured goods that enter into general consumption, and we promise its repeal as one of the beneficent results that will follow the action of the people in intrusting power to the Democratic party. Since the McKinley tariff went into operation there have been ten reductions of the wages of the laboring man to one increase. We deny that there has been any increase of prosperity to the country since that tariff went into operation, and we point to the dullness and distress, the wage reductions and strikes in the iron trade, as the best possible evidence that no such prosperity has resulted from the McKinley act.

" We call the attention of thoughtful Americans to the fact that after thirty years of restrictive taxes against the importation of foreign wealth, in exchange for our agricultural surplus, the homes and farms of the country have become burdened with a real estate mortgage debt of over \$2,500,000,000, exclusive of all other forms of indebtedness; that in one of the chief agricultural States of the West there appears a real estate mortgage debt averaging $165 per capita of the total population, and that similar conditions and tendencies are shown to exist in other agricultural exporting States. We denounce a policy which fosters no industry so much as it does that of the sheriff.

"Section 4. Trade interchange on the basis of reciprocal advantages to the countries participating is a time-honored doctrine of the Democratic faith, but we denounce the sham reciprocity which juggles with the people's desire for enlarged foreign markets and freer exchanges by pretending to establish closer trade relations for a country whose articles of export are almost exclusively agricultural products with other countries that are also agricultural, while erecting a custom-house barrier of prohibitive tariff taxes against the richest countries of the world that stand ready to take our entire surplus of products and to exchange therefor commodities which are necessaries and comforts of life among our own people.

"Section 5. We recognize in the trusts and combinations which are designed to enable capital to secure more than its just share of the joint product of capital and labor a natural consequence of the prohibitive taxes which prevent the free competition which is the life of honest trade, but believe their worst evils can be abated by law, and we demand the rigid enforcement of the laws made to prevent and control them, together with such further legislation in restraint of their abuses as experience may show to be necessary.

"Section 6. The Republican party, while professing a policy of reserving the public land for small holdings by actual settlers, has given away the people's heritage, till now a few railroads and non-resident aliens, individual and corporate, possess a larger area than that of all our farms between the two seas. The last Democratic administration reversed the improvident and unwise policy of the Republican party touching the public domain, and reclaimed from corporations and syndicates, alien and domestic, and restored to the people nearly one hundred million acres of valuable land to be sacredly held as homesteads for our citizens, and we pledge ourselves to continue this policy until every acre of land so unlawfully held shall be reclaimed and restored to the people.

"Section 7. We denounce the Republican legislation known as the Sherman act of 1890 as a cowardly makeshift, fraught with possibilities of danger in the future, which should make all of its supporters, as well as its author, anxious for its speedy repeal. We hold to the use of both gold and silver as the standard money of the country and to the coinage of both gold and silver without discriminating against either metal or charge for mintage, but the dollar unit of coinage of both metals must be of equal intrinsic and exchangeable value or be adjusted through international agreement or by such safeguards of legislation as shall insure the maintenance of the parity of the two metals and the equal power of every dollar at all times in the markets and in the payments of debt; and we demand that all paper currency shall be kept at par with and redeemable in such coin. We insist upon this policy as especially necessary for the protection of the farmers and laboring classes, the first and most defenseless victims of unstable money and a fluctuating currency.

"Section 8. We recommend that the prohibitory 10 per cent. tax on Stat bank issues be repealed.

"Section 9. Public office is a public trust. We reaffirm the declaration of the Democratic National Convention of 1876 for the reform of the civil service, and we call for the honest enforcement of all laws regulating the same. The nomination of a President, as in the recent Republican Convention, by delegations composed largely of his appointees, holding office at his pleasure, is a scandalous satire upon free popular institutions and a startling illustration of the methods by which a President may gratify his ambition. We denounce a policy under which federal office-holders usurp control of party conventions in the States, and we pledge the Democratic party to the reform of these and all other abuses which threaten individual liberty and local self-government.

"Section 10. The Democratic party is the only party that has ever given the country a foreign policy consistent and vigorous, compelling respect abroad, and inspiring confidence at home. While avoiding entangling alliances, it has aimed to cultivate friendly relations with other nations and especially with our neighbors on the American continent, whose destiny is closely linked with our own, and we view with alarm the tendency to a policy of irritation and bluster which is liable at any time to confront us with the alternative of humiliation or war. We favor the maintenance of a navy strong enough for all purposes of national defense, and to properly maintain the honor and dignity of the country abroad.

"Section 11. This country has always been the refuge of the oppressed from every land—exiles for conscience sake—and in the spirit of the founders of our Government we condemn the oppression practiced by the Russian Government upon its Luthern and Jewish subjects, and we call upon our National Government, in the interests of justice and humanity, and by all just and proper means to use its prompt and best effort to bring about a cessation of these cruel persecutions in the dominions of the Czar, and to secure to the oppressed equal rights.

"We tender our profound and earnest sympathy to those lovers of freedom who are struggling for home rule and the great cause of local self-goverement in Ireland.

"Section 12. We heartily approve all legitimate efforts to prevent the

United States from being used as a dumping ground for the known criminals and professional paupers of Europe and we demand the rigid enforcement of the laws against Chinese immigration or the importation of foreign workmen under contract to degrade American labor and lessen its wages; but we condemn and denounce any and all attempts to restrict the immigration of the industrious and worthy of foreign lands.

"Section 13. This convention hereby renews the expression of appreciation of the patriotism of the soldiers and sailors of the Union in the war for its preservation, and we favor just and liberal pensions for all disabled Union soldiers, their widows and dependents, but we demand that the work of the Pension Office shall be done industriously, impartially, and honestly. We denounce the present administration of that office as incompetent, corrupt, disgraceful, and dishonest.

"Section 14 The Federal Government should care for and improve the Mississippi river and other great waterways of the Republic so as to secure for the interior States easy and cheap transportation to tide water. When any waterway of the public is of sufficient importance to demand the aid of the Government—such aid should be extended upon a definite plan of continuous work until permanent improvement is secured.

" Section 15. For purposes of national defense, and the promotion of commerce between the States, we recognize the early construction of the Nicaragua canal and its protection against foreign control as of great importance to the United States.

"Section 16. Recognizing the World's Columbian Exposition as a national undertaking of vast importance in which the General Government has invited the co-operation of all the powers of the world, and appreciating the acceptance by many of such powers of the invitation so extended, and the broadest liberal efforts being made by them to contribute to the grandeur of the undertaking, we are of the opinion that Congress should make such necessary financial provision as shall be requisite to the maintenance of the national honor and public faith.

"Section 17. Popular education being the only safe basis of popular suffrage, we recommend to the several States most liberal appropriations for the public schools. Free common schools are the nursery of good government, and they have always received the fostering care of the Democratic party, which favors every means of increasing intelligence. Freedom of education being an essential of civil and religious liberty as well as a necessity for the development of intelligence, must not be interfered with under any pretext whatever. We are opposed to State interference with parental rights and rights of conscience in the education of children as an infringment of a fundamental Democratic doctrine that the largest individual liberty consistent with the rights of others insures the highest type of American citizenship and the best government.

"Section 18. We approve the action of the present House of Representa. tives in passsing bills for admitting into the Union as States the Terri- tories of New Mexico and Arizona, and we favor the early admission of all the Territories having the necessary population and resources to entitle them to statehood, and while they remain Territories we hold that the officials ap- pointed to administer the Government of any Territory, together with the District of Columbia and Alaska, should be *bona fide* residents of the Terri- tory or District in which their duties are to be performed. The Democratic party believes in home rule and the control of their own affairs by the people of the vicinage.

"Section 19. We favor legislation by Congress and State legislatures to protect the lives and limbs of railway employees and those of other hazardous transportation companies, and denounce the inactivity of the Republican party, particularly the Republican Senate, for causing the defeat of measures beneficial and protective to this class of wage workers.

"Section 20. We are in favor of the enactment by the States of laws for abolishing the notorious sweating system, for abolishing contract convict labor, and for prohibiting the employment in factories of children under fifteen years of age.

"Section 21. We are opposed to all sumptuary laws as an interference with the individual rights of the citizen.

"Section 22. Upon this statement of principles and policies the Democratic party asks the intelligent judgment of the American people. It asks a change of administration and a change of party, in order that there might be a change of system and a change of methods, thus assuring the maintenance unimpared . of institutions under which the Republic has grown great and powerful.''

GROVER CLEVELAND'S LETTER

Accepting the Democratic Nomination for the Presidency in 1892.

To Hon. William L. Wilson and Others, Committee, etc.

GENTLEMEN : In responding to your formal notification of my nomination to the Presidency by the National Democracy, I hope I may be permitted to say at the outset that continued reflection and observation have confirmed me in my adherence to the opinions, which I have heretofore plainly and publicly declared, touching the questions involved in the canvass.

This is a time, above all others, when these questions should be considered in the light afforded by a sober apprehension of the principles upon which our Government is based and a clear understanding of the relation it bears to the people for whose benefit it was created. We shall thus be supplied with a test by which the value of any proposition relating to the maintenance and administration of our Government can be ascertained and by which the justice and honesty of every political question can be judged. If doctrines or theories are presented which do not satisfy this test, loyal Americanism must pronounce them false and mischievous.

The protection of the people in the exclusive use and enjoyment of their property and earnings concededly constitutes the especial purpose and mission of our free Government. This design is so interwoven with the structure of our plan of rule that failure to protect the citizen in such use and enjoyment, or their unjustifiable diminution by the Government itself, is a betrayal of the people's trust.

We have, however, undertaken to build a great nation upon a plan especially our own. To maintain it and to furnish through its agency the means for the accomplishment of national objects the American people are willing through Federal taxation to surrender a part of their earnings and income.

Tariff legislation presents a familiar form of Federal taxaion. Such legislation results as surely in a tax upon the daily life of our people as the tribute paid directly into the hand of the tax-gatherer. We feel the burden of these tariff taxes too palpably to be persuaded by any sophistry that they do not exist, or are paid for by foreigners.

Such taxes, representing a diminution of the property rights of the people, are only justifiable when laid and collected for the purpose of maintaining our government, and furnishing the means for the accomplishment of its legitimate purposes and functions. This is taxation under the operation of a tariff for revenue. It accords with the professions of American free institutions, and its justice and honesty answer the test supplied by a correct appreciation of the principles upon which these institutions rest.

This theory of tariff legislation manifestly enjoins strict economy in public expenditures and their limitation to legitimate public uses, inasmuch as it exhibits as absolute extortion any exaction, by way of taxation, from the substance of the people, beyond the necessities of a careful and proper administration of government.

Opposed to this theory the dogma is now boldly presented, that tariff taxation is justifiable for the express purpose and intent of thereby promoting especial interests and enterprises. Such a proposition is so clearly contrary to the spirit of our Constitution and so directly encourages the disturbance by selfishness and greed of patriotic sentiment, that its statement would rudely shock our people, if they had not already been insidiously allured from the safe landmarks of principle. Never have honest desire for national growth, patriotic devotion to country, and sincere regard for those who toil, been so betrayed to the support of a pernicious doctrine. In its behalf, the plea that our infant industries should be fostered, did service until discredited by our stalwart growth; then followed the exigencies of a terrible war which made our people heedless of the opportunities for ulterior schemes afforded by their willing and patriotic payment of unprecedented tribute; and now, after a long period of peace, when our overburdened countrymen ask for relief and a restoration to· a fuller enjoyment of their incomes and earnings they are met by the claim that tariff taxation for the sake of protection is an American system, the continuance of which is necessary in order that high wages may be paid to our workingmen and a home market be provided for our farm products.

These pretenses should no longer deceive. The truth is that such a system is directly antagonized by every sentiment of justice and fairness of which Americans are pre-eminently proud. It is also true that while our workmen and farmers can, the least of all our people, defend themselves against the harder home life which such tariff taxation decrees, the workingman suffering from the importation and employment of pauper labor instigated by his professed friends, and seeking security for his interests in organized co-operation, still waits for a division of the advantages secured to his employer under cover of a generous solicitude for his wages, while the farmer is learning that the prices of his products are fixed in foreign markets; where he suffers from a competition invited and built up by the system he is asked to support.

The struggle for unearned advantages at the doors of the Government tramples on the rights of those who patiently rely upon assurances of American equality. Every governmental concession to clamorous favorites invites corruption in political affairs by encouraging the expenditure of money to debauch suffrage in support of a policy directly favorable to private and selfish gain. This in the end must strangle patriotism and weaken popular confidence in the rectitude of republican institutions.

Though the subject of tariff legislation involves a question of markets, it also involves a question of morals. We cannot with impunity permit injustice to taint the spirit of right and equity which is the life of our republic; and we shall fail to reach our national destiny if greed and selfishness lead the way.

Recognizing these truths, the National Democracy will seek by the application of just and sound principles to equalize to our people the blessings due them from the government they support, to promote among our countrymen a closer community of interests cemented by patriotism and national pride, and to point out a fair field, where prosperous and diversified American enterprise may grow and thrive in the wholesome atmosphere of American industry, ingenuity and intelligence.

Tariff reform is still our purpose. Though we oppose the theory that tariff laws may be passed having for their object the granting of discriminating and unfair governmental aid to private ventures, we wage no exterminating war against any American interests. We believe a readjustment can be accomplished in accordance with the principles we profess without disaster or demolition. We believe that the advantages of freer raw materials should be accorded to our manufacturers, and we contemplate a fair and careful distribution of necessary tariff burdens, rather than the precipitation of free trade.

We anticipate with calmness the misrepresentation of our motives and purposes, instigated by a selfishness which seeks to hold in unrelenting grasp its unfair advantage under present tariff laws. We will rely upon the intelligence of our fellow countrymen to reject the charge that a party comprising a majority of our people is planning the destruction or injury of American interests; and we know they cannot be frightened by the spectre of impossible free trade.

The administration and management of our Government depend upon popular will. Federal power is the instrument of that will—not its master. Therefore the attempt of the opponents of Democracy to interfere with and control the suffrage of the States through federal agencies, develops a design, which no explanation can mitigate, to reverse the fundamental and safe relations between the people and their government. Such an attempt cannot fail to be regarded by thoughtful men as proof of a bold determination to secure the ascendancy of a discredited party in reckless disregard of a free expression of the popular will. To resist such a scheme is an impulse of Democracy. At all times and in all places we trust the people. As against a disposition to force the way to federal power we present to them as our claim to their confidence and support, a steady championship of their rights.

The people are entitled to sound and honest money, abundantly sufficient in volume to supply their business needs.   But whatever may be the form of the people's currency, national or State—whether gold, silver or paper—it should be so regulated and guarded by governmental action, or by wise and careful laws, that no one can be deluded as to the certainty and stability of its value.   Every dollar put into the hands of the people should be of the same intrinsic value or purchasing power.   With this condition absolutely guaranteed, both gold and silver can be safely utilized, upon equal terms, in the adjustment of our currency.

In dealing with this subject no selfish scheme should be allowed to intervene and no doubtful experiment should be attempted.   The wants of our people, arising from the deficiency or imperfect distribution of money circulation, ought to be fully and honestly recognized and efficiently remedied. It should, however, be constantly remembered that the inconvenience or loss that might arise from such a situation, can be much easier borne than the universal distress which must follow a discredited currency.

Public officials are the agents of the people.   It is, therefore, their duty to secure for those whom they represent the best and most efficient performance of public work.   This plainly can be best accomplished by regarding ascertained fitness in the selection of Government employees.   These considerations alone are sufficient justification for an honest adherence to the letter and spirit of Civil Service Reform.   There are, however, other features of this plan which abundantly commend it.   Through its operation worthy merit in every station and condition of American life is recognized in the distribution of public employment, while its application tends to raise the standard of political activity from spoil hunting and unthinking party affiliation to the advocacy of party principles by reason and argument.

The American people are generous and grateful; and they have impressed these characteristics upon their Government.   Therefore, all patriotic and just citizens must commend liberal consideration for our worthy veteran soldiers and for the families of those who have died.   No complaint should be made of the amount of public money paid to those actually disabled or made dependent by reason of army service.   But our pension roll should be a roll of honor, uncontaminated by ill desert and unvitiated by demagogic use.   This is due to those whose worthy names adorn the roll, and to all our people who delight to honor the brave and the true.   It is also due to those who in years to come should be allowed to hear, reverently and lovingly, the story of American patriotism and fortitude, illustrated by our pension roll.   The preference accorded to veteran soldiers in public employment should be secured to them honestly and without evasion, and when capable and worthy, their claim to the helpful regard and gratitude of their countrymen should be ungrudgingly acknowledged.

The assurance to the people of the utmost individual liberty consistent with peace and good order is a cardinal principle of our government. This gives no sanction to vexatious sumptuary laws which unnecessarily interfere with such habits and customs of our people as are not offensive to a just moral sense and are not inconsistent with good citizenship and the public welfare. The same principle requires that the line between the subjects which are properly within governmental control and those which are more fittingly left to parental regulation should be carefully kept in view. An enforced education, wisely deemed a proper preparation for citizenship, should not involve the impairment of wholesome parental authority nor do violence to the household conscience. Paternalism in government finds no approval in the creed of Democracy. It is a symptom of misrule, whether it is manifested in unauthorized gifts or by an unwarranted control of personal and family affairs.

Our people, still cherishing the feeling of human fellowship which belonged to our beginning as a nation, require their government to express for them their sympathy with all those who are oppressed under any rule less free than ours.

A generous hospitality, which is one of the most prominent of our national characteristics, prompts us to welcome the worthy and industrious of all lands to homes and citizenship among us. This hospitable sentiment is not violated, however, by careful and reasonable regulations for the protection of the public health, nor does it justify the reception of immigrants who have no appreciation of our institutions and whose presence among us is a menace to peace and good order.

The importance of the construction of the Nicaragua Ship Canal as a means of promoting commerce between out States and with foreign countries, and also as a contribution by Americans to the enterprises which advance the interests of the world of civilization, should commend the project to governmental approval and indorsement.

Our countrymen not only expect from those who represent them in public places a sedulous care for things which are directly and palpably related to their material interests, but they also fully appreciate the value of cultivating our national pride and maintaining our national honor. Both their material interests and their national pride and honor are involved in the success of the Columbian Exposition ; and they will not be inclined to condone any neglect of effort on the part of their Government to insure in the grandeur of this event a fitting exhibit of American growth and greatness, and a splendid demonstration of American patriotism.

In an imperfect and incomplete manner, I have thus endeavored to state some of the things which accord with the creed and intentions of the party to which I have given my life-long allegiance. My attempt has not been to instruct my countrymen nor my party, but to remind both that Democratic doctrine lies near the principles of our Government and tends to promote the people's good. I am willing to be accused of addressing my countrymen upon trite topics and in homely fashion, for I believe that important truths are found on the surface of thought, and that they should be stated in direct and simple terms. Though much is left unwritten, my record as a public servant leaves no excuse for misunderstanding my belief and position on the questions which are now presented to the voters of the land for their decision.

Called for the third time to represent the party of my choice in a contest for the supremacy of Democratic principles, my greatful appreciation of its confidence less than ever effaces the solemn sense of my responsibility.

If the action of the Convention you represent shall be endorsed by the suffrages of my countrymen, I will assume the duties of the great office for which I have been nominated, knowing full well its labors and perplexities, and with humble reliance upon the Divine Being, infinite in power to aid, and constant in a watchful care over our favored Nation.

Yours very truly,

GROVER CLEVELAND.

GRAY GABLES, *September 26, 1892.*

CLEVELAND TO WILSON.

The President's Letter of July 2, 1894, on the Tariff.

EXECUTIVE MANSION, *Washington, July* 2, 1894.

MY DEAR SIR: The certainty that a conference will be ordered between the two houses of Congress for the purpose of adjusting differences on the subject of tariff legislation makes it also certain that you will be again called on to do hard service in the cause of tariff reform.

My public life has been so closely related to the subject, I have so longed for its accomplishment, and I have so often promised its realization to my fellow countrymen as a result of their trust and confidence in the Democratic party, that I hope no excuse is necessary for my earnest appeal to you that in this crisis you strenuously insist upon party honesty and good faith and a sturdy adherence to Democratic principles.

I believe these are absolutely necessary conditions to the continuation of Democratic existence.

I cannot rid myself of the feeling that this conference will present the best if not the only hope of true Democracy. Indications point to its action as the reliance of those who desire the genuine fruition of Democratic effort, the fulfillment of Democratic pledges and the redemption of Democratic promises to the people. To reconcile differences in the details comprised within the fixed and well-defined lines of principle will not be the sole task of the conference ; but as it seems to me its members will also have in charge the question whether Democratic principles themselves are to be saved or abandoned.

There is no excuse for mistaking or misapprehending the feeling and temper of the rank and file of the Democracy. They are downcast under the assertion that their party fails in ability to manage the Government, and they are apprehensive that efforts to bring about tariff reform may fail : but they are much more downcast and apprehensive in their fear that Democratic principles may be surrendered.

In these circumstances they cannot do otherwise than to look with confidence to you and those who with you have patriotically and sincerely championed the cause of tariff reform within Democratic lines and guided by Democratic principles. This confidence is vastly augmented by the action under your leadership of the House of Representatives upon the bill now pending.

Every true Democrat and every sincere tariff reformer knows that this bill in its present form and as it will be submitted to the conference, falls far short of the consummation for which we have long labored, for which we have suffered defeat without discouragement; which in its anticipation gave us a rallying cry in our day of triumph, and which, in its promise of accomplishment is so interwoven with Democratic pledges and Democratic success, that our abandonment of the cause or principles upon which it rests, means party perfidy and party dishonor.

One topic will be submitted to the conference which embodies Democratic principle so directly that it cannot be compromised. We have in our platforms and in every way possible declared in favor of the free importation of raw materials. We have again and again promised that this should be accorded to our people and our manufacturers as soon as the Democratic party was invested with the power to determine the tariff policy of the country.

The party now has that power. We are as certain to-day as we have ever been of the great benefit that would accrue to the country from the inauguration of this policy, and nothing has occurred to release us from our obligation to secure this advantage to our people. It must be admitted that no tariff measure can accord with Democratic principles and promises, or bear a genuine Democratic badge, that does not provide for free raw materials. In these circumstances it may well excite our wonder that Democrats are willing to depart from this the most Democratic of all tariff principles, and that the inconsistent absurdity of such a proposed departure should be emphasized by the suggestion that the wool of the farmer be put on the free list and the protection of tariff taxation be placed around the iron ore and coal of corporations and capitalists.

How can we face the people after indulging in such outrageous discriminations and violations of principle?

It is quite apparent that this question of free raw materials does not admit of adjustment on any middle ground, since their subjection to any rate of tariff taxation, great or small, is alike violative of Democratic principle and Democratic good faith.

I hope you will not consider it intrusive if I say something in relation to another subject which can hardly fail to be troublesome to the conference. I refer to the adjustment of tariff taxation on sugar.

Under our party platform and in accordance with our declared party purposes, sugar is a legitimate and logical article of revenue taxation. Unfortunately, however, incidents have accompanied certain stages of the legislation which will be submitted to the conference that have aroused in connection with this subject a natural Democratic animosity to the methods and manipulations of trusts and combinations.

I confess to sharing in this feeling; and yet it seems to me we ought, if possible, to sufficiently free ourselves from prejudice to enable us coolly to weigh the considerations which, in formulating tariff legislation, ought to guide our treatment of sugar as a taxable article.   While no tenderness should be entertained for trusts, and while I am decidedly opposed to granting them, under the guise of tariff taxation, any opportunity to further their peculiar methods, I suggest that we ought not to be driven away from the Democratic principle and policy which lead to the taxation of sugar by the fear, quite likely exaggerated, that in carrying out this principle and policy we may indirectly and inordinately encourage a combination of sugar refining interests. I know that in present conditions this is a delicate subject, and I appreciate the depth and strength of the feeling which its treatment has aroused.

I do not believe we should do evil that good may come, but it seems to me that we should not forget that our aim is the completion of a tariff bill, and that in taxing sugar for proper purposes and within reasonable bounds, whatever else may be said of our action, we are in no danger of running counter to Democratic principle.   With all there is at stake there must be in the treatment of this article some ground upon which we are all willing to stand, where toleration and conciliation may be allowed to solve the problem without demanding the entire surrender of fixed and conscientious convictions.

I ought not to prolong this letter.   If what I have written is unwelcome I beg you to believe in my good intentions.

In the conclusions of the conference touching the numerous items which will be considered, the people are not afraid that their interests will be neglected.   They know that the general result, so far as these are concerned, will be to place home necessaries and comforts easier within their reach, and to insure better and surer compensation to those who toil.

We all know that a tariff covering all the varied interests and conditions of a country as vast as ours, must of necessity be largely the result of honorable adjustment and compromise.   I expect very few of us can say when our measure is perfected that all the features are entirely as we would prefer.   You know how much I deprecated the incorporation in the proposed bill of the income-tax feature.   In matters of this kind, however, which do not violate a fixed and recognized Democratic doctrine we are willing to defer to the judgment of a majority of our Democratic brethren.   I think there is a general agreement that this is party duty.

This is more palpably apparent when we realize that the business of our country timidly stands and watches for the result of our efforts to perfect a ise adjustment, and that a confiding people still trust in our hand their prosperity and well-being.

The Democracy of the land plead most earestly for the speedy completion f the tariff legislation which their Representatives have undertaken, but they emand not less earnestly that no stress of necessity shall tempt those they ust to the abandonment of Democratic principle.

Yours, very truly,

GROVER CLEVELAND.

Hon. WILLIAM L. WILSON.

THE PRESIDENT ON THE NEW LAW.

His Letter of August 27, 1894, to Hon. T. C. Catchings.

EXECUTIVE MANSION,
WASHINGTON, *August 27, 1894.*

Hon. T. C. CATCHINGS.

MY DEAR SIR : Since the conversation I had with you and Mr. Clarke of Alabama a few days ago in regard to my action on the tariff bill now before me, I have given the subject further and most serious consideration. The result is I am more settled than ever in the determination to allow the bill to become a law without my signature.

When the formation of legislation which it was hoped would embody Democratic ideas of tariff reform was lately entered upon by the Congress, nothing was further from my anticipation than a result which I could not promptly and enthusiastically indorse.

It is, therefore, with a feeling of the utmost disappointment that I submit to a denial of this privilege.

I do not claim to be better than the masses of my party, nor do I wish to avoid any responsibility which, on account of the passage of this law, I ought to bear as a member of the Democratic organization. Neither will I permit myself to be separated from my party to such an extent as might be implied by my veto of tariff legislation, which, though disappointing, is still chargeable to Democratic effort. But there are provisions in this tariff bill which are not in the line with honest tariff reform, and it contains inconsistencies and crudities which ought not to appear in tariff laws or laws of any kind. Besides, there were, as you and I well know, incidents accompanying the passage of the bill through the Congress which made every sincere tariff reformer unhappy, while influences, surrounded it in its later stages and interfered with its final construction, which ought not to be recognized or tolerated in Democratic tariff reform counsels.

And yet, notwithstanding all its vicissitudes and all the bad treatment it received at the hands of pretended friends, it presents a vast improvement to existing conditions. It will certainly lighten many tariff burdens that now rest heavily upon the people. It is not only a barrier against the return of mad protection, but it furnishes a vantage ground from which must be waged further aggressive operations against protected monopoly and governmental favoritism.

I take my place with the rank and file of the Democratic party who believe n tariff reform, and who know what it is, who refuse to accept the results embodied in this bill at the close of the war, who are not blinded to the fact that the livery of Democratic tariff reform has been stolen and worn in the service of Republican protection, and who have marked the places where the deadly light of treason has blasted the counsels of the brave in their hour of might.

The trusts and combinations—the communism of pelf—whose machinations have prevented us from reaching the success we deserved, should not be forgotten or forgiven. We shall recover from our astonishment at their exhibition of power, and if then the question is forced upon us whether they shall submit to the free legislative will of the people's representatives, or shall dictate the laws which the people must obey, we will accept and settle that issue as one involving the integrity and safety of American institutions.

I love the principles of true Democracy because they are founded in patriotism and upon justice and fairness toward all interests. I am proud of my party organization because it is conservatively sturdy and persistent in the enforcement of its principles. Therefore, I do not despair of the efforts made by the House of Representatives to supplement the bill already passed by further legislation, and to have engrafted upon it such modifications as will more nearly meet Democratic hopes and aspirations.

I cannot be mistaken as to the necessity of free raw materials as the foundation of logical and sensible tariff reform. The extent to which this is recognized in the legislation already secured is one of its encouraging and redeeming features, but it is vexatious to recall that while free coal and iron ore have been denied us, a recent letter of the Secretary of the Treasury discloses the fact that both might have been made free by the annual surrender of only about $700,000 of unnecessary revenue.

I am sure that there is a common habit of under-estimating the importance of free raw materials in tariff legislation, and of regarding them as only related to concessions to be made to our manufacturers. The truth is, their influence is so far reaching that, if disregarded, a complete and beneficent scheme of tariff reform cannot be successfully inaugurated.

When we give to our manufacturers free raw materials we unshackle American enterprises and ingenuity, and these will open the doors of foreign markets to the reception of our wares and give opportunity for the continuous and remunerative employment of American labor.

With materials cheapened by their freedom from tariff charges the cost of their product must be correspondingly cheapened. Thereupon justice and fairness to the consumer would demand that the manufacturers be obliged to submit to such a readjustment and modification of the tariff upon their finished goods as would secure to the people the benefit of the reduced cost of their manufacture, and shield the consumer against the exaction of inordinate profits.

It will thus be seen that free raw materials and a just and fearless regulation and reduction of the tariff to meet the changed conditions would carry to every humble home in the land the blessings of increased comfort and cheaper living.

The millions of our countrymen who have fought bravely and well for tariff reform should be exhorted to continue the struggle, boldly challenging to open warfare and constantly guarding against treachery and half-heartedness in their camp.

Tariff reform will not be settled until it is honestly and fairly settled in the interest and to the benefit of a patient and long-suffering people.

    Yours very truly,

GROVER CLEVELAND.

TAX LAWS.

An Act to Subject to State Taxation National Bank Notes and United States Treasury Notes.

Be it enacted by the Senate and House of Representatives of the United States of America in Congress assembled, That circulating notes of national banking associations and United States legal-tender notes and other notes and certificates of the United States payable on demand and circulating or intended to circulate as currency and gold, silver or other coin shall be subject to taxation as money on hand or on deposit under the laws of any State or Territory; *Provided,* That any such taxation shall be exercised in the same manner and at the same rate that any such State or Territory shall tax money or currency circulating as money within its jurisdiction.

Sec. 2. That the provisions of this act shall not be deemed or held to change existing laws in respect of the taxation of national banking associations.

Approved, August 13, 1894.

SILVER STATISTICS.

The Law of July 14, 1890, Commonly Called the Sherman Law.

[Public—No. 214.]

An act directing the purchase of silver bullion and the issue of Treasury notes thereon, and for other purposes.

Be it enacted, etc., That the Secretary of the Treasury is hereby directed to purchase, from time to time, silver bullion to the aggregate amount of 4,500,000 ounces, or so much thereof as may be offered in each month, at the market price thereof, not exceeding $1 for 371.25 grains of pure silver, and to issue in payment for such purchases of silver bullion Treasury notes of the United States to be prepared by the Secretary of the Treasury, in such form and of such denominations, not less than $1 nor more than $1,000, as he may prescribe, and a sum sufficient to carry into effect the provisions of this act is hereby appropriated out of any money in the Treasury not otherwise appropriated.

SEC. 2. That the Treasury notes issued in accordance with the provisions of this act shall be redeemable on demand, in coin, at the Treasury of the United States, or at the office of any assistant treasurer of the United States, and when so redeemed may be reissued ; but no greater or less amount of such notes shall be outstanding at any time than the cost of the silver bullion and the standard silver dollars coined therefrom, then held in the Treasury, purchased by such notes; and such Treasury notes shall be a legal tender in payment of all debts, public and private, except where otherwise expressly stipulated in the contract, and shall be receivable for customs, taxes, and all public dues, and when so received may be reissued ; and such notes, when held by any national banking association, may be counted as a part of its lawful reserve. That upon demand of the holder of any of the Treasury notes herein provided for the Secretary of the Treasury shall, under such regulations as he may prescribe, redeem such notes in gold or silver coin, at his discretion, it being the established policy of the United States to maintain the two metals on a parity with each other upon the present legal ratio, or such ratio as may be provided by law

SEC. 3. That the Secretary of the Treasury shall each month coin 2,000,000 ounces of silver bullion purchased under the provisions of this act into standard silver dollars until the 1st day of July, 1891, and after that time he shall coin of the silver bullion purchased under the provisions of this act as much as may be necessary to provide for the redemption of the Treasury notes herein provided for, and any gain or seigniorage arising from such coinage shall be accounted for and paid into the Treasury.

SEC. 4. That the silver bullion purchased under the provisions of this act shall be subject to the requirements of existing law and the regulations of the mint service governing the methods of determining the amount of pure silver contained, and the amount of charges or deductions, if any, to be made.

SEC. 5. That so much of the act of February 28, 1878, entitled : "An act to authorize the coinage of the standard silver dollar and to restore its legal-tender character," as requires the monthly purchase and coinage of the same into silver dollars of not less than $2,000,000 nor more than $4,000,000 worth of silver bullion, is hereby repealed.

SEC. 6. That upon the passage of this act the balances standing with the Treasurer of the United States to the respective credits of national banks for deposits made to redeem the circulating notes of such banks, and all deposits thereafter received for like purpose, shall be covered into the Treasury as a miscellaneous receipt and the Treasurer of the United States shall redeem from the general cash in the Treasury the circulating notes of said banks which may come into his possession subject to redemption; and upon the certificate of the Comptroller of the Currency that such notes have been received by him and that they have been destroyed and that no new notes will be issued in their place, reimbursement of their amount shall be' made to the Treasurer, under such regulations as the Secretary of the Treasury may prescribe, from an appropriation hereby created, to be known as national banks redemption account: but the provisions of this act shall not apply to the deposits received under section 3 of the act of June 20, 1874, requiring every national bank to keep in lawful money with the Treasurer of the United States a sum equal to five per cent of its circulation, to be held and used for the redemption of its circulating notes, and the balance remaining of the deposits so covered shall, at the close of each month, be reported on the monthly public debt statement as debt of the United States bearing no interest.

SEC. 7. That this act shall take effect thirty days from and after its passage.

Approved July 14, 1890.

Commercial ratio of silver to gold for each year since 1867.

Year.	Ratio.	Year.	Ratio.	Year.	Ratio.	Year.	Ratio.
1795	15.55	1820	15.62	1845	15.92	1870	15.57
1796	15.65	1821	15.95	1846	15.90	1871	15.57
1797	15.41	1822	15.80	1847	15.80	1872	15.63
1798	15.59	1823	15.84	1848	15.85	1873	15.92
1799	15.74	1824	15.82	1849	15.78	1874	16.17
1800	15.68	1825	15.70	1850	15.70	1875	16.59
1801	15.46	1826	15.76	1851	15.46	1876	17.88
1802	15.26	1827	15.74	1852	15.59	1877	17.22
1803	15.41	1828	15.78	1853	15.33	1878	17.94
1804	15.41	1829	15.78	1854	15.33	1879	18.40
1805	15.79	1830	15.82	1855	15.38	1880	18.05
1806	15.52	1831	15.72	1856	15.38	1881	18.16
1807	15.43	1832	15.73	1857	15.27	1882	18.19
1808	16.08	1833	15.93	1858	15.38	1883	18.64
1809	15.96	1834	15.73	1859	15.19	1884	18.57
1810	15.77	1835	15.80	1860	15.29	1885	19.41
1811	15.53	1836	15.72	1861	15.50	1886	20.78
1812	16.11	1837	15.83	1862	15.35	1887	21.13
1813	16.25	1838	15.85	1863	15.37	1888	21.99
1814	15.04	1839	15.62	1864	15.37	1889	22.09
1815	15.26	1840	15.62	1865	15.44	1890	19.75
1816	15.28	1841	15.70	1866	15.43	1891	20.92
1817	15.11	1842	15.87	1867	15.57	1892	23.72
1818	15.35	1843	15.93	1868	15.59	1893*	28.52
1819	15.33	1844	15.85	1869	15.60		

* For seven months ending July 31, 1893.

Value of gold coin and bullion imported into and exported from the United States from 1843 to 1892: also excess of imports or exports.

[Compiled from United States Statistical Abstract, 1892.]

Year ending June 30—	Exports.		Total exports.	Imports.	Excess of exports over imports.	Excess of imports over exports.
	Domestic.	Foreign.				
1843 (nine mos.)-1852..		$25,602,569	$25,602,569	$58,465,192		$32,862,623
1853-1862*	$31,044,651	32,264,862	63,309,513	86,596,255		23,286,742
1863-1872	498,264,195	35,442,456	533,706,651	98,954,642	$434,752,009	
1873-1881	236,234,555	19,997,089	156,231,642	310,243,192		54,011,550
1883	8,920,909	2,679,979	11'600,888	17,734,149		6,133,261
1884	35,294,204	5,787,753	41,081,957	22,831,317	18,250,640	
1885	2,741,559	5,736,333	8,477,892	26,691,696		18,213,804
1886	32,766,066	10,186,125	42,952,191	20,743,349	22,208,842	
1887	5,705,304	3,995,883	9;701,187	42,910,601		33,209,414
1888	12,560,084	5,816,150	18,376,234	43,934,347		25,558,083
1889	54,930,332	5,021,953	59,952,850	10,284,858	49,667,427	
1890	13,403,632	3,870,859	17,274,491	12,943,342	4,331,149	
1891	84,939,561	1,423,103	86,362,654	18,232,567	68,130,087	
1892	43,321,351	6,873,976	50,195,327	49,699,454	495,873	
Total	1,060,126,391	164,699,090	1,224,825,481	820,264,931	597,836,027	193,275,477
Total excess of exports					404,560,550	

*Report of domestic shipments commences with 1862.

Value of silver coin and bullion imported into and exported from the United States from 1843 to 1892, inclusive; also excess of exports.

[Compiled from United States Statistical Abstract, 1892.]

Period—Year ending June 30.	Exports.		Total exports.	Imports.	Excess of exports.
	Domestic.	Foreign.			
1843; 9 months-1852	$62,832,863	$33,874,235	$96,707,098	$30,253,698	$66,453,400
1853-1862	400,451,426	25,883,707	426,355,133	42,707,040	383,628,093
1863-1872	188,187,965	49,611,875	237,799,840	60,754,850	177,044,990
1873-1882	186,073,265	58,439,561	244,512,829	113,503,974	131,008,855
1883	12,702,272	7,517,173	20,219,445	10,755,242	9,464,203
1884	14,931,431	11,119,995	26,051,426	14,594,945	11,456,481
1885	21,634,551	12,119,082	33,753,633	16,550,626	17,203,006
1886	19,158,051	10,353,168	29,511,219	17,850,307	11,660,912
1887	17,005,036	9,291,468	26,296,504	17,260,191	9,036,313
1888	20,635,420	7,402,529	28,037,949	15,403,669	12,634,280
1889	25,284,662	11,404,586	36,689,248	18,678,215	18,011,033
1890	22,378,557	12,495,372	34,873,929	21,032,184	13,840,945
1891	14,033,714	8,557,274	22,590,988	18,026,880	4,564,108
1892	16,765,067	16,045,492	32,810,559	19,955,086	12,855,478
Total	1,022,074,280	274,115,520	1,296,189,890	417,327,708	878,862,092

Highest, lowest, and average price of silver bullion, and value of a fine ounce, bullion value of a United States silver dollar, and commercial ratio of silver to gold by fiscal years, 1874 to 1893.

Fiscal years.	Highest.	Lowest.	Average London price per ounce standard .925.	Equivalent value of a fine ounce with exchange at par, $4.8665.	Equivalent value of a fine ounce based on average price of exchange.	Bullion value of a United States silver dollar at average price of silver, exchange at par.	Commercial ratio of silver to gold.
	Pence.	*Pence.*	*Pence.*				
1873–'74....	59⅜	57⅞	58.312	$1.27826	$1.29247	$0.98865	16.17
1874–'75....	58½	55½	56.875	1.25127	1.25022	.96777	16.52
1875–'76....	57⅛	50	52.750	1.15184	1.15954	.89087	17.94
1876–'77....	58½	50¼	54.812	1.20154	1.20191	.92931	17.20
1877–'78....	55⅝	52½	52.562	1.15222	1.15257	.89116	17.94
1878–'79....	52 13-16	48⅞	50.812	1.11386	1.11616	.86152	18.55
1879–'80....	53¾	51⅛	52.218	1.14436	1.14397	.88509	18.06
1880–'81....	52⅞	51	51.937	1.13852	1.13508	.88057	18.15
1881–'82....	52 5-16	50⅞	51.812	1.13623	1.13817	.87880	18.19
1882–'83....	52 1-16	50	51.023	1.11826	1.11912	.86490	18.48
1883–'84....	51⅜	50 5-16	50.791	1.11339	1.11529	.86115	18.56
1884–'85....	50 13-16	48¾	49.843	1.09262	1.09226	.84507	18.92
1885–'86....	49 3-16	42	47.038	1.03112	1.03295	.79750	20.04
1886–'87....	47⅛	42	44.843	.98301	.98148	.76029	21.02
1887–'88....	45 3-16	41⅝	43.675	.95741	.95617	.74008	21.59
1888–'89....	44¼	41 15-16	42.499	.93163	.93510	.72055	22.18
1889–'90....	49	42	44.196	.96883	.96839	.74932	21.33
1890–'91....	54⅝	43⅞	47.714	1.04195	1.04780	.80588	19.83
1891–'92....	46⅜	39	42.737	.93648	.93723	.72430	22.07
1892–'93....	40 3-16	30½	38.375	.84133	.84263	.65063	24.57
July..	34¾	32⅛	33.060	.72471	.72037	.56052	28.52

TREASURY DEPARTMENT,
Bureau of the Mint, August 1, 1893.

Product of gold and silver in the United States from 1792–1844 and annually since.

[The estimate for 1792–1873 is by R. W. Raymond, Commissioner, and since by the Director of the Mint.]

Years.	Gold.	Silver.	Total.
April 2, 1792–July 31, 1834.	$14,000,000	Insignificant.	$14,000,000
July 31, 1834–December 31, 1844.	7,500,000	$250,000	7,750,000
1845	1,008,327	50,000	1,058,327
1846	1,139,357	50,000	1,189,357
1847	889,085	50,000	939,085
1848	10,000,000	50,000	10,050,000
1849	40,000,000	50,000	40,050,000
1850	50,000,000	50,000	50,050,000
1851	55,000,000	50,000	55,050,000
1852	60,000,000	50,000	60,050,000
1053	65,000,000	50,000	65,050,000
1854	60,000,000	50,000	60,050,000
1855	55,000,000	50,000	55,050,000
1856	55,000,000	50,000	55,050,000
1857	55,000,000	50,000	55,050,000
1858	50,000,000	500,000	50,500,000
1859	50,000,000	100,000	50,100,000
1860	46,000,000	150,000	46,150,000
1861	43,000,000	2,000,000	45,000,000
1862	39,200,000	4,500,000	43,700,000
1863	40,000,000	8,500,000	48,500,000
1864	46,100,000	11,000,000	57,100,000
1865	53,225,000	11,250,000	64,475,000
1866	53,500,000	10,000,000	63,500,000
1867	51,725,000	13,500,000	65,225,000
1868	48,060,000	12,000,000	60,000,000
1869	49,500,000	12,000,000	61,500,000
1870	50,000,000	16,000,000	66,000,000
1871	43,500,000	23,000,000	66,500,000
1872	36,000,000	28,750,000	64,750,000
1873	36,000,000	35,750,000	71,750,000
1874	33,500,000	57,300,000	70,800,000
1875	33,400,000	31,700,000	65,100,000
1876	39,900,000	38,800,000	78,700,000
1877	46,900,000	39,800,000	86,700,000
1878	51,200,000	45,200,000	96,400,000
1879	38,900,000	40,800,000	79,700,000
1880	36,000,000	39,200,000	75,200,000
1881	34,700,000	43,000,000	77,700,000
1882	32,500,000	46,800,000	79,300,000
1883	30,000,000	46,200,000	76,200,000
1884	30,800,000	48,800,000	79,600,000
1885	31,800,000	51,600,000	83,400,000
1886	35,000,000	51,000,000	86,000,000
1887	33,000,000	53,350,000	86,350,000
1888	33,175,000	59,195,000	92,370,000
1889	32,800,000	64,646,000	97,446,000
1890	32,845,000	70,464,000	103,309,000
1891	33,175,000	75,417,000	108,592,000
1892	33,000,000	73,697,000	106,697,000
Total	1,937,881,709	1,146,869,000	3,084,750,769

Statement of the production of gold and silver in the   rld since the discovery of America.

rom 1493 to 1895 is from the table of averages for certian periods compiled by Dr
\dolph Soetbeer.   For the years 1886-1892 the production is the annual estimate of
he Bureau of the Mint.]

Period.	Gold.			
	Annual average of period.		Total for the period.	
	Fine ounces.	Value.	Fine ounces.	Value.
3-1520.......................	186,470	$3,855,000	5,221,160	$107,931,000
1-1544.......................	230,194	4,759,000	5,524,656	114,205,000
5-1560.......................	273,596	5,656,000	4,377,544	90,492,000
1-1580.......................	219,906	4,546,000	4,398,120	90,917,000
1-1600.......................	237,267	4,905,000	4,745,340	98,095,000
1-1620.......................	273,918	5,662,000	5,478,360	113,248,000
1-1640.......................	266,845	5,516,000	5,336,900	110,324,000
1-1660.......................	281,955	5,828,000	5,639,110	116,571,000
1-1680.......................	297,709	6,154,000	5,954,180	123,084,000
1-1700.......................	346,095	7,154,000	6,921,895	143,088,000
1-1720.......................	412,163	8,520,000	8,243,260	170,403,000
1-1740	613,422	12,681,000	12,268,440	253,611,000
1-1760.......................	791,211	16,356,000	15,824,230	327,116,000
1-1780.......................	665,666	13,761,000	13,313,315	275,211,000
1-1800.......................	571,949	11,823,000	11,439,970	236,464,000
1-1810.......................	571,563	11,815,000	5,715,627	118,152,000
1-1820.......................	367,957	7,606,000	3,679,568	76,063,000
1-1830.......................	457,044	9,448,000	4,570,444	94,479,000
1-1840	652,291	13,484,000	6,522,913	134,841,000
1-1850.......................	1,760,502	36,393,000	17,605,018	363,928,000
1-1855.......................	6,410,324	132,573,000	32,051,621	662,566,000
6-1860.......................	6,486,262	134,083,000	32,431,312	670,415,000
1-1865.......................	5,949,582	122,989,000	29,747,913	614,944,000
6-1870	6,270,086	129,614,000	31 350,430	648,071,000
1-1875.......................	5,501,014	115,577,000	27,955,068	577,083,000
6-1880.......................	5,543,110	114,186,000	27,715,550	572,931,000
1-1895.......................	4,794,755	99,116,000	23,973,773	495,582,000
16...........................	5,127,750	106,000,000	5,127,750	106,000,000

Statement of the production of gold and silver in the world—Continued.

[From 1493 to 1885 is from table of averages for certain periods compiled by Dr Adolph Soetbeer. For the years 1886-1892 the production is the annual estimate o the Bureau of the Mint.]

	Silver.				Percentage of production.			
Period.	Annual av'ge of period.		Total for the period.		By weight.		By value.	
	Fine ounces.	Coinage value.	Fine ounces.	Coinage value.	Gold.	Silver.	Gold.	Silver.
1493-1520..	1,511,050	$1,954,000	42,309,400	$54,703,000	11.0	89.0	66.4	33.
1521-1544..	2,899,930	3,749,000	69,598,320	89,996,000	7.4	92.6	55.9	44.
1545-1560..	10,017,940	12,952,000	160,287,040	207,240,000	2.7	97.3	30.4	69.
1561-1580..	9,628,925	12,450,000	192,578,500	248,990,000	2.2	97.8	26.7	73.
1581-1600..	13,467,635	17,413,000	269,352,700	348,254,000	1.7	98.3	22.0	78.
1601-1620..	13,596,235	17,579,000	271,924,700	351,579,000	2.0	98.0	24.4	75.
1621-1640..	12,654,240	16,361,000	253,084,800	327,221,000	2.1	97.9	25.2	74.
1641-1660..	11,776,545	15,226,000	235,530,900	304,525,000	2.3	97.7	27.7	72.
1661-1680..	10,834,550	14,008,000	216,691,000	280,186,000	2.7	97.3	30.5	69.
1681-1700..	10,992,085	14,212,000	219,841,700	284,240,000	3.1	96.9	33.5	66.
1701-1720..	11,432,540	14,781,000	228,650,800	295,629,000	3.5	96.5	36.6	63.
1721-1740..	13,863,080	17,924,000	277,261,600	358,480,000	4.2	95.8	41.4	58.
1741-1760..	17,140,612	22,162,000	342,812,235	443,232,000	4.4	95.6	42.5	57.
1761-1780..	20,985,591	27,133,000	419,711,820	542,658,000	3.1	96.9	33.7	66.
1781-1800..	28,261,779	36,540,000	565,235,580	730,810,000	2.0	98.0	24.4	75.
1801-1810..	28,746,922	37,168,000	287,469,225	371,677,600	1.9	98.1	24.1	75.
1811-1820..	17,382,755	22,479,000	173,837,555	224,786,000	2.1	97.9	25.3	74.
1821-1830..	14,807,004	19,144,000	148,070,040	191,441,000	3.0	97.0	33.0	67.
1831-1840..	19,175,867	24,793,000	191,758,675	247,930,000	3.3	96.7	35.2	64.
1841-1850..	25,090,342	32,440,000	250,903,422	324,400,000	6.6	93.4	52.9	47.
1851-1855..	28,488,597	36,824,000	142,442,986	184,169,000	18.4	81.6	78.3	21.
1856-1860..	29,095,428	37,618,000	145,477,142	188,092,000	18.2	81.8	78.1	21.
1861-1865..	35,401,972	45,772,000	177,009,862	228,861,000	14.4	85.6	72.9	27.
1866-1870..	43,051,583	55,663,000	215,25,914	278,313,000	12.7	87.3	70.0	30.
1871-1875..	63,317,014	81,864,000	316,585,069	409,322,000	8.1	91.9	58.6	41.
1876-1880..	78,775,602	101,851,000	393,878,000	509,256,000	6.6	93.4	53.0	47.
1881-1885..	92,003,943	118,935,000	460,019,722	594,773,000	5.0	95.0	45.5	54.
1886.......	93,276,000	120,600,000	93,276,000	120,600 000	5.2	94.8	46.8	53

	In circulation.				From June 1, 1894.	
	June 1, 1893.	July 1, 1893.	June 1, 1894.	July 1, 1891.	Decrease.	Increase.
	Dollars.	*Dollars.*	*Dollars.*	*Dollars.*	*Dollars.*	*Dollars.*
Gold coin	407,945,944 00	403,633,700 00	409,632,485 00	407,873,990 00	1,758,495 00	....
Standard silver dollars	58,053,489 00	57,029,743 00	51,952,691 00	51,191,377 00	761,314 00	....
Subsidiary silver	66,163,602 00	65,400,268 00	58,085,917 00	58,233,311 00	....	117,427 00
Gold certificates	101,469,969 00	92,970,019 00	69,374,549 00	66,344,409 00	3,030,140 00	....
Silver certificates	322,115,592 00	326,489,165 00	329,959,959 00	327,094,381 00	2,865,578 00	....
Treasury notes, act July 14, 1890	132,565,183 00	140,461,694 00	140,074,690 00	134,862,009 00	5,212,681 00	....
United States notes	319,622,323 00	320,875,643 00	270,590,080 00	268,772,371 00	1,817,718 00	....
Currency certificates, act June 8, 1872	16,955,000 00	11,935,000 00	59,250,000 00	58,935,000 00	315,000 00	....
National Bank notes	171,920,799 00	174,731,139 00	199,724,021 00	200,754,351 00	....	1,030,330 00
Total	1,596,151,901 00	1,593,726,411 00	1,678,644,401 00	1,664,061,232 00	14,583,169 00	....

Paper Currency of each Denomination Outstanding June 30, 1894.

Denominations.	United States notes.	Treasury notes of 1890.	National bank notes.	Gold certificates.	Silver certificates.	Currency certificates.	Total.
	Dollars.	Dollars.	Dollars.	Dollars.	Dollars.	Dollars.	Dollars.
One-dollar	3,052,444	12,829,457	357,050	......	22,281,229	......	38,520,180
Two-dollar	2,470,403	10,346,325	174,282	......	15,366,373	......	28,357,383
Five-dollar	52,784,784	33,819,185	61,510,485	......	87,651,885	......	235,766,339
Ten-dollar	84,094,285	41,240,890	66,006,900	......	104,611,711	......	295,953,686
Twenty-dollar	95,125,750	20,110,660	48,685,320	7,464,594	68,849,576	......	240,235,900
Fifty-dollar	14,133,400	1,048,940	10,274,550	4,118,005	13,156,510	......	42,731,365
One-hundred-dollar	23,990,950	11,627,010	19,640,800	5,672,300	24,226,220	......	85,197,270
Five-hundred-dollar	12,039,000	......	133,500	4,546,500	483,000	......	17,202,000
One-thousand-dollar	59,965,000	21,562,000	32,000	8,861,500	522,000	......	90,942,500
Five-thousand-dollar	15,000	......	......	12,185,000	......	395,000	12,595,000
Ten-thousand-dollar	10,000	......	......	23,540,000	......	58,840,000	82,390,000
Fractional parts	......	......	28,143	......	......	......	28,143
Total	347,681,016	152,584,417	206,882,930	66,387,899	337,148,504	59,235,000	1,169,919,766
Unknown destroyed	1,000,000	......	......	......	......	......	1,000,000
Net	346,681,016	152,584,417	206,882,930	66,387,899	337,148,504	59,235,000	1,168,919,766

Financial and commercial statistics of the United States, 1867 to 1893.
[From official data.]

Years.	Population June 30—	Debt, less cash in Treasury. (Per capita.)	Interest paid. (Per capita)	Net ordinary revenue receipts. (Per capita)	Net ordinary expenditures. (Per capita)	Disbursement for pensions. (Per capita.)	Merchandise imported for consumption. (Per capita.)	Customs revenue.			Expenses of collecting customs revenue.
								Duty collected. (Per capita.)	Average ad valorem rate of duty.		
									On dutiable.	On free and dutiable.	
		Dolls.	Dolls.	Dolls.	Dol's.	Dolls.	Dolls.	Dolls.	Per ct.	Per ct.	Per ct.
1867	36,211,000	60 26	3 84	13 55	9 87	$0 51	10 44	4 65	46 67	44.56	3.26
1868	36,973 000	67 10	3 43	10 97	10 21	65	9 33	4 34	48.63	46 49	1.65
1869	37,756,000	64 43	3 32	9 82	8 55	78	10 45	4 68	47.22	44.65	2.99
1870	38,558,371	60 46	3 08	10 67	8 03	72	11 06	4 96	47.08	42 23	3 20
1871	39,555,000	56 81	2 83	9 69	7 39	84	12 65	5 12	43.95	38.94	3.18
1872	40,596,000	52 96	2 56	9 22	6 84	74	13 80	5 23	41.35	37.00	3.21
1873	41,677,000	50 52	2 35	8 01	6 97	70	15 91	4 44	39.07	26 95	3.76
1874	42,796,000	49 17	2 31	7 13	7 07	71	13 26	3 75	38.53	26.58	4 49
1875	43,951,000	47 55	2 20	6 55	6 25	68	11 97	3 51	40.62	28 20	4 47
1876	45,137,000	45 66	2 11	6 52	5 87	63	10 29	3 22	44.74	39.19	4.53
1877	46,353,000	43 56	2 01	6 07	5 21	62	9 49	2 77	42.89	26.68	4.96
1878	47,598,000	42 01	1 99	5 41	4 98	56	9 21	2 67	42.75	27.13	4 48
1879	48,866,000	40 86	1 71	5 60	5 46	69	8 99	2 73	44.87	28.97	3.99
1880	50,155,783	38 27	1 59	6 65	5 34	1 14	12 51	3 64	43 48	29 07	3.23
1881	51,316,000	35 46	1 46	7 01	5 07	98	12 68	3 78	43 20	29.75	3.22
1882	52,495,000	31 91	1 09	7 64	4 89	1 03	13 64	4 12	42.66	30.11	2.95
1883	53,693 000	28 66	96	7 37	4 90	1 13	13 05	3 92	42 45	29.92	3.07
1884	54,911,000	26 20	87	6 27	4 39	1 04	12 16	3 47	41.61	28.44	3.44
1885	56,148,000	24 50	84	5 77	4 64	1 17	10 32	3 17	45.96	30.59	3.58
1886	57,404,000	22 34	79	5 76	4 15	1 13	10 99	3 30	45.55	30.13	3.33
1887	58,680,000	20 03	71	6 20	4 47	1 27	11 65	3 65	47.10	31.02	3.16
1888	59,974,000	17 72	65	6 32	4 33	1 33	11 88	3 60	45.63	29.99	3.27
1889	61,289,000	15 92	53	6 01	7 88	1 45	12 10	3 60	45.13	29 50	3.14
1890	62,622,250	14 22	47	6 44	4 75	1 71	12 35	3 62	44.41	29 12	2.99
1891	63,975,000	13 32	37	6 11	5 55	1 85	13 36	3 34	46.28	25.25	3.17
1892	65,403,000	12 86	35	5 43	5 28	2 16	12 44	2 66	48.71	21.26	3.75
1893	66,826,000	12 55	34	6 91	6 87	2 37	12 64	2 97	49.58	23.19	3.32

Years.	Internal revenue.		Amount of money in the United States per capita.	Money in circulation per capita.	Coin value of paper money July 1.	Commercial ratio of silver to gold.	Annual average price of silver in London per ounce for calender years.	Bullion value of U. S. silver dollar, at average price of silver exchange at par.	Coinage, per capita of—	
	Collected per capita.	Expenses of collecting.							Gold.	Silver.
	Dolls.	Per ct.	Dolls.	Dolls.	Cents.	Ratio.	Dolls.	Cents.	Dolls.	Dolls.
1867	7.34	2.77	20.11	18.28	71.7	15.57	1.328		.66	.03
1868	5.17	4.55	19.38	18.39	70.1	15.59	1.326		.52	.03
1869	4.19	4.59	18.95	17.60	73.5	15 60	1.325		.47	.03
1870	4 79	3.92	18.73	17.50	85 6	15.57	1.328		.60	.04
1871	3.62	5.30	18.75	18.10	89	15.57	1.326		.53	.08
1872	3.22	4.36	18.79	18.19	87.5	15.63	1.322		.54	.06
1873	2.75	4.69	18.58	18.04	86.4	15 92	1.298		1.37	.10
1874	2.39	4 40	18.83	18.13	91.0	16 13	1.278		.82	.16
1875	3.52	3.89	18.16	17 16	87.2	16.59	1.249		.75	.35
1876	2.59	3.38	17.53	16.12	89.5	17.88	1.156		1.03	.54
1877	2.56	2.99	16.46	15.58	94.7	17.22	1 201		.95	.61
1878	2.32	2.96	16.62	15.32	90.4	17.94	1.152		1.05	.60
1879	2.32	3.10	21 52	16.75	100	18.40	1.123		.80	.56
1880	2.47	2.95	24.04	19.41	100	18.05	1.145	88.5	1.24	.55
1881	2 64	3.20	27.41	21.71	100	18.16	1.138	88.1	1.89	.54
1882	2.79	2.80	28.20	22.37	100	18.19	1.136	87.9	1.26	.53
1883	2.69	3.06	30.61	22.91	100	18.64	1.110	86.5	.54	.54
1884	2.21	3.47	31.06	22.65	100	18.57	1.113	86.1	.41	.52
1885	2.00	3 42	32.37	23.02	100	19.41	1.065	84.5	.49	.51
1886	2.03	3.06	31 51	21.82	100	20.78	.995	79.8	.50	.56
1887	2.02	3.22	32.39	22.45	100	21.13	.978	76 0	.41	.60
1888	2.07	2 92	34.40	22.88	100	21.99	.940	74.0	.52	.57
1889	2.13	2 88	33.86	22.52	100	22.09	.936	72.1	.35	.58
1890	2.24	2.65	34.24	22.82	100	19 76	1.046	74.9	.33	.63
1891	2.28	2.75	34.31	23.41	100	20.92	.988	80.6	.46	.43
1892	2 35	2 52	36.21	24.44	100	23 72	.871	72.4	.53	.19
1893	2.41	2.57	34 75	23.97	100	26.19	.790	65.0	.85	.13

FINANCIAL AND COMMERCIAL STATISTICS OF THE UNITED STATES, 1867 TO 1893.

Years	Domestic merchandise.		Imports and exports of merchandise carried in American vessels.	Consumption per capita of—							
	Exports (per c'pita).	Exports of agricultural products (per cent of total exports).		Wheat.	Corn.	Sugar.	Coffee.	Tea.	Distilled spirits.	Malt liquors.	Wines.
	Dolls.	75.34	Per cent.	Bush.	Bush.	Lbs.	Lbs.	Lbs.	Proof gallons.	Galls.	Galls.
1867...	7.73	75.34	33.87	3.92	23.52	24.1	5.01	1.09	......	5.31	....
1868...	7.29	70.19	35.11	5.36	20.44	30.9	6.52	.96	......	5.15	...
1869...	7.99	75.85	33.18	5.21	23.79	35	6.45	1.08	1.69	5.21	...
1870...	9.77	78.40	35.59	5.41	22.62	33	6	1.10	2.07	5.31	.32
1871...	10.83	70.74	31.87	4.69	27.40	36.2	7.91	1.14	1.62	6.10	.40
1872...	10.55	74.13	29.15	4.79	21.09	40.4	7.28	1.46	1.68	6.66	.41
1873...	12.19	76.10	26.37	4.81	22.86	39.8	8.87	1.53	1.63	7.21	.45
1874...	13.31	79.87	27.17	4.46	20.95	41.5	6.59	1.27	1.51	7	.48
1875...	11.36	76.95	26.21	5.58	18.66	43.6	7.08	1.44	1.50	6.71	.45
1876...	11.64	71.67	27.67	4.69	25.14	35.2	7.81	1.85	1.83	6.88	.45
1877...	12.72	72.68	26.91	5.01	26.18	38.9	6.94	1.23	1.28	6.58	.47
1878...	14.39	77.07	24.81	5.72	26.37	36.4	6.24	1.33	1.09	6.68	.47
1879...	14.29	78.12	22.09	5.58	26.61	40.7	7.42	1.21	1.11	7.05	.50
1880...	16.43	83.25	17.43	5.35	28.88	42.9	8.78	1.39	1.27	8.26	.56
1881...	17.23	82.69	16.49	6.09	31.64	44.2	8.25	1.54	1.38	8.65	.47
1882...	18.97	75.31	15.77	4.98	21.92	48.4	8.80	1.47	1.40	10.03	.49
1883...	14.98	77	16.04	6.64	29.24	51.1	8.91	1.80	1.46	10.27	.48
1884...	13.20	78.98	17.16	5.64	27.40	53.4	9.26	1.09	1.48	10.74	.37
1885...	12.94	72.96	18.29	6.77	31.04	51.8	9.60	1.18	1.26	10.62	.39
1886...	11.60	72.82	15.52	4.57	32.60	56.9	9.36	1.37	1.6	11.20	.45
1887...	11.98	74.40	14.30	5.17	27.08	52.7	8.53	1.49	1.21	11.23	.55
1888...	11.40	78.23	13.68	5.62	23.86	56.7	6.81	1.40	1.26	12.80	.61
1889...	11.92	72.87	14.34	5.34	31.28	51.8	9.16	1.29	1.32	12.72	.56
1890...	13.50	74.51	12.87	6.09	32.09	52.8	7.83	1.33	1.40	13.67	.46
1891...	13.63	78.69	12.46	4.58	22.79	66.1	7.99	1.29	1.42	15.28	.45
1892...	13.53	78.69	12.34	5.91	30.33	63.5	9.63	1.37	1.50	15.10	.44
1893...	12.44	74.05	11.54	4.85	23.66	63.4	8.25	1.32	1.51	16.08	.48

Years.	Consumption of wool.		Per cent. of domestic production exported.				Tonnage of vessels. Per cent. annual increase or decrease (x or —).	Immigration. Per cent. of annual increase of population.
	Total per capita.	Per cent. foreign.	Cotton.	Wheat.	Corn.	Mineral oil.		
	Pounds.							
1867....	5.45	19	68.32	12.50	1.85	46.58	—.14	....
1868....	5.14	11.9	66.90	18.45	1.63	52.34	x1.10	39.23
1869....	5.78	17.8	57.01	30.92	.94	60.01	x4.76	36.04
1870....	5.43	22.7	65.98	22.50	.24	61.37	x2.41	43.95
1871....	5.73	29.4	72.89	22.80	.98	69.62	x.85	38.71
1872...	6.75	45.3	57.44	16.88	3.60	54.60	x3.62	30.87
1873....	5.67	38.2	65.47	20.80	3.68	57.85	x5.82	37.45
1874....	4.81	17.5	70.08	32.54	3.86	51.23	x2.23	41.09
1875....	5.28	23.1	70.69	23.60	3.53	46.50	x1.10	27.13
1876....	5.21	18.3	70.75	25.34	3.86	68.69	—11.83	19.18
1877....	5.16	16.3	68.97	19.73	5.66	64.54	—.86	13.98
1878....	5.28	16.9	71.23	25.29	6.49	54.02	—.70	11.39
1879....	5.03	14.2	67.74	35.16	6.33	50.42	—1.02	10.92
1880....	6.11	34.9	65.73	40.18	6.43	31.41	—2.43	13.78
1881....	5.66	17.3	68.47	37.38	5.46	44.29	—.35	39.40
1882....	6.36	19	67.23	31.82	3.71	39.21	x2.66	56.78
1883....	6.62	18.7	67.20	29.33	2.58	54.18	x1.67	65.86
1884....	6.85	20.6	67.56	26.49	2.90	53.55	x.84	49.53
1885....	6.69	18	68.96	25.86	2.95	61.11	—.12	41.92
1886....	7.89	28.9	64.68	26.48	3.85	54.21	—3.16	31.48
1887....	6.68	37.4	68.71	33.66	2.48	50.67	—.60	26.19
1888....	6.31	28.9	65.83	26.23	1.74	49.87	x2.10	37.87
1889....	6.33	31.8	69.33	21.31	3.57	46.09	x2.74	41.59
1890....	6.03	27	68.15	22.81	4.85	36.06	x2.71	33.84
1891....	6.43	30.8	67.86	29.60	2.15	29.73	x5.88	33.66
1892....	6.72	33.1	65.13	36.88	3.72	35.10	x1.71	39.24
1893 ...	7.05	35.7	65.99	37.20	2.89	39.55	x.79	43.79

VALUE OF MERCHANDISE IMPORTED INTO, AND EXPORTED FROM, THE UNITED STATES FROM 1844 TO 1893, INCLUSIVE: ALSO ANNUAL EXCESS OF IMPORTS OR OF EXPORTS—SPECIE VALUES.

Year ending June 30—	Exports			Imports.	Total exports and imports.	Excess of exports over imports.	Excess of imports over exports.
	Domestic.	Foreign.	Total.				
	Dollars.	Dollars.	Dollars.	Dollars.	Dollars.	Dollars.	Dollars.
1844........	99,531,774	6,214,058	105,745,832	102,604,606	208,350,438	3,141,226	....
1845........	98,455,330	7,584,781	106,040,111	113,184,322	219,224,433	....	7,144,211
1846........	101,718,042	7,865,206	109,583,248	117,914,065	227,497,313	....	8,330,817
1847........	150,574,844	6,166,754	156,741,598	122,424,349	279,165,947	34,317,249	....
1848........	130,203,709	7,986,806	138,190,515	148,638,644	286,829,159	....	10,448,129
1849........	131,710,081	8,641,091	140,351,172	141,206,199	281,557,371	....	855,027
1850........	134,900,233	9,475,493	144,375,726	173,509,526	317,885,252	....	29,133,800
1851........	178,620,138	10,295,121	188,915,259	210,771,429	399,686,688	....	21,856,170
1852........	154,931,147	12,053,084	166,984,231	207,440,398	374,424,629	....	40,456,167
1853........	189,869,162	13,620,120	203,489,282	263,777,265	467,266,547	....	60,287,983
1854........	215,328,300	21,715,464	237,043,764	297,808,794	534,847,558	....	60,760,030
1855........	192,751,135	2,158,208	218,909,503	257,808,708	476,718,211	....	38,899,205
1856......	266,438,051	14,781,372	281,219,423	310,482,310	591,651,733	....	29,212,887
1857........	278,906,713	14,917,047	293,823,760	348,428,342	642,252,102	....	54,604,582
1858........	251,351,033	20,660,241	272,011,274	263,338,654	535,349,928	8,672,620	....
1859........	278,392,080	14,509,971	292,902,051	331,333,341	624,235,392	....	38,431,290
1860........	316,242,423	17,333,634	333,576,057	353,616,119	687,192,176	....	20,040,662
1861........	204,899,616	14,654,217	219,553,833	289,310,542	508,864,375	....	69,756,709
1862........	179,644,024	11,026,477	190,670,501	189,356,677	380,027,178	1,313,824	....
1863........	186,003,912	17,960,535	203,964,447	243,385,815	447,300,262	....	39,371,368
1864........	143,504,027	15,333,961	158,837,988	316,447,283	475,285,271	....	157,609,295
1865........	136,940,248	29,089,055	166,029,303	238,745,580	404,774,883	....	72,716,277
1866........	337,518,102	11,341,420	348,859,522	434,812,066	783,671,588	....	85,952,544
1867........	279,786,809	14,719,332	294,506,141	395,761,096	690,267,237	....	101,254,955
1868........	269,389,900	12,562,999	281,952,899	357,436,440	639,389,339	....	75,483,541
1869........	275,166,697	10,951,000	286,117,697	417,506,379	703,624,076	....	131,388,682
1870........	376,616,473	16,155,295	392,771,768	435,958,408	828,730,176	....	43,186,640
1871........	428,398,908	14,421,270	442,820,178	520,223,684	963,043,862	....	77,403,506
1872........	428,487,131	15,690,455	444,177,586	626,595,077	1,070,782,663	....	182,417,491
1873........	505,033,439	17,446,483	522,479,922	642,136,210	1,164,616,132	....	119,656,288
1874........	569,433,421	16,849,619	586,283,040	567,406,342	1,153,689,382	18,876,698	....
1875........	499,284,100	14,158,611	513,442,711	533,005,436	1,046,448,147	....	19,562,725
1876........	525,582,247	14,802,424	540,384,671	460,741,190	1,001,125,861	79,643,481	....
1877........	589,670,224	12,804,996	602,475,220	451,323,126	1,053,798,346	151,152,094	....
1878........	680,709,268	14,156,498	694,865,766	437,051,582	1,131,917,298	257,814,234	....
1879........	698,340,790	12,098,651	710,439,441	445,777,775	1,156,217,216	264,661,666	....
1880........	823,946,353	11,692,305	835,638,658	667,954,746	1,503,593,404	167,683,912	....
1881........	883,925,947	18,451,899	902,377,846	642,664,628	1,545,041,974	259,712,718	....
1882........	733,239,732	17,302,525	750,542,257	724,639,574	1,475,181,831	25,902,683	....
1883........	804,223,632	19,615,770	823,839,402	723,180,914	1,547,020,316	100,658,488	....
1884........	724,964,852	15,548,757	740,513,609	667,697,693	1,408,211,302	72,815,916	....
1885........	726,682,946	15,506,809	742,189,755	577,527,329	1,319,717,084	164,662,426	....
1886........	665,964,529	13,560,301	679,524,830	635,436,136	1,314,960,966	44,088,694	....
1887........	703,022,923	13,160,288	716,183,211	692,319,768	1,408,502,979	23,863,443	....
1888........	683,862,104	12,092,403	695,954,507	723,957,114	1,419,911,621	....	28,002,607
1889........	730,282,609	12,118,766	742,401,375	745,131,652	1,487,533,027	....	2,730,277
1890........	845,293,828	12,534,856	857,828,684	789,310,409	1,647,139,093	68,518,275	....
1891........	872,270,283	12,210,527	884,480,810	844,916,196	1,729,397,006	39,564,614	....
1892........	1,015,732,011	14,546,137	1,030,278,148	827,402,462	1,857,680,610	202,875,686	....
1893........	831,030,785	16,634,409	847,663,194	866,400,922	1,714,064,116	....	18,737,728

NO. 95.—UNITED KINGDOM.

879........	346,485,881	2,342,558	348,828,439	18,638,423	89,900,389	108,538,812	−240,289,627
880........	450,994,244	2,802,253	453,796,497	30,789,424	179,824,270	210,613,694	−243,182,803
881........	477,450,619	3,684,459	481,135,078	25,080,499	169,908,193	195,588,692	−306,641,340
882........	404,248,031	4,099,124	408,347,155	25,680,499	169,908,193	195,588,692	−212,758,463
883........	420,433,473	4,390,701	425,424,174	27,324,440	161,298,179	188,622,619	−236,801,555
884........	382,717,159	3,521,227	386,238,386	27,586,708	134,962,900	162,549,608	−223,688,778
885........	394,925,925	3,177,278	398,103,203	24,495,559	112,206,321	136,701,780	−261,401,323
886........	344,927,973	3,525,727	348,453,700	27,345,468	126,808,586	154,254,054	−191,199,646
887........	363,101,143	3,209,536	366,310,679	26,732,749	138,234,694	165,067,443	−201,243,236
888........	358,238,799	3,276,643	361,515,702	30,695,422	147,202,553	177,897,975	−183,017,728
889........	379,990,131	2,991,543	382,981,674	28,205,963	150,063,104	178,269,067	−204,712,607
890........	444,459,009	3,436,653	447,895,662	30,046,069	155,342,887	186,488,956	−261,406,706
891........	441,599,807	3,814,219	445,414,026	36,418,430	158,304,832	194,723,262	−250,690,764
892........	493,957,868	5,357,464	499,315,332	35,367,178	120,933,703	156,300,881	−343,014,451
893........	414,966,094	6,168,457	421,134,551	43,166,473	139,692,296	182,859,769	−238,274,782

STATISTICS ON WOOL.

Extract from Speech of Hon. Peter J. Somers, of Wisconsin, in the H. of R., August 13, 1894.

SAVING IN THE WOOL AND WOOLEN SCHEDULE.

By the adoption of this bill you save to the people of this country more than $141,-000,000, as is shown by the statement I herewith present, made by the deputy appraiser of the port of New York:

A statement showing the amount saved to the consumer by the adoption of the Senate bill in place of the McKinley act, Schedule K. wool and woolens, prepared by J. Schoenhof, deputy appraiser of the port of New York.

English cloth made in Leeds, imported into the port of New York, wool and cotton warp, 60 inches wide, weighing 11¼ ounces per yard: Cost per yard 1s 3d less 5 and 5 per cent discount, 27 cents net per yard:

	Cents.
McKinley duty (38½ cents per pound –- 40 per cent per yard)	39.80
Senate duty (40 per cent per yard)	10.80
Saved to consumer	29.00

The samples No. 1 to No. 6 attached to the respective statements represent actual importations made in the current year. The prices are the actual invoice prices, as passed by the appraiser's department in New York.

English cloth, wool and cotton warp, imported into the port of New York, 54 inches wide, weight 13 ounces per yard: Cost per yard 1s 2½d., less 7 per cent, 27 cents net per yard:

	Cents.
McKinley duty (38½ cents per pound –- 40 per cent per yard)	42.00
Senate duty (40 per cent per yard)	10.40
Saved to consumer	31.60

English overcoatings, wool and cotton warp, imported into the port of New York, 50 inches wide, weight 26 ounces per yard: Price 1s. 9d. net per yard:

	Cents.
McKinley duty (33 cents per pound –- 40 per cent per yard)	70.45
Senate duty (40 per cent per yard)	16 80
Saved to consumer	53.65

Worsted coating, Bradford, England, imported into the port of New York, 57 inches wide, weight 20 ounces: Cost 2s. 9d. per yard, less 7 per cent., 62½ cents per yard:

	Cents.
McKinley duty (44 cents per pound –- 50 per cent per yard)	86½
Senate duty (50 per cent) per yard	31½
Saved to consumer	55

French cashmere, imported into the port of New York, 45 inches wide: Cost 0.95 francs per meter net, 18 cents per yard:

	Cents.
McKinley duty (12 cents per square yard - - 50 per cent), per yard	.24
Senate duty (50 per cent), per yard	.9
Saved to consumer	.15

French dress goods, challies, all wool, imported into the port of New York, 30 inches wide, weight 2¼ ounces per yard : Cost per yard, 20¼ cents net :

	Cents.
McKinley duty (12 cents per square yard -- 50 per cent) per yard	.20
Senate duty (50 per cent), per yard	.10
Saved to consumer	.10

Balance sheet showing the amount saved to the consumer by the adoption of the Senate bill in place of the McKinley act.

1892-'93.	Imports of manufactures of wool		$36,993,000
	Duties		36,448,000
	Import value, duty paid		73,441,000
1889-'90.	Census year, domestic manufactures:		
	Woolen goods	$133,577,000	
	Worsted goods	79,194,000	
	Hosiery and knit goods $67.241,000		
	Deduct cotton hosiery 17,000,000		
		50,241,000	
	Carpets	47,770,000	
			310,782,000
	Value of domestic manufactures		384,223,000
	Add 33⅓ per cent to cover wholesale and retail profits		128,074,000
	Cost of wool manufactures to consumers		512,297,000
	Cost of wool manufactures under Senate bill on same amounts :		
	Importations	$36,993,000	
	Duty, 45 per cent	16,665,000	
		53,658,000	
	Value of domestic manufactures, $310,000,000, reduced from an average of 100 per cent duty to 45 per cent rate as a result of free wool	224,525,000	
		278,183,000	
	Add 33⅓ per cent as profits	92,728,000	
			370,911,000
	Amount saved to consumers on the woolen schedule only under Senate bill		141,386,000

INDEX.

www.ingramcontent.com/pod-product-compliance
Lightning Source LLC
Chambersburg PA
CBHW030406270326
41926CB00009B/1298